YURI VERKHOSHANSKY
NATALIA VERKHOSHANSKY

SPECIAL STRENGTH TRAINING
MANUAL FOR COACHES

Published by Verkhoshansky SSTM
2011 – Rome, Italy

Special Strength Training
Manual for Coaches
© Copyright: Yuri Verkhoshansky, Natalia Verkhoshansky

Reprinted October 2013
Final English review: Daniel Raimondi

Published by Verkhoshansky SSTM©
www.verkhoshansky.com

PREFACE

Dear reader,

The Special Strength Training (SST) presented in this manual is mainly addressed to coaches of Olympic sport athletes; it is also useful for strength & conditioning coaches in any sports where it is necessary to have strength in conjunction with highly efficient movements.

I was a coach for many years, and still am in my mind and in my heart. I understand coach's problems very well and, with this manual, I would like to share my knowledge and experience.

The initial idea for this book came to me when I discovered that in many Western countries bodybuilding training methods were used to improve the specific strength preparedness of athletes in Olympic sport disciplines. This came as a surprise to me as there is a fundamental difference between the training of Olympic sport athletes and bodybuilders. *The final aim of bodybuilding is the perfection of bodily shape. The goal in Olympic sports is the perfection of bodily movements.*

Bodybuilding methods are employed to perfect muscular harmony, elegance of pose, and volitional muscle control. Bodybuilding methods are ideal for these purposes; they are very finely detailed and scientifically justified. However, these methods involve mechanisms of the muscle contractile function which are not specific for the Olympic sports. In Olympic sports, where victory hinges on speed of movement, power of muscular effort, and physical endurance, strength training entirely based on the use of bodybuilding methods cannot be effective.

Special Strength Training for Olympic sport disciplines is based on different principles from those used in bodybuilding. Many of these principles were developed in the Soviet Union towards the end of the last century when I was more actively involved in the field of sports training. I have written this manual in order to set out these principles in an attempt to inform coaches and facilitate their understanding of Special Strength Training Methodology.

What are the distinctive features of Special Strength Training Methodology?

The main distinctive feature of Special Strength Training in Olympic sports is that in the training process resistance exercises are focused not simply on the development of muscle strength; above all, they intensify the functional activity of the human motor system and, consequently, the functional activity of the body's physiological system. Correctly applied, SST changes the morpho-functional characteristics of the athlete's body, thereby allowing the athlete to execute his or her specific competition exercise with greater power output. This is the foundation for improving an athlete's technical-tactical mastery and physical performance. SST, therefore, is not simply a useful extra. In every sports discipline it is an integral part of the whole training system; it is one of the main contributors towards excellence in sports achievement.

Often we may observe an unjustified opposition towards resistance exercises among coaches and in the literature. It is proposed by some that resistance exercises negatively influence speed of movement. The training effect of every exercise, however, depends on the methods. When the SST methods are used correctly, resistance exercises promote not only an increase in speed, but also perfection of coordination, motor reaction, quickness and frequency of movement, muscular relaxation ability, local muscular endurance, and improved maximum anaerobic power.

It is important to note that SST is characterized by the use of training means integrated into a system. In the past, coaches were searching for the 'best exercise' that could easily ensure improvements in an athlete's performance. Later, it was understood that a single exercise cannot guarantee the best increase in a specific performance, but that results are achieved by a group of different exercises integrated in a system. In this manual, readers will find useful information about how such integrative training systems can be created.

Integrating the training means into a system inevitably requires that the coach has to know the methodological principles of organizing the training process. I have tried to transfer, in a concise way, my knowledge of these principles so that this manual can be a tool to develop rational SST programs and organize a training process with the optimal use of an athlete's time and energy.

Even though the contents of this manual are mainly addressed to Olympic sports athletes, they are useful to coaches working with young athletes. The training of young athletes is aimed not only towards the improvement of their performance in current competitions, but also, and above all, to their preparation for highly intensive and specialized training in the future. Besides these recommendations, coaches can see what is to be expected of young athletes in the future, gradually preparing them in advance, using the time available constructively.

Why did I decide to publish a second edition of the manual?

After the first edition was published I received many questions, many of which showed me the difficulties Western readers had in understanding the practical applications of SST. Theoretical explanation was lacking in the old edition because I assumed readers were already familiar the principles of SST. Because of this I decided to revise the book content entirely and publish a new edition in which the methodological fundamentals of SST would be presented not only in few pages like the first edition, but they would be described in a clearer and more detailed form. Furthermore, to respond to the most frequently asked questions, I have completely revised the section of the book explaining the organization of the training process with more detailed descriptions of the Block Training System.

For this new edition I have relied on the help of my daughter, Natalia. She is the person who understands my work best. She grew up in a Track & Field stadium, between the jumping pit where I was coaching and the throwing field where her mother was coaching. She studied at the Central State Institute of Physical Education and Sport and worked on her baccalaureate thesis in my laboratory where she witnessed many of my burning ideas, many of which she based her PhD thesis on. She participated in a number of scientific discussions, defended these ideas, and put them into practice as a coach of the Soviet national female tennis team in the1980s, the Italian national female basketball team, and the junior national fencing team in the late

1990s. She is the author of several scientific articles and a professor at the Rome University Tor Vergata. She has given her own significant professional contribution to this work. Several new sections of the manual come from her previous publications or material used at the University where she teaches. For these reasons she is the co-author of this edition.

We have tried to standardize and bring uniformity to the terminology and to describe the SST means, methods, and training programs in more detail; we have also added new training programs which were not in the first edition. The result is a completely new book.

Final remarks

All the SST programs illustrated in the manual came from experiments and have been successfully employed in sports practice by Olympic sport athletes. Based on these proven programs (and using the manual as a guide) I believe coaches can work out their own programs for any sports discipline.

Some of the programs are very intense as they were created for top level athletes. If you are not at this stage of development please pay attention to the volume of loads. Do not use them or, at least, try to start at the lowest level of loads indicated.

Be careful and I am sure that success will be yours.

Sincerely yours,

EDITOR'S NOTE: The main part of the book was already finished when Prof. Verkhoshansky passed away; this preface is proposed as it was written by him.

FOREWORD

WHO WAS YURI VERKHOSHANSKY?

Yuri Verkhoshansky is mainly known to most readers in the West as the Russian researcher who invented plyometrics training (the Shock Method). Many coaches and sports scientists around the world, however, recognize Y. Verkhoshansky as a prominent figure in the field of explosive strength training, an expert sports training theory, and one whose ideas were implemented and expanded to include the Methodology of Special Strength Training and Special Physical Preparation, Long Delay Training Effect, Conjugate–Sequence System, and Block Training System.

To few sports training experts, he is known as the first scientist who applied the physiology of adaptation in the analysis of the sports training process and the scientist who, more than 20 years ago, introduced a new approach for planning the training process, "Programming of training", based upon the innovative methodology presently known as System Analysis & Design and Structured Process Modeling.

Yuri Verkhoshansky started his career in the late 1950s after graduating from the State Central Institute of Physical Culture and Sport as a Track & Field coach and Physical Education teacher. He started to work at the Moscow Institute of Aeronautical Engineering. In just two years he achieved incredible results, transforming 12 not-athlete university students belonging to his sports group into high-level Track & Field jumpers (Masters of Sport). Soon thereafter he became the head coach of the Moscow United Team in sprint and jump events. He prepared Boris Zubov, a record holder in sprint events of the European and Soviet Union. He was also a training consultant to the Soviet athletic leaders Valery Brummel and Igor Ter Ovanesijan, and the Soviet triple jump champion Oleg Fedoseev.

In 1961 he published his first book, *Triple Jump*. A few years later, in 1963, he prepared and defended his first dissertation 'The experimental substantiation of the use of speed-strength training means in relation to the bio-dynamics of sports exercises' to earn his first Russian scientific title, equivalent to a PhD.

In the late 1960s Y. Verkhoshansky began his work at the Central State Institute of Physical Education and Sport as an adjunct professor of Track & Field and associate professor of Biomechanics. During this period he started to research how to optimize the training process.

Y. Verkhoshansky's work in this regard was strongly influenced by the ideas of N.A. Bernstein (the founder of the New School of Physiology of Coordination and the author of *Physiology of Activity*). The legendary Soviet scientist formulated the fundamental theory of a self-regulated motor system, in which he expressed the basic ideas of cybernetics twenty years before Norbert Viner.

Expanding on Bernstein's ideas, Y. Verkhoshansky began to use a systemic approach to analyze the training process, creating a new method of programming training.

In 1973 Y. Verkhoshansky prepared his second dissertation, 'Optimization of the training process of elite athletes in the strength-speed sport disciplines'. He obtained the title of Doctor Habilitatus (Doc Hab., the highest scientific degree in Eastern Europe) and, later, the title and honor of Academic Rank Professor.

For one year he was the vice-director of the Central Institute of Physical Culture for scientific studies and, for many years, he was the head of the Institute's Problematic Research Laboratory where the main agenda was "The optimization of the training of high level athletes and the physiology of sports work capacity".

During these years with his collaborators he helped prepare the Soviet national sports teams for the Olympic Games and other international competitions by introducing new training methods, new training models, and the means for their practical implementation (see table below)[1].

SPORT DISCIPLINE	WHO (National Team Coach)	WHAT (Prof. Verkhoshansky introduced in their training system)	WHEN
Track & Field Jumping	Ter-Ovanesiyan, Kreer Mironenko	SST Methodology, Shock Method, BTS, Programming of Training	From 1960's to 1990's
Track & Field Sprint	Korneliuk	SST Methodology, Programming of Training, BTS	1980's
Track & Field Throwing events	Kusnetzov, Konstantinov	SST Methodology, Shock Method	1980's
Track & Field Decathlon	Ushakov	SST Methodology, Shock Method, Programming of Training, BTS	1980's
Track & Field Middle distance running	Kulitcenko	SST Methodology, BTS, Programming of Training	1980's
Boxing	Filimonov	SST and SSP Methodology, Shock Method, Programming of Training	1970's
Ice-skating	Vasilkovsky, Muratov	SST and SPP Methodology, Programming of Training	1970's
Figure Skating	Zjuk	SST and SPP Methodology, Shock Method	1970's
Hand ball	Evtushenko	SST and SPP Methodology, Shock Method	1970's
Basketball	Gomelsky	SST and SPP Methodology, Shock Method	1970's
Ice Hockey	Tarasov, Tichonov, Yurzinov	SST and SPP Methodology, Shock Method, Programming of Training	1980's
Rowing	Drachevsky	SST and SPP Methodology, Shock Method, Block Training System	1980's
Cycling	Kusnetzov	SST and SPP Methodology	1980's
Gymnastic	Arkaev	Shock Method	From 1970's to 1990's
Weight lifting	Rigert	SST Methodology, Shock Method	1980's
Skiing	Stenin	SST and SPP Methodology	1980's

[1] Y. Verkhoshansky also assisted the national teams of China, DDR, Italy, Sweden, Brazil, and Bulgaria.

For the series of publications, "Highly-Qualified Sportsmen Training Programming and Control", Professor Verkhoshansky was awarded the gold medal of the State Committee for Sports in the USSR.

During the 1980s he was a member of the Scientific Council of the Institute and member of the Soviet Union Central Supreme Commission of Scientific Graduation.

He was the head of the commission that led the Institutes of Physical Education and Sport in scientific research for the USSR. These institutes elaborated the training systems for elite athletes and allowed others to benefit from their research and findings.

In the late 1980s, he worked as an associate professor at the Central Elite Coach School, the most important centre for the education of national team coaches.

In the early 1990s he headed the Theoretical and Methodological Centre at the Russian Research Institute of Sport, becoming Vice-President of the International Information Academy.

In 1992, he was elected President of the International Association on Theory and Methodology of Training in Elite Sports at the International Sports Scientific Congress in Israel.

For many years, Professor Verkhoshansky lectured on the philosophy, physiology and methodology of sports training and the programming of training in Russia and other countries including: Austria, USA, Spain, Yugoslavia, Greece, Israel, South Africa, Germany, Italy, France, Holland, Portugal, and Bulgaria.

Professor Verkhoshansky wrote more than 500 scientific papers and more than 20 monographs. His work has been translated into 22 foreign languages and published in 29 countries. He was an associate editor of the NSCA Journal, Journal of Applied Sports Science Research, Fitness and Sports Review International (USA) and Leistungssport (Germany). He was also a member of the International Sports Sciences Association (ISSA) in the USA.

In 1995, Professor Verkhoshansky became a scientific consultant for the Italian National Olympic Committee.

On June 23, 2010, Yuri Verkhoshansky passed away in Rome, Italy at the age of 82, after a lifetime of dedication spent improving sports science and collaborating with coaches in order to improve the competition results of athletes. For this reason I wish to dedicate the foreword of this book to his professional path.

FROM COACH TO SCIENTIST

Because Professor Yuri Verkhoshansky has passed away nobody can ask him how he originally developed his interest in sport training. During his youth, he was interested in engineering, photography, writing novels, and playing the piano. After school, he finished classical music college. Impassioned by Glenn Miller, he organized the jazz band in which he performed on sax, clarinet, and piano. Sport was part of his life only because he participated in Track & Field and Cross Country Skiing competitions as many young Soviet boys did.   However,
he was successful in sports and, maybe because of this, sports became his greatest passion. Instead of becoming a music teacher, he decided to be a sport coach. In 1947, he became a student of the Moscow Central State Institute of Physical Culture and Sport (see his photo of this period on the right).

During the 1950's, Yuri Verkhoshansky was an unknown Track & Field coach and great admirer of famous coach and scientist Vladimir Dyachkov[2]. Dr. Dyachkov authored the first scientifically based

---

[2] Vladimir M. Dyachkov (1904–1981, Doctor Habilitatus was an athlete, coach and scientist. In the 1930s, he won the Soviet high jump and pole vault championships for a total of 11 times. Later he served as the Soviet na-

training principles for the jumping events. In addition, he is also credited as the first to use weight training exercises in the preparation of high jumpers.

Dyachkov did not regularly publish his training methods after he began his tenure as the Soviet national coach. In fact, the use of resistance exercises in speed-strength sports events were described for the first time in 1961 by Verkhoshansky. In that year he published the article, "The barbell in the training of track & field jumpers"[3], illustrating the unexpected results of the new training concept he had discovered accidentally.

Photo on the right, Dr. Dyachkov with his most prolifically decorated athlete, the high jumper Valery Brumel. Brumel won the silver medal in the 1960 Olympic Games and the gold medal at the 1964 Olympic Games.

At the end of the 1950s, Yuri Verkhoshansky was training a small group of Track & Field jumpers made up of students from the Aeronautical Engineering Institute. At that time, the institute did not have an indoor athletic facility for training during the harsh winters. Verkhoshansky was relegated to training his pupils in the cramped space under the institute's staircase and in its meager corridors. By doing this, the training would not be interrupted by the weather conditions. It was here that the accidental discovery of an old barbell led to Verkhoshansky's first use of exercises with weights.

"Because of the lack of space, the athletes were divided into two groups. While one group did barbell exercises, the other did jumping exercises in the corridor. The most frequently used jumping exercise consisted of trying to touch the ceiling with a vertical jump, executed after a short run-up and a double leg take-off. Soon it was noticed that by using this exercise, the athletes — who at first were only able to brush against the ceiling with their fingertips — began touching the ceiling with the palm of their hand. We were euphoric as if we were gold fossickers who had struck it lucky. We began 'elaborating' this new knowledge with great enthusiasm, trying to improve the methodological use of barbell exercises. Improvement in this work was given a great stimulus by V. Djachkov's advice". (Excerpt taken from the paper "The barbell in the training of track & field jumpers").

In the beginning athletes only did traditional weightlifting exercises. As the training progressed, more specific exercises were developed. These exercises were based on Verkhoshansky's analysis of the biomechanics of Track & Field's jumping events.

Though now seen as groundbreaking, the 1961 article "The barbell in the training of Track & Field jumpers" was skeptically received by coaches. At that time, barbell exercises had never been used before in the training of track & field jumpers and runners. Training with weights had always been associated with increasing muscle mass and were thought to have a negative influence on speed. The thinking of the time was that *"a runner must have the muscles of a deer, not a buffalo"*. Only years later did

---

tional team head coach for the Olympic Games in 1960, 1964 and 1968. Dyachkov also was the personal coach of Olympic high jump champions, Valeriy Brumel and Robert Shavlakadze. He also was the coach of Olympic medallists Taisia Chenchik and Antonina Okorokova in addition to European champion Valentin Gavrilov.

[3] Y. Verkhoshansky, "The barbell in the training of track &field jumpers" in Track & Field Review, n.6, 1961.

they discover that it was possible to obtain 'the muscles of a deer' by correctly practicing the barbell exercises. Using appropriate methods, barbell exercises elicited improvements not only in the length and height of the jumps, but also in running speed.

In the 1960's Verkhoshansky was conducting research on the biodynamic structure of the triple jump technique. He discovered that the forces during the last contact phase reached upwards of 300kg. This discovery led him to start the search for an exercise that reproduced the same conditions. He began his inquiry by having the athletes perform half squats instead of full squats because the abbreviated range of movement allowed for an increase in the barbell weight. Unfortu-

Y. Verkhoshansky with his high jumpers Gerard Sorokin and Arcadiy Slobodskoy.

nately, this exercise immediately caused lower back pain in his lanky jumpers. His second attempt had the athletes perform a variation of the leg press. This exercise had the barbell placed on the feet and pressed vertically while two assistants prevented the barbell from falling. The athletes found they were unable to maintain control of the heavy barbell, and the exercise was deemed too dangerous to continue.

Verkhoshansky returned to reflect on the incredible strength effort of the triple jump and how he could replicate it in training. He contemplated that it would be possible to obtain such a strength effort by using the kinetic energy of the falling human body. To find a practical way to actualize this, he took his idea to the modest space available to him at the institute.

It was in this setting that the most revolutionary training exercise of the 20th century was created, the Depth Jump. Sometime later, this new discovery was adapted further to use falling weight's kinetic energy to increase the strength effort in upper body explosive movements. Verkhoshansky named his discovery the "The Shock Method." Fred Wilt[4] would later coin the more cosmopolitan term "plyometrics" used in the West. During the 1960's Fred Wilt was a friend and colleague with whom Verkhoshansky often corresponded.

After the publication of Verkhoshansky's paper in 1961, barbell exercises became an essential part of the physical preparation of Track & Field jumpers and sprinters. Coaches became so accustomed to weight exercises that the Depth Jump was regarded as child's play. It wouldn't be till the 1970's that the exercise came to be considered the most powerful training means for improving explosive strength. 1962 marked the year that Djachkhov finally published a paper in which he presented his "conjugated

Fred Wilt, the famous U.S.A. athlete, coach, and scientist

---

[4] Fred Wilt (1920–1994) was a U.S. distance runner. He was member of the 1948 and 1952 Olympic teams and famous for his legendary indoor mile encounters with Wisconsin's Don Gehrmann. After retiring from the FBI, Wilt coached the women's running teams at Purdue University. He edited the publication *Track Technique* and advised various athletes. His star pupil was 1964 Olympian Buddy Edelen, who held the world marathon record with the time of 2:14:28. In the 1960s and 1970s, Fred Wilt became a famous writer. His book, "How They Train", was a long-time best seller. His most popular book, "Run, Run, Run…" is an incredible collection of articles on science, history, and methods of running, reflecting his passion and desire to bring real knowledge to the people.

method" of using barbell exercises in training. Djachkov's training program consisted of using weight exercises in order to improve the technical skill of high jumpers. He used exercises with weights to increase the force efforts in the accentuated phases of the specific movements. Verkhoshansky sought to explore Djachkov's idea thoroughly and formulated the criteria for selecting these weight exercises. In 1963, Verkhoshansky published the "Principle of the dynamic correspondence between weight exercises and the biodynamic structure of the competition exercise". It is important to note that Verkhoshansky's and Djachkov's application of their principles were different with regard to their implementation. Though both were respected colleagues, Djachkhov and Verkhoshansky had different approaches with regard to the application of the means in which their training was prescribed. They conducted their training in different environments altogether. This was due to their different positions in the coach's hierarchy. Djachkhov was the head coach of the Soviet national team, and Verkhoshansky was only the coach of a Moscow student's team. This hierarchical difference meant that Djachkhov could have at his disposal the resources to conduct his training sessions throughout the year. Verkhoshansky, on the other hand, had limited resources and he did not have access to an indoor facility in the winter time. Djachkhov had the opportunity to train his athletes on an indoor high jump surface all year. This allowed them to perform specialized exercises that focused on improving the biodynamic structure of high jumping. Therefore, weight exercises were used as a part of the athlete's technical preparation. In direct contrast, during the winter months Verkhoshansky had to spend entire training sessions concentrating only on weight training.

Verkhoshansky's method of using barbell and jumping exercises in the same training session was more suitable to the goals of specific physical preparation: the prescribed training was directed towards increasing the ability of the athlete to produce a maximal strength effort in minimal time. In addition, Verkhoshansky observed that the cumulative training effects of the barbell and jumping exercises could be obtained when they are used in both the same and subsequent training sessions. Verkhoshansky also noted that the cumulative training effects of these exercises did not represent the sum of their training effect because the effects of previous training means change the training flow of subsequent means. The influence of subsequent means depend on their temporal sequencing and rest periods between. Finally, he ascertained that the training influence of every training exercise decreases in future training sessions if it is used over a long period of time.

These observations were the starting point of Verkhoshansky's principle "**Integration of Training Means into a System**". This principle stated that in order to ensure an increase in a parameter of an athlete's physical preparedness, the cumulative effect of exercises with different training emphasis must be applied in harmony with specific exercises that adhere to the principle of dynamic correspondence. These exercises must be correctly selected, integrated into a training plan, and used in one set sequence. Research on the application of this principle led to the development of the new SST Methodology. This is based on three new concepts: Conjugate-sequence system, Long-lasting Delayed training effect, and Block Training System.

Before the discussion of how these concepts were developed, it is necessary to look at how the professional career of Yuri Verkhoshansky evolved. In the 1960's, twelve of his athletes, students at the Moscow Institutes of Aeronautic Engineering, obtained the title "Master of Sport". According to the traditions of the Soviet track & field federation, their coach had to be appointed "Honored Coach of Russia". For such a young coach, this acknowledgement was considered "incredible". The coaches responsible for granting this commission considered Verkhoshansky's success a chance occurrence. On their recommendation, the nomination was withdrawn. They said of Verkhoshansky, "Let him work a bit more."

Verkhoshansky then took the opportunity to become the head coach of the Moscow United Team in the sprinting and jumping events.

In 1964, Verkhoshansky's athlete Boris Zubov, a student at Moscow University, became both the European and Soviet record holder in the sprint events. With Verkhoshansky's earlier success, he again was to be nominated for the title of "Honored Coach of Russia." But, similar to his earlier circumstances, the nomination was again withdrawn. The official reason for the withdrawal was "because of missing documents.". Unintentionally this decision became the best course of action for the development of sports science. Verkhoshansky decided that after again being unfairly denied his accreditation, he would discontinue his coaching career and concentrate his work on scientific research. His short but exemplary coaching career became of great benefit to his scientific career as much of his research was stimulated by his previous empirical findings.

The first of his scientific achievements was the discovery of the **Conjugate-Sequence System**.

The starting point of this concept was the powerful training effect of the Depth Jump. Verkhoshansky observed the effects of this training when his jumpers used it for the first time. After months of the usual heavy work with a barbell, they perceived this new exercise as joke. They enjoyed the ease of the exercise so much that they carried out a great number of Depth Jumps. The following day, none of the athletes came to practice. Their legs were incapable of executing any kind of exercise.

Soviet javelin thrower Jānis Lūsis used the depth jump during his preparation for the 1972 Olympics in Munich. This training means was introduced in his training by Verkhoshansky's friend Vladimir Kouznetsov, head coach of the Soviet national javelin team (see Appendix 4). Lūsis was determined to reclaim gold after winning it at the 1968 games with an Olympic record of 90.10m.

Lūsis obtained a tremendous increase in explosive strength from his training. The increase was so great that the javelin technique he used in competition became inadequate to his new level of physical preparedness. He did not have enough time to adjust his technique before the Olympics and, consequently, claimed only silver in Munich. His performance though was nothing short of spectacular. The competition was the closest javelin in history, with Lūsis losing by only 2cm. Lūsis had throws of 88.88m, 89.54m, and 90.46m. These throws marked 3 of the 4 longest throws of his Olympic career. In addition, his 90.46 surpassed the Olympic record, bested only by the winning throw of his competitor.

Jānis Lūsis - Latvian athlete who won three Olympic medals: bronze in 1964, gold in 1968 and silver in 1972.

Verkhoshansky would later surmise that Depth Jumps must be carried out with minimal quantity. In addition, they should be included only at the end of the winter strength stage or following the conclusion of the entire preparation period.

At the end of 1960s, his research was directed at studying the Shock Method and its implementation in the training system of speed-strength sport events. The results from these studies demonstrated that only four sets of ten depth jump repetitions were required to increase explosive strength when compared to a higher number of traditional bounds and jumps.

In the article "Depth jumps: are they useful?" (1967), he wrote: "…*The quantity of depth jumps to use in a single training session is related to the level of the athlete's preparedness. High level athletes may use these jumps two times a week but not more than 40 jumps. Low level athletes must use no more than 20-30 depth jumps only once a week in two series: first series includes 10 jumps from the height of 0.75 m; second series – 10 jumps from the height of 1.1 m. Athletes who want to increase the training effect by increasing the height of depth jump can be compared to those zealots who follow the principle: instead of taking 15 drops of medicine two times per day, it's better to drink the whole bottle immediately*".

What was overlooked by the researchers was that the powerful training effect of the Shock Method is expressed well when depth jumps are used after a predetermined period of traditional jump training: *"Depth jumps are a very powerful training exercise. For this reason, it must be gradually introduced in the training process. The best training exercises for the preliminary preparation are: multiple standing jumps and Kettlebell squat jumps... The young sportsmen shouldn't use depth jumps at all. Multiple jumps and bounds are more useful for them..."*

This led to the idea that every training mean (a training exercise executed according to a given method) has a specific training potential: the capacity to increase a definite parameter of the athlete's motor function until that function reaches a certain level. During the systematic use of training means the related motor function increases. However, the training potential of the training means used decreases. Therefore a logical application of training means is necessary: it is more suitable to use the training means with lower potential first, followed sequentially by those having a high training potential.

This finding led to the first application of the Conjugate-Sequence system: the training means having the same training direction, but different training potentials, should be incorporated in the training plan in a definite sequence: in relation to the gradual increase of their training potential.

Years later, Verkhoshansky deduced that training means having different training directions could be concentrated in different training stages of the preparatory period, incorporated in the training plan in a definite sequence ("conjugated in a sequence"). One observation of his preceding coaching experience stuck with him.

Though the harsh winter weather of Moscow eventually subsides into spring, the training conditions for the track & field athletes continue to be difficult. Each spring the Soviet athletes would move their training camp to Batumi (Georgia) to train in the warm air that moves westerly from the Black Sea. Here the preparation for the summer competition stage would begin. When Verkhoshansky and his athletes went in Batumi after the first winter dedicated to weight training, his Georgian colleagues re-

marked, *"Yuri, what happened to your athletes? They have different legs compared to the past years!"* His athletes obtained an unexpectedly high level of specific performance during the spring which followed the winter phase. Indecently, the winter phase was wholly dedicated to strength training.

After a long Russian winter spent enjoying quality time on a daily basis with their "new iron **Batumi, Georgia, spring of 1951. The group of Verkhoshansky's jumpers (photo on the left). The coach Verkhoshansky with Arcadiy Slobodskoy.**

friend", the athletes wanted nothing more to do with the barbell. They were indeed happy to finally begin their jumping and running training. Their training started with the execution of a variety of jumping exercises and bounds. They then gradually moved on to more specific exercises and technical event work. The conglomeration of training, and its systematic implementation was "concentrated" or localized in different training stages, or blocks. These blocks were organized sequentially based on when the implementation of the barbell exercises, jump training, and technical work was executed. Following this spring preparation, his athletes started to achieve incredible performances.

Nearly a decade later, Verkhoshansky sought to organize an experiment where the same "concentrated load" phase training was replicated. A primary reason for this was that he had in his laboratory new equipment which would allow him to measure the dynamics of strength parameters: the Universal Dynamometric Stand.

In the 1970's, Verkhoshansky was appointed the head of the research laboratory for optimizing the training of elite athletes at the Central State Institute of Physical Culture and Sport. It was during this time that he started to search for new, more powerful methods that would be able to ensure an increase in the performance of high level athletes. The initial research dedicated to this project showed that the high total volume of training loads couldn't ensure the adequate increase in sport results, most notably because the athletes used the complex-parallel form of temporal organization of training loads of different emphasis. The high total volume of the loads, having complex composition, cannot ensure the high intensity of training stimuli because it causes a moderate reaction within the organism, in which the training effect of one means can negatively affect the training effect of another. The innovative idea of Verkhoshansky consisted of their selective "concentration", directed primarily towards only one training objective. This would create a focused training stimulus, able to influence the most important factor of increasing sport performance.

In order to prove this idea in an experiment, a group of high level T&F jumpers began to use a training program which included only barbell exercises, finalized towards an increase in maximal strength: the barbell exercises, which were usually uniformly distributed over time, were concentrated in the limited training stage.

The research began with the athletes carrying out the block of barbell exercises as Verkhoshansky's athletes had ten years prior. Unexpectedly the UDS test showed a decrease in strength parameters. According to the current methodological beliefs, these results indicated that the program was not effective. This methodology was based on the Periodization concept of L. Matveev, which postulated that a correctly organized training process ensures a constant increase in an athlete's physical preparedness. Verkhoshansky found himself at a crossroads. Either cancel the experiment, or continue it in spite of the test results. For a while he didn't take any action. His hope was that he could discover something wrong with the test procedure. As is the case with most circumstances, fate finds a way to intervene. One of Verkhoshansky's test subjects informed him that she had become pregnant and would have to drop out of the experiment and stop training. Verkhoshansky complied with her request, but asked that she continue to be evaluated for the time being. Remarkably, after her respite from training her strength parameters showed an unexpected increase. "*It is impossible!*" exclaimed Verkhoshansky. Hoping to rule out the anomaly of pregnancy, he decided to complete the experiment and evaluate the other participants along the same parameters as the young woman. These results brought about the same exclamation, "*It is impossible!*". What he observed was the first instance of the classic "Supercompensation" curve illustrated by a final performance increase of 30%. He immediately organized new experiments to confirm these exceptional results.

Further experimentation and subsequent results led to the discovery of the **long-term delayed training effect (LDTE)**[5]. The concentrated strength loads caused temporary deficits in the Maximal and Explosive Strength parameters; after concluding the stage of their use, the strength parameters, in the beginning, returned to their initial level and, subsequently, reached an exceedingly high level, which was never achieved by the athletes in his precedent experience. Furthermore, the total volume of barbell exercises carried out by each athlete during the concentrated loads stage was less than the their total volume carried out in the whole preparatory period of the previous yearly cycle, in which all these loads were uniformly distributed over time and used together with other training means.

---

[5] Verkhoshansky Y.V. Long lasting delay training effect of the strength loads. Theory and Practice of Physical Culture, 1982, n.1, p.14.

Subsequent studies of the practical application of LDTE led to the creation of an innovative yearly cycle model for speed-strength sport disciplines. In the 1980s, this training model came to be called the 'Conjugate-Sequence System'. It was successful and soon became the dominant model used in training elite Soviet athletes.

Although they were praised as innovative, the aforementioned discoveries were specific only to the speed-strength sports. The endurance disciplines relegated the use of resistance exercises exclusively to the athlete's general physical preparation. Furthermore, the use of barbell exercises as a means of special physical preparation was dismissed as ineffective. It would take advanced physiological research data to break these convictions.

In the 1970s many research experiments deduced that physiological parameters from laboratory tests characterize the athletes' physical fitness level more precisely than endurance parameters estimated through motor tests. At the time maximum oxygen consumption (VO2 max) was considered to be the most important indicator of endurance motor ability. Therefore, all research utilized the Vo2 increase index as the most effective parameter of evaluation of endurance training. It would be a decade until physiological research data showed that the capacity to consume a larger quantity of oxygen was less important than the capacity of the muscles to use oxygen more effectively during prolonged physical exercise. This concept came to be known as Local Muscular Endurance (LME). LME is dependent on the physiological characteristics of the muscle fibers: the specific composition of the fibers involved in the work, the oxidative capacity, and the contractile ability of the fibers.

Moscow, end of the 1970's. Y. Verkhoshansky with Igor Ter-Ovanesian, head coach of Soviet Track & Field National Team (jumping events) and Valerij Podluznij (8.18m long jump bronze medalist, Moscow Olympic Games, 1980). They were the first in applying the Block Training Sys-

Verkhoshansky's research showed that LME could in fact be influenced by the use of resistance exercises carried out in an interval regime. He advocated that it would be most effective if used in combination with prolonged aerobic exercise. Logic then led to the conclusion that the Conjugate-Sequence System could also be applied effectively to endurance sports[6].

In the 1980's, Verkhoshansky began to elaborate the new training models for endurance sports and for sport games. However, his ideas was negatively accepted by Soviet experts in the theory and methodology of sports training: *"In the entire history of modern sport nobody brought to mind the absurdity of organizing the long term preparatory period of training on the basis of the consecutive use of loads with the same training emphasis united into several week-long stages or 'blocks'. The pseudoscientific character of this theoretical approach is evident."*[7]

In the late 1980's, Verkhoshansky was deprived of the possibility of experimental work; his work on

---

[6] For the first time the Block Training System for endurance sports was described in the articles of Y.Verkhoshansky, published in the Sport Science Bulletin "Nauchno-sportivny vestnik" in 1984 (n.3), 1985 (n.1), 1986 (n.4) and later, a German version in "Ein neues Trainingssystem fur zyklische Sportarten. Ein neuer Weg der Gestaltung und Programmierung des Trainingprozesses", Philippka-Verlag, 1990.

[7] Platonov V. N., Super-compensation, training loads, adaptation and other related issues to sports science (parte II), SdS-Scuola dello Sport, 2005, Italy

the new training models could not be concluded. Notwithstanding this, many coaches of elite athletes in endurance sports and sport games were enthusiastic with Verkhoshansky's ideas. They began to apply Verkhoshansky's experimental model as the basis for their yearly plans. The Conjugate-Sequence System was named by them the "Block Training System."

Years of discussion and consideration were required to clarify the concept of the Block Training System. Verkhoshansky finally reached the conclusion that it was necessary to approach the training process from another angle. The nature of the training process would be completely changed in its approach. The perspective of the biological sciences is where he would draw the concepts and evaluations that were to be applied, not from the traditional pedagogical perspective. This led to a change in the conceptual framework of sports training methodology. Verkhoshansky had supplanted its basic paradigm[8].

LAST CONSIDERATIONS

A Coach is a person who can transform an ordinary person into an athlete. Like the artist who thoughtfully applies his brush to a blank canvas, the coach "creates" the future champion through a 'cause-effect' process, in which the 'cause' is the training program the coach selects for his/her athlete and the 'effect' is the improvement of the athlete's performance. Every day, the coach has to make decisions, based on the presumed results. What will help a coach make the correct decisions?

The coach can read articles about the study of this 'cause and effect' relationship, in which numerous single "causes" are reproduced in experiments; their "effects" are statistically elaborated upon and concluded with the following practical recommendations: *if the coach makes a particular decision, with a certain statistical probability, then a particular result or a specific change in an athlete's performance will be obtained.*

Considering the variables and sometimes the unpredictability of the athlete's response to the training program, making the correct decisions depends on the depth of the coach's personal experience. Over the years, many cases of 'cause and effect' enable a coach to analyze the results of his decisions. What the coach learns from this analysis can be applied to the subsequent training programs. Applying the knowledge gained in the process of trial and error in subsequent training programs will help the coach expand their knowledge further. The coach can also learn from other coaches' training experiences, reading their publications and accumulating their knowledge to increase the robustness of their program from year to year.

Almost all rules and principles of sports training methodology are formed and based on empirical data and verified by the results of experiments. However, in order to know *how* to improve the athlete's performance it is necessary to know *what* exactly must be improved and *why*. The understanding of why will result in the 'effect' and can guide the coach's professional intuition towards the correct decision. So, the coach's theoretical background and his general 'attitude' towards the training process are the most important factors of his professional success. For the coaches who are interested only in "practical" aspects of sport training, it may be useful to know that "*There is nothing more practical than a good theory*". It is the famous phrase of the Italian physicist Alessandro Volta (1745-1827), who invented the most practical thing in the

Rome, 2000s. Y. Verkhoshansky with Oreste Perri, Italian National Canoeing Team coach.

[8] About this issue, see Appendix 4

world - the voltaic battery.

Much has been written for coaches, most by great coaches who had decided to reveal their professional secrets and confide to others how they had obtained successful results. Each detail of their training experience is important and may be used directly by athletes and by other coaches working in the same sports disciplines. This book is different. The main aim of this manual is to give the reader practical information about how to use strength exercises in order to improve performance in a given sports discipline. The manual describes various means of training, methods and programs, which are related to the basic question, "How to train?". However, it is important to note

Rome, 2006, Y. Verkhoshansly with Gianpiero Ventroni, at that time physical preparation coach of the Italian soccer team "Juventus F.C.".

that the manual also includes theoretical observations that seek to answer the questions "What to train?" and "Why?".

Y. Verkhoshansky was not only a coach, but also one of the greatest experts in the field of sports training who worked, for most of his professional life, with coaches. He did not teach them how to train their athletes; he worked with them so that coaches and their athletes were able find solutions together.

Rome, 2008-2009. On the left - Y,Verkhoshansky with Nils Holmdahl, Sweden National Volley Ball Team coach. On the right – with Mark Bennet, fitness coach of Welsh National Rugby Team.

The main part of the training programs for different sports disciplines described in this manual were elaborated in collaboration with these coaches and approved of by their athletes. This is neither a recipe book nor is it a series of prescriptions; it is a frame of reference for a creative coach.

To find ways of successfully putting these programs into practice, it is necessary to try and fully understand how these programs have been compiled, and why they guarantee better results with respect to other programs. Their successful interpretation through your own coaching and training experience depends on highlighting two points: the essence of these programs which cannot be changed and the variable details which may be adapted to your particular sport discipline.

Natalia Verkhoshansky

Acknowledgments

The people involved in this new edition have been very precious in supporting us in this project. Our appreciation goes first to James Smith, who assisted us in conveying the original version to the English text. James has been very precious in his contributions because of his familiarity both with our previous works and with the current English sport terminology due to his professional background: former University of Pittsburgh Football Assistant Physical Preparation Coach, founder of Powerdevelopmentinc.com, and author of many articles and manuals about sports training.

We also would like to thank several others who were involved at various stages of the project: Riccardo Barros for his contribution in preparing Appendix 3; Nils Holmdahl, Sweden's national volleyball team coach, for his suggestions on Chapter 1, and Nate Davis, Assistant track & field coach at the University of Wisconsin, for his final text review of the Preface and Appendix 4.

One year after publication many readers notified us of the need for an English review of the text. Knowing the difficulties and the knowledge needed in doing this job, we asked Danny Raimondi, Research Assistant at the University of Minnesota, to help us in this endeavor.

The result is an easier to understand text, especially for English readers. Thanks, Danny.

TABLE OF CONTENTS

METHODOLOGICAL FOUNDATIONS OF SPECIAL STRENGTH TRAINING

Special Strength Training (SST) essentially means using specialized resistance exercises to improve the athlete's competition performance in his sports discipline.

The use of resistance exercises is not a recent practice; dating back to the Greek Olympians, some ancient drawings clearly show exercises with external resistance which are very similar to those used today. The most common method of increasing external resistance is still by means of weights (weighted objects placed on the shoulders, fastened to the legs, held in the hands, or thrown). Special equipment is also used to change the vertical vector of the force of gravity, and to oppose the force of muscle contraction.

Resistance exercises are traditionally referred to as 'strength exercises' because their main purpose is to stimulate the improvement of strength ability. However, as we will find out in this manual, the influence of these exercises on the body is more substantial: they stimulate the exertion of specific motor functions and, due to the corresponding morphological-functional transformation of the athlete's organism; they ensure the adaptation increase in these functions.

SST may be used not only in Olympic sports and in sports training in general, but also in any kind of activity which requires a high level of physical performance.

Regardless of the professional field or sports discipline, the fundamental rule when applying SST is an awareness of the particular conditions of the activity, the factors that influence and determine its efficiency, and how SST acts on these factors.

The famous Russian dancer Vladimir Shubarin used the SST methods reported in Y. Verkhoshansky's book 'Triple Jump'. From 1960-1970, his incredible leaps amazed the fans of the classic and pop dancing genre.

1.1. SPORT RESULT AND FACTORS DETERMINING ITS IMPROVEMENT

1.1.1. SPORT RESULT AS POWER OUTPUT OF COMPETITION EXERCISE

The essence of sports activities lie in the movements of the human body. Sports movements are not simply changes of bodily positions in space: in every sport discipline, without exception, they represent a **complex motor action** aimed at completing determined **motor tasks**. It can be a single motor task, such as obtaining a quantitative goal in certain Track & Field sports disciplines, or a qualitative goal, determined by the experts (sports referees), as in gymnastics and figure skating. In team sports and combat sports, it is necessary to solve several motor tasks, which conform to the rules of competition in order to achieve the final goal - win the match or beat the opponent.

Solving the motor task of complex motor action is accomplished through appropriate *motor pattern* – the sequence of movements arranged in space and time. In sport, it is the competition exercise, which represents a rationally organized system of movements aimed at achieving a specific goal, in specific conditions, under the competition's rules.

The main quantitative characteristic of sport results are, in general, maximum speed of acyclic movements or the maximum average speed of cyclic locomotion. In fact, the success of the weightlifter's completed lift, the wrestler's clinch, the boxer's punch, the fencer's lunge, or the race of a sprinter / marathon runner, is the speed at which these movements are performed. The speed of execution in the competition exercise, however, is only an 'external' characteristic of the sport result. In fact, to change bodily position (gravitational centre of the body mass) or modify limb position in space, an athlete has to overcome the forces of gravity and inertia, acting against them in an effort to accomplish the motor task in the shortest possible time.

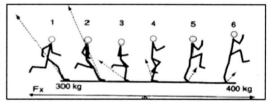

Fig. 1.1 - Interaction between the athlete's body and the base of support during the long jump take off movement. The arrows indicate the resulting force vector's interaction with the base of support (I.Ratov, V.Muraviov).

In order to increase the speed, the athlete must develop an adequate level of force. For example:

- a long jumper, in order to ensure the necessary speed of flight at the end of the run-up, has to execute a powerful push-off on the support base to overcome the force of gravity of his body weight (Fig. 1.1);
- a weightlifter develops strength by interacting with the support base and the barbell to overcome the force of gravity related to its weight (Fig. 1.2);
- a swimmer develops the traction force in the stroke movements to propel his body through the water, interacting with water resistance (see Fig. 1.3).

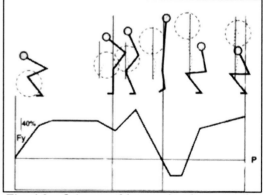

Fig. 1.2 - Scheme of interaction between the athlete's body, the base, and the barbell during the execution of a Weightlifting exercise (first part of Jerk): Fy – vertical component of interaction between the athlete's body and the support base, P – the sum of the athlete's body weight and the weight of barbell.

Therefore, the final goal of competition exercises in Olympic sports ('Citius, Altius, Fortius' – 'Faster, Higher, Stronger') may almost always be related to the capacity to express power produced by the speed of movements and by the force of overcoming external resistance. Consequently, a training process focused on improving the sports results represents the process of increasing the **power output** of competition exercises.

Fig. 1.3 – Interaction between the athlete's body and water resistance

1.1.2. DETERMINING FACTORS IN INCREASING THE POWER OUTPUT OF COMPETITION EXERCISES

"Virtually all human movements are aimed at achieving something in the environment. In any case, each and every movement takes place in an environment. Mechanically, the environment influences movements through the forces from the environment that act on the body[9]."

From a biomechanical perspective, human movement represents an interaction between the human body and the external environment (A. Bernstein). The competition exercise represents a system of movements in which the simultaneous and successive displacements of the body's segments are arranged in relation to the final goal. To achieve this goal, the movement system must be executed according to pre-determined spatial-temporal characteristics, which ensure the possibility of overcoming external and internal forces formed for solving the motor tasks.

Thus, increasing the working effect (power output) of competition exercises requires the acquisition of specific skills to control the bodily movements and the body's capacity to generate the active force to overcome the external and internal opposition.

From a physiological perspective, human movement represents an interaction between the *human organism* [10] and the external environment. The theory of Functional Systems (P. Anokhin) explains the physiological mechanism which ensures the possibility to accomplish this interaction. To achieve the goal of the complex motor action, several structural elements of the physiological systems (such as the central nervous system, the neuro-muscular system, and the energy-supply system) are activated and gathered into a **Functional System** 'focused on' and 'determined by' this goal.

While improving the athlete's sports mastery, these elements of the physiological system undergo an accelerated transformation process which guarantees the stabilization of their functional characteristics at a higher level:

- for the central nervous system, it means increasing the capacity to produce the necessary intensity of the volley of impulses from the central motor area to the motor periphery and to ensure the central motor plan parameters of intramuscular coordination;
- for the neuromuscular system, it means improving the function of the motor apparatus in accordance with the work regime;
- for the energy supply system, it means the enhancement of energy producing mechanisms and set-

---

[9] Gerrit Jan van Ingen Schenau, Arthur J. van Soest. On the Biomechanical basis of dexterity. In the book: "Dexterity and its development" edited by M.L. Latash and M. T.Turvay . Lowrence Erlbown Associates, Inc. Publishers.

[10] The word "organism" means "an organized body", a system regarded as analogous in its structure or functions to a living body. In this manual the term ' human body' is used when it refers to the human body as an anatomical system; the term 'human organism' is used in reference to the human body as a physiological system.

ting up bidirectional links between them.

All these adaptive changes, taking place on different levels, are very specific and depend on the demands imposed on the body during a sports activity. For example:

- in speed-strength sport events, an increase in the power output is mostly dependent on the increase in the functional level of the Central Nervous System (CNS) and the neuromuscular system;
- in endurance sport events, an increase in the power output is mostly dependent on enhancing energy producing mechanisms.

The stabilization process of the functional characteristics sets up at higher levels a **Specialized Morpho-Functional Structure** in the athlete's organism, a stable mutual connection between the physiological systems, ensuring an optimal level of the athlete's specific **work capacity** related to his sports discipline. It must be pointed out that the Functional System is the mechanism assigned to solve the motor action goals on call, while the Specialized Morpho-Functional Structure is a time stabilizer[11]. Thus, the increase in the power of muscular contractions during competition exercise is assured by the increase in the functional level of physiological systems. The higher the athlete's level of sports mastery, the more specialized this mechanism is.

The characteristics of the power produced by muscle contractions are determined by the specific *working regime* typical of every sports discipline: the typology of the sports discipline determines whether it is important to be able to express maximal power in the shortest period of time or maintain a high level of average power over a set period of time. Despite the differences between these two working regimes, the power output of competition exercise is always determined by the *muscular capacity to produce the greatest quantity of mechanical energy per unit of time*. This capacity is called 'the functional power of the motor system' or **motor potential**. The athlete's motor potential determines his work capacity related to the specific regime of sports discipline; this 'specialized work capacity' is expressed through the organism's Specialized Morpho-Functional Structure.

The resulting power-output of the competition exercise also depends on the athlete's skill to organize movements in a rational way such that the total energy produced by muscular contractions is wholly

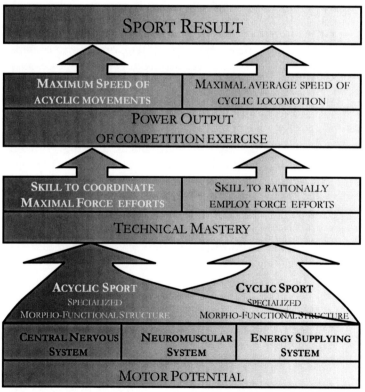

Fig. 1.4 – The determining factors for increasing the power-output of competition exercise

---

[11] For further information about this issue see Appendix 4 ("The basic mechanism assuring versatility of human motor function")

used to execute specific technical gestures for achieving the final result.

The athlete's ability to effectively express his motor-potential in competition is called **technical mastery**.

In speed-strength sport disciplines, technical mastery, characterized by the <u>skill to coordinate maximal force efforts</u>, is ensured by the immediate and full employment of one's motor potential.

In endurance sport disciplines, technical mastery is characterized by the <u>skill to rationally employ force-efforts</u>, both in the organization of every single cycle of movement and in competition exercise as a whole. In team and combat sports, technical mastery is characterized by both of these skills.

The increase in power output of sports exercise, therefore, is caused by the adaptation of the whole organism to the specific muscular work which is accomplished by:

- increasing the functional level of physiological systems involved in the execution of competition exercise;
- improving the specific function of the motor control system, ensuring the athlete's capacity to organize the competition exercise movements in a rational way.

In another words, an increase in sports results is ensured by two main factors (Fig. 1.4):

- increasing the athlete's special work capacity (motor potential);
- perfecting the athlete's skill to effectively realize his motor potential in competition exercise performance (technical mastery).

1.2. SST ROLE IN THE TRAINING PROCESS

1.2.1. MAIN COMPONENTS OF THE TRAINING PROCESS

The essence of long-term training in sport is shown in Fig. 1.5.

The improvement of sports result (S) is directly connected to:

1) the increase in the athlete's motor potential, that is, the level of special work capacity (A);

2) the improvement of an athlete's skill to effectively use his motor potential, that is, his technical mastery (B).

From the graph, we can deduce that for elite athletes able to fully use their motor potential (lines A and B drawn closer), further increases in sport results (S) can be achieved mainly by increasing their motor potential (A). This is the main task in the training of high level athletes.

Since sport results have to be obtained in a given period

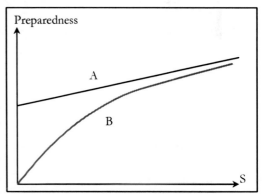

Fig. 1.5 - Dynamics of an athlete's motor potential (A) and technical mastery (B) in relation to the sport's result (S)

of time (the days of competition), the training process aimed at improving sport results is referred to as 'preparation'.

The task of increasing the athlete's motor potential is resolved by the so-called **Special Physical Preparation (SPP)**. The Special Strength Training (SST) is an important component of SPP.

The task of improving the athlete's skill to effectively realize his motor potential in the competition exercise is accomplished by the **technical** and **tactical preparation**.

In speed-strength sports, the main purpose of technical preparation is to maximize the realization of muscle strength potential in the specific regime of competition exercise.

In endurance sports, the main purpose of technical preparation is to economize movements, improving the skill of exploiting the so-called non-metabolic energy between the active and reactive movement phases.

Although sport motor actions are always aimed at maximizing the expressed power level, the athlete has to reach not only a rational space-time coordination of movements (which, in itself, is quite difficult), but he also has to execute these movements employing a certain power in order to overcome external and internal opposition which clash with the human organism. In other words, it is a matter of control, not so much of movements, but of the force efforts that initiate and regulate them. Thus, the improvement of the athlete's technical mastery is based on the improvement of the athlete's capacity to coordinate the force-effort. Considering that this capacity depends, first of all, on the capacity to overcome external resistance, the improvement in technical mastery is also based on an increase in the athlete's motor potential.

According to one of the most important training rules, an increase in the athlete's motor potential must precede the improvement of his capacity to utilize it in his specific sport regime.

In the preparation period, the SST means must precede the technical preparation exercises executed at the maximal level of power output.

This approach does not mean overestimating the role of SST. On the contrary, it should be regarded as a rational approach, which guarantees favorable conditions to accomplish the technical-tactical preparation tasks. Based on this we can assert (without negating the importance of other aspects) that the main role for improving sports mastery belongs to SST.

1.2.2. SST - INCREASING THE MOTOR POTENTIAL

Motor potential is the total quantity of mechanical work that can be produced by the human body's motor system while performing certain movements.

The motor potential can be recognized as general or specific. The general motor potential pertains to the capability of achieving a mechanical output in every kind of muscular work (e.g. the general motor potential of the male body is higher than that of the female body). The specific motor potential pertains to the capability of achieving a mechanical output in specific movements of a given muscular work.

In physics mechanical work is the amount of energy transferred by force acting through a distance. The specific motor potential of an athlete, therefore, depends on the total quantity of mechanical work that can be produced by his motor system, transforming the force of muscular contractions into specific movements, which compose the competition exercise. Thus, to increase the athlete's motor potential it is necessary to increase the force-generating capacity of the muscles involved in the execution of the competition exercise.

As mentioned above, the competition exercise represents a system of movements in which the simultaneous and successive displacement of the body's segments is arranged in relation to the final goal. These movements are organized in a defined *kinematic*[12] structure in conformity with the anatomical and functional structure of the human motor apparatus.

The human motor apparatus allows executes a wide range of different movements; these can be subdivided in three levels of complexity:

---

[12] *Kinematics* - dealing with the implications of observed motions without regard for circumstances causing them.

1) single-joint movements involving two actively combined adjacent links (kinematic pair);
2) multi-joint movements including a combination of several body links (kinematic chain);
3) conjugate-sequence combination of several multi-joint movements (kinematic system).

To accomplish each of these movements, the traction force must be developed by muscle contractions. The prime movers, primarily responsible for generating the voluntary movements in a kinematic pair, are the *muscle–agonists*: the muscle groups, anatomically designed to fulfill single joint movements via limb leverages. To accomplish the multi-joint movements in a kinematic chain and kinematic system, the muscles–agonists do not work alone; when the motor action involves the whole body, the other muscles ensure displacement of the body mass and its segments in a given direction, maintaining the body's posture during these displacements.

To obtain a given kinematic characteristic of the complex motor action, the motor control system operates not at the level of a single muscle, but at the level of innate functional components of the human motor apparatus, called **working mechanisms**. The most important working mechanism of the human motor apparatus refers to the so named **muscle synergy**.

The concept of muscle synergy was proposed by N.Bernstein as a neural strategy of simplifying the control of multiple degrees of freedom[13], as a pattern of co-activation of muscles recruited by a single neural command signal. One muscle can be part of different muscle synergies, and one synergy can activate multiple muscles. Few muscle synergies are combined at different proportions to form a continuum of muscle activation patterns for smooth motor control during various tasks. These synergies work together to cause movements.

Initially it was thought that the main function of muscle synergy was eliminating the redundant degrees of freedom (mechanics) by constraining the movements of certain joints or muscles. A more recent hypothesis proposes that the central nervous system does not eliminate the redundant degrees of freedom, but instead uses all of them to ensure flexible and stable performance of motor tasks.

The main muscle synergies are constituted by:

- the muscle groups, agonists and antagonists, whose synchronized contractions propel the movement of body segments in a given direction;
- the muscle groups that ensure *elementary postural reflexes* (the involuntary force efforts helping to maintain posture during the displacements of the centre of body mass and its links).

There are also two other working mechanisms, which help to ensure flexible and stable performance of motor tasks. They are:

1) *rational succession of different muscle's recruitment* - the particular system of reflexes, ensuring the rational subsequent activation of the muscles specific to different body segments during the execution of complex movements;
2) *elastic properties of muscles* - the force stored in the muscle complex as elastic energy;
3) *muscular system tonus* - a stable state of muscle's contraction, which ensures the readiness of the whole muscular system to execute movements.

The working mechanisms are created and fixed in the human genotype as a result of evolution of the human motor apparatus. In the execution of competition exercise, the ratio of the working mechanisms involvement depends on its spatial-temporal characteristics (kinematic structure). Sport training does not change these mechanisms, but it may increase their functional level (force-generation capacity) and optimize their reciprocal interrelations in the specific movement coordination. Therefore, to increase the athlete's motor potential, it is necessary to increase not only the strength potential of the muscles, but the force generation capacity of the working mechanisms involved in the execution of

[13] Bernstein N. The Coordination and Regulation of Movements. Pergamon Press. New York, 1967.

competition exercises; this guarantees the increase in the quantity of mechanical energy expressed. The higher quantity of mechanical energy each of these working mechanisms is able to ensure, the higher total quantity of mechanical energy will be available to the athlete in the competition exercise (i.e. the higher will be his specific motor potential).

The increase in the force generation capacity of the working mechanisms involved in the execution of the competition exercise can be obtained by the SST means, appropriately selected for the given sport discipline. Resistance exercises are able to increase the traction force of the main muscular synergies involved in competition exercise. First of all, they can increase the traction force of the muscle synergies producing the so named *anti-gravitational force*. In the speed-strength sports, these muscle synergies produce powerful anti-gravitational force efforts in the final phase of competition exercise, whereas in endurance sports it is the *body propelling force-effort* in each cycle of locomotion (ground propulsion in running or water propulsion in swimming and rowing). Free-weight exercises are also able to improve the elementary postural reflexes and increase the tonus of the muscular system as a whole. Jump exercises are able to improve the effectiveness of utilizing the reactive capacity of the muscles.

1.2.3. SST - IMPROVING THE ATHLETE'S SKILL TO RATIONALLY USE THE MOTOR POTENTIAL

The resulting power output of competition exercises depends not only on the total quantity of mechanical energy the athlete's body produces in specific movements (motor potential), but also on the athlete's skill to rationally use this mechanical energy during the execution of the whole competition exercise (see Fig. 1.5).

The competition exercise is a system of movements organized to solve a given motor task; each of these movements is the result of interactions between the body and the external environment. The complexity of all these interactions with the external environment can be represented by a **strength field**.

Analyzing every competition exercise from a *kinetics*[14] perspective, it may be assumed that the strength field includes not only the *active* forces produced in the movements, but also the *reactive* forces, which are activated consequently by the impact of active forces to the external environment. These forces can be external or internal to the body and, depending on their directions, may assist or resist the movement.

'In order to achieve a desired motor goal accurately and within a reasonably short time, one must get ready to counteract (or to use)... external forces and object motions as well as reactive forces, i.e., forces emerging due to joint-coupling' (M. Latash, 1998)[15].

Depending on the character, origin, and direction of forces, the strength field includes several different components which may be identified as follows:
- active driving forces produced by muscular contractions;
- gravitational forces (bodyweight or its links);
- reactive forces arising as a result of the interaction between the active forces and the environment;

---

[14] *Kinetics* - one of the branches of dynamics, concerned with what body movements are produced under the action of particular forces. It is not to be confused with kinematics, the study of motion without regard to force or mass.

[15] Mark Latash. Progress in Motor Control. Volume 1: Bernstein's Traditions in Movement Studies. Human Kinetic, 1998, pp 408.

- force of the body's (or its links) inertia;
- force stored in the muscle-complex as elastic energy during the preparatory phases of movements. Each one of these components is involved in the process of solving the motor task and has a distinct influence on the result. During the process of assimilation of the correct technique, in the strength field, some phases of active and reactive dynamics (force application) become more accentuated with the change of electrical activity of the muscles involved. In the electrical activity of the muscles, the following changes can be observed (Fig. 1.6 and 1.7):
- an increase in the total level of electrical activity and synchronization of moto-neuron impulses;
- a concentration of muscle-agonist electrical activity in specific phases of movement.

In the beginning, when the athlete is still learning the techniques of the competition exercise, these accentuated phases of active and reactive dynamics are expressed weakly and are irregularly distributed over the time of exercise execution. When the athlete achieves a certain level of technical mastery, these elements of the strength field become more accentuated in specific phases of exercise execution and more interrelated. They aggregate in a stable system of interactions, i.e. a specific pattern made by simultaneous and sequential actions, called the **biodynamic structure**.

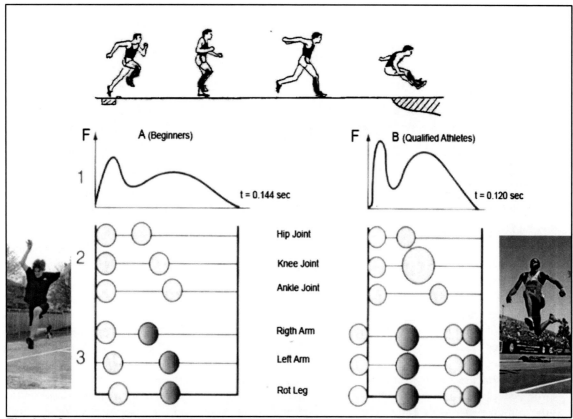

Fig. 1.6 - Sequence of accentuated active and reactive dynamics of the motor system for the second take-off in the triple jump: 1. resulting force-time curve; 2. accentuation in the tension of the relevant hip and knee muscles, and the ankle joints of the support leg (measured with a myotension meter); 3. accentuation of active and reactive (shaded circles) dynamics of rotary movement associated with the swinging arms and leg. The white circles refer to active, concentrated voluntary effort. (Y. Verkhoshansky, 1970).

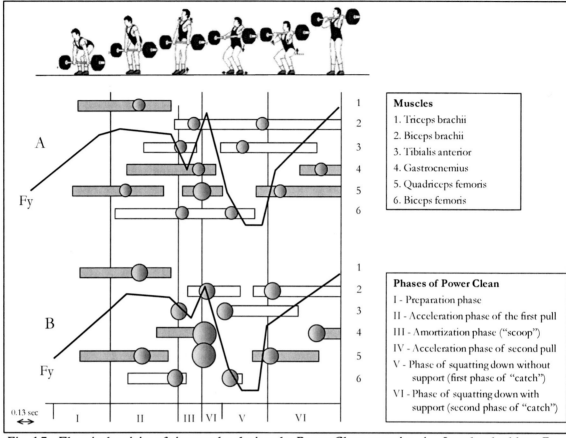

Muscles

1. Triceps brachii
2. Biceps brachii
3. Tibialis anterior
4. Gastrocnemius
5. Quadriceps femoris
6. Biceps femoris

Phases of Power Clean

I - Preparation phase
II - Acceleration phase of the first pull
III - Amortization phase ("scoop")
IV - Acceleration phase of second pull
V - Phase of squatting down without
    support (first phase of "catch")
VI - Phase of squatting down with
    support (second phase of "catch")

Fig. 1.7 - Electrical activity of six muscles during the Power Clean exercise. A – Low level athlete. B – High level athlete. Fy vertical component of ground reaction. (V. A. Podlivaiev, 1975)

The biodynamic structure of competition exercise constitutes the basic framework of the movement system; it is the main mechanism for an efficient realization of the athlete's motor potential during its performance.

HOW CAN THE BIODYNAMIC STRUCTURE BE IMPROVED?

There is an established hierarchical scheme of relationships among the elements of a biodynamic structure - some elements hold dominant roles while others hold subordinate positions. The biodynamic structure of the competition exercise can be divided into two fundamental components:

1) the key-elements, crucial for managing motor tasks, as well as for producing the resulting power output;

2) secondary elements, which assist the key-elements during the competition exercise's execution.

For example, the mechanical energy required to execute the Track & Field long jump is built up during the run-up phase (Fig. 1.8), a result of horizontal acceleration and the displacement of the athlete's body mass. The take-off movement ensures the vertical rotation of the horizontal force vector due to the contraction energy of the leg extension muscles and the elastic energy accumulated in the stretched muscles during the phase of amortization. The effectiveness of the long jump execution depends on the athlete's capacity to perform the take-off movement with the correct angle of the force vector rotation (with minimal reduction in horizontal speed), maintaining the body's equilibrium during the flight phase. The force-effort of the final take-off movement plays a dominant role in the organization of the whole movement system and in determining the power output expressed in the complete exercise: increasing the force effort in this key-movement causes the increase in power output of the competition exercise as whole.

To improve the biodynamic structure of a given competition exercise, it is therefore necessary to:

I. identify its key movements;

II. increase their **working effect** (see the following paragraph);

III. improve the efficiency of interactions between key-movements, and between the key-movements and the secondary movements.

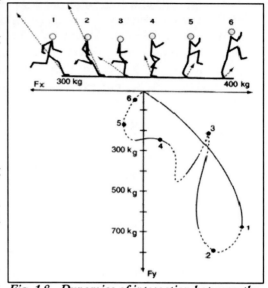

Fig. 1.8 - Dynamics of interaction between the athlete's body and the support base during the long jump take off movement. The arrows indicate the resulting force vector of interaction with support base (I.Ratov, V.Muraviov)

To <u>identify the key-movements</u>, it is necessary to analyze the biodynamic structure of the competition exercise. The most common key-movements could be identified in three groups:

1) Displacements of the body mass centre from a determined body position in a determined direction. For example:
   - ground propulsion force efforts, aimed at overcoming the external ground-reaction force in the take-off phases of running and jumping;
   - water propulsion force efforts, in the swimming stroke movements or in the movement of the propulsion devices in rowing.

2) Displacement of the 'active' body limb:
   - in the phases of the contact between the active body limb and ball, in the in the final phase of kicks (volleyball and soccer);
   - in the phases of the contact between the two sport devices in the final phase of the stroke (tennis, cricket, golf, baseball);
   - in the final movement of throwing (track and field throwing and in the throwing movement of sport games);
   - in the kick movements of combat sports (box and karate).

3) Synchronized displacement of the body mass and 'active' body limb in the final movements of the competition exercise (throwing) and in the final movements of the main technical-tactical elements of the competition activity in sport games and combat sport.

To <u>increase the working effect of the key-movements</u> of a competition exercise, the so named **local exercises**, having single motor structure, must be used. The local exercises are chosen based on the best similarity of their strength fields to those of the key movements (**dynamic correspondence**, see § 1.4.3.1). These exercises are executed with determined training methods and are the most important group of SST means. Their main task is to increase the athlete's strength capabilities which determine the working effect of the key-movements (see the following § 1.3.1).

To <u>improve the efficiency of interactions</u> between the key-movements and the secondary movements of a competition exercise, the so named **global exercises**[16], having complex motor structure, must be used. The global exercises should reproduce the competition exercise as a whole or the main technical-tactical elements of the competition activities under more difficult conditions.

Also, the training methods of technical preparation are used for improving the efficiency of interactions between the key-movements and the secondary movements of competition exercise.

1.3. TASKS OF SST

1.3.1. IMPROVING THE ATHLETE'S STRENGTH CAPABILITIES

As was underlined before, to increase the power output of the competition exercise, it's necessary to increase the working effect of its key-movements.

What is the working effect of movement and what does its increase determine?

1.3.1.1. IMPROVING THE WORKING EFFECT OF MOVEMENT

The **working effect of movement** is the mechanical work produced by movement as a result of active interaction between the body and the external environment. The working effect of movement is determined by the character (evolution over the time) of the force effort developed by the muscles involved in the movement.

If we don't consider the type of movement (its direction, the body segment that executes the movement, and the muscular work regime), the character (evolution over the time) of the force effort developed could be represented by the curve F/t in figure 1.9. The working effect is determined by the amplitude of the impulses of force ($I = F \times t$) overcoming the external resistance force. In figure 1.9, the working effect of force effort is recognized as the area below the curve F (t) and above the line (P) which indicates the weight or the opposing resistance force which has to be overcome. The increase in the working effect of a movement develops by increasing this area.

From an abstract point of view, the working effect of a movement can be increased by increasing the maximal magnitude of the force developed (the highest point of the curve F in figure 1.9) and/or by increasing the time (T1-T2) of the force employed to overcome the external resistance (P).

The increase in the time of force

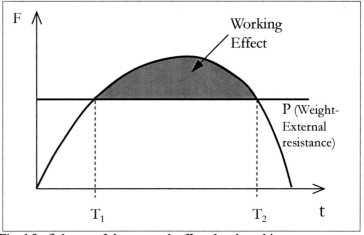

Fig. 1.9 - Scheme of the strength effort developed in a movement

---

[16] The terms 'global' and 'local' are usually used to identify, respectively, the exercises involving a large volume or small volume of muscles. In our contest these terms are referred to the motor structure of competition exercise.

employment (T1-T2) may be obtained by decreasing the velocity of movement. Decreasing the velocity of movement, however, is in contrast with the nature of competition exercise: the main qualitative characteristics of sport result are the maximum speed of acyclic movements or the maximum average speed of cyclic locomotion. For this reason, the force effort of key movements of competition exercise must be applied in a limited or short time.

The results of research (see Fig. 1.10 and 1.11) confirmed this assumption: the increase in an athlete's sports mastery is strictly correlated to the increase in the maximal magnitude of force-effort of key movements, and to the decrease the time in which the force-effort employed overcomes the external resistance (T1-T2).

In speed-strength sport exercises, in order to increase the working effect of the displacement of the body (the centre of body mass) or of the displacement of the sports device (in throwing), the athlete has to increase the maximal force effort in the shortest amount of time. As sports mastery increases, the magnitude of the force-effort increases and the time to achieve the force level, equal to the opposing resistance force (weight of the body or the sports device), decreases (Fig. 1.10).

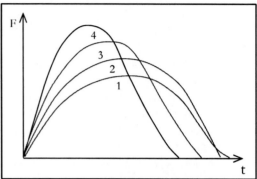

Fig. 1.10 - The evolution of the maximal explosive force effort in the track & field take off movement of an athlete during the process of his sport mastery improvement (the evolution goes from curve 1 to curve 4)

In cyclic exercises (running, swimming, rowing), in order to increase the working effect of the body mass centre's displacement, the athlete must increase the magnitude of the ground propulsion or the water propulsion force-efforts during the active phases of each cycle, with alternate deep and quick muscular relaxations during the passive phases. As sports mastery increases, the magnitude of each force-effort increases, the time of its employment decreases (the period of active phases decreases) and the period of the relaxation phase increases because of the higher distance covered in each cycle of locomotion due to the higher maximal force effort employed in the active phase (Fig. 1.11). As a result, the number of cyclic repetitions of movement decreases slightly, along with the decrease in the time of the execution of the whole exercise.

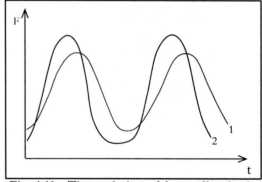

Fig. 1.11 - The evolution of force effort in the cyclic movements of an athlete during the process of improving his sport mastery (from curve 1 to curve 2)

The results of this research pointed out a common characteristic to be achieved for the improvement of results in both cyclic and acyclic sports: increase the magnitude of force-effort employed in the key movements and decrease the time of its employment. In other words, improvement in performance is ensured by the same changes in the character of the force effort in the key-movements of competition exercise, but the different conditions under which the neuro-muscular system works during the sports activity requires different mechanisms for ensuring these changes.

What are the neuro-muscular mechanisms for ensuring the needed changes in the character of force effort development in a given sport key-movement?

1.3.1.2. BASIC STRENGTH CAPABILITIES

Long term research carried out in the Sport Research Laboratories of Moscow[17] showed that the athlete's capacity to perform specific movements with maximal force output in a minimal amount of time is not a 'blending' of separately developed speed and strength motor abilities (see Appendix 4), but is determined by several relatively independent characteristics of the neuro-muscular system which interact in an orderly manner to accomplish a common motor task. At the same time, they maintain their individuality and readiness to enter into any functional combination that may be required under the changing conditions of the performed activity. These functional characteristics of the motor apparatus were identified as the **basic strength capabilities**[18]:

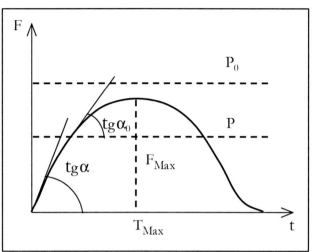

Fig. 1.12 - The force-time curve of a maximal explosive effort and its parameters determining the basic strength capabilities.

- **Maximal Strength (P_0)**[19] – is the greatest magnitude of the voluntary force-effort that the athlete displays in the isometric regime when there is no time limit to complete the task (Fig. 1.12).
- **Explosive Strength (J)** - is characterized by the athlete's capacity to achieve the maximal force-effort (F_{MAX}) in the shortest time (T_{MAX}): $J = F_{MAX}/T_{MAX}$.
- **Starting Strength (Q)** - characterizes the athlete's capacity to produce rapid increases in force-effort at the beginning of the muscular tension. It is measured by the tangent ($tg\alpha$) to the curve $F(t)$ at the point of the force effort beginning.
- **Accelerating Strength (G)** - characterizes the athlete's capacity to rapidly achieve the maximal value of the force effort (F_{MAX}) in the final phase of muscular tension. In a dynamic regime, the final phase begins when the magnitude of force effort achieves the level of the external resistance (P). It is measured by the tangent ($tg\alpha_0$) of the curve $F(t)$ when it intersects the line P.

The results of the research, carried out for the majority of Olympic sports, pointed out that:

1) basic strength capabilities are rarely displayed separately in sports movements. In a given sport's key-movement, each strength capability may have specific relevance to obtain the highest working effect. (e.g. Fig. 1.13);
2) each of the basic strength capabilities can be effectively improved using SST means in an appropriate regime, i.e., an appropriate level of external resistance, an appropriate ratio between the magnitude of the force-effort and the rate of force development, and an appropriate regime of

---

[17] 340 athletes of different sport disciplines participated in the research. The minimal sample group, for each sport discipline, included 18 athletes.

[18] For further information about strength capabilities see Y. Verkhoshansky's "The Fundamentals of Special Strength Training".

[19] In earlier publications, Verkhoshansky referred to the magnitude of voluntary maximal strength efforts (Po) as 'Absolute Strength'. This deserves clarification: the term 'Absolute Strength' should only be used when the maximal strength effort is provoked by an electrical impulse. For this reason, in this book, the term 'Maximal Strength' has been adopted in place of 'Absolute Strength'.

muscular contraction.

In summation, it is possible to assert that:

1) in the execution of different competition exercises the neuro-muscular system works under different conditions: the force-effort of the key-movements of a given competition exercise is ensured by using different functional options of the athlete's motor apparatus (strength capabilities), which interact in an orderly manner to accomplish a common motor task.

2) each strength capability can be effectively improved using determined resistance exercises in an appropriate regime (i.e. according to an appropriate method).

Therefore, to increase the force effort of the key-movement of a given competition exercise, it's necessary to use a combination of different training exercises, integrated in a training means system (see § 1.4.3.2).

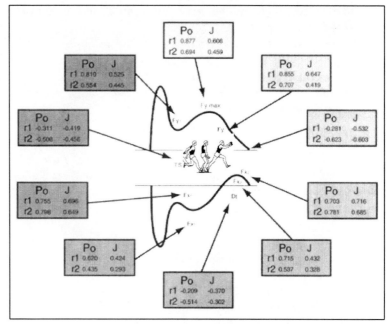

Fig. 1.13 - Correlations between the accentuated phases of active and reactive dynamics in the take-off phase of the Track & Field long jump execution and the basic strength capabilities of athletes (maximal and explosive strength – Po and J), evaluated in the one-leg Leg Press - r1, and the Seated Calf Rise – r2

1.3.1.3. STRENGTH CAPABILITIES RELATED TO THE REGIME OF MUSCULAR CONTRACTION

It's possible to identify another group of strength capabilities as the particular abilities to generate the strength effort in a specific regime of muscular contraction. Each of these strength capabilities is strictly related to one of the basic strength capabilities.

Before describing these strength capabilities, it is necessary to make some clarifications regarding the terms used to identify the muscle contraction regimes.

The following terms are used to identify the different contraction regimes:

1) *Isometric*, when the length of the muscle remains the same, while undergoing tension. The isometric regime of muscular contraction is usually associated with the term '*static regime*'.

2) all the other contraction regimes are associated with the term '*dynamic*':
   - *Isokinetic*, when the muscle contraction velocity remains constant, while force is allowed to vary;
   - *Isotonic*, when the tension in the muscle remains constant despite a change in muscle length;
   - *Miometric*, when the length of the muscles shorten while undergoing tension;
   - *Pliometric*, when the length of the muscle elongates, or lengthens, while undergoing tension.

Starting in 1959[20], the terms 'concentric' and 'eccentric' were used instead of the terms 'miometric' and

---

[20] Karpovich PV. Physiology of Muscular Activity. Philadelphia, PA: Saunders, 1959. Rodahl K, Horvath SM,

'pliometric'. Recently, the terms 'concentric' and 'eccentric' have been challenged by the scientific world:

"...In correlating muscle contractions with the movements of the limbs during walking and running, Hubbard and Stetson[21] recognized that muscles underwent contractions during three different 'conditions'. The three conditions were termed 'miometric', 'isometric', and 'pliometric' by coupling the Greek prefixes 'mio' (shorter), 'iso' (same), and 'plio' (longer) to the noun 'metric', defined as pertaining to measures or measurement. The definitions of 'concentric' as 'having the same centre' and of 'eccentric' as 'not having the same centre' are consistent with hypertrophy or the remodeling of the heart muscle, but are inappropriate to describe the contractions of skeletal muscles. The adjectives 'concentric' and 'eccentric' are misleading and inappropriate and should not be used to describe the contractions of skeletal muscles"[22].

To solve this terminological problem, in this book we adopt the terminology used in the Russian sports literature: muscular contractions in the miometric ('concentric') regime are referred to as '**overcoming**', while muscular contractions in the pliometric ('eccentric') regime are referred as '**yielding**'.

The capacity to generate maximal force in the isometric and dynamic regimes of muscular contraction is caused by different neuromuscular mechanisms, which are relatively independent of each other in their functional display and development. For this reason, *static strength* and *dynamic strength* are considered to be two different strength capabilities.

Static Strength is usually indentified as Maximal Strength (P_0) – the basic strength capability to generate the greatest magnitude of the voluntary isometric force-effort when there is no time limit to complete the task.

Dynamic Strength is identified as the ability to generate the greatest strength effort during the execution of a given movement. In the dynamic regime, the maximal strength effort depends on the conditions of movement execution and, first of all, on the level of external resistance.

When the force-effort is displayed in high speed movements with a small external resistance, its magnitude is determined by the so-called **High-Speed Strength** (Fv). The results of research showed that this capability is strictly correlated with the Starting Strength (Q), but with the increase of the external opposition, other basic strength capabilities play a dominant role.

In specially organized experiments, the role of different basic strength capabilities in the maximal explosive movements performed with different external resistance was studied. The strength capabilities of the athletes were evaluated in two maximal force efforts performed in isometric and in dynamic regimes: the Leg Press and the Seated Calf Raise (Fig. 1.14).

In the isometric regime, the athletes had to achieve maximal strength without a time limitation. In the dynamic regime, athletes had to perform a maximal explosive effort in the shortest time overcoming five different levels of external resistance: 20%, 40%, 60%, 80% and 100% of their maximal isometric strength Po, as evaluated in an isometric regime. In the experiment,

Fig. 1.14 - The test schemes using the Seated Calf Raise and the Leg Press

and Risch MPS. Muscle as a Tissue. New York: McGraw-Hill, 1962. Knuttgen HG, Petersen FB, and Klausen K. Exercise with concentric and eccentric muscle contractions. Acta Paediatr Scand Suppl 217: 42-46, 1971.

[21] Hubbard AW and Stetson RH. An experimental analysis of human locomotion. J Physiol 124: 300-313, 1938.

[22] Faulkner, J.A. Terminology for contractions of muscles during shortening, while isometric, and during lengthening. Journal of Applied Physiology 95: pp 455-459, 2003.

special equipment, the Universal Dynamometric Stand - UDS was used to record the curve F(t).

The statistical analysis of the tests showed that Maximal Strength, Explosive Strength, Starting Strength and Acceleration Strength had no equal relevance in generating the maximal explosive force effort with a change in the level of external opposition: one capability or another assumes the primary role. In explosive movements executed with low resistance, Starting Strength is of primary importance. As resistance increases, Explosive, and later Accelerating, Strength becomes more important.

Thus, in achieving the maximum speed of explosive movements, the relevance of Maximal Strength (P_0) depends on the level of external opposition to be overcome: the higher the external opposition, the higher the level of Maximal Strength necessary to ensure the maximal speed of movement. Figure 1.15 summarizes the results of this experiment:

- Y-axis: the generality coefficient r^2 ($r \times 100\%$).
- X-axis: the level of external resistance to overcome (% of maximal strength).
- The curve P_0/V_P shows the trend of correlation between maximal strength (P_0) and maximal speed of loaded movement (V_P) with the increase in the external resistance.
- The curve V_0/V_P shows the trend of correlation between the maximal speed of unloaded movement (V_0) and maximal speed of loaded movement (V_P) with the increase in the external resistance.
- Zones 1, 2, and 3 indicate the spectrum of movements with different external resistance, in which the

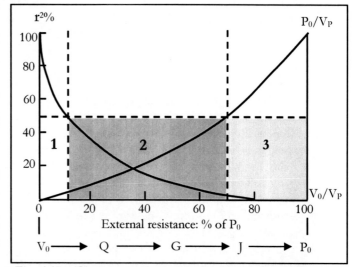

Fig. 1.15 - Changes in the level of correlation (coefficient of generality) between maximal strength and maximal speed of movement with the increasing of the external resistance

role of P_0, the maximal strength, is low (white zone), middle (dark gray zone) and high (light gray zone).

Below the graphic it is shown the relevance progression of the strength capabilities in assuring the maximal speed of the movements with the increase in the external resistance; the relevance of Q (starting strength) at a low percentage of external opposition, relevance of G (accelerating strength) and J (explosive strength) with a progressively higher external opposition, till the relevance of P_0 (maximal strength) when the external opposition is higher than 70% of P_0.

An important consideration to keep in mind is that sports movements are usually executed in a mixed regime of muscular contractions. For instance, during a single explosive movement in which the athlete has to displace a heavy load from a standing position, before initiating the movement, the muscles work in isometric regime. As soon as the developing isometric force effort achieves the level of the external resistance force, the movement starts and the muscles begin to work in dynamic regime.

In the so-called 'starting movements' executed without a 'countermovement' against heavy resistance (e.g. the body's static inertia), the main role is played by the maximal isometric and explosive isometric muscular strength. When the explosive movement is executed with a 'countermovement', i.e. in the combined 'yielding-overcoming' regime, a major role is played by explosive strength expressed in the overcoming regime. If the overcoming contraction follows the mechanical stretching of the muscles, the elastic potential of mechanical muscle stretching provides with an extra source of energy facilitating the enhancement of the subsequent muscular contraction. This particular characteristic of the motor apparatus is termed the *Reactive Ability*.

Reactive Ability (R) is the characteristic of the nervous-muscular system to display a powerful explosive effort immediately after the occurrence of a sharp mechanical stretching of the muscles by an external force (i.e., in the rapid transition from the yielding to the overcoming regime of muscular work).

1.3.1.4. STRENGTH ENDURANCE

Strength Endurance is usually defined as:
- a specific form of strength displayed in activities which require a relatively long duration of muscle tension with minimal decreases in efficiency,
- the ability to resist a force over time or to make repeated muscle contractions against a force,
- a measure of the ability of a muscle or muscle group to work continuously. It has a meaning similar to muscle endurance, but with Strength Endurance there is a greater emphasis on the amount of force which can be resisted.

Strength Endurance can thus be defined as the ability to maintain a high level of muscular contraction or contractions under work conditions of long duration. Since the work conditions and duration could be different, it's not possible to establish in general what determines Strength Endurance, but it is possible only in reference to the given typology of exercise. Strength Endurance could be understood as the ability to maintain a high level of a single force effort, holding a given position of posture (*Static Strength Endurance*) or as the ability to reproduce the utmost level of repetitive force efforts during a certain period of time (*Dynamic Strength Endurance*). In each of these types of muscular functioning, the resulting power output is determined by different forms of mutual connections among different components of the neuro-muscular and energy supply systems.

Static Strength Endurance is the athlete's ability to maintain a constant level of muscular tension, holding a given position of posture for a certain time (*postural stability*). This strength capability is important in such sports as Skating and Alpine Skiing and also in Wrestling.

Some research showed that in certain muscle groups, Maximal Strength and Static Strength Endurance are directly related: the higher the Maximal Strength, the longer is ability to maintain the static tension with a given level of external opposition. Electro-miographic analyses have shown that the capacity to maintain the isometric muscular contraction is determined by the particular mechanism of the motor unit's coordination, which ensures the possibility of alternating the activation of different motor units in the working muscles.

Dynamic Strength Endurance is the ability to reproduce the utmost level of repetitive force-efforts during a certain period of time. It is typically associated with cyclic exercises in which considerable tension is repeated without interruption during each cycle of movement.

It is not possible to establish what determines Dynamic Strength Endurance in general, but only in relation to the duration of exercise. The power output in cyclic exercises of different durations is determined by different forms of interactions among the neuro-muscular and energy supply systems. Since there are two main energy supply systems, aerobic and anaerobic, the term Dynamic Strength Endurance is advisable to refer to:
- **Maximum Anaerobic Power** (**MAP**) to identify the ability to effectively execute short-term (10-15 sec) anaerobic work at the maximum level of power output.
- **Local Muscular Endurance** (**LME**) to identify the ability to maintain muscle contractile capacity for a long period of time in the aerobic regime.

Research has shown that the determining factor of sport results in cyclic disciplines is the muscle's capacity to express the utmost force effort in the main body propelling movement during the execution of the given cyclic locomotion:

- at maximal speed level (maximal power of work in an anaerobic regime);
- at the speed level at which the anaerobic threshold is achieved (maximal power of work in an aerobic regime).

In most endurance sport disciplines, both abilities are strictly correlated with the magnitude of the maximal explosive force effort (F_{MAX}). For example, the most important specific characteristics of Track & Field middle distance running are:

- the maximal average stride length while running at maximal speed;
- the maximal average stride flight phase time while running at maximal speed;
- the maximal average stride length while running at speeds of anaerobic threshold;
- the minimal average stride support phase time while running at speeds of anaerobic threshold.

A special experiment was carried out with the goal of discovering what strength capabilities are correlated with these specific characteristics of Track & Field running. The strength capabilities expressed in the Seated Calf Raise and the Leg Press were valuated with the UDS. The results of this experiment showed that the magnitude of the maximal explosive force-effort (F_{MAX}) in the Leg Press has the highest level of correlation with the above mentioned running characteristics. In the following experiment, it was shown that the increase in F_{MAX}, obtained after a specially organized training stage with the use of SST means, ensures the increase in these specific running characteristics.

Another important result that came from these experiments was that the SST means allow not only the improvement of the strength capabilities, which ensure a higher working effect of the main propelling movement, but also an increase in the power output of cyclic locomotion executed in a determined metabolic regime. This aspect is another task (purpose) of SST: improving the energy transformation efficiency of the working muscles, intensifying the muscle work in the specific regime.

This is an important concept which requires further explanation.

1.3.2. INTENSIFICATION OF THE MUSCLE'S WORK IN A SPECIFIC REGIME

From a physiological perspective, resistance exercises cause an increase in the level of exertion of the neuro-muscular system: each exercise influences specific functional characteristics of the motor apparatus (strength capability). Therefore, the purpose of these exercises can be seen as the intensification of the muscular system's work during the training process.

In cyclic sports, resistance exercises may be used with a more specific purpose: intensifying the muscular system's work in the specific regime of cyclic locomotion. There are two ways to realize this purpose.

The first is related to the use of specific resistance exercises (see Fig.1.16), which consist of the repetitive execution of the main body propelling movement with a given external resistance in a given metabolic regime. Depending on the method of such resistance exercise execution (the level of external opposition, the number and the rate of movement repetitions, and the duration of rest intervals), the mobilization of the strength potential of the muscular system affects dif-

Fig. 1.16 - Specific resistance exercise for canoe, carried out by B. Bonomi (Olympic silver medal in Atlanta, 1996) using an isokinetic device.

ferent muscular fibers and different metabolic substrates, which ensure the needed energy supply of muscular contractions.

The second way is the execution of the specific competition exercise under more difficult conditions (see figures 1.17 and 1.18). The execution of specific locomotion (walking, running, swimming, rowing) usually represents

Fig. 1.17 - Running in more difficult conditions: towing an automobile wheel and with the resistance of a partner.

the main training exercise used in cyclic sports. The training influence of exercises on determined energy systems of the organism is managed by changing the speed (intensity), the duration of exercise, and the regime of its execution (continuous, interval, or intermittent). By increasing the external resistance with spring and hydraulic devices, or by performing uphill exercises, it's possible to increase the training influence of an exercise on the given energy supply system by increasing the mobilization of skeletal muscles involved in the exercise. When the external resistance is increased, the central nervous system (CNS) is stimulated to generate a more powerful flow of impulses activating the working muscles. As a result, an increased number of motor units are involved during the execution of the movements.

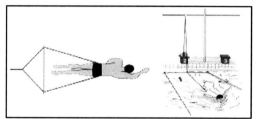

Fig. 1.18 - Swimming while towing the float (brake) and swimming with a pulley device.

The execution of competition exercises under more difficult conditions helps to solve the same tasks as the repetitive execution of the main body propelling movement with added external resistance, but the rationale of using such a method consists in the intensification of the motor system work for the entire movement structure.

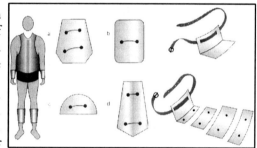

Fig. 1.19 - Additional resistance fastened to the athlete's body

In the acyclic (speed-strength) sports, the execution of competition exercises with additional external resistance (see Fig. 1.19) is associated with the Conjugate Method, pioneered by Vladimir Djachkov. However, to use this method successfully, it is important to correctly choose the level of external resistance so as not to provoke drastic changes in the biodynamic structure of the movement system. Considering the limits of increasing the weight of an additional overload, this method is used, first of all, to improve the interaction efficiency between the key elements and the secondary elements in the motor structure of competition exercise.

1.4. APPLYING SST IN THE TRAINING PROCESS

1.4.1. GENERAL CHARACTERISTICS OF TRAINING MEANS AND TRAINING PROCESS

The main goal of sports training is to improve the athlete's performance in competition (to increase the working effect of the competition exercise). Competition exercises, in every sports discipline, are complex motor actions having a highly defined motor structure, the performance of which requires a motor skill. Therefore, the training process can be seen as a process of improving an athlete's *skilled motor function*.

Improving the skilled motor function is usually seen as the process of motor learning: *acquisition of skills and the control of movements*[23] or as the pedagogical process of *motor learning*. However, sports activities, especially in elite sports, facilitate the maximal exertion of the human motor function. For this reason, in order to improve an athlete's sports results, it is necessary not only to improve their level of skill acquisition, but also to increase the functional power of the body (motor potential). Consequently, *the sports training process is to be seen as an adaptation process of the athlete's skilled motor function to the more intensive regime of muscular work.*

In designing the training (adaptation) process, the coach has to fulfill two interrelated tasks:
1) the exertion of the athlete's motor function, loading his organism to stimulate the adaptive processes that lead up to the required morphological-functional transformations in his body;
2) the adjustment of the athlete's technical mastery in relation to his increased motor function (his increased physical capabilities) i.e., to improve his capacity to control specific movements within the new power conditions of the body.

To suit the needed adaptation responses of the athlete's organism, the coach manipulates the athlete's motor behavior during the training process, using different options to change the training influence on the athlete's organism. These options regard the selection of the appropriate:
- training means;
- training methods;
- training means/methods combinations in a training session and
- ways to organize the training means/methods temporally in the training process as whole.

A **training means** is an exercise (a complex motor action with a defined motor structure) used in the training process for a specific purpose. In order to fulfill this purpose, the exercise has to be executed in an appropriate way, i.e. using an appropriate **training method**, which is identified by:
1) the character of exercise execution (the regime of muscular contraction and the level of power output);
2) the number of exercise repetitions in each set;
3) the number of sets in each series;
4) the duration of rest intervals between sets and between series.

The use of a training means induces a training stimuli that provoke a specific adaptive response of the athlete's organism, the **training effect**.

The training effect of every training means has a defined qualitative and quantitative characteristics that determine:
- the main emphasis of its influence on the body - the **training means direction**;
- the level of this influence - the **training potential**.

The **training means direction** is the qualitative characteristic of its training effect. Each training means produces specific training stimuli, which have the primary influence on a defined characteristic of the athlete's motor function and on the defined structures of the athlete's organism.

The **training potential** is the quantitative characteristic of the training effect; which the training means is capable of inducing. The use of every training means stimulates the exertion of an athlete's defined motor function, causing an improvement of this function (as a result of the adaptive reaction to its exertion). The higher the level of exertion (and, as a consequence, the level of improvement of the motor function), the higher the training potential of the training means. Essentially, the training potential regards the level of intensity of the training stimuli that the training means is able to induce.

---

[23] S. Kelso. 'Human motor behavior,' J.P. Peack 'Motor behavior and Human Skill' in Human Kinetic, 1998.

There can be limits to training potential: after a certain period of time, the means used in training can become obsolete and no longer effective. This occurs when the training exercise ceases to produce the same training effect as before.

As a result, the training potential of the training means can be 'powerful', but not 'persistent': i.e., the use of the exercise is effective, but only over a limited time interval. It depends not only on the training means itself, but also on the decrease in the capacity of the athlete's body to respond to the influence of this means. The training effect of the training means decreases when the level of the athlete's motor function increases through the use of this means.

Therefore, if the training means has the same direction of influence and can cause different quantitative responses in the athlete's body, then it can be said that training means have different training potentials.

Every training means is the component of a continuous training process: the repetition of every exercise during the training process leads, via accommodative morphological transformation, to the growth of the functional capacity of cellular structures - tissues, organs, and the body as a whole. Therefore, the training effect of training means is recognized as follows:

1) **immediate (acute) training effect** - working activation of the physiological system involved in the exercises leading to the destruction of the enzymatic and structural proteins in the body tissues;

2) **delayed training effect** – resulting in a re-synthesis of the enzymatic and structural proteins, their number increasing beyond and above their former level, due to the phenomenon of super-compensation.

In the training process, when the use of training means has different training directions, the acute (or delayed) effects result in a **cumulative effect**, which unites different kinds of adaptive reactions. In this way, the desired morphological-functional improvement in the athlete's organism can be obtained by using a determined training means system.

The cumulative training effect, obtained by this training means system, is not the sum of the training effects of different training means used, but depends on the sequence of their use (the form of their temporal organization) in a training session and also in the training process as a whole (this issue is discussed in the following paragraphs).

1.4.2. GENERAL CHARACTERISTICS OF SST MEANS

Special Strength Training is the part of Special Physical Preparation characterized by exercises using additional external opposition. Referring to their macro structure and to their operating objectives (the operating objectives occur in reaching the final aim of SST), the SST means can be divided in two categories:

- global SST exercises have complex motor structures, which reproduce the whole competition exercise or its elements;
- local SST exercises having simple motor structures, which reproduce key-movements of the competition exercises or movements which involve muscle groups used in the key movements.

The following schema synthesizes the structure of SST objectives and the related means.

SST EXERCISE CATEGORIES	SST OBJECTIVES		MEANS FORMING THE SST MEANS SYSTEM
GLOBAL SST EXERCISES HAVING COMPLEX MOTOR STRUCTURES	Increasing the Power Output of the whole competition exercise (Example: Track & Field)		Exercises reproducing the whole competition exercise carried out with additional external resistance
			Exercises reproducing specific phases of the competition exercise carried out with additional external resistance
	Increasing Power Output of the main components of the competition activity (Example: Sport Games and Combat Sports)		Exercises reproducing the main components of the competition activity carried out with additional external resistance
LOCAL SST EXERCISES HAVING SIMPLE MOTOR STRUCTURES	Increasing the Working Effect of the key movements	Increasing the main Strength Capability expressed in the key movement (for example: increasing Explosive Strength)	Exercises reproducing the key movement with additional external resistance selected on the base of Principle of Dynamic Correspondence. The exercises are carried out according to the method which ensures the increase in the main Strength Capability.
		Increasing the Strength Capabilities which are at the base of the increase in the main Strength Capability expressed in the key movement (for example: increasing Maximal Strength)	Exercises having the same kinematic structure of the key movement but with different kinetic structure. The exercises are carried out according to the method which ensures the increase in the Strength Capabilities at the base of the increase in the main Strength Capability expressed in the key movement.
		Enforcement of muscle synergy involved in the key movements	Exercises which do not have the same kinematic structure of a key movement but act on the same muscle groups involved in the key movement
	Increasing the Power Output of cyclic movements in specific metabolic regimes (Cyclic sports)	Increasing Maximal Anaerobic Power and/or improving Local Muscular Endurance	Repetitive execution of key movements with additional external resistance in a given metabolic regime

In global SST exercises having complex motor structures, the additional external opposition is constituted by weights situated on the athlete's body, spring and hydraulic devices, or by executing the exercise under more difficult conditions (see § 1.3.2).

In local SST exercises having simple motor structures, the additional external opposition is constituted by 'free weights' (barbell, dumbbells, Kettlebell), weights fixed on a block apparatus, and by using the kinetic energy of the athlete's falling body. They may be divided into the following two groups:

- resistance exercises (Chapter 2);
- jump exercises (Chapter 3).

The main purpose of the local SST exercises having simple motor structure is the improvement of the athlete's strength capabilities. Each strength capability can be effectively improved:

- executing resistance exercises in an appropriate way (choosing the appropriate level of external resistance, rate between the magnitude of the force-effort and rate of force development, and the regime of muscular contraction)
- carrying out resistance exercises in an appropriate training regime (choosing the appropriate: number of repetitions in a set, number of sets, and duration of rest interval).

All of these parameters constitute the **method**.

The correct method results in the necessary training effect.

For example, resistance exercise with different weights, number of repetitions per set, number of sets, and duration of rest intervals result in training effects with different directions (see table 1).

OVERLOAD WEIGHT (% 1 RM)	NUMBER OF REPETITIONS (APPROXIMATE)	NUMBER OF SETS	DURATION OF REST INTERVAL	DIRECTION OF TRAINING EFFECT (WHAT CAN BE OBTAINED)
80 - 100	1 - 3	4 - 8	3 - 4 min	Maximal Strength and Explosive Strength expressed against great external opposition
70 - 90	3 - 10	4 - 8	3 - 4 min	Explosive Strength expressed against moderate (low - middle) external opposition
70 - 80	6 - 12	3 - 6	1 - 2 min	Maximal Strength and muscle hypertrophy
50 - 70	10 - 15	4 - 6	3 - 4 min	High Speed movement expressed against a great external opposition
50 - 70	20 - 40	2 - 4	45 - 90 sec	Local Muscular Endurance expressed against a great external opposition
30 - 60	30 - 50	2 - 4	45 - 90 sec	Local Muscular Endurance expressed against a moderate (low - middle) external opposition
30 - 50	10 - 15	4 - 6	3 - 4 min	High Speed movements expressed against a low external opposition
15 - 30	15 - 20	3 - 5	3 - 4 min	Rapid and frequent movements without overload

Table 1 - The Primary Emphasis of Resistance Exercises Executed with Different Overload Weights, Repetitions, Number of Sets, and Different Rest Interval Durations

The training effect of SST means also depends on the working regime of the exercise, which is characterized by the rate of force employment.

To obtain an increase in a determined strength capability, SST exercise should emphasize its desired outcome (e.g. to increase Explosive strength, the force effort of the exercise has to be developed explosively; to increase maximal strength (Po) the time of force employment in the execution of the exercise must not be limited). The Barbell Squat executed in different ways, for example, may elicit increases in different strength capabilities (see the following table 2).

DIRECTION OF TRAINING EFFECT	MUSCLE RELAXATION BETWEEN REPS	SPEED OF MOVEMENTS	RATE OF REPS	WEIGHT (% OF RM)	NUMBER OF REPETITIONS PER SET	NUMBER OF SETS PER SERIES	REST BETWEEN SETS	NUMBER OF SERIES	REST BETWEEN SERIES
MAXIMAL STRENGTH WITHOUT HYPERTROPHY	+	Low	Low	90	2 - 3	2 - 3	4 - 6 minutes	-	-
MAXIMAL STRENGTH WITH HYPERTROPHY	-	Low	Low	80	8 - 10	3 - 5	From 2-3 to 4-5 minutes	-	-
				85 - 90	Maximal with 2-3 movements of cheating	2 - 3	Free	-	-
EXPLOSIVE STRENGTH	+	Maximal in the overcoming phase	Low	60 - 80	5 - 6	2 - 3	4 - 6 minutes	2 - 3	6 - 8 minutes
HIGH-SPEED STRENGTH	+		Low	30 - 50	6 - 8	2 - 4	3 - 4 minutes	2 - 3	6 - 8 minutes
STRENGTH ENDURANCE	-	High	High	50 - 60	5	4	4 - 6 minutes	-	-

Table 2 - The training effects of the Barbell Squat executed in different ways

Therefore, each SST means ensures a specific influence on the athlete's motor function (i.e. its specific training effect). Qualitatively, the specific training effect of SST means is recognized as the training means direction: its capacity to increase a determined strength capability. Quantitatively, the training effect of SST means is recognized as its training potential: the level of increasing this strength capability. To improve a motor function, specific for a given sport discipline, it is needed to use SST means with a specific training effect that corresponds to the specific demands of the sport discipline.

1.4.3. GENERAL PRINCIPLES TO FOLLOW IN SELECTING SST MEANS

For each sports discipline and for each athlete, the SST means have to be selected for achieving the following aims:
1) the improvement of strength capabilities and functional properties (contractile, oxidative, elastic) of the muscles involved in the competition exercises;
2) the improvement of the biodynamic structure of competition exercise; it means, increasing the force efforts applied in the key-movements, improving the efficiency of interaction between key-movements and between the key movements and the secondary movements.
To increase the force efforts applied in the key-movements, it is needed to enforce the working mechanisms involved in the key movements.
Therefore, to select the SST means for a given sport discipline, the first step is to analyze the kinematic and kinetic characteristics of the competition exercise and individualize:
- the key-movements of competition exercise;
- the muscle groups involved in the key-movements;
- the character of the force effort in the key movement;

- the strength capabilities, which ensure the increase in the specific working effect of the key movements.

To complete the frame, it is needed to recall some concepts illustrated in the preceding paragraphs:

1) to increase the working effect of the key-movement, it's necessary to increase specific strength capabilities which determine the character of the force effort in this movement.

2) in relation to the character of the force effort of a given key movement, each strength capability can have specific relevance in obtaining its highest working effect;

3) each strength capability can be effectively improved using determined SST exercises in an appropriate regime (i.e. according to an appropriate method).

Therefore, to increase the working effect of a given sport movement, one can use the combination of several SST means finalized at increasing the strength capabilities more relevant for improving that sport movement. In other words, an increase in the working effect of a given sport movement can be obtained by the cumulative training effect of several SST means, having various training effect directions.

The first step in selecting the SST means is the evaluation of their:

- **training direction**, the strength capability/ies that they are able to improve;
- **training potential**, their capacity to increase the level of a given strength capability.

The second step in selecting the SST means regards the choose of the most specific exercises for a given sport discipline. The choose is made on the base of the **principle of Dynamic Correspondence** between the motor structures of the SST means and the key-movement of the competition exercise (see the following paragraph).

The third step in selecting the SST means regards the choose of other exercises to be included in the training program. The main principles to follow is the **principle of Integrating Training Means in a System** (see § 1.4.3.2).

1.4.3.1. PRINCIPLE OF DYNAMIC CORRESPONDENCE

The principle of Dynamic Correspondence is applied in selecting the local SST means finalized at increasing the working effect of the key-movements of competition exercise: the SST means have to be selected on the criterion of the similarity to the characteristics of the key-movements of competition exercise.

This selection is made based on the following criteria:

1) muscle groups involved in the exercise;
2) amplitude (ROM) and direction of movement;
3) accentuated part of the movement's amplitude;
4) magnitude of force-effort and time of its application;
5) regime of muscular contraction.

The application of the 1st, 2nd and 3rd criteria implies the correct selection of the starting position of the SST exercises.

An example of selection of SST means for track & field's sprints and long jumps is illustrated in figures 1.20 and 1.21. In this case, the key-movement of competition exercise is the propulsive force-effort of the take-off leg, synchronized with the swing movement of the other leg.

To increase the power output of the swing movement, the exercise is often used with a barbell plate shown in figure 1.20-B. This exercise choice is not correct because it does not correspond to the movement of the competition exercise illustrated in figure 1.20-A: the direction and amplitude relative to the hip joint do not correspond; neither does the accentuated part (the shaded portion) at which the maximum effort is developed. The track & field runner or jumper who wants to increase the power output of the swing movement should practice the exercise shown in figure 1.20-C.

However to increase the working effect of key-movements the most useful SST means is the exercise in which the swing leg movement is combined with the force-effort of the take-off leg, as in Fig. 1.21.

In all of these exercises, the force-effort is accentuated at the beginning of the movement and has the same direction as in the competition exercise of track & field running and jumping.

Each of the basic strength capabilities can be effectively improved using training exercises in an appropriate regime, i.e., an appropriate level of external resistance, an appropriate rate between the magnitude of the force-effort and the rate of force development and an appropriate regime of muscular contraction.

Fig. 1.20 - The working amplitude of the specific swing movement and illustration of the incorrect (B) and correct choice (C) of SST exercise.

Fig. 1.21 - Examples of SST exercises combining swing leg flexion with the take-off leg extension from the hip joint. Left: SST exercise for track & field runner. Right: SST exercise for track & field high jumper.

The 4th criterion (magnitude of force-effort and time of its application) implies that the character of force effort in SST exercises should ensure improvement of the specific strength capability which is essential to increasing the working effect of the key movement of competition exercise.

The 5th criterion implies that SST exercises aimed at increasing the working effect in the key-movement of competition exercise must be executed in the same muscle work regime.

For example, in downhill Alpine skiing, the key movement of the competition exercise is maintaining the determined position. As in wrestling, the capacity to keep the force effort in a given body position is an important element of the competition activity. In these cases, the SST exercise must be executed in the isometric regime. In sport disciplines where the key movement of competition exercise is a powerful dynamic force effort, the SST exercises should be executed in a dynamic regime.

When, in the key movement, the athlete must perform the maximal force effort acting against great external resistance, at the beginning of movement, the muscles work in an isometric regime. In this case, the SST exercises in isometric regime are useful.

The regime of muscle contraction is very important to obtain a specific training effect. Different regimes of muscular contraction during exercise (isometric, dynamic, miometric, pliometric, isokinetic) ensure different responses of the locomotor system. For example, as we will see from the results of Bravaja's experiment, illustrated in Chapter 2, resistance exercises executed in an isometric regime have a negative influence on the working effect (force momentum) expressed by the same muscle group in the dynamic (isokinetic) regime; the exercises, executed in the isokinetic regime at high speed, do not produce an increase in the maximal isometric strength.

A particular characteristic of many weight training exercises is the *ballistic*[24] *regime* of muscle contraction. The ballistic weight training exercises are useful for the most of sport disciplines in which the key movements of competition exercise are performed in the ballistic regime. However, the ballistic weight exercises are less specific for the aquatic sport disciplines, in which the character of force application during propulsion movements is more similar to *isokinetic* regime (about this regime see § 2.2.2.3).

1.4.3.2. PRINCIPLE OF INTEGRATING THE TRAINING MEANS IN A SYSTEM

As stated above, the specific character of force-effort in the key-movements of every competition exercise is determined by the activation of different functional properties of the neuro-muscular apparatus (strength capabilities), which interact to fulfill a common motor task. Each strength capability can be improved by using training exercises in an appropriate regime, i.e. the level of external resistance (force-effort magnitude), rate of force development, and regime of muscular contraction (isometric, dynamic, miometric, and pliometric).

When different training means are used in the training process, their combination elicits an integrated morpho-functional adaptation, the Cumulative Training Effect. Therefore, determined combinations of different training means can be used to improve the working effect of competition exercises. These training means represent a **training means system**[25] in which each training means solves its specific motor task, but the combined effect of them results in a global training task aimed at increasing the power output of competition exercises. The following study illustrates how the SST means system can be formed.

The aim of this study was to find out the training means able to increase the speed of specific tennis displacements. Tennis displacements are characterized by the complex (compound) trajectory with frequent stops and immediate changes of the running direction. The take-off movements during specific running are executed with flexed legs. As it was presumed, to perform these kinds of displacements without losing speed, the athlete should have a high level of isometric strength of the main muscle synergies involved in the lateral and frontal changing directions.

In the experiment, 19 high level tennis players performed two groups of tests: specific speed running tests and strength tests.

The specific speed running tests consisted of performing the most typical tennis game's displacements[26] (see Fig. 1.22):

1) forward run of 10 meters distance with a stop at the finish point ('Advance to the net');
2) run of 48 meters distance with different trajectories:
    -   'Long Shuttle', 6 × 8 meters with 5 lateral (side-to-side) changes of directions;
    -   'Short Shuttle', 12 × 4 meters with 11 lateral changes of directions;
    -   'Fan', 12 × 4 meters with 11 both lateral and frontal changes of directions.

---

[24] *Ballistic movement* - a forced movement initiated by muscle action, but continued by the momentum of the limbs.

[25] *System* (from Latin systēma, in turn from Greek σύστημα systēma) is a set of interacting or interdependent entities, real or abstract, forming an integrated whole. The concept of an "integrated whole" can also be stated in terms of a system embodying a set of relationships which are differentiated from relationships of the set to other elements, and from relationships between an element of the set and elements which are not a part of the relational regime. System thinking is based on Aristotle's idea that 'The Whole is more than the sum of the parts'.

[26] These forms of tennis displacements were individuated, in a preceding study, as the most frequently used during the tennis matches of high level players.

In the strength tests, the level of basic strength capabilities were evaluated using the UDS: Maximal (P_0), Explosive (J) and Starting strength (Q) expressed in the maximal isometric strength efforts and maximal explosive isometric strength efforts of the Leg Press and Seated Calf Raise.

Table 3 shows the correlations between the results of the running and strength tests. The correlations indicate that the higher the level of explosive strength (J) of the tennis player, the higher is their capacity to run rapidly on a court. So, to increase specific speed ability in tennis, the athletes should use SST means able to increase Explosive Strength expressed in the take-off movements, primarily, jumping exercises.

The results also showed that the athletes who expressed a higher value of P_0 in the Seated Calf Raise (but not in Leg Press) showed a high level of speed ability. This means that to increase the speed it is advisable to use a training method able to increase the weight of 1RM in the Seated Calf Raise exercise.

As we can see, the results of specific running tests are not correlated directly with Maximal Strength as expressed in the Leg Press. However, the correlations between the parameters of strength capabilities (Table 4) show that the higher the level of Maximal Strength (P_0), the higher is the level of Explosive Strength (J). This means that to increase the level of Explosive Strength in the Leg Press and, consequently, to increase the speed of specific tennis displacements, it's necessary to increase the maximal strength expressed in the Leg Press. This means that to increase the speed it is advisable to use a training method able to increase the weight of 1RM in the Leg Press exercise (barbell squat).

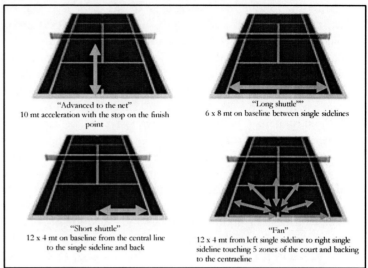

"Advanced to the net"
10 mt acceleration with the stop on the finish point

"Long shuttle"
6 x 8 mt on baseline between single sidelines

"Short shuttle"
12 x 4 mt on baseline from the central line to the single sideline and back

"Fan"
12 x 4 mt from left single sideline to right single sideline touching 5 zones of the court and backing to the centraeline

Fig. 1.22 - Scheme of tennis drills. The changes of direction in the left-right placements must be executed without rotating the body – the athlete must always face the net.

	LEG PRESS			SEATED CALF RISE		
	Po	J	Q	Po	J	Q
ADVANCE TO THE NET	0.075	**-0.536**	-0.156	**-0.503**	**-0.541**	**-0.442**
SHORT SHUTTLE	0.086	**-0.593**	0.018	**-0.488**	**-0.511**	**-0.446**
LONG SHUTTLE	0.185	**-0.595**	-0.308	**-0.442**	**-0.454**	**-0.437**
FAN	-0.299	**-0.513**	-0.149	**-0.436**	**-0.485**	**-0.446**

Table 3 - The correlations between the execution time of specific the tennis test and basic strength capabilities. R = 0.433, n = 19 (N. Verkhoshansky, 1984).

		LEG PRESS			SEATED CALF RISE		
		Po	J	Q	Po	J	Q
LEG PRESS	Po	1					
	J	**0.803**	1				
	Q	0.354	**0.692**	1			
SEATED CALF RISE	Po	0.332	**0.545**	0.461	1		
	J	0.140	**0.499**	0.533	**0.837**	1	
	Q	0.047	0.399	**0.588**	**0.692**	**0.880**	1

Table 4 - The correlation between the strength capabilities in the tennis players group. R = 0.433, n = 19. (N. Verkhoshansky, 1984)

During the running test procedures, it was evidenced that the tennis players, involved in this experiment, had different levels of the specific skill of performing tennis displacements. This difference could influence the level of correlation between the speed and strength tests.

To evaluate the level of this influence, another experiment was done which analyzed the correlations between the results of the 'Long Shuttle' and 'Short Shuttle' and the tests of Explosive Strength in the Leg Press and on Maximal Strength in the Seated Calf Raise for two groups of athletes: a group of tennis players and a group of athletes specialized in other sport disciplines (8 rowers, 2 skiers, 7 Track & Field runners, 6 boxers, and 2 gymnasts). As we can see in the figure 1.23, the results of the group of tennis players showed a very high level of correlations, while the results of the group of other sports athlete didn't show any correlation. The athletes, specialized in other sports, had a higher level of strength preparedness than the tennis players. Notwithstanding this, they were not able to realize their motor potential in the motor structure of the specific tennis displacements.

This indicates that the speed of the specific tennis displacements depend also on the specific technical skill, which can be improved through the execution of specific tennis running exercises.

Summarizing the results of this study, it's possible to assert that, in order to improve the specific speed ability, tennis players should use combinations of several training means: barbell exercises, jump exercises and specific speed running exercises. These means can be combined in the same training session or in different training sessions of the same microcycle, and can be used also in the Block Training System (see § 8.7, "SST program aimed at increasing the speed of tennis displacements").

Thus, in every sport discipline, the increase in power output of competition exercise may be obtained by the improvement of several strength parameters combined in a specific structure. In order to improve each of these parameters, it is possible to use different training means or a combination of them. A SST means system should include not only training means focused on improving determined strength capabilities (maximal strength, explosive strength, high-speed strength), but also focused on increasing the strength potential of the main muscle synergies involved in the competition exercise. In

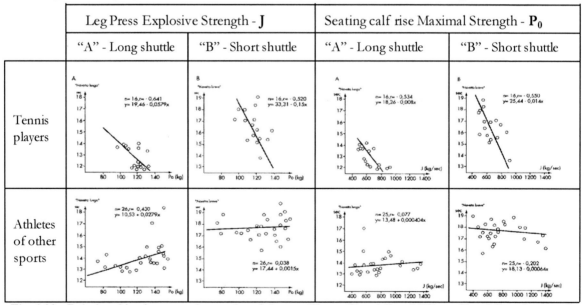

Fig. 1.23 - Relationships between the results of the test "Long Shuttle" and "Short Shuttle" and strength capabilities (P0 and J), in two groups of athletes: tennis players (above) and athletes of other sports (below). N. Verkhoshansky, 1984.

endurance sports, combat sports, and team sports, the SST means system should also include exercises aimed at improving Maximal Anaerobic Power and Local Muscular Endurance.

So, there could be many SST means at the disposal of a coach to improve the power output of competition exercise. The choice of the SST means will effectively fulfill this task only when the means are:

- integrated in a system in which the training task of every means is designed in relation to the other tasks;
- integrated in a common system of training, i.e. the means are rationally combined with the other means used in the training process.

The main goal of the whole system can only be achieved when, in the training process, the means are temporally organized in such a way that each of them effectively fulfils its own particular task, and at the same time, all of them together, allow the athlete to achieve the required level of special work capacity with the minimum expenditure of time and energy.

1.4.4. RULES OF APPLYING SST MEANS IN THE TRAINING PROCESS

1.4.4.1. RULE ONE: FORMULATING THE MOTOR TASK BEFORE EXECUTING SST MEANS

> To obtain the necessary training effects, the athlete must clearly understand the motor task which is to be achieved through the execution of the exercise.

This rule emphasizes the pedagogical aspect of sports training: the task of the coach is not only in selecting the correct training means and methods, but also in choosing the best communicational and motivational forms in transferring to the athlete the information of the exercise's correct execution.

Why is this rule important for the successful implementation of SST?

Each exercise, used in the training process as a 'training means', represents a complex motor action; its working effect is determined by the goal that the athlete has to reach through its execution.

"Similar to how the brain creates a reflection of the real external world, an actual external situation, an earlier memorized situation that happened in the past, it must also be able to 'reflect' (actually, to construct) a situation pertaining to a near future which has not yet become reality and which the brain tries to bring into existence led by its biological needs. Only such a clear image of a desired future can be used to formulate a problem and create a program for its solution" (N. Bernstein, 1961[27]).

"...Goal, understood as an encoded in the brain model of a desired future, defines processes that should be considered as goal oriented" (N. Bernstein, 1966)[28].

According to the Bernstein's vision, the coach, first of all, should correctly formulate the 'image of the desired future', explaining not only which specific movement and how the athlete must execute it, but also what motor task he must solve and what goal he has to reach. The following example may help to understand its application in SST. The methods used in SST can be divided as either 'intensive' or 'extensive':

- **intensive methods** are characterized by maximum power and a small amount of work;

[27] N.A. Bernstein, Routes &Problems of the Physiology of Activity, in Problems of Philosophy, 6:1961 pp77-92,. See 'Progress in motor control', Vol. 1,'Bernstein's traditions in Movement Studies' in Human Kinetics, 1988, p. 90 (translated from Russian by Mark L. Latash).

[28] N.A. Bernstein, Essays on the Physiology of Movements and Physiology of Activity, Moscow, 1966. See 'Progress in motor control', Volume 1, 'Bernstein's traditions in Movement Studies' in Human Kinetics, 1988, p. 91 (translated from Russian by Mark L. Latash)

- **extensive methods** are characterized by moderate (sub-maximal) power and an optimal amount of work.

In order to obtain the necessary training effect, the athlete has to clearly understand the motor task and be motivated to reach the final goal:

1) When intensive training methods are used the athlete should be motivated to execute the exercise 'as quickly as possible' or 'as powerfully as possible'.

2) When extensive methods are used the athlete should to be motivated to maintain the correct technique and fluidity of movements.

Athletes have different temperaments, mentalities, characters, intellectual levels, levels of motor control, and motor learning capacities. For each type of athlete, the coach must find an appropriate description of the motor task and an appropriate reason for letting him carry out the task in the best possible way.

Therefore, the athlete must never start a SST exercise without having a clear idea of the exercise's primary objective; furthermore, the athlete must always receive feedback from the coach regarding the progress of the exercise's execution.

1.4.4.2. RULE TWO: MAINTAIN SCHEDULED LENGTH OF REST INTERVALS USING ACTIVE REST

In order to obtain the necessary training effects of the SST means, it is very important to respect both the length of the rest between sets and series, and the athlete's activity during these periods.

> 1. The rest periods have to be strictly observed as prescribed by the training method.
> 2. The rest periods must include exercises capable of facilitating the recovery processes by increasing the blood's circulation in the working muscles and ensure their relaxation.

Because of this, the rest is the most important element of the training method. The length of the rest period determines a specific organism's functional reaction to the entire volume of work (specific training effect; examples of this influence can be observed in tables 1 and 2).

It must be taken into account that an athlete does have difficulty in keeping the prescribed length of the rest period between the repeated work efforts. Considering the high emotional involvement typical of this type of training session, it is up to the trainer to pay attention to this particular aspect of the training.

During the rest periods the athlete's motor activity must ensure the recovery of the organism's functional condition before executing each follow-up working effort.

Every time the training exercise is repeated, the muscle's contractile function decreases because of lactate accumulation. For example: in cyclic work, during the subsequent force efforts greater than 20% of 1RM, the level of Lactate accumulation increases with the increasing level of force effort. For this reason, it is important to eliminate lactate from the engaged muscles during the break, in order to accelerate the recovery of the organism's work capacity.

In well-prepared athletes, the most active site of lactate oxidation is not so much in the liver and myocardium (of the heart muscle) but in the working skeletal muscles.

If muscular work is carried out in the rest periods, the speed of lactate removal increases with the increase in the work intensity up to the level equal to approximately 60-70% (until 80%) of the individual's maximum oxygen consumption ($VO2_{Max}$). The study of L. Hermansen and J. Stenvold shows that during the rest period, after 3 bouts of maximal work 'to failure' (refusal), the blood lactate level decreases faster with work involving the same muscles stressed during the training exercises (see Fig. 1.24).

Work at an intensity of 75% of $VO2_{MAX}$ ensures approximately a 75% lactate turnover (conversion to glycogen) through the oxidation process in the skeletal muscles. The differences of the lactate turnover process, corresponding to three different muscle activities used during the rest pauses, were the object of an experiment in which the blood lactate concentration of runners was measured at the end of 8-minute rest intervals between repeated 4×1200 m runs (Fig. 1.25).

The three variants of the work during the rest intervals were the following:
1) walking (a);
2) jogging with the heart rate (HR) at 120 beats per minute (b);
3) running with the HR at 140 beats per minute (c).

The results showed that in the third case (c) the blood lactate concentration is considerably less.

It is now possible to draw two conclusions:
- First, it is necessary to pay attention to the recommended duration of rest both between sets as well as between series. Under no circumstances should these recommendations be neglected; time economy leads to a loss in training efficiency;
- Second, in the rest periods it is necessary to execute active work by the same muscle groups to which the training is directed and which receive the major training influence. Gradual accelerations (long build-ups) and non-intensive jump exercises during the rest periods between sets, and particularly between series, help to maintain the athlete's special work capacity at an optimal level and increase the efficacy of the training effect on the organism. During the rest periods, dynamic stretching exercises, known as 'Russian warm-ups', can also be used; they are described in Appendix 3.

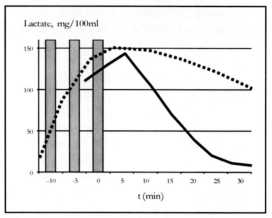

Fig. 1.24 - Blood lactate concentration before, during, and after 3 bouts of maximal work "to failure". A- Passive rest , B- Active rest. (L. Hermansen, J. Stenvold, 1972)

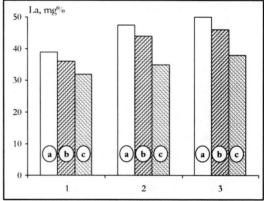

Fig. 1.25 - Concentration of lactic acid in the blood at the end of the rest pause between repeated runs of 4×1200 m. Three different activities were used during the rest pauses: a – walking, b – jogging with the heart rate at 120 bpm, c – running with the HR at 140 bpm.

1.4.4.3. RULE THREE: USING SST MEANS IN SPECIALLY ORGANIZED TRAINING SESSIONS OR SÉANCES

> In a training session, never use SST means as an additional supplement to other training means, but integrate them in a specific training unit *(training séance)* with a specific training task.

A training séance[29] is a one-time portion of training loads with a specific target in focus. The training séance is a closely measured structure of the training impacts on the athlete's organism. The impact has the same training direction and is organized over the time based on a rational combination of work and recovery.

SST means must be organized in training units ('threads') aimed at fulfilling determined training tasks such as the increase of Maximal or Explosive Strength, Reactive Ability, Maximal Anaerobic Power or Local Muscular Endurance.

If there are other tasks to be accomplished in the same training session (for example: technical preparation), the SST means must be separated from other means with different training directions by a prolonged rest interval. They must be seen by the athlete as an extra training session. SST séances must be completed before and not after technical work.

The most important application of the concept of a training séance is in the Combined Methods of SST (see Chapter 4). Examples of training séances including jump exercises are described in the § 3.5. Experiments have shown that rationally organized training séances appreciably raise the efficacy of the training's impact on the organism, reducing energy expenditure.

1.4.4.4. RULE FOUR: ENHANCING THE TRAINING POTENTIAL OF SST MEANS

> The SST means having a high training potential must be gradually introduced into the training process after training means with a lower training potential.

First and foremost, it is not appropriate to use high-intensity training stimuli (training means having high training potential) at the beginning of the training process (multi year training process or preparation period), since the organism is not yet ready, from a functional point of view, to give an adequate adaptive response to their use.

Second, the training effect of any means will decrease proportionally to the athlete's increase in the level of special physical preparedness. In order to avoid 'stagnation', it is necessary to constantly and gradually increase the training stimuli. In another words, it's necessary to enhance the training potential of SST means: when the training means ceases in ensure the increase in the corresponding parameters of the special work capacity (i.e. its training potential has already been realized/depleted), this means must be gradually substituted by a new means having a higher training potential.

The SST means must be individually selected for each athlete. The criteria of this selection have to be related to the level of his/her sports mastery and to the current level of his/her preparedness:
-   athletes with a low level of motor function require a training means with low training potential;
-   athletes with a high level of motor function require a higher stimulation level of motor function during the training process. Similarly, the training potential of the SST means must also be higher.

Therefore, in order to keep up the SST efficiency as a whole, training means with the same direction, but different motor potential, must be correctly placed in the training process (see the following paragraphs).

1.4.4.5. RULE FIVE: INCREASING THE SPECIFICITY OF SST MEANS' TRAINING STIMULI GRADUALLY

The training process, especially of high level athletes, must be highly specialized: the athlete must not

---

[29] The French word "séance" has the same meaning as the English word "session" - the interval of time covering a non-interrupted performance of work or process.

perform useless activities that can't positively contribute to the attainment of the specific objective.

This does not mean that each training exercise must reproduce the competition exercise; the specific aim must be attributed to the whole training means system and to the whole training stimuli system of training loads used in the preparation period.

As outlined above, the SST means system should include a large spectrum of exercises aimed at improving different determining factors for increasing the power output of competition exercises. So, these training means should have different training directions (for improving different strength abilities and different functional properties of different muscle groups), different training potential levels, and different levels of specificity (level of dynamic correspondence to the competition exercise).

There are two aspects of the training means specificity that must be considered.

The first aspect regards the <u>correspondence of the training means to the motor structure of competition exercise</u>.

The training means included in the SST means system can have two levels of specificity; they should be used in the preparation period in the following sequence:

- less specific exercises, for preparing the athlete's motor apparatus (the working mechanisms of his body) to more specific exercises with higher training effects and for helping to avoid injury;
- highly specific exercises, for ensuring the increase of the force-efforts in the key movements;

The second aspect regards the training means' <u>correspondence to the specific character of the power output in the competition exercise</u>.

Each training means included in the SST system must ensure an increase in those functions of the organism which determine increasing the power output of muscular work in the specific regime (characteristic of the given sport discipline). Since power is determined by two components, force and velocity, the training means included in the SST means system must be able to emphasize:

- the magnitude of the force-effort in specific movements;
- the velocity of increasing the magnitude of the force effort.

Considering these two aspects, the rule of the gradual increase in the training stimuli's specificity implies that, in the preparation period, the SST means must be introduced in such a sequence to solve the following training tasks:

1) enforcing the main muscular synergies and the other body's working mechanisms involved in the competition exercises;

2) increasing the magnitude of force effort in the key movements;

3) increasing the speed of the force employment in the key movements.

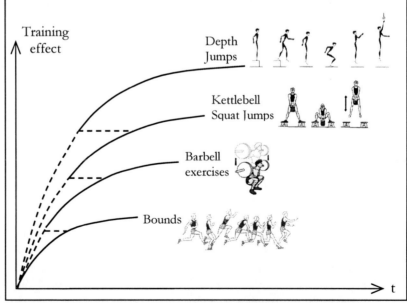

Fig. 1.26 - Conjugate-Sequence System of SST means finalized at the improvement of explosive strength of Track & Field jumpers (Y. Verkhoshansky, 1970).

61

In Fig. 1.26, it can be seen how this rule is applied to increase power output in the Track & Field jumps through the following phases:
1) bounds - for getting the motor apparatus ready to execute the subsequent training loads;
2) barbell squats - for increasing the force component of the take-off power output;
3) barbell and kettlebell jumps - for increasing the speed component of the take-off power output;
4) depth jumps - for increasing both the force and speed components of the take-off power output through the use of highly intensive training stimuli.

This rule also implies that one type of exercise is gradually replaced by another. The previous SST means must ensure the functional-morphological basis so that the positive training effect of the subsequent SST means is felt. At this stage, the exercises which follow continue to further enhance the adaptive changes acquired by the organism on a higher level of specificity. This schedule of training loads is called the Conjugate-Sequence System.

A similar approach was used to create a Conjugate-Sequence System for Track & Field throwers and middle distance runners (Fig. 1.27).

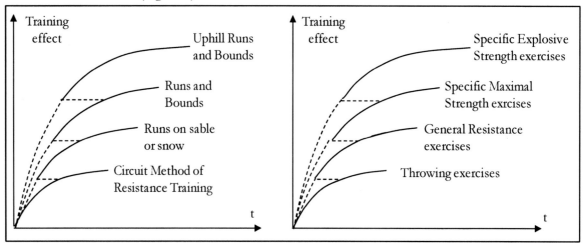

Fig. 1.27 - The schema of the Conjugate-Sequence method using SST means: right - for Track&Field throwers (P.Tshine, 1978), left - for Track&Field middle distance runners (A. Nurmekivi, 1974)

1.5. GUIDELINES FOR PLANNING SST

A synthetic schema of activities for SST planning that is not exhaustive of all activities and data involved in the process includes:
1) the definition of the main SST goals;
2) the selection of the SST means and methods (for setting-up the SST means system);
3) the analysis of the competition calendar (for setting up the duration of the preparation cycle);
4) the selection of the temporal organization of SST means (see Chapter 5);
5) the definition of the total work volume for each training means, fixing it based on the training load volumes reached in the previous preparation period of training.

The SST means system should be set-up based on the biomechanical and physiological characteristics of the given sport discipline.

The following five data (parameters) must been defined for designing a SST program:

REGIME ⇒ MEANS ⇒ METHODS ⇒ ORGANIZATION ⇒ VOLUME

The sequence of activities for setting the corresponding parameters are:
1) to analyze the working regime of the organism and the motor system that is predominantly inherent to the given sport discipline;
2) to select the SST means that are adequate to this regime;
3) to select the most effective SST methods for ensuring the necessary training influence on the athlete's body;
4) to set-up the best form of temporal organization of SST means, in such a way that their cumulative effect will ensure the task of the SST at the optimum expenditure of the athlete's time and energy;
5) to define the volume of the SST means that is necessary for solving the SST tasks.

In this sequence, it is mandatory to pass to the next phase only after having completed the previous activity, analyzing every possible choice (based on the personal know-how and other documentary and informative sources):
- it is not effective to seek any SST methods without first searching for the appropriate means;
- it is unwise to define the volume of the SST loads without first working out the effective organization form of the SST means.

The selection of the work volumes for each training means must be based on the training load volumes reached by the athlete in the previous preparation periods of training. In order to have this information, the coach must faithfully record all training loads used by his athletes in each training session.

Usually for this purpose a training diary is used; after each training session, the coach wrote what exercises have been performed and how much work has been carried out.

An example is shown in the following tables in which all training loads are classified according to their training goal (or training method used).

TRAINING MEANS / DATE	1	2	3	4	5	6	Micro cycle Total	...	Monthly Total
Executions of the competition exercise (number)									
Standing Jumps and intensive short bounds (number of take-offs)									
Long bounds (distance, m)									
Running exercises (m)									
Sprints (number)									
Resistance exercises (total tones):									
- executed with maximal weight									
- executed with the weight of …%									
Etc…									

Training means/ months	X	XI	XII	I	II	III	IV	V	VI	VII	VIII	IX	Monthly Total
High jumps (number of competition exercise executions)	60	80	140	420	200	100	120	380	260	140	60	40	2000
Jump exercises (number of take-offs)	4000	3600	2400	1000	600	2600	2600	1000	1000	600	400	200	20000
Barbell exercises (tons)	40	128	176	32	16	112	176	32	32	32	24	-	800
Sprints (km)	2.4	2.7	3.0	5.4	2.4	1.8	2.4	5.1	2.1	1.2	1.2	0.9	30

A 'mandatory activity' is to monitor the athlete's state through objective control tests used in the given sport discipline.

A monthly recording of the dynamic of the athlete's state in a Personal Card and the volumes of the training loads (the above tables) allows to 'visualize' the trend of training process and to effectively evaluate the effect of the training strategy selected by the coach for the preparation period.

1.6. CONCLUSIONS

> Special Strength Training is the systemic use of a complex of specialized resistance exercises aimed at increasing the power output of the competition exercise in a given sport discipline.

Why is SST needed for improving sports results?
The final aim of sport training is the improvement of sport result, which is expressed by the power output of competition exercise. The power output of competition exercise depends on the athlete's motor potential and on the athlete's capacity to utilize it.
The SST ensures both increasing the motor potential of the athlete and improving the athlete's capacity to utilize the motor potential during the execution of competition exercise:
- increasing the working effect of key movements of competition exercise through the improvement of correlated strength capabilities;
- intensifying the muscular work in a specific regime.

What do we need to know about our sports discipline to create a SST that will improve our sports results?
The coach, first of all, should have a good knowledge of biomechanics and physiology of his/her sport in order to answer the following questions:
1. What are the key movements of competition exercise?
2. What are the strength capabilities that need developing to improve the working effect of these movements?
3. In what way is it possible to intensify the muscle system's work?

Beyond that, the coach should have a good knowledge of the strength training methodology in order to answer the following questions:
1. What are the SST means and methods which may ensure the development of these strength capabilities?
2. What are the SST means and methods which may ensure the intensification of the muscle system's work in a specific regime?
3. How should these SST means be scheduled in the training process?

The following Chapters 2, 3, 4 and 5 will help the reader to get the answers of the second group of questions.
In Chapters 6, 7 and 8 the reader will find examples of practical applications of SST means and methods for different sports.

SST MEANS AND METHODS: RESISTANCE EXERCISES

2.1. GENERAL CHARACTERISTICS OF RESISTANCE EXERCISES USED IN SST

The most important means used in SST are the resistance exercises, referred to as exercises with overload. Resistance exercises are also termed 'weight training' because the majority of resistance exercises are executed with weights (additional external opposition to increase the force of gravity) e.g. 'free weights' (barbells, dumbbells, etc…) or weights fixed by a system of blocks/stacks in a cable apparatus (lever operated machines).

In selecting SST means for a given sport discipline, it is necessary to consider two main groups of resistance exercises:

1) exercises aimed at increasing the working effect of the key movements of the competition exercise;

2) exercises aimed at preparing the athlete's motor apparatus so that the first group of exercises can be carried out with a higher training effect and with less injury potential

In the training load schedule during the preparatory period, the second group of exercises must precede the exercises of the first group.

The resistance exercises of the first group should be selected by strictly applying the principle of dynamic correspondence (see § 1.4.3.1). Resistance exercises of the second group have to be selected according to their capability to prepare the athlete's body to carry out the exercises of the first group and to increase their training effect.

WHAT EXERCISES ARE INCLUDED IN THE SECOND GROUP?

These exercises are usually referred to as the means of General Physical (Strength) Preparation. This is not a right definition of them. The general preparation training means do not have a specific task, but rather an 'over-all' purpose: to develop the athlete's organism in order to give it a basic preparation for any kind of specific activity (or for a large list of specific activities). Instead, the SST exercises of the 2nd group have to ensure the preliminary preparation to effectively carry out the first group of exercises, which are highly specific. It is more appropriate to refer to these exercises as *preliminary SST exercises*.

These means are usually aimed at increasing the level of maximal strength of the primary muscle groups involved in competition exercise; they are fundamental for the subsequent increase in the working effect of the main force producing movements of competition exercise.

The main criteria for selecting the preliminary SST exercises, therefore, is their capacity to enforce the working mechanisms of the body (above all, the main muscle synergies - see § 1.2.2) involved in the execution of highly specific exercises of the first group.

The muscle work regime in the preliminary SST exercises may differ from competition exercises.

For example, if the athlete needs to increase the power output of the leg's ground contact during competition sprinting or jumping, he needs to increase the level of maximal explosive force effort of similar movements using highly specific explosive strength exercises (jumps). Before the use of these highly specific explosive strength exercises, it is necessary to enforce the main muscle synergies which ensure improvement in the capacity to oppose the force of gravity: barbell squats, standing calf raises and more specifically, the Seated Calf Raise. These preliminary exercises are aimed at increasing maximal strength; they should be executed slowly with high overload ranging from 80% to 93% 1RM. In order to safety execute these exercises with high overload (see § 2.2.1.1 - Maximal Effort Method), it is necessary to carry them out starting from a lower load and gradually increasing it (see § 2.2.1.2 - Repeat-Serial Method).

Furthermore, the range of movements in preliminary SST exercises may differ from competition exercises. For example, in isometric training, to increase the maximal strength produced in a specific joint angle, the force-efforts must be performed with the same joint angle. However, performing force-efforts with a more 'closed' joint angle causes an increase in force-effort maximal strength across almost every angle of this joint. It is also important to consider that the more 'open' the working joint angle is, the higher the maximal force-effort level is produced (see the end of § 2.3).

This information about isometric training is useful when dynamic strength exercises are used with heavy overload. To increase the force-effort level of maximal strength in a more 'open' joint angle, it is, therefore, necessary to use heavier overloads. The magnitude of these overloads must be heavier than those required to increase the maximal strength level in force-efforts with a more 'closed' joint angle. These points must be considered when selecting overload exercises i.e. the same exercise, carried out with a different range of movement, may be used for different training purposes.

The following problem often arises during coaching discussions:

IS IT BETTER TO USE A BARBELL SQUAT AS A FULL SQUAT OR HALF SQUAT?

This problem does not arise if the full squat and the half squat are considered to be two different exercises; both are useful, but for different purposes. The heavy weight barbell squat with complete closing of the knee-angle (full squat) can be used as a preliminary exercise; it is effective for enforcing the 'anti-gravitational' muscles of the body.

The barbell squat executed with less leg flexion (the half squat or the flexing of the legs until a desired knee angle is reached) can be used as a highly specific training mean aimed at increasing the maximal strength effort in the main force producing movements of competition exercise. In this exercise, however, the athlete should use heavier overload weights compared to those used in the full squat.

The full squat, therefore, is an optimal exercise for preparing the athlete for the half squat:

1) the use of the heavy weighted full squat ensures an increase in the maximal strength of the muscle synergies, involved in the execution of the half squat as well;
2) the use of the full squat is less harmful to the body (assuming the athlete possesses the required joint mobility to safely perform the exercise).

The following is another problem that often arises during coaching discussions:

SHOULD, OLYMPIC WEIGHTLIFTING EXERCISES (SNATCH, CLEAN AND JERK, PUSH JERK, POWER CLEAN, ETC.) BE USED AS SST MEANS FOR THE PREPARATION OF OTHER SPORTS DISCIPLINES?

These exercises are highly specific training means for Olympic weightlifters; however, if any correspond to the motor structure of competition exercise of other sports discipline, then these exercises could be used as highly specific SST means. Otherwise, they may be used for general physical (strength) preparation: they are very effective exercises to develop the body and to improve practical experience in working with weights.

Resistance exercises may be subdivided in three groups: dynamic exercises, isometric (static) exercises and exercises executed in a combined regime.

2.2. DYNAMIC EXERCISES

2.2.1. METHODS OF USING DYNAMIC EXERCISES

The training effect of dynamic resistance exercises on the athlete's body depends on the condition of the movement's execution, usually determined by the following load parameters:

1) amount of external resistance - defined as the overload weight or other external resistance which makes the movement more difficult;
2) number of repetitions in one set;
3) number of sets;
4) number of series;
5) rest between sets;
6) rest between series.

A given combination of these parameters represents the *method* or how dynamic resistance exercises are performed. Depending on the method used, the training effect of resistance exercises can be oriented towards the development of:

- Maximal Strength;
- Explosive Strength;
- High Speed Strength;
- Strength Endurance;
- Maximal Anaerobic Power;
- Local Muscular Endurance.

Resistance training methods can be classified according to the type of exercises performed, the number of repetitions per set, the number of sets, and the duration of the rest intervals.

According to the character of the exercise's execution, two different training methods may be classified: Maximal Effort Method and Refusal Method.

The **Maximal Effort Method** allows an athlete to perform the exercise at a high level with one or another characteristic of movement, e.g. speed or power. The common quality of each repetition is its repeatable execution with good form. The repetitions cease the moment in which an appreciable decrease in these characteristics occurs, which is tied in with the onset of fatigue. The rest periods between sets should be of sufficient duration to restore the body back to an optimal condition that maintains quality performance of the exercise. This method is used for development of Maximal, Explosive, Starting Strength, and Reactive Ability.

If the resistance exercise allows one to execute a specific number of repetitions in the form of a repetition maximum, until failure, it is recognized as the **Refusal Method**.

This method is used mainly for the development of Strength Endurance. The key factor of this method is to use a resistance that allows one to execute a specific number of repetitions in the form of a repetition maximum e.g. a 10RM prevents an 11th rep. The work is performed, for example, in 4 to 6 sets with the rest between varying from 2 minutes to 30 seconds. If the 'work to failure' method is executed with more sets, as for example 6 to 8, the amount of resistance must be reduced in order that only 10 repetitions are executed in each set. Depending on the length of the rest periods between each set, two different methods may be classified: Repeat Method and Interval Method.

If the rest period between sets of exercises is of sufficient duration for the restoration of the body back to an optimal condition (i.e. one that maintains quality performance of the exercise), it is recognized as the **Repeat Method**.

If the rest pause between sets is not of sufficient duration for the restoration of the body back to an optimal condition, it is recognized as the **Interval Method**.

The Interval Method is used for the development of Strength Endurance and to increase the capacity of energy acquisition sources involved in extended cyclic work that requires the display of significant muscle effort. In comparison to the Repeat Method, this method is characterized by sub-maximal work power as well as a large number of repetitions separated by short rest periods between sets.

If resistance training is planned for the execution of several series of exercises, each of which includes the same number of sets, it is regarded as the Serial Method. Between series it is necessary to maintain rest periods that are sufficient to restore the body until it is capable of having a qualitative performance in the following series.

The Serial Method in formula form is as follows:
Where:

$$\frac{n \times X}{t_1} \times \frac{m}{t_2}$$

- X - number of repetitions of the exercise in one set;
- n - number of sets in one series;
- m - number of series;
- t_1 - the rest between sets;
- t_2 - the rest between series.

For example:

$$\frac{4 \times 6}{4_{min}} \times \frac{3}{8_{min}}$$

In this example there are four sets of six repetitions with a rest period of four minutes in between each set. This constitutes one series. There are then three series with a rest of 8 minutes in between.

In training, there are two forms of the serial method: repeat-serial and interval-serial.

The use of several sets of the same exercise, executed via the Repetitive Method, is recognized as the **Repeat-Serial Method**. The use of several sets of the same exercise, executed via the Interval Method, is recognized as the **Interval-Serial Method**.

In the SST the most important methods used are:
1) Maximal Effort Method;
2) Repeat-Serial Method;
3) Interval-Serial Method.

2.2.1.1. MAXIMAL EFFORT METHOD

The Maximal Effort Method is usually used for the development of maximal and explosive strength without significant increases in muscle size. The peculiarity of this method is high intensity with limited volume of training. It causes adaptations in the CNS mechanisms of muscular tension regulation, improves anaerobic energy systems, optimizes the speed of muscle relaxation, and improves motor unit synchronization in order to generate a powerful muscular force effort.

The Maximal Effort Method is used with rest periods (between sets of the exercise) of sufficient duration for the restoration of the body back to the optimal condition, so it is recognized also as the Repeat Method.

The main variant of the Maximal Effort Method is 2-3 repetitions with 90-95% of 1RM with obligatory muscle relaxation between repetitions. Training sessions consist of 2-4 sets with 4-6 minute rest periods.

The muscle relaxation exercises are conducted between individual repetitions of a single set. For instance, when using this method with the back squat exercise the athlete would perform one squat repetition, rack the barbell, and perform the relaxation movements. The athlete then un-racks the barbell and performs another single squat repetition followed by re-racking of the barbell and additional relaxation movements (and perhaps one more cycle of this for a third repetition). This series of events equals one set.

Periodically, once every 2-3 weeks during the off season and once every 1-2 weeks during the preseason, a different method can be used. After the warm up, complete lifts with 90, 95 and 100% 1RM, then 95, 100, and higher. Between each lift, rest 4-5 minutes. The rest between the second set of lifts is regulated depending on how the athlete feels.

Both methods could be used to support an athlete's speed-strength potential during the competition season.

2.2.1.2. REPEAT-SERIAL METHOD

This method is characterized by sub-maximal work intensity and volume. The exercise is executed for the same number of sets, and with optimal rest periods. This constitutes one series. Each series is repeated the same number of times. The rest periods between series are longer than between sets.

The number of reps in the series, the number of series, and the duration of rest between them is determined by the current condition and level of preparation of the athlete, the tasks of the training, and the regime of exercise execution.

This method is used predominantly for activation of morphological rebuilding in the body. It is also used to increase the amount of power generating substances available and the development of adaptive reactions to stabilize the body on a new functional level.

In general, this method of training creates a load slightly lower than the previous Maximal Effort Method. It includes a few variations divided by the sought after training adaptation which is regulated by the amount of resistance, velocity and tempo of movement, as well as the length of the rest periods.

VARIANT 1- **Increasing Maximal Strength** with muscle hypertrophy:
- Resistance 75-80% 1RM;
- Execute slow movements until desired fatigue is reached;
- Perform 2 sets with 2 minute rest periods for 2 to 3 muscle groups. If working only one muscle group, do 3 sets.

This method is not effective for improving speed, but it is useful at the beginning of the off-season training to prepare the muscles for heavier workloads.

VARIANT 2 - **Increasing Maximal Strength** with minor muscle hypertrophy:
- Complete 3 sets: 80% 1RM, 90% 1RM, and 93% 1RM
- 2 - 4 minute rest periods between sets.
- During one training session, perform 2 to 3 series separated by 6 to 8 minute rest periods.
- As the strength of the athlete increases, increase resistance by 5%.

In each of the two variants of the Repeat-Serial Methods, the muscles must not be relaxed between the movements (repetitions). Unlike the Maximal Effort Method, all repetitions of a single set are performed continuously.

VARIANT 3 - **Increasing High Speed Strength:**
- The overload weight is limited to 30-70% 1RM depending on the resistance to be overcome in the particular sport discipline.
- Perform 6 to 8 reps with maximum velocity in the miometric (overcoming) regime and moderate tempo in the pliometric (yielding) regime, relaxing muscles in the most advantageous bio-

mechanical position after each repetition.
- There are 2 to 3 sets in each series separated by 4 to 6 minute rest periods.
- There are 2 to 3 series in each training session separated by 8 to 10 minute rest periods.

VARIANT 4 - Increasing speed and frequency of unloaded movements:
- Resistance 15-20% 1RM.
- Execute the movement at maximal speed.
- If emphasizing speed, then frequency of movement has to be moderate and muscle relaxation movements are to be performed in between repetitions.
- If emphasizing frequency of movement, then the exercise has to be performed at maximal movement tempo.

Each series consist of 2-3 sets. Each set includes 8-10 reps. The rest between sets is 2-4 minute in the case of movement speed maximization, and 4-6 minutes in the case of movement frequency maximization[30].

VARIANT 5 - Improving reaction speed and muscle coordination:
- Training exercises are to simulate competition movements.
- Resistance 30-40% 1RM.
- Emphasis on quick start movements on the specific competition signal, i.e. visual, tactile, etc...
- Sets include 4-6 reps with long pauses.
- There are 2-3 series in one training session separated by 4-6 minute rest periods.
- In some cases, exercises can be performed with explosive isometric muscular tension (see § 2.3).

VARIANT 6 - Improving Dynamic Strength Endurance:
- Resistance 90-93% 1RM.
- Exercises performed at slow movement speed.
- 3 sets of 2-3 repetitions separated by 4-6 minute rest periods.
- Sets are not performed to failure, but until the athlete can repeat the movements at the same rate as at the beginning.
- After that, another 2-3 sets should be performed with the weight of external resistance decreased by 5%.

2.2.1.3. INTERVAL-SERIAL METHOD

This method uses repeated sub-maximal intensity exercises with shorter rest periods than in the Repeat-Serial Method. This method increases the power and capacity of energy supplying mechanisms[31].

VARIANT 1 - Increasing Maximal Anaerobic Power and the capacity of CP (Creatin-Phosphate) mechanisms:
- Work for 10 seconds with maximal effort.
- Resistance is limited to 30-40 % 1RM - the work must not lead to fatigue, evident when the speed and frequency of movement decrease.
- Tempo is one movement per second.
- Rest periods are 30 sec initially, but with an athlete's improvement in performing the exercise, it should gradually be decreased to 10 sec.

At the beginning of the workout, only 5-6 reps should be performed. Over the course of contin-

---

[30] The movement speed characterizes the speed of execution of individual repetitions. Alternatively, the movement frequency characterizes the speed of repetitions in succession.

[31] For the definition of power and capacity of energy supplying mechanisms, see § 7.1.

ued training sessions the number of repetitions has to be gradually increased until 8 - 10.

Each workout should consist of 2 - 3 sets separated by 8 - 10 minute rest periods between each series.

VARIANT 2 - Increasing power and capacity of glycolytic mechanisms.
-   Work for 30 seconds with moderate effort.
-   Rest period = 60 seconds.
-   Resistance is the same as in Variant 1.
-   Tempo = one movement per second.
-   There are 6-8 repetitions in each set.
-   In each training session there are 2 to 3 series separated by 10 to 12 minute rest periods.

In both variants, the training effect of exercises has to be increased by:
1) increasing external resistance (weight of overload) while preserving the same tempo of repetitions;
2) increasing the tempo of repetitions using a constant overload weight.

2.2.2. REGIMES OF DYNAMIC EXERCISE EXECUTION

As was underlined before, different regimes of muscular contraction cause different responses of the locomotor system even in the execution of the same exercise.

A 'classic' study carried out by Assmussen et alt. in 1965 showed that:
-   in the case of dynamic muscular contraction, the muscles never develop a force effort as high as what can be developed in an isometric contraction;
-   at any muscle's contraction velocity, the dynamic force is less than the isometric force;
-   during the maximal overcoming force effort, the higher the speed of movement, the less is the developed strength;
-   the maximal force achieved in a yielding dynamic contraction is always higher than the maximal isometric force; the difference, between them, increases if the movement speed (speed of muscle lengthening) increases.

In the 1960s and 1970s, Y. Verkhoshansky and his collaborators carried out studies to find out the training regime which could ensure the highest increase in the level of maximal strength effort in the take-off movements of Track & Field jumpers. The results of these studies confirmed Asmussen's research and, at the same time, revealed new information: the highest levels of maximal strength were obtained when dynamic exercises were executed in combined regimes of muscle contraction.

In one of these studies, carried out by G.Semenov in 1968, an athlete performed maximal strength efforts from a standard starting position with a knee angle equal to 120° using different regimes of muscular contraction:
-   maximal isometric strength effort in Leg Extension;
-   maximal dynamic strength effort in Leg Extension (overcoming regime);
-   maximal dynamic strength effort in pliometric ('eccentric') regime yielding under great opposition;
-   maximal dynamic strength effort in yielding regime after executing a maximal isometric tension in the starting position, with a knee angle equal to 120°;
-   maximal dynamic strength effort in reversible movements (the overcoming movement was preceded by a maximal strength effort in the yielding regime).

When the athlete executed the maximal dynamic strength effort with a slow movement overcoming great resistance (miometric regime), the strength effort magnitude was less than in the maximal isometric strength effort. The value of the maximal strength effort in a yielding regime was higher than the overcoming regime.

The greatest value of maximal strength effort was observed when a slow movement was performed in yielding regime after executing a maximal isometric tension in the starting position, with a knee angle equal to 120°. However, the value of maximal strength effort was also high when the movement was performed in the reversible regime.

The results of the other studies showed that it is possible to increase the influence of exercise on the athlete's body not only when using the appropriate variations of the muscle work regimes in the same exercise but also performing in sequence the same exercise in different regimes.

The transfer of this research results to the training practice needed to solve the following issues:

1) Most resistance exercises are carried out in a dynamic regime with repetitions of reversible movements in the yielding and the overcoming regimes. The rate of the reversible movement's repetition may vary in a range; how does the change in rate influence the training effect of the exercise?

2) When only one of the reversal movements (yielding or overcoming) is executed with overload (by using special equipment), what case will give the exercise better results?

3) When resistance exercises are carried out in sequence with different regimes, which regime's combination causes the highest cumulative effect?

To answer the questions above new research was carried out. In the following paragraphs the results of this research will be discussed.

2.2.2.1. DYNAMIC EXERCISES EXECUTED WITH DIFFERENT MOVEMENT RATES

The training effects of dynamic strength exercises are very different when they are executed at different movement rates.

In 1975 Lelikov recorded the rate of movements of 169 weightlifters carrying out the same barbell exercises (Squat, Snatch, Clean and Jerk), over 16 weeks, three times a week. The aim of their training sessions was to increase maximal strength: the maximal weight of the barbell (RM).

According to the movement rate at which they carried out these exercises, the athletes were divided into three groups: the first group used a high movement rate, the second a middle movement rate, and the third group a low movement rate.

The total volume of the training load in each group was the same, equal to 720 lifts at 80% of RM. At the end of the training period (after 16 weeks), the increase in maximal weight of each group was evaluated for the Squat, Snatch, and Clean and Jerk exercises.

All three groups obtained improvements; the best improvement was obtained by the second group which carried out the exercises with middle rate of movements (see Fig. 2.1). This result led to the thought that execution of resistance exercises with different movement rates involves different physiological

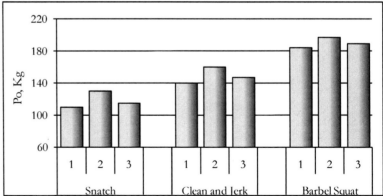

Fig. 2.1 - Increases in RM weight in Snatch, Clean, Jerk and Squat, in the three groups of weightlifters: Group 1 - using high rate of movement; Group 2 - using middle rate of movement; Group 3 - using low rate of movement.

mechanisms and different energetic resources. It is therefore likely that the combination of exercises executed with different movement rates would ensure the highest results.

This was in fact confirmed by the results of a follow-up experiment in which 4 groups of weightlifters used the Barbell Squat with different movement rates (high, middle, low and very low) and the 5th group performed exercises in combinations of equal proportion of all four different movement rates.

As can be seen from the results in Fig. 2.2, the highest increase in Maximal Strength was obtained by the 5th group of athletes.

In this experiment, particular attention was given to the dynamic of the increase in the level of maximal strength for the first four groups. After every 15 training sessions, the increase of RM was measured for each athlete.

The results, expressed as a percentage increase in RM, showed the following (see Fig. 2.3):

- the middle rate exercises had the highest training potential, according to the increase of Maximal Strength which lasted for a longer period of time (until the 30th training session);
- the very low rate exercises had a lower training potential, with respect to the middle-rate exercises, but this training potential was higher with respect to the low-rate and high-rate exercises;
- the very low rate and the high-rate exercises caused an increase in Maximal Strength up to the 15th training session only;
- the low rate exercises had the lowest level of training potential, but they were able to maintain their training effect for a longer time with respect to the other exercises (up to the last training session).

2.2.2.2. DYNAMIC EXERCISES EXECUTED ONLY IN OVERCOMING OR YIELDING REGIME

Athletes and coaches, as well as sport scientists, have always been interested using overcoming (miometric) and yielding (pliometric) regimes separately, especially in training aimed at increasing

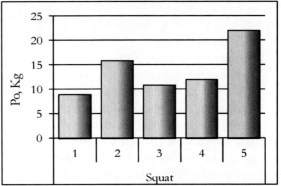

Fig. 2.2 - Increase in the RM weight of the Barbell Squat in five groups of weightlifters: Group 1 using a high rate; Group 2 using a middle rate; Group 3 using a low rate; Group 4 using a very low rate; Group 5 using high, middle, low and very low rates (in equal proportions).

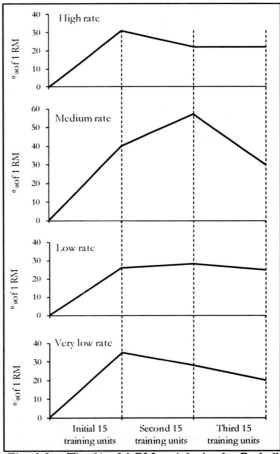

Fig. 2.3 – The % of 1 RM weight in the Barbell Squat increasing in four groups of weightlifters.

maximal strength.

Particular attention has been directed to the yielding ('eccentric') regime of muscular contractions.

In 1929, A. Bethe[32] established that the active force expressed in the overcoming regime, as a rule, is considerably less (in general, 1.2 to 1.6 times) than the passive force expressed in the yielding regime. The research carried out by Assmussen et alt. (1965) also showed that the maximal force achieved in a yielding dynamic contraction is always higher than the maximal isometric force.

This led to the theory that resistance exercises carried out in a yielding regime could lend particular advantages in increasing muscular strength in comparison to the other regimes.

The experiment of B.Pletnev studied the influence of resistance exercises, executed in different regimes, on the maximal strength expressed in Leg Extension. Leg Extension is the most important component of the key-movement of competition exercise in most sport disciplines.

Four groups of 14 weightlifters carried out the same volume of resistance exercises over a 12 week period (three training sessions in a week):

- the first group used exercises only in the overcoming regime (only the overcoming phase of the Barbell Squat);
- the second group – only in the yielding regime (only the yielding phase of the Barbell Squat);
- the third group – only in the static regime (overcoming isometric force efforts from a sitting position with a 90° knee angle against an immobile barbell on the shoulders);
- the forth group used all three of the above regimes (the exercises used by the 1st, 2nd and 3rd groups) in equal proportion.

At the end of the training period, the increase in the level of maximal isometric and dynamic strength, expressed via the Leg Press (i.e., in an overcoming regime) from the bent-leg position of a 90° knee angle, was evaluated in each group. The results of the experiment are presented in Fig. 2.4. The second group (which used only 'yielding exercises') didn't obtain the highest increase in the overcoming maximal strength. The results of this experiment also revealed that the highest increase in both isometric and dynamic strength was obtained by the forth group, which performed the resistance exercises in all three different regimes.

The results of the first 3 groups using only one regime in their training, showed that:

- the first group, which used only overcoming work, obtained a higher increase in the overcoming regime (both in the dynamic and isometric) in comparison to the second (yielding exercises) and third group (isometric exercises);
- the third group, which used only isometric exercises, obtained the highest increase in the isometric Leg Press and the lowest in the dynamic Leg Press.

Thus, in the first 3 groups, the greatest increase, both in dynamic and isometric strength, was observed in the corresponding regime used in the training.

Since the use of the combination of resistance exercises, executed in all three different mus-

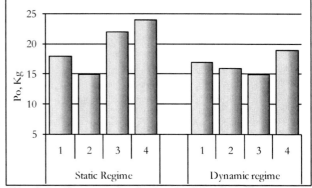

Fig. 2.4 – Increase in the level of the Leg Press maximal strength, expressed in the dynamic regime and isometric regime, in four groups of weightlifters who used the barbell squat according to the three different regimes.

[32] Bethe A Aktive und passive Kraft menschlicher Muskeln. Pfluegers Arch. (1929) 222: 334-349.

cular work regimes, produced the best increase in Maximal Strength, it was interesting to determine the best proportion between these exercises. In a follow-up experiment, therefore, the weightlifters were divided into 6 groups each using a combination of exercises in the overcoming, yielding, and isometric regimes in different proportions (see Table 5). In the 1st, 2nd and 3rd group the exercises executed in each of these three different regimes were used in proportion 1-1-2 (25% - 25% - 50%). In the 4th, 5th and 6th groups, the volume of the overcoming exercises prevailed (80%, 70%, and 50%).

	OVERCOMING REGIME	YIELDING REGIME	ISOMETRIC REGIME
1ST GROUP	50%	25%	25%
2ND GROUP	25%	25%	50%
3RD GROUP	25%	50%	25%
4TH GROUP	80%	10%	10%
5TH GROUP	70%	10%	20%
6TH GROUP	60%	20%	20%

Table 5 - The combinations of three different regimes of barbell squatting, used by six groups of weightlifters during the experiment

The results of this experiment showed (see Fig. 2.5) that the best increase in maximal dynamic strength (in an overcoming movement) was obtained by the 4th group, which carried out 80% of the resistance exercises in the overcoming regime.

The 5th and 6th groups, which carried out 60-70% of the exercises in the overcoming regime, reached a greater increase in Maximal Strength than the 1st, 2nd and 3rd groups, which carried out only 25% of the exercises in the overcoming regime.

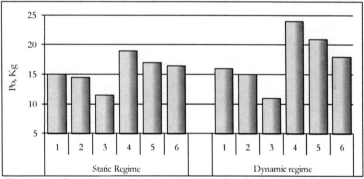

Fig. 2.5 - Increase in the level of maximal strength in the Leg Press in the dynamic and isometric regimes (from the 90° knee-angle position) of 6 groups of weightlifters who executed the Barbell Squat in different regimes (Table 5)

In the first three groups, which carried out no more than 50% of the exercises in one of the three regimes, the 1st ('overcoming' group) reached a greater increase (both in dynamic and isometric strength) than the 2nd ('isometric' group) and the 3rd ('yielding' group). The final result of the 3rd group was the lowest. The yielding exercises, therefore, executed in conjunction with other different regimes, don't elicit a positive effect if their volume is equal to or greater than the others. Thus, when resistance exercises, executed in different regimes, are used in various combinations, the use of the yielding regime in these combinations doesn't offer particular advantages.

Resistance exercises executed in yielding regime also produce a negative effect on muscular tissues. High muscular tension during yielding contractions can cause harmful changes in muscles, e.g., mechanical lesions of muscular tissues and their contractile tissue elements.

Nevertheless, we cannot deny that strength exercises executed in the yielding regime could be very effective, especially when a strong external opposition is to be overcome.

Another experiment evaluated the training effect of resistance exercises, executed in different regimes, on Explosive Strength (Vertical Jump) and on Maximal Strength expressed by dorsal muscles in trunk extension, in the Barbell Squat (the weight of 1RM).

For 3 months, 3 groups of athletes carried out the same volume of resistance exercises:
- the first group executing them only in the yielding regime;
- the second group executing them only in the overcoming regime;
- the third group executing them only in the static (isometric) regime.

The results of this experiment (Table 6) show that:
- a greater increase (15 Kg) in the Barbell Squat was obtained by using the yielding regime while the lowest increase (9 Kg) was obtained using the static regime;
- the best increase in Maximal Strength of the dorsal muscles was caused by the exercises executed in the static regime (30.2 Kg);
- the best increase in Explosive Strength, measured through the increase in vertical jump height, was caused by the exercises executed in an overcoming regime, while the static and yielding regimes produced a negative effect.

GROUPS USING DIFFERENT REGIMES	BARBELL SQUAT (KG)	MAXIMAL STRENGTH OF DORSAL MUSCLES (KG)	VERTICAL JUMP (CM)
1. YIELDING	**+ 15.0**	+ 21.5	- 1.6
2. OVERCOMING	+ 12.2	+ 14.6	**+ 3.7**
3. STATIC	+ 09.2	**+ 30.2**	- 5.4

Table 6 - The changes in the level of Maximal and Explosive Strength, after executing resistance training with different regimes of muscular work.

This experiment showed that resistance exercises in the yielding regime ensure mostly an increase in Maximal Strength and don't influence, or negatively influence, Explosive Strength.

2.2.2.3. ISOKINETIC EXERCISES

The use of the isokinetic regime to develop muscular strength widely spread between the end of the 1960s and the beginning of the 1970s, especially in the United States. The main idea of this method consists in the possibility to automatically change – thanks to a special device – the external opposition to the movement, by limiting its speed and ensuring the same load on the muscles for the entire amplitude of movement. In isokinetic exercises, the velocity of movements has to be set, unlike in the weight exercise, where the level of external opposition (overload weight) is set. The use of isokinetic exercises offers some practical advantages:
1) The isokinetic device adapts itself to an athlete's ability to execute the movement (it's not the athlete who adapts himself to a prefixed opposition). The isokinetic device automatically changes the level of external opposition when the athlete is not able to maintain the necessary force efforts (as a strained muscle or the sensation of pain), so that the possibility of accidents is reduced.
2) Isokinetic exercises do not require a long warm-up, which is usually required before weight training; only five minutes of warm-up may be enough to perform an efficacious training session.

3) In a training group, even if the athletes are characterized by different levels of strength, it's not necessary to adapt the device to each athlete and this leads to heightened training time economy.

4) In isokinetic training, the needed training effect may be reached using a lower number of movement repetitions, thanks to the device which automatically adapts the level of external opposition to the developed force effort. In this way, in each repetition, the muscles are loaded enough for the entire amplitude of the movement.

5) The isokinetic device provides a feedback of the athlete's result on a screen, which helps the athlete to adjust his effort in order to reach the desired result.

In comparison with other work regimes, the isokinetic regime is characterized by higher electrical muscular activity and by a better increase in movement speed and muscular strength, which are reached over shorter periods of time, and by a longer preservation of these effects after the training. Exercises executed in an isokinetic regime produced a training effect with a high level of functional specificity, i.e. isokinetic exercises executed at a certain speed ensure a high increase in maximal force effort expressed with the same movement at the same velocity and a lower influence on the same movement executed with a different velocity.

In 1984, D. Bravaya studied the functional specificity of isometric and isokinetic strength training.

Three homogeneous groups of athletes carried out 5 times a week, over 4 weeks, the same number of maximal force efforts in ankle joint flexion in different regimes of muscular contraction:

-   Group 1 in an isometric regime;
-   Group 2 in a low-speed isokinetic regime (angular speed 40 degrees/sec);
-   Group 3 in a high-speed isokinetic regime (angular speed 160 degrees/sec).

Before and after the four weeks of training, the momentum of force in Maximal Strength effort, of ankle joint flexion, was measured in 5 different tests:

1) Maximal isometric strength effort;
2) Maximal strength effort in an isokinetic regime at an angular speed of movement 40 degrees/sec;
3) Maximal strength effort in an isokinetic regime at an angular speed of movement 80 degrees/sec;
4) Maximal strength effort in an isokinetic regime at an angular speed of movement 120 degrees/sec;
5) Maximal strength effort in an isokinetic regime at an angular speed of movement 160 degrees/sec.

The results of this experiment, expressed as % of change of force momentum with respect to the initial level before the four weeks of training, are shown in Fig. 2.6.

The first group, trained in the isometric regime, obtained the greatest increase in the isometric regime. At the same time the athletes showed a decrease of dynamic strength at angular speeds of movement from 40 to 160 degrees per second.

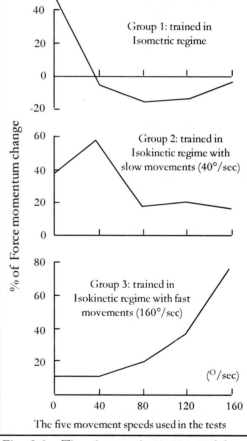

Fig. 2.6 - The changes in moment of force (after 4 weeks training) in the ankle joint developed as result of different regimes of training.

The second group, trained in isokinetic regime at a low speed (40 degrees/sec.), improved both isometric and dynamic strength when displayed in low speed movements. The third group, trained in an isokinetic regime at a high speed (160 degrees/sec.), improved dynamic strength displayed mainly at high speeds (120 and especially 160 degrees/sec.)

Thus, the greatest increase in the moment of force is observed in the training regime. As such, isometric training has a negative influence on force moment in the dynamic regime and that may negatively influence the speed of muscle contraction. High speed training (160°/sec) in the isokinetic regime does not produce an increase in isometric force.

The results of this experiment showed that isokinetic exercises increase the working effect only in those movements executed in the same regime. The isokinetic exercises could be effectively applied in the SST of those sport disciplines in which the force effort, expressed in the key movements, is finalized to use the opposing force produced by the environment (or device) against which the force effort is applied for a longer period of time compared to the time needed to complete the full key movement. A swimmer or canoeist, for example, applies his force effort in their propulsive phase of the stroke, against the environment (water) to employ the opposing force of water to move forward. In this example, the environment (water) makes a stand to the transformation in kinetic energy (displacement of water) of the applied force (athlete' force effort).

Only few sport disciplines have key movements that could be compared with the isokinetic regime: most sport movements are executed in a ballistic regime. This limit of application of isokinetic training in sport was asserted by P.O. Astrand[33]: *"With the possible exception of swimming, isokinetic exercises do not stimulate natural movements, and therefore the value of isokinetic training is difficult to evaluate."*

In fact, a study on the relationship between isokinetic strength of knee extensors/flexors, jumping, and anaerobic performance[34], showed that the maximal isokinetic strength of the knee extensors/flexors, evaluated at 60, 120 and 180°/sec, was not correlated with Squat Jump height.

Other studies[35] showed that the torques of the sub-maximal and maximal isokinetic efforts of the knee extensors at angular velocities of 60 and 180°/sec were moderately correlated with vertical jump height.

On the other hand, the study of C. Bosco[36] showed that the peak torque, produced during isokinetic contraction of the leg extensor muscles, is correlated with:

- the height of vertical jump executed from a static position SJ ($r=0.71$, $p<0.01$);
- the height of counter-movement vertical jump CMJ ($r=0.74$, $p<0.005$);
- the height of Depth Jump DJ ($r=0.60$, $p<0.05$),
- the result of the 15 sec Maximal Anaerobic Power test ($r=0.70$, $p<0.01$) and
- the result of the 60 sec anaerobic power test ($r=0.68$, $p<0.01$).

If the above results are not completely convergent, all of the studies show that isokinetic exercises, executed with the aim to obtain a maximal peak torque, could be used also to increase the working effect of ballistic movements in combination with more specific SST means (in a SST means System).

---

[33] P.O.Astrand, K.Rodahl, H.Dahl, S.B.Stromne Textbook of Work Physiology.Human Kinetics, 2003

[34] Hayriye Çakır Atabek, Gülsün Aydın Sönmez, İlker Yılmaz. The relationship between isokinetic strength of knee extensors/flexors, jumping and anaerobic performance. Journal "Isokinetics and Exercise Science". Volume 17, Number 2, 2009.

[35] P. Malliou, I. Ispirlidis, A. Beneka, K. Taxildaris, G. Godolias. Vertical jump and knee extensors isokinetic performance in professional soccer players related to the phase of the training period. Journal "Isokinetics and Exercise Science" Volume 11, Number 3, 2003

[36] C. Bosco, P. Mognoni and P. Luhtanen. Relationship between isokinetic performance and ballistic movement. European Journal of Applied Physiology and Occupational Physiology Volume 51, Number 3, 357-364, 1983.

2.3. ISOMETRIC EXERCISES

In the isometric regime the strength effort is developed without muscle shortening, i.e., when the muscles are under active tension with no visible movement.

This type of resistance training causes muscle group tension by applying push-off or traction force to a motionless object and maintaining this tension for a certain period of time. Muscle length does not change and the traction or push-off force remains relatively steady.

In the field of sport, the popularity of isometric exercises spread in the middle of the 1950s. This spread was due to the search for methods to develop muscular strength and characterized by a high saving and a high efficiency. T. Hettinger and E. Muller (1953, 1955) established that 10 weeks of daily execution of isometric tensions at 2/3 of the maximum level, for a length of 6 seconds, leads to a weekly increase of 5% in muscular strength.

Positive results, obtained thanks to the isometric training, caused a chain reaction in the field of research. Naturally, the aim of most of that research was centered on the question:

What is the most efficacious type of training: isometric or dynamic?

This research produced quite conflicting results, but the general conclusions, which can be drawn by analyzing the collected data, is that isometric training can be more efficacious than dynamic training particularly for those sport disciplines in which the external opposition in the competition exercise is high. In sports that require high speed movements against low external opposition, isometric training is less efficacious than dynamic training. The following advantages regarding isometric training need to be pointed out:

- basic equipment is only required;
- it produces a local effect on any muscular group in a precise joint angle, while during dynamic work, the movement passes very quickly through the position in which the muscular tension may produce its greatest effect;
- it requires less time and less energy; the training effect of each isometric tension can be compared to one produced by dozens of dynamic contractions (the length of maximum strength efforts in an isometric exercise lasts 6 seconds, in dynamic exercise, no longer than 0.1 seconds).
- Isometric exercises provide better visual and kinesthetic memorization of movement images than the dynamic regime of muscular work. This is why the isometric method is very useful in teaching and correcting mistakes.

If a high number of isometric exercises are executed in the training session, they can have the following negative effects:

- excessive fatigue of nervous and cardiovascular systems;
- decrease in coordination capacity and speed of movement;
- reduction of muscle elasticity.

The negative effects of isometric training may be avoided by using:

1) correct breathing patterns during the exercise's execution;
2) muscle contraction lengths no longer than 6 seconds (some authors suggest a limit of 10 seconds);
3) relaxation exercises during the recovery breaks.

The use of isometric exercises for a long period leads to a remarkable growth of intramuscular connective tissues. This increases muscle stiffness, that is, it decreases their elasticity (flexibility). This is why in disciplines involving high velocity dynamic muscle work, prolonged use of isometric overloads is not suitable.

There are two types of isometric regimes.

1) EXPLOSIVE ISOMETRIC REGIME: this isometric muscular contraction has an explosive character; it is

carried out by emphasizing the speed of tension developed up to a maximum of 80-90%. This ensures the development of Explosive and Starting Strength, expressed in a dynamic regime with a great external opposition.

2) NON EXPLOSIVE ISOMETRIC REGIME: this isometric muscular contraction is performed in order to achieve a given magnitude of strength effort without time limits and maintaining the level of tension as long as possible. Fig. 2.7 shows the time ranges in which it is possible to keep the isometric muscular contraction in relation to the magnitudes of strength effort. This regime promotes the development of Maximal

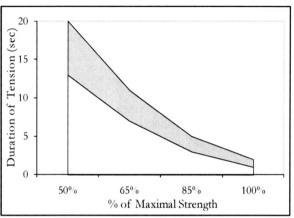

Fig. 2.7 - Duration of isometric muscle tension depending on the magnitude of strength effort (% of Maximal Strength)

Strength and Static Strength Endurance. In non explosive isometric exercises, it is necessary to:
- gradually develop the strength engagement applied to a motionless object;
- use 5-10 seconds rest between repetitions;
- limit the duration of isometric training to 10 minutes per work-out;
- finish the isometric training with relaxation exercises.

The problem with isometric exercises is that the magnitude of strength effort can only be determined subjectively. To solve this problem, non explosive isometric exercises should be executed holding a determined weight for the given period of time. The combined regime (quasi-isometric) could be also used to solve the aforementioned problem (see § 2.4.1).

The training effect of isometric exercises depends on the joint angle, i.e. the position in which the isometric tension has been applied. Isometric tension executed in a given joint angle ensures a 'specific' training effect: increasing the maximal force effort expressed with the same angle. It also causes a 'collateral' training effect for the force effort expressed in other angles.

In 1974, L. Raitzin carried out an experiment on the <u>flexion exercises</u>, studying the training effects of isometric tensions performed with different joint angles. Two groups of athletes executed isometric exercises aimed at increasing maximal isometric strength in arm flexion. The first group executed the isometric exercises with a wide (open) joint angle, the second group – with a closed joint angle. After the training period, the increase in the Maximal Strength of arm flexion was evaluated measuring the maximal magnitude of isometric force effort expressed in different joint angles.

The results showed that isometric training with an open joint angle caused less increases in maximal isometric strength, but a relatively higher transfer to joint angles not trained. On the contrary, isometric training with a closed joint angle elicits a higher increase in maximal isometric strength, while its relative transfer on the untrained joint angles is lower than isometric training with an open joint angle.

T.Kitai and D.Sale (1989)[37] studied the training effects on isometric strength of the <u>extension isometric exercises</u> (anatomical plantar flexions) executed at an ankle joint angle of 90°. Isometric strength was measured at the training angle and at additional angles: 5°, 10°, 15°, and 20° intervals in plantar flexion and dorsiflexion. The results of this research showed that isometric training mainly strengthens the

---

[37] T. A. Kitai and D. G. Sale. Specificity of joint angle in isometric training. European Journal of Applied Physiology and Occupational Physiology. Volume 58, Number 7, 744-748, DOI: 10.1007/BF00637386

muscle at the specific joint angle in which the isometric exercise occurs, with some increases in strength at joint angles up to 20° in either direction depending on the joint trained.

B.A. Pletnev (1979) studied the influence of extension isometric exercises (trunk extension and leg extension) on the maximal dynamic strength expressed in the corresponding movements. The results showed that, for the trunk extension, the isometric exercises executed with a 90° joint angle ensure a greater increase in dynamic strength than isometric exercises executed with joint angles of 120° and 150°. For the leg extension, isometric exercises executed with a 90°joint angle ensure the greatest increase in dynamic strength.

The results of these experiments provide only one consensus: isometric exercises should be executed at a joint angle corresponding to the same position (angle) of the maximal force effort expressed in the competition exercise. For example, research (V. Kuznetzov at al., 1980) showed that for ski jumpers, the isometric squat exercises are useful if executed in the positions with the knee joint angles equal to 80°, 110° and 140°, which corresponds to the position in which the maximal force effort has to be expressed in key movements of the competition exercise.

In summation, it is possible to outline the following GUIDELINES FOR ISOMETRIC TRAINING:

1) It is necessary to execute isometric exercises in specific positions (postures) that are appropriate to the moment of display of maximum effort in the competitive exercise.

2) Isometric training is especially effective when the competition exercise requires displaying high levels of strength. Isometric training is less effective and can even create a negative influence on speed of muscle contraction when the competition exercise requires high-speed movements against a relatively small external resistance.

3) Prolonged application of isometric exercises leads to significant expansion of the connective tissue. As a consequence, the muscle's elasticity decreases. For competition exercises requiring fine movement coordination or high speed in cyclic movements, the high volume and the extended duration of isometric exercises are not advisable.

4) It is effective to combine isometric tensions with the dynamic regime (quasi-isometric exercises).

5) It is necessary to perform relaxation and dynamic stretching exercises of moderate intensity between sets and at the end of isometric training.

2.4. RESISTANCE EXERCISES IN COMBINED REGIMES

2.4.1. STATIC-DYNAMIC REGIME

In the static-dynamic regime, isometric and dynamic regimes are sequentially combined into one exercise. There are three different types of exercises executed in the static-dynamic regime:

1) Quasi-isometric exercises;
2) Explosive static-dynamic exercises;
3) Slow dynamic exercises with reduced amplitude of movements.

2.4.1.1. QUASI-ISOMETRIC EXERCISES

Quasi-isometric exercises are executed with a considerable weight and include the combination of dynamic strength effort (lifting of weight) and static strength effort (pushing or holding the weight for a given period of time).

The 'pushing' version of the quasi-isometric exercises is known as Hoffmann's method. It consists of lifting the weight, followed by a push against a permanent support with an isometric contraction (on the left of Fig. 2.8).

Exercises are performed involving isometric tensions lasting from 6 to 8 seconds, executed after previously lifting a barbell to a pin. Raise the weight and move it slowly along an overhead trajectory until the limiting device, and push it to create isometric tension. At the beginning of this exercise, there is a short dynamic phase which gives the athlete some indication regarding the intensity level. The overload can

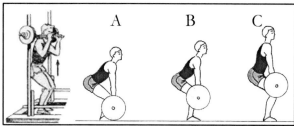

Fig. 2.8 - Muscle work exercises in the static-dynamic regime. Quasi-isometric exercises, pushing and holding version: A, B, and C positions in which isometric tension is developed.

be lifted more than once in the space between the sequence of limiting devices and, after completing the last lift, an isometric tension can be used for as long as required.

The 'holding' version of quasi-isometric exercises consists of lifting a heavy weight along a long trajectory, with stops of 5 - 6 seconds of isometric tension (on the right of Fig. 2.8). Raise the weight and move it slowly along an overhead trajectory, interrupting the movement at set intervals of the range of motion. This allows the tension to act on muscles along the whole trajectory and to assess the strength increase based on of the increases in the overload.

2.4.1.2. EXPLOSIVE STATIC-DYNAMIC EXERCISES

Explosive static-dynamic exercises consist in alternating isometric and explosive dynamic strength efforts. At the beginning of the exercise, the isometric tension is held for a few seconds and then replaced by dynamic explosive strength efforts. Three variants of exercise execution are usually used:

1) The first variant includes performing isometric tensions of 5 to 6 seconds, holding a weight equal to 80% of the maximal, and subsequent explosive dynamic work effort with a weight equal to 50-60% of the maximal. This variant is used for developing Explosive and High-Speed Strength.

2) In the second variant, a steady overload equal to 75-80% of the maximum is used for both dynamic and isometric components of exercise. For example an athlete, with the barbell on his/her shoulders, passes from a stationary upright position to a semi-squat position, maintaining it for 3-5 seconds, and, afterwards, jumping upwards at maximum speed. The exercise is repeated after landing. This variant is used for developing Explosive and Maximal Strength.

3) In the third variant, the muscles are slowly stretched in the isometric regime until a level equal to 70-80% of the maximum. Subsequently, the external resistance is suddenly eliminated (thanks to a special device). Muscles begin shortening and their previous potential of tension is used against an external opposition equal to about 30-40% of the maximum. In this way, a very high power of muscular work is developed; it is much higher than that which can be developed without a previous isometric muscular tension.

4) The third variant is known as the **Tear Regime**. It may be referred to as the regime of the 'sudden release' of the stretched muscle, and has been taken into account by experimental neuromuscular physiology (Jewel, Wilkie, 1958). It represents a specific method of intensifying the muscle's contractile function. In the first phase of the exercise there is an isometric tension which creates a higher excitability of the central nervous system. Subsequently, after the sudden elimination of the external opposition, an instantaneous explosive muscular contraction against a quite weak external opposition takes place. Naturally, the practical use of the Tear Regime requires the development of a new special device. An experimental verification showed that the Tear Regime is very effica-

cious at improving High-Speed Strength and Explosive Strength, both used against a moderate external resistance.

2.4.1.3. SLOW DYNAMIC EXERCISES WITH REDUCED AMPLITUDE OF MOVEMENTS

At the beginning of the 1980s, sport physiologists understood that increasing the power output of cyclic movements at the level of anaerobic threshold was the most important factor in improving sport results in cyclic sports. Researchers began searching for training methods that solved this task. Y.Verkhoshansky proposed in the 1980s enforcing the Creatine Phosphate shuttle mechanism, which allows increasing contractile and oxidative capacity of the muscles involved in competition exercise (execution of standing jumps with overload and hip flexion resistance exercise in a definite interval regime, see § 7.5.1.1). The theory of V.Seluyanov, proposed in the 1990s[38], was based on increasing the contractile capacity (strength) in the slow twitch fibers, ensuring their hyperplasia (the process of forming new fibers, see § 7.5.1.2).

The problem is that traditional resistance exercises, which are usually executed in dynamic regimes with wide amplitude of movements, cannot be effective for increasing the contractile capacity of the slow twitch fibers; only the fast twitch fibers are stimulated enough to ensure a training effect. According to V.Seluyanov, this happens because such regime allows contractions and relaxations of the muscles during the exercise's execution ensuring an adequate blood flow to the oxidative fibers while there is not an accumulation of hydrogen ions (without acidosis there is no training effect in these fibers). Therefore it is necessary to impair the blood circulation in the slow twitch fibers during the exercise, by keeping them tense and avoiding relaxation.

In order to facilitate the process of forming new muscle fibers (hyperplasia) one has to impair blood flow through the working muscles. If resistance exercises are executed in a regime which does not let the muscle relax and keeps the capillaries compressed, it facilitates hyperplasia in the slow twitch muscle fibers. To increase the contractile capacity of the slow twitch fibers, Seluyanov proposed the following method, taken from the bodybuilding community:

- the overload weight is 10-40% of RM;
- the resistance exercises are performed without muscle relaxation between the reversal phases of movements;
- the amplitude of movements is reduced: each overcoming phase of the reversal movement must be executed from a joint angle flexion position starting from 90% until the angle of 110% is reached;
- the rate of movements repetition is very low;
- the speed of movement is constant: in each reversal phase, the movements are executed without weight acceleration (without accentuation of the force effort at the starting phase of movement).

These exercises are usually executed in super-series in which different resistance exercises for the same muscle group may be also executed:

- 3-5 sets of 30-40 sec duration (until the pain sensation is reached) are repeated with 30-40 sec active rest intervals between sets;
- after the conclusion of these 3-5 sets, a longer interval of active rest (5-10 minutes) is done and the athlete executes the other resistance exercises for the same muscle group in the same regime as the previous one;
- in the super-series, the total number of sets should not exceed 7-12;

---

[38] Seluyanov V.N., Erkomayshvili I.V. Adaptation of skeletal muscles and the Theory of Physical Preparation. "Messenger of Sport science", 1990, p. 3-8 (in Russian).

- in the training session, only one super-series is carried out;
- the super-series can be repeated only after 3-5 days.

Research based on computer modeling explored the possibility of using these exercises to improve Local Muscular Endurance in cyclic sports. As the authors of this research predicted, the use of these exercises ensures the hyperplasia of the myofibrils in the slow twitch fibers and increases the level of power output of cyclic exercise at the anaerobic threshold level [39].

2.4.2. SHOCK REGIME

The Shock Regime is characterized by a sharp, sudden force effort of muscles stretched by a former short, powerful impact against an external opposition. It is used to develop Explosive Strength, Reactive Ability, and Maximal Strength. This regime is characterized by a great training effect on the motor and neuromuscular system and on the central mechanism that regulates muscle contractile function. At the end of the 1960s, after having verified its efficacy in sport practice, it was adopted as a special training regime for high-level athletes only.

The Shock Regime was thoroughly investigated in Y.Verkhoshansky's research in 1960s [40]. The idea behind this method is in the use of the body's (or training device) kinetic energy, accumulated in its free fall, to stimulate neuromuscular tension. The neuromuscular tension is provided at the contact after dropping from a specific measured height. The landing causes a relatively short phase of amortization that causes a sharp (shock) stretching of the muscles. That results in two interrelated reactions of the neuromuscular system:
- increasing the motor neuron's stimulation intensity;
- creating an elastic potential of muscle tension.

This ensures an increase in speed of the subsequent muscle contraction during the fast switching from pliometric (yielding) to miometric (overcoming) regime.

In the USA, the Shock Regime was identified as the so called *plyometrics*. This term was invented by Fred Wilt, a former Olympic runner, National Collegiate Athletic Association champion, and Purdue track coach, author of several books about Track & Field training.

The word 'plyometric' is very nice and, maybe for this reason, it became a popular 'brand' not only referred to the Shock Method, but also to the use of all jump exercises.

"Despite suggestions for other terminology for this type of conditioning by Komi[41] and later by Knuttgen and Kraemer[42], the popularity of 'plyometrics' and the use of the term have increased dramatically."[43]

According to John A. Faulkner*"...the increased use of the term "plyometrics" for conditioning with high-power jumps that involve repeated, rapid, and forceful shortening and lengthening actions during almost max-*

[39] Mjakinchenko E.B, Seluyanov V.N. Developing the Local Muscular Endurance in the cyclic sports. – Moscow.: TVT "Division", 2005 (In Russian)

[40] Y. Verkhoshansky "All about Shock Method", published in Brazil and Italy.

[41] Komi PV. Physiological and biomechanical correlates of muscle function: effects of muscle structure and stretch-shortening cycle on force and speed. In: Exercise and Sport Science Reviews, edited by Terjung RL. Lexington, MA: Collamore, 1984, p. 81-121.

[42] Komi PV. Physiological and biomechanical correlates of muscle function: effects of muscle structure and stretch-shortening cycle on force and speed. In: Exercise and Sport Science Reviews, edited by Terjung RL. Lexington, MA: Collamore, 1984, p. 81-121

[43] Faulkner, J.A. Terminology for contractions of muscles during shortening, while isometric, and during lengthening. J Appl Physiol 95: 455-459, 2003.

imum activation of large muscle groups" is *"an additional deterrent to the use of the term pliometric"*.

According to Y. Verkhoshansky, the use of the term 'pliometric' to define the Shock method is not correct; the principal training factor involved in this method is not simply the former muscle's stretching in a yielding regime, but rather the fast switching from sharp shock stretching to vigorous contraction.

The simplest form of performing the exercise in the Shock Regime is the Depth Jump: a vertical double leg jump after a drop down from a carefully measured height (see Fig. 2.9; for a complete description of this exercise see § 3.4). Exercises shown in Fig. 2.10 and 2.11 are for training the upper body muscles.

A particular form of the Shock Regime exercises for training different muscle groups is shown in Fig. 2.12. At the start, the weight is freely lowered, approximately 2/3 of the total range of movement, and followed by a sharp downwards-upwards movement. The consequent fast twitching of the muscles, from a yielding to overcoming regime, produces a vigorous acceleration of the load. In order to avoid injury it is necessary to provide limiting devices to block the movement of weight from going further than necessary.

In the preparation of the exercise's execution, consider the following:

- The starting position is selected after taking into consideration the position of the body at which the maximum working effort is expressed in the competition exercise.
- The initial pathway should be minimal but sufficient to create the shock tension in the muscles.
- The size of the shock effect is determined by the overload weight and by the height from which it falls. The optimal combination of these two factors has to be empirically determined. However, preference should always be given to greater height rather than greater weight.
- The exercises in the Shock Regime should be executed only after an adequate warm up.
- The dosage for shock exercises depends on the 'quality' of execution and should not exceed 4 sets

Fig. 2.9 - The take-off after the drop down in the Depth Jump

Fig. 2.10 - Push up Depth Jumps. An example of a shock regime exercise for training the arm extensor muscles

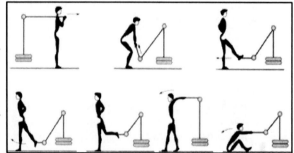

Fig. 2.11 - Examples of exercises in the shock regime of developing effort

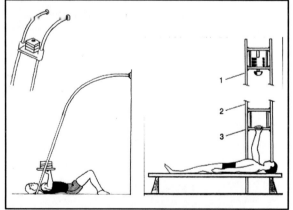

Fig. 2.12 - Special devices for training arm extensors by the shock method

of 10 repetitions. When the athlete executes this exercise for the first time, the dosage should not exceed 2-3 sets of 5-8 repetitions.

The Fig. 2.13 illustrates some specialized training devices for the Shock Regime exercises.

It must be emphasized that the Shock Method is not to be taken lightly. Recently, mainly in the USA, variants of Depth Jumps have been presented by many authors. They often suggest exceeding the optimum dosage of Depth Jumps and the recommended height of the drop-down, as well as their use for low level athletes.

The Shock Method has an extraordinarily strong training effect on the neuro-muscular system, considerably stronger than any other natural method of stimulation of the contractile activity of the muscles. It is, therefore, inadmissible to exceed the optimum dosage and duration of

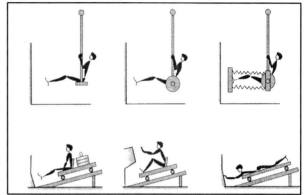

Fig. 2.13 - Training devices to achieve the Shock Regime of muscular work (Laboratory of V. Kousnetzov)

Depth Jumps used in the training process, as well as the recommended height of the drop-down. Depth Jumps have a strong training effect on the ligaments and joints and, consequently, it is necessary to:

- prepare the athlete in advance, performing jumping and resistance exercises;
- study the technique of executing exercises in the Shock Regime, especially when the muscles are working in the push-off (take-off) after the drop down. This is not as simple as it may seem initially;
- never use the Shock Regime when tired (when muscles are sore), when undergoing the treatment for injuries or in combinations of resistance exercises in different regimes.

The Shock Method is for high-level athletes; it should never be applied in the training of low-level athletes. For them, there are different and sufficiently effective SST means.

It is incorrect to overestimate the possibilities of the Shock Method. It is only one of many ways for intensifying the work of the neuromuscular system. The Shock Method cannot be used alone, but must be applied together with other means and methods and must have a definite place in the SST system.

SST MEANS AND METHODS: JUMP EXERCISES

3.1. GENERAL CHARACTERISTICS OF JUMP EXERCISES USED IN SST

Because of the training effect they yield to the organism, jump exercises represent a universal means of SST. According to the character of execution and how it is combined with other means, jump exercises improve:
- Maximal Strength, Explosive Strength, and Reactive Ability;
- Local Muscular Endurance and Maximal Anaerobic Power;
- nimbleness (lightness, looseness) of movements (muscle's ability to relax immediately after the execution of powerful motor efforts);
- ability to coordinate the movements and the force efforts.

Moreover, in Track & Field running and team sports (which include running as a main component of competition activity), jump exercises ensure an increase in the power output of the take-off force-efforts, and consequently, increase the running stride length that facilitates a speed increase in the starting acceleration and the maximal average speed on competition distance. Among jump exercises, the following main types could be characterized:

1. Jump exercises executed without additional external resistance (weights), which include:
   a. Single Standing jumps,
   b. Multiple take off jumps without forward displacement (Standing Jumps and Box Jumps);
   c. Multiple take off jumps with forward displacement:
      - with moderate forward displacement (Jumps over boxes or hurdles);
      - with active forward displacement (Bounds)
      - with active upward-forward displacement (Stadium Jumping);
2. Jumps with weight (Barbell Jumps and Kettlebell Jumps), which include:
   a. Consecutive Barbell Jumps;
   b. Consecutive Kettlebell Squat Jumps;
   c. Vertical Jumps with Barbell
3. Depth Jumps or Shock Method Jumps (because their training effect is so powerful, they are considered a particular type of jump exercise).

Each of these groups of jump exercises can be used for a specific purpose (increasing Explosive Strength, Reactive Ability, and Local Muscular Endurance etc.).

By 'quantitative' point of view, they provoke different levels of exertion of the athlete's neuro-muscular function i.e. a different level in the intensity of the training stimuli, determined by the power output in the take-off force efforts. According to these criteria, jump exercises can be hierarchically organized as shown in the following figure 3.1.

JUMPS WITHOUT OVERLOAD (standing jumps and bounds) $\Rightarrow$ JUMPS WITH OVERLOAD (consecutive Barbell Jumps, Kettlebell Squat Jumps and Vertical Jumps with Barbell) $\Rightarrow$ DEPTH JUMP.

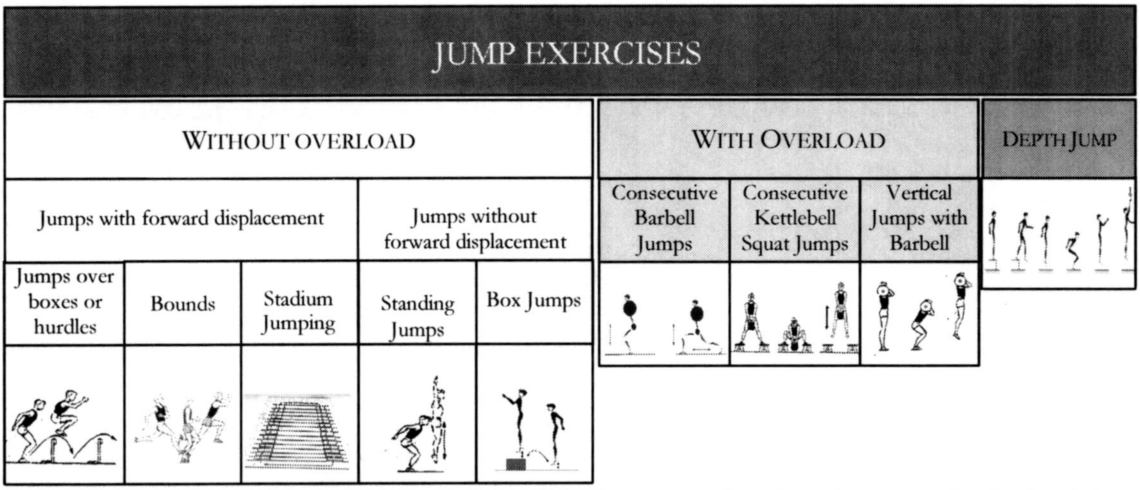

JUMP EXERCISES
WITHOUT OVERLOAD
WITH OVERLOAD
DEPTH JUMP
Jumps with forward displacement
Jumps without forward displacement
Consecutive Barbell Jumps
Consecutive Kettlebell Squat Jumps
Vertical Jumps with Barbell
Jumps over boxes or hurdles
Bounds
Stadium Jumping
Standing Jumps
Box Jumps

Fig. 3.1 - Approximate hierarchical sequence of the jump exercises based on their level of training stimuli intensity (the power output in take-off force efforts).

This sequence can be used to elaborate a Conjugate-Sequence System for introducing jump exercises in the multi-years training process and also in the preparation period of high level athletes (see Fig. 3.2).

TRAINING STIMULI INTENSITY
DEPTH JUMP
Vertical Jumps with Barbell
JUMPS WITH OVERLOAD
Consecutive Kettlebell squat Jumps
Consecutive Barbell Jumps
MULTIPLE JUMPS WITHOUT FORWARD DISPLACEMENT
Box Jumps
Standing Jumps
MULTIPLE JUMPS WITH FORWARD DISPLACEMENT
Stadium Jumping
Bounces
Double leg jumps
SINGLE STANDING JUMPS

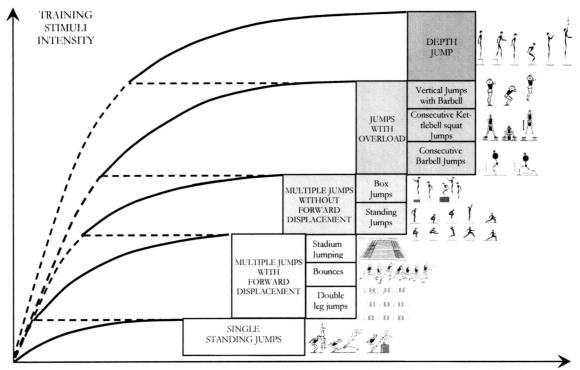

Fig. 3.2 – Conjugate-sequence system using jump exercises: in the training process and in the preparation period.

Jump exercises also have another peculiarity: they elicit an increase in the excitability of the central nervous system. For this reason they are used as a warming-up component which help to increase the training effect of the subsequent speed exercises.

In special studies, it was shown that in the preparation of sprinters and middle distance runners, the use of jump exercises in the warm-up ensures an increase in running speed during the subsequent training session.

In the 7 week training of sprinters, the experimental group used alternating bounds (3×60 meters) at a sub-maximal intensity during the warm-up, while the control group made the traditional running warm-up activity. In a 60 meter run with flying start test, the experimental group obtained a 4.2% increase in maximal speed while the control group reached only a 2.1% increase. In the training of middle distance runners, the experimental group, using alternating bounds (3×100 meters), obtained a 2.2% increase in the 1,200 meter race, while the control group reached only a 1.1% increase.

3.2. JUMP EXERCISES WITHOUT OVERLOAD

3.2.1. SINGLE AND MULTIPLE TAKE OFF JUMPS WITHOUT FORWARD DISPLACEMENT

3.2.1.1. SINGLE TAKE-OFF JUMPS

Standing jumps with double leg take offs (box jump, vertical jump, and long jump, see Fig. 3.3), are useful for improving Explosive and Starting Strength. These jump exercises should be executed with maximal effort using the Repeat-Serial method e.g. in sets of 8-10 jumps (take-offs) with an arbitrary rest period. In the double leg jumps onto a box, the height of the box should be maximal; an important element of this exercise is active leg flexion during the flight phase.

Fig. 3.3 - Examples of jumping exercises with double leg take-offs: vertical jump, long jump, and box jump

3.2.1.2. MULTIPLE STANDING JUMPS

Multiple consecutive standing jumps represent the multiple repetitions of vertical jumps and jumps onto a box; they are used to improve Reactive Ability, Maximal Anaerobic Power, and Local Muscular Endurance. Each exercise represents a group of consecutive vertical double leg takeoffs, executed at the optimal level of intensity using the Repeat or Interval method.

The multiple consecutive jumps include two groups of exercises:
- Multiple Standing Jumps;
- Box Jumps.

Multiple Standing Jumps are SST means useful not only for improving Local Muscular Endurance, Reactive Ability, and Maximal Anaerobic Power, but also for improving coordination and to strengthen the trunk muscular fascia (in figure 3.4 - 1 and 2 are variants using these exercises).

These jumps, if well-executed, are especially useful for sport game players, wrestlers, and boxers. Each exercise is executed 10 times. Jogging is performed during the rest interval between exercises (1.5 min). The trainer has to check the length of the recovery interval, explain the exercise, and instructs how it is to be carried out. The entire session lasts 10 minutes. It is recommended to periodically change the composition of the exercises as a whole.

Fig. 3.4 - Two variants of multiple standing jumps composition

Box Jumps are consecutive jumps up onto a box and down onto the floor. It is a very effective training mean for improving Reactive Ability, but only if carried out in the correct way.

Unlike single jumps onto a high box, multiple Box Jumps require a stronger vertical push, executed 'springy', with the force impulse coming mainly from foot work. Only if the exercise is executed in this condition is the athlete able to primarily use the Reactive Ability and, as a consequence, able to perform the exercise with a great number of take offs. If the landing is 'hard', the Reactive Ability will not improve and, if the number of repetitions is too great, the legs risk injury.

At the beginning of using this exercise, the athlete should jump onto a low box (0.30-0.40 m), economizing the force efforts of the knee extensors and emphasizing the involvement of the feet in the take-off force efforts (the legs should be quite straight, see Fig. 3.5). Moreover, it's very important to be relaxed both during the take off and the flight phases, maintaining equilibrium and landing in the correct places. Trying to maintain these conditions in the execution, the athlete should gradually increase the number of take offs in each exercise, building them up to 40-50 consecutive take offs onto a box.

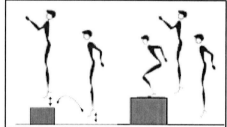

Fig. 3.5 - Box Jumps onto and down off a low box (left) and high box (right).

Once the athlete is able to continue this exercise without difficulty for an extended period of time, (his legs working like 'springs', without great voluntary force effort), this exercise can then be carried out with a more precise training objective: to improve the speed (decreasing the length of the ground contact phases), to increase the take off speed, or to improve the take off power using a higher box (see for example, the Training Program

Starting position   1   2   3   4

Fig. 3.6 - Consecutive Jumps onto and down off a high box

for Top Level Rowers, § 7.8).

When a higher box is used, the height must be gradually increased during the training stage from 0.4 to 0.8 m (see for example, the Training Program to Develop Explosive Strength and Reactive Ability for American Football players, § 8.6).

To keep the correct exercise execution it's very important that the athlete maintains the ability to perform the take off exercise in a 'springy' fashion even when the height of the box is higher. In figure 3.6 is shown a correct execution of this exercise using a box of 0.8 m.

For a correct execution of this exercise it's important to note the following characteristics:

- In the phase of jumping onto the box, the athlete must use mainly the take off force effort, not leg flexion; the angle of knee flexion in phase 2 should not reach 90°.
- After landing onto the box the subsequent take off movement must be directed upwards, not down (phase 3).
- During the flight phases, the athlete must be relaxed.

3.2.2. CONSECUTIVE JUMPS WITH FORWARD DISPLACEMENT

This group of jumping exercises includes:

1) Consecutive double leg jumps over vaulting boxes, over hurdles, and over low benches;
2) Bounces
3) Stadium Jumping.

3.2.2.1. CONSECUTIVE DOUBLE LEG JUMPS OVER VAULTING BOXES, OVER HURDLES, AND OVER LOW BENCHES

Consecutive double leg jumps onto/over the vaulting boxes (Fig. 3.7), are executed at a moderate pace, the take-off force efforts are accentuated.

Consecutive jumps over hurdles or low benches (Fig. 3.8) are executed at a higher speed: the rate of force development is accentuated during take-off while the time of the contact phase is minimized.

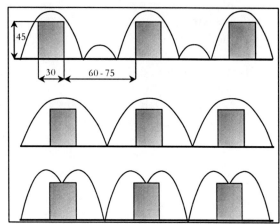

Fig. 3.8 - Takeoffs with two legs on and over vaulting boxes at a moderate pace.

3.2.2.2. BOUNDS

Bounds (or Bounces) are multiple consecutive jumps executed with great forward momentum (Fig. 3.9). They can be performed:

- with take-offs on one leg (one leg bounces);
- with take-offs on two legs ('frog');
- alternating the legs in each subsequent take-off (alternate leg to leg bounces);
- alternating two-three take-offs on the right leg and two-three take-offs on the left one (alternate two-three take-offs bounces).

Fig. 3.7 - Double jumps over low hurdles and an exercise bench; double and single-leg jumps advancing along the length of the bench ('slalom').

While executing one leg bounces it is necessary to accentuate the upward takeoff via the slight forward trunk lean with momentum.

While executing alternate leg to leg bounces, make sure that:

- the quick forward movement of the free thigh is coordinated with the arm action;
- the landing is on the whole foot, leaning upon the heel;
- the shoulders do not lean forward excessively from the trunk.

The bounds can be subdivided in two categories:

1) 'Short' bounding exercises are bounds executed over a short distance; they belong to the means of intensive training action and are used to increase the power output in the take-off movements. The load of the 'short' bounds, usually defined as leg to leg standing jumps, is calculated by the number of take offs.

2) 'Long' bounding exercises are bounds executed over a long distance; they belong to the means

Fig. 3.9 - Alternate leg to leg bounds, subsequent bounds on one leg and two leg bounds ("Frog")

of extensive training action and are used to enforce the body's working mechanism involved in the take-off movements and formation and stabilization of the morphological transformations in the muscles and in the joint tissues. 'Long' bounds are executed, over 50 to 200 meters at an effort less than maximal, maintaining a relatively motionless trunk. The load of 'long' bounds is calculated by measuring the distance covered in each bounding exercise.

Bounding exercises can be carried out not only from a standing position but also after a brief run-up (3-5 jogging steps):

1) Long jumps with a single take-off with one leg;
2) 'Short' bounds, executed with maximal effort in different variants, e.g.:
    - Triple (3 fold), quintuple (5 fold) and decuple (10 fold) alternate jumps;
    - Bounds on one leg (right or left) with 4-6 take-offs;
    - Bounds, two on the right leg, two on the left leg (6-8 total take-offs on each leg);

There is also another kind of bounding, **Bounding runs**, which may be classified as a speed running exercise because it must be performed over a distance of 50m with maximal speed (the correct execution of this exercise is described in § 7.3.4.3). This exercise is very efficacious for sprinters, hurdlers, long distance runners, triple jumpers, and decathletes. The time of the 50 m Bounding run execution is strictly connected ($r = 0.93-0.97$) to the results of 60 and 100 sprint run.

A particular form of bounce is also used in skating: the bounds with lateral-forward takeoffs - 'herringbone' (see Fig. 3.10). This exercise triggers the active leg muscles, which are involved both in the flexion and in the extension of the coxo-femoral articulations. This exercise can also be used for increasing power at the take-off movement in the

Fig. 3.10 - Skater's exercise: alternate bounds with lateral-forward takeoff

track & field running.

Bounds should not be executed with additional overload (for example, by overloading with a belt or a jacket) because it can cause damage to the ligaments and to the foot joints. To increase the training effect of these exercises, they can be executed on a slight slope or on the stairs of a stadium (Stadium Jumping).

3.2.2.3. STADIUM JUMPING

Stadium Jumping is a particular form of bounce, which is executed on the long stairway of a stadium tribune. For example, leg to leg stair bounds with 6-10 active take-offs over 2-3 steps. This exercise can be executed as 2-3 series of 4-6 repetitions in the following way: after jumping up the staircase, the athlete descends on another staircase while 'shaking up' the leg muscles. After, he returns to the initial starting position with easy walking, the following jumping set is repeated (Fig. 3.11).

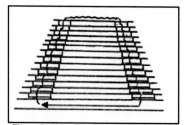

Fig. 3.11 - Jump exercises on the stadium stairs

3.2.3. METHODS OF USING JUMP EXERCISES WITHOUT OVERLOAD

The methods used with jump exercises are: the Repeat method, the Interval method, and the Serial method (Repeat-Serial and Interval-Serial).

Each method yields a particular training effect on the organism: the Repeat and Interval methods yield intensive demands while the Serial method yields extensive demands.

In the **Repeat method**, the exercises are executed with a high (maximal) level of effort and with few repetitions. The rest interval between the repetitions should be long enough for the organism and its locomotor system to recover in progress. This method is used to increase the power output in the take-off movements as well as to increase Maximal Anaerobic Power.

In the **Interval method**, the exercises are executed with sub-maximal efforts and with shorter rest intervals between repetitions than in the Repeat method. This method is mainly used to increase the functional level of energy supplying mechanisms.

In the **Serial method**, several jump exercises (set) are carried out in several series.

The training effect of jump exercises carried out with the Serial method is regulated by three parameters:

- the level of power output in each exercise;
- recovery time between exercise repetitions in a set, between sets, and between series;
- the load volume, which includes the number of exercise repetitions in a set, in all of the sets and in all of the series.

The number of sets in a series, the number of series, the recovery time between exercise repetitions in a set, between sets, and between series, is strictly regulated according to the athlete's level of preparation and to the training goals. In relation with the length of the rest periods between sets, this method has two variants: Repeat-Serial and Interval-Serial.

The load volume is calculated using the following formula: $\left[n(t_n) \times m(t_m) \right] \times k(t_k)$

Where:

- n = number of exercise repetitions in a set
- m = number of sets
- [n × m] = series executed in a repeat or interval method regime

- k = number of series repetitions
- (t_n) = recovery duration between exercise repetitions in a set, between sets (t_m), and between series (t_k)

For example the formula for the Standing Triple jump [5(0.5) x 4(5) x 3-4 (8)] indicates that:

- 5 standing triple jumps are executed with 0.5 minute recoveries between repetitions in a set.
- 4 sets, with 5 minutes rest between them, are executed in the series.
- 3-4 series are executed with 8 minutes recovery between them.

The **Combined method** offers a wide array of choices in creating a specific training effect using different combinations of jump exercises.

The concept of this method is contained in the interconnected use of 'short' and 'long' bounding exercises in adjacent training sessions. For example, 'short' bounding exercises are executed on Mondays and Thursdays, while 'long' bounding exercises are executed on Tuesdays and Fridays. Such a combination facilitates an adequate general reaction of the organism including functional signs of both training actions.

An experiment was conducted on three groups of middle-level sprinters trained for three months using different combinations of bounces: group A used only 'short' bounces, group B used only 'long' bounces, and group C used a combination of 'long' and 'short' bounces.

The aim of the experiment was to evaluate the training effects of 'short' and 'long' bounces and the cumulative effect of training with their combined use.

The experiment yielded the following results (Fig. 3.12):

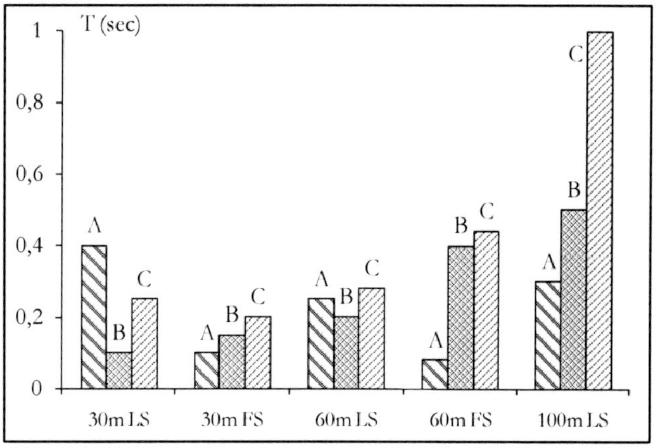

1) 'Short' bounces ensure a much higher increase in running speed in the initial part of a 100m distance in comparison with 'long' bounces, but a lower increase in the running speed to cover the flying 30 and 60 meters distance that is yielded by 'long' bounces.

Fig. 3.12 –Sprinter's improvement in running to cover different distances (30, 60, and 100 m) after the use of "short" (A), "long"(B) bounds and their combination (C). "LS" indicates the runs executed from the low start position, "FS" - flying starts.

2) 'Long' bounces allow a much higher increase in a flying race (particularly to cover a flying 60 meters distance) in comparison with 'short' bounces, but they allow a lower increase in race starting speed in comparison with 'short' bounces.

3) The Combined method ensures a good increase in all of the control distances and particularly in the competition distance (100 meters race); on average, the sprinters of group C improved their results in 100 meters race from 11.5 to 10.5 seconds.

The Combined method, which combines the use of 'short' and 'long' bounces, turned out to be excellent in the preparation of sprinters' and high-level jumpers.

In summation, the experiments gave clear indication for the use of the Combined Method in the preparation of sprinters, hurdlers, long jumpers, triple jumpers, and decathletes.

3.3. JUMP EXERCISES WITH OVERLOAD

A particular group of jump exercises consists of standing jumps with overload: Consecutive Barbell Jumps, Kettlebell Squat Jumps, and Vertical Jumps with a Barbell. The methods to use these exercises in different sport disciplines, including the rules in choosing overload weight, the number of series, sets, and repetitions, are determined by the desired goal and are described in Chapters 6, 7, and 8.

3.3.1. CONSECUTIVE BARBELL JUMPS

Consecutive barbell jumps consists of the completing 10-20 of one of the two following jumps (Fig. 3.13):

- Barbell Squat jumps, also termed Parallel Squat jumps with the bar on the shoulders, executed by bending the knees at least until the thighs are parallel to the floor, and then jumping upwards.
- Barbell Scissor-lunge jumps, jump out from a lunge (stride) position with a switch in the legs during the fly, alternating them on every jump.

Fig. 3.13 - Barbell Squat jump and Barbell Scissor-lunge jump

In the single exercise, these jumps are executed with constant height, degree of leg flexion, and vertical back position, without pausing between them and maintaining an optimal height and frequency of jumps.

These exercises are excellent means for increasing the level of Maximal Anaerobic Power and for improving Local Muscular Endurance. The training effect of these exercises depends on:

- the level of force effort in each jump;
- the frequency of jumps;
- the number of jumps in a set;
- the length of recovery intervals.

For example, 10-20 consecutive Barbell Squat Jumps, performed in an aerobic regime are used to improve Local Muscular Endurance; they may also be used as a means of developing Explosive Strength for athletes with:

- a low level of special strength preparedness;
- a high level special strength preparedness, at the beginning of the preparation period.

The Barbell Scissor-lunge jump may also be executed in a 'low' position (without the vertical jump component) and with maximal frequency (as fast as possible). This variant is used to improve Maximal Anaerobic Power and should only be implemented with high level athletes who have adequate physical preparedness.

3.3.2. KETTLEBELL SQUAT JUMPS

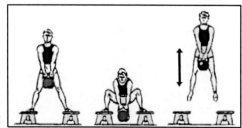

Kettlebell Squat Jumps (Fig. 3.14) are a very effective exercise in improving Explosive Strength, Reactive Ability, and Maximal Anaerobic Power.

The athlete performs a series of consecutive vertical jumps standing on two parallel benches or plinths. During the execution of this exercise, the kettlebell must almost

Fig. 3.14 - Kettlebell Squat Jump

reach the floor without touching it; in this way a standard leg flexion angle is guaranteed, determined by the height of the plinths. The weight (16, 24, 32 kg) is chosen according to the athlete's preparedness. If Russian Kettlebells of suitable weights are not available, a dumbbell (although not very comfortable to hold) is just as effective and may be found in nearly any gymnasium which supports athletic preparation. Kettlebell Squat Jumps are preferable in comparison to the Barbell Squat Jump for two reasons:

1) a reduced risk of a vertebral column injury. In Kettlebell Squat Jumps, the opposing force vector influencing the vertebral column has a backwards directional component. In order to counter this force vector, the athlete uses the abdominal muscles to maintain the vertical position, thereby saving the lumbar curve so that the vertebral column sustains much less trauma;

2) a deeper stress on the leg muscles due to the vertical jumps executed from the lowest position at the end of the yielding phase. It is easier to maintain balance during the execution of this exercise since the weight is below the center of body mass.

3.3.3. VERTICAL JUMPS WITH A BARBELL

Vertical Jumps with a Barbell (Fig. 3.15) are excellent means for developing Explosive Strength.

Vertical Jumps with a Barbell, different from the Barbell Squat Jump presented earlier, must not be executed as consecutive jumps, but as a 'set' of single jumps, which include the following phases:

1) place the barbell on the back of the shoulders, position feet about hip-width apart;

Fig. 3.15 - Vertical Jumps with Barbell

2) quickly squat down and jump straight up as high as possible,

3) stop and relax (shake) the legs, one after another (the athlete can also rack the barbell).

This exercise is sometimes referred to as the Barbell Squat Jump, but it is a different exercise from when performed as described above. For this reason, it should be termed differently. The term 'Vertical Barbell Jump' is more suitable for indicating the correct motor orientation of the athlete.

The athlete must focus on obtaining a maximal jump height without being concerned about the knee angle at the end of the yielding phase. As is the case with the normal vertical jump, the previous yielding phase must be executed in such a way that the best jump height is 'automatically' ensured, thanks to the athlete's correct understanding of the motor trend of this exercise.

Vertical Jumps with a Barbell must be executed with a weight selected according to the athlete's preparedness, within the limits of 30-60% of his maximum. In one set there can be 4-6 squat jumps performed with the aim of jumping as high as possible.

Vertical Jumps with a barbell must always be performed with a supportive belt because it may be very harmful for the vertebral column if the athlete does not have perfect technique of execution. In this case, it's strongly recommended to acquire a good technique of execution in the previous training periods by practicing the squat jump with a light barbell.

Barbell Squat Jumps, Kettlebell Squat Jumps, and Vertical Jumps with the barbell can be used to increase Explosive Strength.

The following general considerations may help in placing these exercises in a correct sequence of the initial introduction into the training process as well as in avoiding injury:

1) 5-10 consecutive (sequential) kettlebell jumps standing on two parallel high benches and 5-10 se-

quential barbell squat jumps, used with the same overload weight, have a similar training effect. These two exercises can be used for the development of Explosive Strength, varying them from one training session to another in order to avoid the monotony of the training process.

2) Kettlebell and Barbell Squat jumps may both be dangerous for the vertebral column if the athlete does not maintain perfect technique during their execution: a correct vertical position of the back (lumbar curve maintained) and a correct (soft/low impact) landing. For this reason, these exercises should be introduced very gradually into the training process after a period of performing non-overloaded standing jumps and bounces. In this manner it's possible to gradually strengthen the muscles of the back and the disc ligaments in the vertebral column and to avoid injuries. In this period it's very important to pay close attention to the technical execution of the exercises.

3) When the athlete already has a high level of Explosive Strength but needs to further increase it, he should use another exercise: the Vertical Jump with a barbell (4-6 single-sequential jumps with an overload of 50-60 %, executed with brief relaxations of the legs between each jump).

3.4. Depth Jump

The Depth jump or Shock Method jump is a very effective means for developing Explosive Strength and Reactive Ability. At the present time this is a training means that is popular and its use is widespread all over the world. Although it has acquired many take-off execution variants, its main form is the vertical two leg take-off.

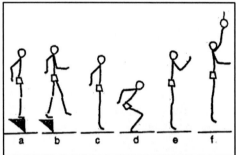

Despite its apparent simplicity, the execution technique of the Depth Jump is quite complex and, in many cases, it is performed incorrectly. First of all, this can lead to an excessive load to the knee and tibio-tarsic joint, creating a trauma risk. Secondly, it can reduce the training effect of this exercise on the organism.

Fig. 3.16 - The phases of the Depth Jump's execution

This is the reason why when beginning to use the Depth Jump it's worth illustrating the correct execution of this exercise. After, the athlete must not think about it: the correct execution of this exercise will be obtained thanks to the athlete's correct understanding of the motor trend of this exercise.

Drop phase - from 'a' to 'c' positions (Fig. 3.16). The Drop jump (stepping off an elevated surface) is an important particular of the technique that greatly influences the correct execution of the whole exercise.

The athlete must not step off with both the legs, but rather take a step forward with one leg and, at the beginning of the fall, bring the other leg forward, reuniting the two legs. The athlete must not bend the legs prior to stepping off the elevated surface (legs must be straight) and must not jump, but drop forward - the fall trajectory must be perpendicular to the ground.

Landing phase - from 'c' to 'd' positions. The athlete must land on both legs, on the ball of the feet, and then quickly lean back on the heels. Landing should be flexible with a substantial passage to cushion and then to takeoff.

Cushioning and take-off phase - from 'd' to 'e' positions. The passage from cushioning to take-off is very quick. Before the landing both the arms are put backward (position 'c' and 'd') and at the moment of the take-off they should move upwards with a quick and powerful thrust (position 'e'). The cushioning and take-off phases should be executed as a single action with a powerful concentrated effort.

Flight after the takeoff phase - position 'f'. To reach the highest point of flight after the take-off, the athlete should fix a point of reference (for example, a small flag) to reach for, trying to touch it with one or both hands. After the flight, the athlete should gently land on the balls of both feet with a flexible cushioning.

'**Land with a spring and then fly as high as possible**' - this should be the motor trend that the athlete should acquire for facilitating the correct technical execution of the exercise. The athlete's understanding of the Depth Jump's motor trend determines the correct execution of all its phases and its training effect on the neuromuscular system. The visual point of reference (small flag) is a very important element; it emphasizes the final goal of this exercise.

The Depth Jump has a very powerful effect on the central nervous system and on the musculo-skeletal system. This is why it should be used, above all, in the training of well-prepared athletes and only after a preparation period that includes a substantial volume of bounding exercises and jumps with an overload.

The athlete should begin with low drop heights, from 0.4 to 5m, and gradually work up to reaching the optimal height of 0.75m. He must not use other jump exercises after the Depth Jump, especially when tired or suffering muscle pain or traumas that have yet to heal.

3.5. ORGANIZING JUMP EXERCISES IN TRAINING SÈANCES

As it was underlined before, SST means must be organized in the training system aimed at solving a defined training task. They must be separated from other exercises by a prolonged rest interval and perceived by the athlete as another training session - the training séance.

The following jump training séances, or only parts of them, can be used by high level sprinters, long jumpers, and sport game players.

INCREASING EXPLOSIVE STRENGTH

1) Single maximal takeoffs with single leg execution (single leg upward take off imitates long jump):
   - 5-6 takeoffs should be executed in a 60-70 meters distance while walking or jogging in between each takeoff.
   - 5-6 repetitions per set
   - One series may include 2-3 sets separated by 3-4 minute rest periods
   - 2-4 series in total separated by 4-5 minute rest periods.
2) Vertical takeoffs with double leg jumps after 2-3 steps of jogging between each jump:
   - 4-5 takeoffs per set separated by rest periods of optional duration
   - 4-6 sets per series separated by 4-5 minute rest periods
   - 4 series in total separated by 5-6 minute rest periods.
3) Triple (3 fold) or quintuple (5 fold) jumps with maximal effort, initiated from either a standing start or with 2 or 3 supports of jogging:
   - 4-5 repetitions per set with rest periods of arbitrary duration.
   - 2-3 sets per series separated by 4-5 minute rest periods.
   - 2-3 series in total separated by 6-8 minute rest periods
4) One leg bounds. Subsequent quintuple jumps (5 jumps in succession) with a very strong takeoff, initiated by a standing takeoff or with 2-3 supports of jogging:
   - 2-3 repetitions on each leg per set separated by rest periods of arbitrary duration.
   - 2-3 sets per series separated by 4-5 minute rest periods.
   - 2-3 series in total separated by 6-8 minute rest periods.

5) Standing octuple bounds (8 fold) (two with the right leg and two with the left one x 2):
   - 3-4 repetitions per set separated by 2-3 minute rest periods.
   - 2-3 sets per series separated by 5-6 minute rest periods.
   - 2-3 series in total separated by 6-8 minute rest periods

6) Vertical Jumps with barbell (the weight is 30-40% of the barbell squat maximum):
   - Wear a supportive belt
   - Every jump should be executed with a quick passage to takeoff.
   - After each jump you should relax the leg muscles, one after the other.
   - 5-6 jumps with maximal effort per set.
   - 3-4 minute rest periods after every two sets.
   - 4-5 sets per series separated by 4-5 minute rest periods.
   - 2-3 series in total separated by 8-10 minute rest periods.

7) Kettlebell Squat Jumps with 12-24 kilogram weights.
   - 5-6 jumps per set with strong effort
   - 1-2 minute rest periods between each set.
   - 2-3 sets per series separated by 5-6 minute rest periods.
   - 2-3 series in total separated by 10-12 minute rest periods.

INCREASING HIGH SPEED STRENGTH

1) Alternate decuple bounces (10 fold alternate leg takeoffs):
   - Project yourself forward after each takeoff.
   - 3-4 repetitions per set separated by 3-4 minute rest periods.
   - 2-3 sets per series separated by 2-3 minute rest periods.
   - 2-3 series in total separated by 4-5 minute, or 6-8 minute, rest periods.

2) Alternate bounds over 20-30 meters, executed with an accelerated pace and very quick forward takeoffs:
   - 3-4 repetitions per set separated by 2-3 minute rest periods.
   - 2-3 sets per series separated by 4-5 minute rest periods
   - 2-3 series in total separated by 6-8 minute rest periods

3) Alternate bounds (with sub-maximal, but very quick, forward takeoffs).
   - Start with 30-40 meters distance and gradually increase to 60-80 meters over a number of workouts.
   - 2-3 repetitions per set separated by 2-4 minute rest periods.
   - 2-3 sets per series separated by 4-6 minute rest periods.
   - 2-3 series in total separated by 10-12 minute recovery breaks.

   Each recovery break between series - execute slight running (jogging) during the first 4 minutes, then perform easy alternate bounds 2-3 times for the remaining time, concluding with walking about and executing relaxation and flexibility exercises.

4) Two bounds on the right leg and two bounds on the left leg with quick forward takeoffs.
   - Start with 20-30 meters distance and gradually increase to 60-80 meters over a number of workouts.
   - Begin with 2-3 repetitions, and then work towards 5-6 repetitions.
   - 5-6 minute rest periods between repetitions.
   - One series of work in total.

5) 'Bounding runs', alternate bounds, executed over 50 meters distance with maximal speed:
   - Repeat 3-4 times with very quick forward takeoffs (with periodic time recording by a chro-

nometer).
- 2-3 repetitions per set separated by rest periods of arbitrary duration.
- 2-3 sets per series separated by 4-6 minute rest periods.
- 2 series in total separated by 8-10 minute rest periods.

IMPROVING REACTIVE ABILITY
1) Depth Jumps:
   - For high-level athletes the optimal height of a depth jump is 0.75 meters
   - Athletes of high preparation - dosage in a training session should not exceed 4 series with 10 takeoffs.
   - Athletes of lesser preparation- 2-3 series with 6-8 repetitions, with 60 centimeters height.
   - The 4-5 minute rest periods between series consists in jogging and relaxation and flexibility exercises.
   - During the preparation period, the takeoff exercises after the depth jump should be executed in a fixed quantity, 2 times (at most 3 times), and only after the preparation of preliminary strength (with overload) and the preparation of jumps and bounds.
   - During the competition period they represent an effective means to maintain the achieved level of special physical preparation. In this period one should include them in training once a week and then reduce their training frequency to once every 7-8 days before competitions.
2) Kettlebell Squat Jumps (with 16-32 kilogram weight):
   - 4-5 jumps with maximal takeoff per set.
   - 3-4 sets per series separated by 4-5 minute rest periods.
   - 2-3 series in total separated by 8-12 minute rest periods.
3) Consecutive jumps over vaulting boxes or over low hurdles at a moderate pace.
   - 3-4 jumps per set separated by a 2 minute rest period.
   - 2-3 sets per series separated by 4-5 minute rest periods.
   - 2-3 series in total separated by 8-10 minute rest periods
4) Multiple jumps with two legs off of a takeoff board (or any other object of low height-0.4m)
   - Execute at a moderate pace.
   - 3-4 sets of 15-20 jumps per series separated by 5-6 minute rest periods.
   - 2-3 series in total separated by 10-12 minute rest periods.

INCREASING MAXIMAL ANAEROBIC POWER
1) Standing alternate uphill bounds:
   - Slope need only have a low incline
   - Execute with powerful long forward-upward takeoffs
   - Quick and vigorous movements of legs and arms.
   - 6-8 takeoffs are executed with the final takeoff transitioning into easy running and returning to the start position.
   - 2-3 repetitions per set separated by 4-5 minute rest periods.
   - 2-4 sets per series separated by 6-7 minute rest periods.
   - 2-4 series in total separated by 8-10 minute rest periods.
2) The same as above but with a short run-up:
   - 2-3 repetitions per set separated by 4-5 minute rest periods.
   - 3-4 sets per series separated by 8 minute rest periods.
   - 2-3 series in total separated by 10 minute rest periods.

3) 2 uphill bounds on the right leg and two bounds on the left leg over a distance of 12-20 meters, executed with powerful takeoffs:
   - 3-4 repetitions per set separated by 2-3 minute rest periods.
   - 3-4 sets per series separated by 3-4 minute rest periods.
   - 2-3 series in total separated by 8-10 minute rest periods.
4) Stadium Jumping:
   - Execute 6-8 powerful takeoffs (each takeoff covering 2-3 steps).
   - 4-6 repetitions per set separated by a rest period lasting no longer than 1 minute.
   - 3-4 sets per series separated by 8-10 minute rest periods.
5) Uphill bounds or bounding runs on a moderate inclination:
   - Execute by using the body's inertia that is developed via a quick run-up (10-12 running supports on flat ground leading up to the incline).
   - Uphill running (6-8 long strides) is executed with powerful forward-upward takeoffs (the strides must always be long).
   - 3-4 repetitions per set separated by rest periods lasting no longer than 1 minute.
   - 2-4 sets per series separated by 10-12 minute rest periods.
6) Kettlebell Squat Jumps with weights of 16-14 kilogram:
   - 3-4 repetitions of 5-6 jumps per set separated by 20-30 second rest periods.
   - 3-4 sets per series separated by 6-8 minute rest periods.

IMPROVING LOCAL MUSCULAR ENDURANCE
1) Alternate bounds (or two on the right leg and two on the left leg):
   - Sub-maximal effort takeoffs over a distance of 50-60 meters
   - Gradually increase the distance up to 100 and 150 meters over a number of workouts.
   - 3-4 repetitions separated by 8-10 minute rest periods.
2) Alternate bounds (or two on the right leg and two on the left leg):
   - Execute takeoffs at an intermediate intensity and a moderate forward momentum on a slight inclination of 80-100 meters.
   - At the end of the slope perform easy running (jogging) and return to the starting position.
   - 2-3 repetitions separated by 8-10 minute rest periods.
3) Two bounds on the right leg and two bounds on the left leg:
   - Execute with maximal effort takeoffs over a distance of 20-30 meters.
   - 3-4 repetitions per set separated by 8-10 minute rest periods.
   - Gradually increase the distance up to 50 meters over a number of workouts.
   - As the workouts progress, the rest periods between repetitions should be reduced to 30 seconds while the rest periods between series increases up to 10-12 minutes.
4) A group of 5 different standing jump exercises (see Fig. 3.4):
   - Each variant is repeated 10 times with sub-maximal effort.
   - 1.5 minutes of jogging, relaxing, and stretching exercises for the legs muscles are executed during the rest periods between exercises.
   - The entire workout lasts 10 minutes.
   - All of the exercises should be executed in succession.
   - The trainer says, in a loud voice, the subsequent exercise in the series; gives the command for its execution, and times the rest periods between exercises.
   - Occasionally the composition of jump exercises should be changed.
5) Kettlebell Squat Jumps (16-24 kg):

- 8-10 jumps per set executed with sub-maximal effort.
- 2-4 sets per series separated by 4-6 minute rest periods.
- 2-4 series in total separated by 8-10 minute rest periods.

6) Intensive leg to leg bounds (3-5 maximal takeoffs on one leg and then the other in succession) followed by running:
   - 3-4 repetitions per set separated by a 20-30 second rest periods.
   - 2-4 sets separated by 6-8 minute rest periods.
   - According to the increase in the athlete's level of preparation, the number of takeoffs increases up to 10, the number of repetitions per set increases up to 5-6, and the number of sets increases up to 4-5.

7) 15-20 alternate standing bounds:
   - Execute takeoffs with sub-maximal effort and transition into running to finalize each repetition.
   - 2-4 repetitions per set separated by a 1 minute rest period.
   - 2-3 sets separated by 8-10 minute rest periods.
   - The number of repetitions of bounds in a set should be gradually increased up to 4-5 and the rest period between bounds in a set should be reduced down to 30 seconds.

8) Bounding Runs:
   - Record the amount of time it takes to cover the distance.
   - 8-10 repetitions separated by 1 minute rest periods of slow running.
   - Perform one series.

COMBINED METHODS OF SST

Combined Methods of SST consist of combinations of different SST means in order to ensure a determined cumulative training effect.

Depending on what means are used, how they are performed, and how they are temporally combined, it is possible to differentiate the following Combined Methods:

1) Complex Method;
2) Stimulation Method;
3) Contrast Method;
4) Circuit Method;
5) Strength-Aerobic Method.

4.1. COMPLEX METHOD

The Complex Method consists of a combination of SST means having the same primary emphasis but different characteristics of their training effects. These training means are carried out in the same training session, as a special *training séance* (see § 1.4.4.3), or in adjoined training sessions.

The Complex Method has been already illustrated in § 2.2.2.1 where dynamic resistance exercises with different movement rates were used in Lelikov's experiment. This method was used by the 5th group, which carried out resistance exercises with high, low and middle repetition rates (combined in equal proportion). This group reached the highest increase in Maximal Strength, in comparison with the results reached by the other three groups that carried out the same resistance exercises using, respectively, only the high, the low, and the middle rate of movement repetition.

Another example of the Complex Method has been illustrated in § 2.2.2.2, where the training effect has been evaluated of resistance exercises executed in various regimes of muscular work in the experiment of B.Pletnev. In this experiment, the 4th group performed resistance exercises in overcoming, yielding, and isometric regimes, combined in equal proportion, reaching the highest increase in Maximal Strength in comparison with the results reached by the other three groups, which performed the same exercises, respectively, only in overcoming, yielding, and isometric regimes.

Therefore, it's possible to assert that the Complex Method utilizes the body's capacity to utilize the adaptive reactions of different training stimuli in the resultant training effect, which is greater than the sum of the training effects of each exercise. These exercises must have the same training effect direction, but different characteristics of their training influence.

For example, the following means may be combined to increase 'jump force':

- Barbell Squat jumps and Kettlebell Squat Jumps;
- 'Short' bounces and 'Long' bounces;
- Jump exercises with a takeoff on one or both legs;
- Depth Jumps from different heights.

In the Complex Method, different SST means can be adjusted not only in the same training session, but also in conjunction with other training sessions.

For example, in an experiment involving three groups of cross country skiers, the athletes used the same volume of resistance exercises aimed at increasing the level of Strength Endurance:
- the 1st group carried out exercises according to the Refusal Method;
- the 2nd group carried out exercises according to the Circuit Method;
- the 3rd group carried out exercises according to the Refusal Method and Circuit Method in two adjacent training sessions.

The 3rd group, which used the combination of the two methods, reached the highest increase in sport results (10.9%) and in the level of recovery capacity (34.4%). The 1st and 2nd groups, which used only one of the two methods, obtained a 5% increase in sport result and a 9.5% increase in the level of recovery capacity.

It's very important to note that to obtain a positive cumulative training effect it's necessary to select the means having the same training emphasis; the cumulative training effect, otherwise, will be diminished. This phenomenon could be illustrated by the results of the following experiment.

Three groups of athletes carried out three different resistance training programs aimed at increasing the force momentum in isokinetic movements:
- group A carried out isokinetic exercises at an angular velocity of 60°/sec.
- group B carried out isokinetic exercises at an angular velocity of 300°/sec.
- group C carried out the combination of isokinetic exercises at an angular velocity of 60°/sec and 300°/sec.

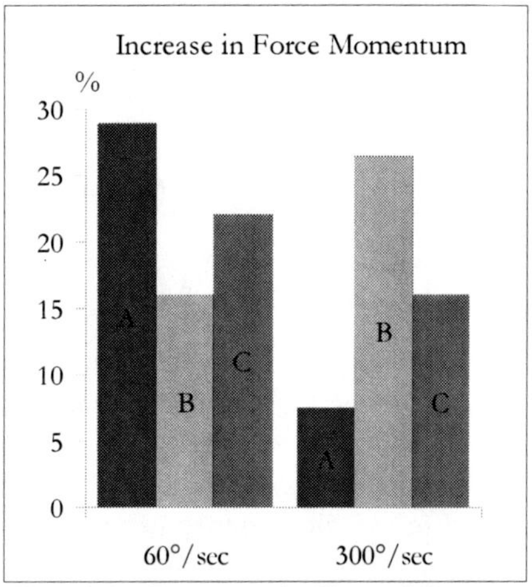

At the end of the training, the increase in the force momentum was verified by performing isokinetic exercises executed at an angular velocity of 60°/sec and at an angular velocity of 300°/sec (sees Fig. 4.1).

In both tests group C didn't obtain the best results because training with angular velocities of 60°/sec and 300°/sec have different training directions: the first exercise increases maximal strength, while the second increases high-speed strength.

In the next section we will see how group C's results could have been improved had the two exercises been carried out in a determined sequence: first the exercise at 60°/sec and after the exercise at 300°/sec.

Fig. 4.1 - Increase in Force Momentum in movements executed with a speed of 60°/sec and 300°/sec of the three groups trained with exercises executed at different speeds: Group A, at a speed of 60°/sec; Group B, at a speed of 300°/sec; Group C, with a combined work at a speed of 60°/sec and 300°/sec.

4.2. STIMULATION METHOD

The Stimulation Method can be illustrated by an experiment conducted by V. Nedobivailo.

Three groups of athletes used three different resistance training programs aimed at increasing the power output in the vertical jump:
- the first group carried out slow Barbell Squats with a weight equal to 90% of 1RM;
- the second group carried out Barbell Vertical Jumps with a weight equal to 50% of 1RM;
- the third group carried out a combination of the two exercises used by the 1st and 2nd group, in the same training session with the following sequence: 1) slow movements with a weight of 90%

1RM; 2) Barbell Vertical Jumps with a weight of 50% 1RM. The highest increase in power output was obtained by the third group (see Fig. 4.2).

The result of another experiment showed that executing the Barbell Squat ensures a notable increase (until 7.8 %) in the subsequent vertical jump height if the time interval between these two exercises is between 3 and 6 minutes (see Fig. 4.3).

These experiments concluded that the Stimulation Method maximizes the training effect of a speed-strength exercise using a CNS stimulating effect produced by the previous tonic exercise.

Usually resistance exercises are used as tonic (stimulating) exercises executed via the Maximal Effort Method. If the athlete is still not able to execute the Barbell Squat using the Maximal Effort Method, he may use the Kettlebell Squat Jump as a tonic exercise.

Increasing Explosive Strength in the take-off movements, for example (jump force), five combinations of two exercises listed in Table 7 can be used. These variants of the Stimulation Method have different training potentials, increasing from variant I to variant V. Only one of these variants may be used in a training session.

In the Stimulation Method, the following isometric exercises may also be used as tonic exercises:

1) pushing against an immobilized object;
2) holding a weight in a fixed position.

The second variant of isometric tension is very effective when it is performed with a forced lengthening of the contracted muscles. In this case, isometric tension is produced:

-   in joint flexion, acting against the external force applied to the 'open' the joint;
-   in joint extension, acting against an external force applied to 'close' the joint.

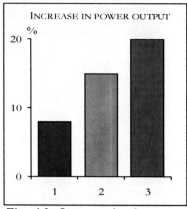

Fig. 4.2- Increase in the power output of the standing vertical jump after 6 weeks of training with various weights

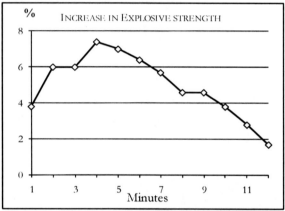

Fig. 4.3 - The increase in Explosive Strength, expressed by a Leg Extension maximal explosive effort after squatting with a heavy bar, in relation to the duration of rest between their executions.

An experiment conducted by P. Mironenko showed that isometric contractions of the lengthening thigh muscles ensure a reliable increase ($p < 0.005$) in the standing vertical jump: 3% in the maximal height of a single vertical jump. An increase of 18% was also observed in the maximal power output of repeated vertical jumps and a 14% decrease in support time.

A similar phenomenon of increasing the vertical jump height, after execution of an isometric exercise, was also observed by Andrew Darqui, who used the isometric trunk back extension (see Fig. 4.4).

Fig. 4.4 - An example of tonic isometric exercise: the "Iso Extension Stim" created by Andrew Darqui.

STIMULATION METHOD VARIANTS	FIRST EXERCISE	REST BETWEEN EXERCISES	SECOND EXERCISE	NUMBER OF COMPLEX REPS	REST BETWEEN COMPLEX REPS
I VARIANT	KETTLEBEL SQUAT JUMPS Weight = 6-24 Kg 2 of 6-8 jumps Rest between sets 3-4 min	3-4 min	LEG TO LEG BOUNCE 6–8 take-off 2 sets of 5-6 bounces Rest between series 3-4 min	2-3	6-8 min
II VARIANT	BARBELL SQUAT Weight = 70-80% 2 sets of 5-6 rep. Rest between sets 2-4 min	4-6 min	STANDING TRIPLE JUMP 2-3 sets of 6-8 jumps Rest between sets 4-6 min	2-3	6-8 min
III VARIANT	BARBELL SQUAT Weight = 80-85% 2 sets of 2-3 rep. Rest between sets 3-4 min	3-5 min	KETTLEBELL SQUAT JUMPS Weight = 16-24-32 Kg 2-3 sets of 4-6 jumps Rest between sets 3-4 min	2-3	6-8 min
IV VARIANT	BARBELL SQUAT Weight = 90% 2 sets of 2-3 rep. Rest between sets 3-4 min	4-6 min	VERTICAL JUMPS WITH BARBELL Weight = 30% 3 sets of 6-8 jumps Rest between sets 3-4 min	2-3	8-10 min
V VARIANT	BARBELL SQUAT Weight = 90-95% 2 sets of 2 reps. Rest between sets 2-4 min	4-6 min	DEPTH JUMP H = 0.75 m. 2 sets of 6-8 jumps Rest between sets 4-6 min	2-3	8-10 min

Table 7 - Five variants of Stimulation Method aimed at increasing Explosive Strength in the take-off movements.

The Stimulation Method is used predominantly for increasing Explosive Strength, but it is also effective for increasing High-Speed Strength and the speed and frequency of unloaded movements.

To increase Explosive Strength, the following two variants of the Stimulation Method are the foundation for devising other combinations of exercises. These exercises should be chosen based on the similarity of their characteristic movements to those of their own sport discipline.

Stimulation Method Variants	First Exercise	Dosage of 1st Exercise	Second Exercise	Dosage of 2nd Exercise	Dosage of Series
I VARIANT	MAXIMAL STRENGTH EXERCISE. Execute 2-3 slow movements with a weight of 90-95% of maximal.	2 sets with about 3-4 minutes rest.	EXPLOSIVE STRENGTH EXERCISE. Execute 6-8 maximal dynamic explosive efforts with a weight of 30% of maximal, with compulsory relaxation of the muscles between repetitions.	3 sets with 3-4 minutes rest	2-3 series with 8-10 minutes rest
II VARIANT	ISOMETRIC EXERCISE. Increase gradually isometric tension to the maximum and hold for 6 seconds in the position in which maximum effort is displayed in competition excises.	2-3 repetitions with a rest until the muscles are fully relaxed.	EXPLOSIVE STRENGTH EXERCISE. Execute 4-6 maximal dynamic explosive efforts with a weight of 40-60% of maximal.	2 sets with 3-4 minutes rest	2 series with 4-6 minutes rest

Table 8 - Two variants of the Stimulation Method for increasing Explosive Strength

To increase High-Speed Strength, the following exercises are used:
- one series includes 2 sets of 3-4 repetitions with a resistance of 50-75% 1RM;
- followed by 2-3 sets of 6-8 reps with a resistance of 30% RM performed with maximum speed and muscular relaxation between repetitions;
- 4-6 minute rest intervals between sets and 8-10 minutes between series.

To improve the speed and frequency of unloaded movements the following combination is used:
- 2 sets of 3-4 reps at a moderate tempo with 50-70% 1RM;
- followed by 2-3 sets of 8-10 reps using 15% 1RM (either by increasing the speed of movement in the overcoming phase with moderate yielding tempo and relaxation between sets, or by increasing the frequency of movements with maximum tempo, respectively).

Since the Stimulation Method has a very strong effect on the body, especially on the musculo-skeletal system, close attention must be paid to its use in training. More specifically:
1) To apply the Stimulation Method, it is necessary to prepare the leg muscles by using barbell and jump exercises during the preceding training stage.
2) The training effect of the Stimulation Method is reduced considerably if it is carried out while fatigued.
3) Since the Stimulation Method utilizes much energy, it should not be used before a workout which requires precise coordination of effort, high movement speed, and display of Explosive Strength

or endurance.

4) It is better to use the Stimulation Method in a separate training session and only with 'fresh' forces, when the energy potential of the body has not been spent in other work.

5) It is important to comply with the recommended rest periods between sets and series. If the exercise is repeated when the muscles are not fully restored, its execution changes the training effect toward the development of Strength Endurance.

6) Between series, it is necessary to execute free wide amplitude swinging movements by the loaded muscle groups.

7) If the SST program is executed to increase the 'jump force', in between series, it is necessary to perform 2-3 non-intensive running accelerations (long build-ups) in combination with easy jump exercises. In addition, swinging leg movements and exercises for muscle relaxation (shake-ups) should be performed.

4.3. CONTRAST METHOD

The Contrast Method is used mainly for increasing High-Speed strength. This goal is achieved by creating a contrast of the kinesthetic sensations, performing, at maximal power output, a complex movement in alternating conditions, more or less difficult in comparison to the normal.

For a better understanding and employment of this method, it is necessary a closely examine the physiological mechanism involved and the related concepts of *motor engram* and *kinesthetic feedback*.

Every motor action begins with an idea about the purpose of this action (its goal) and with a range of possible ways to accomplish it, which are stored in the brain as hypothetical variables of the movement execution. N. Bernstein called these hypothetical variables of the movement's execution, motor engrams[44]; they are memorized motor patterns, stored in the motor area of the brain, used to perform a movement. A motor engram is a set of instructions which are used by the body for executing a specific movement.

The higher the motor experience of an individual, the more precise and unambiguous these instructions are. However, these instructions are quite imperceptible for the conscious effort. During a repetitive exercise's execution, the *kinesthetic sensations*[45] (afferent feedback-impulses from the body to the brain) inform the brain about the current movement pattern in order to achieve the goal of motor action. Such kinesthetic feedbacks allow the body to make adjustments during subsequent repetitions of the motor action, altering unconsciously the movement pattern until the desired pattern is achieved. However, when the correct motor patter has been already acquired, it's difficult to obtain adjustments which could ensure a further increase in the working effect of motor action.

If the athlete repetitively performs the same sport exercise, with the aim of executing it at the highest power output, his motor control system always uses the same engram. The kinesthetic sensations of the needed magnitude of force efforts and speed of movements are fixed in the brain and became an archetype. Because of this 'archetype, the athlete encounters great difficulty in changing the biodynam-

---

[44] N. A. Bernstein. *The Co-ordination and Regulation of Movements*. Pergamon Press, Oxford, 1967.

[45] *Kinesthetic sensations* are sensory inputs which recognize the orientation of different parts of the body in relation to other parts as well as the rates of movements of the body parts. *Kinesthetic sense* is an ability to be aware of muscular movement and position by providing information through receptors about muscles, tendons, joints, and other body parts. *Kinesthetic sense* is a kind of *proprioception* (the ability of central nervous system to communicate and coordinate parts of your body with each other) that indicates whether the body is moving with required effort, as well as where the various parts of the body are located in relation to each other.

ic structure of exercise when he repetitively strives to increase its power output. In addition, the same training stimuli, repeated consecutively, provokes a sensorial adaptation and a desensibilization (decrease in the sensibility) of the nervous system to these stimuli, ceasing to produce the same training effect.

If the athlete executes the exercise with the same goal (maximal power output) but in different external conditions, the kinesthetic feedback adapts the motor structure to these conditions and the new motor engram remains in the brain. The new condition could be more difficult when the athlete has a higher level of external resistance to overcome, or easier, when the level of external resistance is less and the athlete can execute the movements with a higher speed. If the athlete, immediately after the exercise's execution in the changed conditions, performs the exercise in the normal conditions, he will use the new motor engram formed by the preceding exercise executed under more difficult or easier conditions. This may allow performing the exercise in the normal conditions with a higher force effort or with a higher speed. In addition, the execution of the same exercise in different conditions causes a decrease in the level of sensorial adaptation to the same consecutively acting external stimuli.

There are many ways to vary the conditions of the competition exercise's execution.

In the **speed-strength sport** disciplines, the Contrast Method is often used in the training of Track & Field throwers, executing the final movement of competition exercise (or the competition exercise as whole), with different weights of the sport device. The use of light weights causes an execution with a higher speed and ensures the transfer of this senso-motor image on the subsequent exercise performed with a standard weight. In the same manner, the use of a heavier weight facilitates the activation of a higher force effort such that when this force effort is applied to the normal weight device during the subsequent exercise's execution, it ensures a higher speed of movement. Usually, after the throwers perform exercises with a very heavy weight, it is advisable to perform 2-3 repetitions of the exercise under normal conditions.

In **combat sports** the freestyle and classic Olympic wrestlers use specific exercises performed with heavier or less heavy sacks (the opponent's 'body') or with a partner of a higher or lower weight category.

The Contrast Method is also used in the training of the **cyclic sport** disciplines. In a rower's training a hydrodynamic brake can be used to alternate between difficult and easier conditions (see Fig. 4.5). In a cyclist's training, athletes alternate tracks with different speeds (on the road and on the track) and tracks (uphill/downhill) with different gears. In a swimmer's training an elastic rope can be towed (see Fig. 4.6) until it is completely extended (10-15 strokes) followed by a short swim of 10-15 m under normal conditions (without external opposition). This combination is repeated 6 to 10 times. Another effective method consists of alternating short swims (15-20 m) at maximal speed under normal conditions, with a swim towing the athlete with an elastic rope (using traction force until 110-120% of maximal speed).

Track & Field sprinters can execute speed running exercises on a track of 30-40 m with a slightly downward slope, followed by a flat track. The run on the flat track, after the downhill phase, is executed with the same speed and stride length. Middle distance runners use

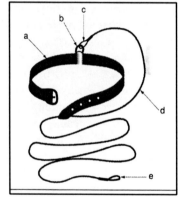

Fig. 4.5 - Elastic rope used in swimming.

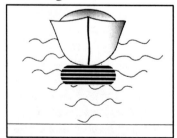

Fig. 4.6 - Hydrodynamic brake used for rowing.

this exercise on a track having 50-60 m downward slope.

The efficacy of the above use of runs on tracks with alternate conditions has been experimentally proven. The training effect is influenced by different combinations of running tracks (see Fig. 4.7): the combination 4-5-2-3 and the combination 5-2-3-4 promote an increase in maximal speed while the combination 3-4-5-2 promotes an improvement in the capacity to maintain speed during the distance.

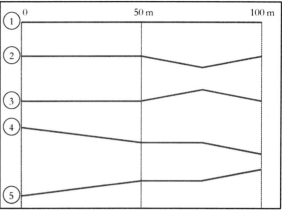

Fig. 4.7 - Variants of trails outlined used in the Contrast Method.

In this experiment, two groups of Track & Field sprinters carried out speed running exercises: the experimental group used the Contrast Method slope-flat running exercises; the control group used flat surface running exercises.

The experimental group achieved a 6.8% increase in the results of the 100 m sprint and a 6.5% increase in the 200 m sprint, while the control group only achieved a 4.3% and a 3.8% respectively.

An increase in speed was obtained in other experiments involving 400 runners and soccer players who executed the following system of run exercises: uphill - flat - downhill.

To create easier conditions for speed running, the renowned Russian biomechanics professor L.Ratov created a special device which decreased the force of gravity during the run (see Fig. 4.8). Thanks to this device, the athlete can reach a maximal speed 5-7% higher of that reached under normal conditions. In the laboratory of professor V.Kousnetzov (see Appendix 4), this method was adapted for use with treadmill running (using only the vertical elastic traction fixed between the ceiling and the belt). In this case it was also possible to fix the athlete's maximal speed (it is also useful for the so named 'leading method').

Fig. 4.8 - The scheme of I. Ratov's special device: 1 - rail; 2 - bogey; 3 - vertical elastic traction device; 4 - belt.

How to create a more difficult or easier condition is also a matter of experience and is often suggested by the need to overcome difficulties in applying the method in different environments or by the will to evaluate one's own intuition.

"When I was coach of Track & Field sprinters I used a simple variant (of the exercises described before)*: I fasten an elastic shock absorber to a belt putted on the athlete. Initially I ran following the athlete creating a resistance at the starting acceleration or during the running (sometimes I used a sledge or a tire). The training method scheduled a session with 'my opposition' followed by two sessions without opposition or two session with opposition followed by 2-3 in normal condition. When I was exhausted to run following my athletes I started to think how I could organize this training without been killed by it; it has been the need to survive that pushed me to ideate the so called 'sudden release method*

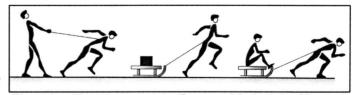

Fig. 4.9 – Exercises used in Contrast Method for Track & Field sprinters

(tear regime)'. The idea behind this method is quite simple. I was seated on a sledge towed by my 'unlucky' athlete (see Fig. 4.9). When he reached a good speed, I pulled a slope fasted to the clamp of his bell, releasing the shock absorber to which my sledge was tied. At that moment the athlete was 'uncorked' increasing sharply his speed. The sequence of alternating conditions was the same used before.

Despite its simplicity, this method showed its high efficacy in developing the starting acceleration and the running speed. This method has been successfully applied by many coaches and, after many years of its use, its efficacy has been experimentally confirmed and further improved.[46] "

One of these experiments was made by N. Lavrilenko; he used special equipments to create the following alternate conditions:

- run with an external opposition of 8% of the athlete's weight;
- run in the tear regime: the athlete starts with an opposition of 8-10% of his weight and, after the opposition has been removed, he runs at maximal speed;
- towed run (easier condition) with a traction force of 3-4% of the athlete's weight, the increase in maximal speed not greater than 1 m/s.

The duration of another experiment was of 10 months involving two groups of high level sprinters: a control and experimental group, each made up of 12 athletes (6 women and 6 men). Both groups performed speed work 3 times per week: the control group with the traditional methods; the experimental group using the alternate conditions. The experimental group used the following method:

- 3-4 repetitions of 2 x 60-100 m runs with an external opposition of 8% of the athlete's weight followed by 1 x 60-100 m run under normal conditions;
- 2-3 repetitions of 2 x 60-80 m run in a tear regime followed by 1 x 60-80 m run under normal conditions;
- 1-2 repetitions of 2 x 80-100 m in a towed run (easier condition) with a traction force of 3-4% of the athlete's weight followed by 1 x 80-100 m run under normal conditions.

The results of this experiment showed that the combination of the alternate conditions and the standard condition ensure an increase in maximal speed and an improvement in the capacity to maintain the speed during the distance.

In swimming, the Contrast Method is utilized at the end of the preparation period or in the competition period, using a combination of sprint exercises, executed under normal and more difficult conditions: swimming with a brake, swimming with small shovels (200x100 mm), or swimming with big shovels (200x200 mm).

A series includes the following exercises:

1) 25 m swimming at maximal speed without shovels;
2) 25 m swimming at maximal power of strokes with big shovels;
3) 12-25 m swimming at maximal frequency of strokes with big shovels;
4) 25 m swimming at maximal speed without shovels;
5) 25 m swimming at maximal power of strokes with small shovels;
6) 12-25 m swimming at maximal frequency of strokes with small shovels;
7) 25 m swimming at maximal speed without shovels.

The rest interval between the exercises is 1-2 minutes. In one training session, 4 series are carried out with rest intervals of 2-3 minutes.

---

[46] Y. Verkhoshansky "La Preparazione Fisica Speciale", CONI-Scuola dello Sport, 2001, Roma-Italy, pag. 123.

4.4. CIRCUIT METHOD

The Circuit Method is well known in sport practice. In this method the exercises, affecting different muscular groups, are carried out sequentially (circuit) and the sequence is repeated several times (Fig. 4.10). The interval between exercises is usually of a short duration in order to execute the exercises of the training séance in an aerobic regime. In this way both muscular system and cardio-vascular system are stimulated.

This method mainly helps to increase the capacity of the energy systems, to perfect the functional capabilities of various muscle groups, and to activate the morphological reorganization of the body. This method is widely applied in sport games and combat sports. Practical examples are shown in § 8.3.3.

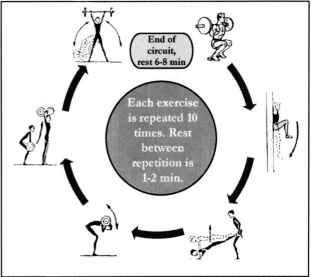

Fig. 4.10 - Example of organizing strength exercises using the circuit method.

4.5. STRENGTH-AEROBIC METHOD

The main characteristic of the strength-aerobic method lies in the strength development of both the fast and the slow muscle fibers.

VARIANT 1 is similar to the Complex Method. It includes two resistance exercises executed with the same muscle groups, but using different methods. For example, one could use several sets of the first exercise (using the Maximal Effort Method) and several sets of the second exercise (using the Repeat-Serial Method or Interval Method). If the resistance exercises are carried out with heavy weights and few repetitions, mainly the fast twitch fibers are involved. To stimulate the slow twitch fibers, the resistance exercises must be executed with long lasting sets and with relatively lower weight. The basic premise of this variant consists of combining these two types of exercise so that the maximal mobilization of muscle fibers is achieved: the first exercise is executed with a weight of 80-90% 1RM. The same exercise is then executed with a weight of 40-50% 1RM.

The following two combinations are used:

COMBI-NATIONS	FIRST EXERCISE	DOSAGE OF 1ST EXER-CISE	REST BETWEEN SETS	SECOND EXERCISE	DOSAGE OF 2ND EXERCISE	DOSAGE OF SERIES
I	Weight = 80-90% In one set there are 2-3 repetitions executed slowly	3 sets with about 3-4 minutes rest	2-4 minutes	Weight = 40-50% In one set there are 15 repetitions executed slowly	4 sets with 2-4 minutes rest	2-3 series with 8-10 minutes rest

COMBI-NATIONS	FIRST EXERCISE	DOSAGE OF 1ST EXER-CISE	REST BETWEEN SETS	SECOND EXERCISE	DOSAGE OF 2ND EXERCISE	DOSAGE OF SERIES
II	Weight = 80-90% In one set there are 2-3 repetitions executed slowly	3 sets with about 3-4 minutes rest	2-4 minutes	INTERVAL METHOD Weight = 40-50% The set duration is 15-20 seconds, the repetitions are executed slowly	4 sets with 2-4 min rest. The cardiac frequency must not overcome 120-140 beats/minute	2-3 series with 8-10 minutes rest

VARIANT 2 is similar to the Circuit Method, but includes more specific exercises executed in a more intensive interval regime, which further induces accentuated stimulation of the aerobic mechanism.

The work includes several specific resistance exercises for various muscle groups, selected according to principle of Dynamic Correspondence. These exercises are executed according to the interval regime, but without evident fatigue:

- 8-10 specific resistance exercises, for different muscular groups, are executed consecutively with a rest interval of 1 minute.
- The duration of the work is 20 minutes.
- Two consecutive exercises must not be executed by the same muscular group.
- For each exercise, the weight of overload is selected in such a way that permits execution of a set of 30-60 seconds duration without evident fatigue.
- Cardiac frequency during the work must not surpass 120-140 beats/minute.

ORGANIZATION OF SST IN THE TRAINING PROCESS AND THE BLOCK TRAINING SYSTEM

5.1. INTRODUCTION

For 'organization of the training process' here we mean the optimal distribution of training loads, over the time, in accordance with the target objectives. Organizing the training process can be seen as the process of *managing the motor behavior* of an athlete, utilizing the adaptation process in a way to obtain the desired sport result at a determined moment in time (the day of competition).

Every single training mean, carried out by the athlete during the training process, subjects his organism to the adaptation stimuli, spurring a determined motor function with its 'load' (for this reason we often use the words 'training means' and 'training loads' as synonyms). Nevertheless, the single training mean is never used alone in the training process but it is always placed among other training means whose training effects act on the same object (the athlete's organism), activating an integrated process of adaptation. For these reasons, the coach must not organize the training process basing upon the training effects of the single training mean, rather on the training effects of the *training loads* within a determined unit of time (training session, training day, microcycle, training stage and preparative period).

In the sport training literature, the training loads are traditionally characterized by two main characteristics:
- **Volume**, identifying the amount of work;
- **Intensity**, measuring the effort applied.

However, these characteristics pertain more the training means carried out by the athlete, rather than their influence on his organism which is the reference point in organizing (designing) the training process. Recently, in sport training literature, the characteristics of training load have been distinguished in two categories: *'external'* (training work) and *'internal'* (exertion of the athlete's organism).

According to this classification, the speed of exercise execution, usually associated to the concept of load intensity, pertains to the 'external' load intensity; thus it doesn't always coincide with the "internal" load intensity. The execution of a training exercise at the same level of speed could provoke, in different athletes, different levels of organism exertion. Increasing the speed of exercise execution could bring to a change in the training load orientation (emphasis); for instance, in cyclic sports - a change of energy supply mechanism from the aerobic to the anaerobic, in acyclic sports - from Maximal Strength to High Speed Strength. Thus, it will be more correct to use the following three main parameters to characterize the 'internal' training load:
- **Emphasis** - the qualitative characteristic indicating the main direction of the training stimuli (influence on a given characteristic of the human motor function and influence on the physiological systems related to this function);
- **Volume** - the quantitative characteristic indicating the total number of training stimuli;
- **Intensity** - the quantitative characteristic indicating the level of exertion of a given motor function

under the influence of training stimuli.

How can the "internal" load intensity be increased?

In Physics, intensity is a measure of energy flux, time averaging action over the period function of the wave. If we interpret the influence of training load on the athlete's organism as the wave of energy flow (training impact), the increase in its intensity may be obtained in two ways:

- increasing the 'magnitude' of the training impact (influence), using training means with higher training potential;
- increasing the 'frequency' of a given training impact (number per time unit), as, for example, in the concentrated training load (see § 5.4.1).

In the training process, every training influence of a single training load has a functional interrelations with the other based upon the laws of adaptation of the human organism to intensive muscular activity[47]. Training loads spur the adaptive processes in the physiological systems involved in the execution of the exercise (*'short term adaptation'*) leading up to the morphological-functional transformations of the athlete's organism (*'long term adaptation'*). Considering these two interrelated adaptation mechanisms, the organization of the training process reveals itself in two main forms:

1) through the organization of training loads in the micro-cycle, training day and training session, based on the short term adaptation mechanism;
2) through the organization of training loads in the yearly cycle and preparatory period, based on the long term adaptation mechanism.

The ability to find the most rational form of the temporal organization of training loads, and to implement it within a given time framework, is the gauge of excellence of a coach's professionalism. This ability is based on his knowledge and his experience.

1) To find the optimal form of training loads organization in micro-cycles, training days and training sessions, it is necessary to keep in mind the mechanisms of short term adaptation in choosing:
   - the optimal dosage of means in single training sessions;
   - the optimal ratio between 'work-recovery' process.
2) To find the optimal form of the training load organization in the yearly cycle and preparatory period, it is necessary to keep in mind the mechanisms of long term adaptation when:
   - choosing the directions of training impacts (objectively necessary for the development of the adaptation process in a given sport), and develop corresponding criteria for the differentiation of training loads;
   - selecting specific (to a given sport) training loads and grouping them according to their training direction and training potential;
   - elaborating a method of objective control over the dynamics of athlete's state to set up the adaptation strategy.

The full explanation of these issues goes beyond the purpose of this manual focused on the Special Strength Training. Furthermore, the actual knowledge of their practical application is still very limited in the field of sport science. Notwithstanding this, it's also impossible to discuss about the SST methodology without touching on the problems of the organization of the training process as whole, because, the purposes of SST are realized only when the SST means are effectively organized in the training process.

In searching for ways to solve this conundrum, two famous phrases could be useful: *"The knowledge of some principles easily compensates for the ignorance of some facts"* (C.A. Helvétius, French philosopher)

---

[47] For more detailed information about the laws of the process of adaptation to the intensive muscular activity, see the Addendum 1 of "Supertraining" Sixth Edition expanded version, Italy, 2009.

and "… *a clear image of a desired future can be used to formulate a problem and create a program for its solution*" (N.A. Bernstein).

So, in order to give the readers useful information about the organization of SST in the training process, is possible to help them giving the fundamentals of training loads organization (*knowledge of some principles*) and ideal solutions (*a clear image of a desired future*) so that will be possible to perceive the related problems which the coach will face in the practical applications. According to this idea, in the following paragraphs will be illustrated:

1) the fundamentals of training loads organization in the training process:
   - the basic conditions for the development of the adaptation process during sport training (these information help to identify the main problems related to the organization of the training process);
   - the main principles of organizing the training process (these information help to see the ideal solutions to these problems);
2) the model of training load organization in the preparatory period of high level athletes (the Block Training System) to give a practical example on how these principles could be realized.

5.2. BASIC CONDITIONS FOR ATHLETE'S IMPROVEMENT

The human adaptation to every kind of change in the external environment is based on the body's reaction in establishing a new status of equilibrium between the external environment and the body itself.

The sport training process represents the artificially reproduced process of the organism's adaptation to intense muscular activity, finalized at obtaining the highest increase of the athlete's physical performance. For this reason, it has particular characteristics compared to the adaptation process to other types of change in the external environment (climatic, geographical, social and so on):

- The adaptation stimuli are selected and organized artificially, in such a way to act on those physiological systems 'responsible' of increasing sport results in a given sport discipline.
- The adaptation stimuli, provided by the training loads, do not act on the athlete's organism with continuity, but intermittently during the regime of 'work – recovery'.
- The adaptation stimuli should ensure an increase in the athlete's performance in a limited period of time (preparation period).

The constructive effect of adaptation has its basis in three phenomena:

1) specificity of protein synthesis during the post-work period, conditioned by the type of work executed, its intensity and its source of energy;
2) super-compensation of the substrates used up during the workout (substrates serving as sources of energy) and different structural and enzymatic proteins;
3) a positive correlation between the catabolic and anabolic processes, brought about by muscular work.

In managing the adaptation process during the sport training, the following three basic conditions must be taken into consideration:

1) the specificity of the training stimuli;
2) the optimal ratio of the 'work-recovery' process;
3) the optimal training load quantity.

5.2.1. SPECIFICITY OF TRAINING STIMULI

The base mechanism of the athlete's progress in physical performance, during the training process, is the intensified synthesis of structural and enzymatic proteins in the active cells (short term adaptation), leading, via morphological transformations, to the growth of the functional capacity of the cellular structures and, consequently, of tissues, organs, and the body as a whole (long term adaptation).

Short term adaptation transitions gradually into long term on the basis of multiple short term training effects on the body. In this way, there are multiple short term repetitions of the utilization of the body's plastic reserves that are used for repairing the physiologically worn out structures, as well as for adaptive synthesis of structural and enzymatic proteins, ensuring temporary increases in the ability of the cells in doing their functions. As a result of long term repetition, the effects of these changes are strengthened and become more expressed. In this way, in place of the temporary redistribution of the plastic reserves of the body during short term adaptation, there is development of stable, stronger reformation-long term adaptive restructuring.

The peculiarity (specialty) of the organism's reaction to the training stimuli (training loads flow), triggered by the use of given exercises, is determined by the so-called 'metabolic trace'. That is, in fact, the accumulation of metabolism's intermediate products (metabolites), which represent the main inductors of protein synthesis, which takes place shortly after the muscular work. Metabolites specifically determine the pool of proteins whose synthesis is caused by a given muscular activity. The stimulated protein synthesis concerns those proteins that are used to build active cellular structures and those enzymes that catalyze the biochemical reactions, which are specific to the trained cell function In this way, the qualitative correspondence between the athlete's motor activity and the morphological-functional improvement in his organism is ensured (Fig. 5.1).

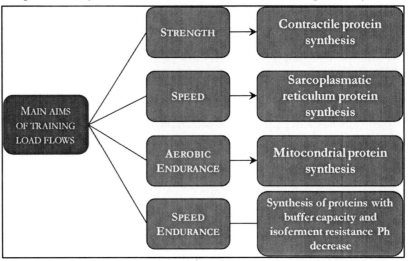

Fig. 5.1 - Scheme of the specific training flow of different kind of load, and the related adaptive protein synthesis (A. Viru, 1988 - reviewed)

In relation to the typology of exercises, in the muscles there is either:

- strengthening the anaerobic resynthesis of ATP (creatine kinase and gylcolitic) and a progression in the speed of the contractile process, or
- an increase in the respiratory re-synthesis of ATP with an increase in endurance for long term work, or
- an increase in the mass of the contractile proteins and their ATP activity, which leads to an increase in strength.

As a result, the muscles acquire the functional properties adequate to the work regime of specific sports activities.

From here, in a formal relationship to the determined task and content of the training process, it is logical to assume that, in order to develop strength it is necessary to use strength exercises, in order to increase speed it is necessary to perform speed work, in order to develop endurance, it is necessary to perform endurance exercises, etc.

However, the training means act on the athlete's organism not as a separated elements, but as components of the training load of a determined training time unit (training sessions, training days, microcycle and training stage).

The training effect of the training load is caused not only, and not so much, by the sum of the training effects of the single training means, but mainly by their combination, their sequence, and the time interval between them. The rearrangement of the chronological sequence of the training means, included in each load, considerably changes the training effect. The training effect of the load used in the prior training stage, changes the organism's functional reaction and, therefore, the training effect of subsequent load.

Thus, the targeted organism's reaction to the training stimuli could be obtained by using given combinations of different training exercises in the same training session and also by using these different exercises in subsequent training sessions, or concentrating them in different subsequent training stages. We must then consider that the development of the adaptation process follows a definite *heterochronicity* in the formation of accommodative body restructuring which is linked to the specific consecutiveness of the adaptation reactions and development of morpho-functional restructuring in different physiological systems of the human body.

For these reasons, in order to obtain the required specific changes in the athlete's body, which ensures an increase in the sport results in a given sport discipline, the training loads must be organized and ordered as elements of a system of training stimuli, artificially created for a specific purpose (see § 5.3.1 - The principle of the systemic organization of training stimuli). Training loads must be carefully selected and their interaction should be programmed to ensure the formation of peculiar quality of the training effect (specificity), required by the training strategy, at the moment in time where the athlete should participate in the most important competition of the season.

To summarize, in order to obtain the necessary increase in the athlete's sport results, the training process must ensure the specific adaptive reactions, which correspond to the particular needs of a given sport discipline. The athlete should not spend time and energy uselessly; performing exercises whose training effects do not contribute towards the final increase in the power output of the competition exercise. However, the final training effect is not the just sum of the training effects of each single training means. Even the exercise which may not seem to be very specific to a sport discipline can, instead, be efficacious as an element of the entire specific system of training means. Considering that the cumulative effect of different training means depends on their temporal sequences and on the rest periods between them; the specificity of a single exercise's training effect could be further increased under the influence of the training flow of subsequent, more specific exercises.

So, when the coach searches for useful information to design the training program for his athletes, he should not only study articles, which regard the training effects of single exercises, rather the entire training models, specifically designed for athletes at the same competitive level, where not only the training means are described, but also their temporal organization.

When learning to cook a new dish from a recipe, a inexpert cook catches mostly the quantity of ingredients, whereas an expert cook – rather catches the way and the sequence of their addition.

5.2.2. OPTIMAL RATIOS OF 'WORK AND RECOVERY' PROCESSES

The relationship between 'work and recovery' during training process has the main role of letting the biological mechanism of adaptation to be understood and therefore allowing the elaboration of the principles of the training process organization.

During physical work, the dominant processes of scission and oxygenation of biochemical substrates in the muscles are necessary for energetic provisioning. After a workout, the consumed resources are restored thanks to different type of synthesis. The biological synthesis includes the renewal of the proteins of the cellular structures, involved in the work, the supplementary synthesis of the ferment's proteins and the provision of the protein re-synthesis, with the 'material of construction': amino-acids and the precursors of nucleic acids.

In the rest period after work, the chemical substances, which are destroyed during work, are not simply recovered, i.e. returning to the initial level, rather the process of their restitution always crosses the phase of super-compensation (Fig. 5.2). The level of such super-compensation depends on the intensity of the consumption of chemical substance during the workout as well as its duration.

The processes of restitution of all chemical substances and structures that are destroyed during muscular work, pertains to the phenomenon of super-compensation: the restitution of creatine-phosphate and glycogen contents, of the enzymatic and structural protein contents, as well as the restitution of the quantity of mitochondrial

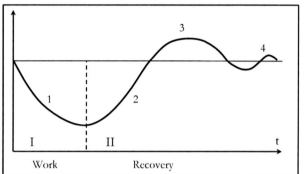

Fig. 5.2 - The scheme of Jiakovlev, 1988; the process of energy sources consumption during the work and their restitution during the recovery: 1. consumption, 2. restitution, 3. super-compensation, 4. the return to the initial level.

in the muscular fibers (Jakovlev 1983). The multiple repetitions of this process represent the base of the morpho-functional specialization of the organism and the growth of the athlete's working capacity.

In the period of recovery following muscular work, a re-synthesis of creatine-phosphate and the elimination of excess lactate occur. Later, the restitution of glycogenic content is completed, and even later, the synthesis of proteins and phospholipids.

Protein synthesis has consumption energetic cost; therefore, it does not begin immediately after training, but only after the restitution of the energetic potential of the muscular fibers; for which the ATP consumption is necessary. ATP is the energetic source of biological synthesis, which occurs at the same speed as its scission. Immediately after the completion of a workout, a slightly emphasized and very short-lasting phase of ATP super-compensation may be observed. This intense ATP activity disappears soon after, since the consumption of ATP is necessary for the reparative synthesis.

For this reason, protein synthesis, in relation to the intensity and the duration of the workout, may occupy a prolonged time frame: from 12 to 24 hours, or in the case of a very heavy workout, from 48 to 72 hours (Jiakovlev 1983, Viru, Kirge 1983, A.Viru 1985).

How the process of protein synthesis develops, as well as the final result of this process, depends on the interval between the previous and the subsequent training influences (Fig. 5.3):

-   If the new training influence comes at the moment when the protein synthesis, induced by the previous influence, is still at the beginning (arrow A), the effect of the preceding influence is untouched.

- If the new training influence comes at the moment when protein synthesis, induced by the precedent influence, is still not terminated (arrow B), the effect of the preceding influence is only partly attained.
- If the following training influence coincides with the moment of termination of protein synthesis induced by precedent influence (arrow C), the attainment of positive results of the training effect of the preceding load is more likely.
- Finally, if the new training influence is delayed (arrow D), the training effect of the preceding load remains unattained.

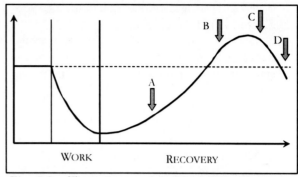

Fig. 5.3 - The scheme of A. Viru, 1988, illustrating the dynamics of protein synthesis after the work with four different intervals between the previous and subsequent training influence (for the explanation see the text)

Therefore, to ensure the specificity of the organism's adaptive reactions, it's necessary to:

- consider the physiological effect ('the metabolic trace') caused by the chosen training load;
- select correctly the length, for the immediate follow-up period, which are objectively necessary so that the process of re-establishment, and in particular the process of protein synthesis, may develop and be completed.

To summarize, the coach must understand that - *when the athlete sleeps, his organism works*. The time between two training sessions is not simply a period of rest necessary for recovering the optimal status of the athlete, but rather, the necessary time for 'digesting' the preceding workout. Only during this period the biochemical processes develop, allowing the development of the organism's immediate adaptive reactions into new morphological-functional particularities.

5.2.3. OPTIMAL QUANTITY OF TRAINING LOADS

Prolonged powerful muscular work can alter the basal physiological status of the human organism (homeostasis) and provoke a series of pathological changes; finally leading to the disruption of the adaptation process.

A fundamental role in the process of adaptation belongs to the endocrine and immune systems: they influence every type of exchange of the chemical substances in the organism and control the maintenance of homeostasis.

The endocrine and immune systems, together with the SNC, are the *general managers* that control the complex adaptation syndrome in all phases of this process.

The endosecretory system is responsible for the so called non-specific adaptation mechanism: it ensures the favorable conditions for the realization of specific homeostatic reactions and the mobilization of the organism's defensive system. In regards to the mobilization of energetic resources of the organism, the primary role belongs to the noradrenalin system.

The mobilization of the plastic reserves of the organism, in the case of the stress brought by intense physical work, is ensured by the managing function of the ipofiso-adrenocortical system located in the suprarenal cortex. This function consists in the creation of a 'pool' of free amino acids necessary for the plastic provisioning for the process of protein synthesis. The attainment of stress resistance is based on morpho-functional changes that are realized at cell tissue and subcellular structures level. This ensures a superior functional power in different cellular structures of the entire organism and its systems. This process determines the development of long term adaptation.

Under the influence of prolonged muscular work, three phases (Fig. 5.4) of changes of the state of the noradrenalin system can be described (Kassil, 1978):

1) the immediate activation phase, characterized by a 'strengthened flow' of adrenaline in the blood immediately after beginning the workout; with no lowering of the contents in the adrenal ganglions.

2) the stable and prolonged activation phase, characterized by an increasing upsurge of adrenaline secretion in the blood with the gradual lowering of the content in the adrenal ganglions.

3) the exhaustion phase, characterized by the lowering of noradrenalin activity, externally evident in that there is a drop in the level of the athlete's work ability.

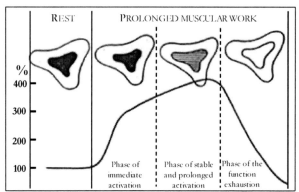

Fig. 5.4 - The phases of the noradrenaline system responding to the influence of prolonged muscular activity, evaluated on the basis of the change in the content of adrenaline in the adrenal ganglions. In the drawings above: the adrenal cortex with a large content of adrenaline at the beginning of this activity (in black), the subsequent lowering (in grey) and the final exhaustion (in white). The curve points out the change in the concentration of adrenaline in the blood (Kassil and others, 1973).

It is very important to note: the drop in the athlete's level of work ability does not necessarily coincide with the fall in the adaptation function of his organism. In other words, the athlete may be able to maintain the necessary level of work output at the same time his noradrenalin system has already entered into the exhaustion phase of its function.

For example, as far back as 30 years ago, an inexplicable phenomenon was verified in the preparation of elite Soviet rowers: the athletes, who obtained the highest results in the physical fitness tests, prior to competition, did not succeed in reaching the intended result for that competition. The following investigations analyzed the state of the endo-secretory system of these athletes and verified the lowering of noradrenalin level along with the reduction in volume of the adrenal ganglions.

In fact, the fitness parameters used to control the athlete's state during the training process (the results of motor tests) did not reflect the current adaptation process; but rather, the intermediate results of this process: the already received morpho-functional changes of the athlete's organism. The trend of the adaptation process, which causes these morphological-functional transformations, may be characterized by other parameters, which regard the development of protein synthesis in the organism's structures (organs and tissues), involved in the training work, and the endocrine and immune systems response to the work itself[48].

The signs of overcoming the bearable limit of the physical load may be found in the form of alterations in the parameters of the immune system: *myogenic leukocytosis*[49].

Immune defense is the base mechanism of the process of adaptation. Sport activity is characterized by stressful influences on the organism: prolonged loads of elevated volume and high levels of physical and psycho-emotional tension, presented particularly in the series of commercial competition, can

---

[48] About this issue, see the book of Atko Viru and Mehis Viru "Biochemical Monitoring of Sport Training", Human Kinetics, 2001.

[49] *Myogenic leukocytosis* – the pronounced increase in leukocytes provoked by intensive muscular activity (see the book of A. Viry and M. Viru "Biochemical Monitoring of Sport Training", Human Kinetics, 2001

overcome the organism's ability to provide a suitable answer. In these cases, the power of the factors that influence the organism, and their systematic repetition, generate a chronic stress and the disruption of adaptation. Such disruption, in this case, is verified not by a decrease in performance parameters, rather, and primarily, in the form of alteration in the functions of the immune system or via immuno-depression.

The most frequent consequences of immuno-depression are infectious illnesses and a decrement of recovery abilities. The alteration of the immune system may linger for a prolonged period after the end of the annual cycle of training. In this case, the loads influence of the following annual cycle may overlap with the depressed status of the organism's immuno-system, possibly leading to illness prior to the introduction of intensive training loads.

The point of primary focus is that the immuno-depression of athletes doesn't represent the 'cost of adaptation', rather the premature sign of the disruption of the adaptation process provoked by training loads that are too intensive and poorly organized.

Unfortunately, sport science is still at the beginning of studying the adaptation in the training process. So, in order to find the optimal organization of training loads, coaches are still only guided by their personal experience and intuition.

The most frequent coaching error occurs when striving to obtain an increase in the athlete's physical fitness level as soon as possible by increasing the training loads volume. However, *"nine pregnant women together cannot ensure the baby's birth after one mount"*. Every type of physiological process in the human organism has its own period of expression and rate of development, which cannot be accelerated. It's impossible to accelerate the adaptation process by increasing the training loads volume or intensity. The possibility to obtain a greater adaptive reaction, as a response to a higher level of training influences, has certain limits, which are specific for every athlete and may also be different within the diverse states of his organism. The quantitative benchmarks, which can help to find these limits, are the values of the training loads used by the athlete in the preceding yearly cycle (the data of the training diary): the total volume of training loads, which was already 'assimilated' by the athlete's organism in a similar preparation period, and also the maximal volume in a single microcycle of said period.

The total SST load volume in the following yearly cycle could remain the same, as in the preceding, and an increased fitness level of the athlete may be obtained by increasing the intensity of training stimuli: introducing into the training process the training means having a higher training potential or using the concentrated form of training loads (see § 5.4.2.1).

5.3. MAIN PRINCIPLES OF TRAINING LOADS ORGANIZATION IN TRAINING PROCESS

5.3.1. PRINCIPLE OF SYSTEMIC ORGANIZATION OF TRAINING STIMULI

The main general principle of organizing the training process is the Principle of Systemic Organization of Training Stimuli. This principle expresses one of the basic concepts of modern sport training methodology that considers the training load not simply as a 'set' (complex) of different means and methods, but as a monolithic unit (system) of training stimuli on the organism; chronologically gathered in a certain way.

The use of the term 'systemic' underlines the fact that different training stimuli are gathered in a system: each component of this system (the single training mean stimuli) interacts with the other components (the other training means stimulus), so, their resulting effect may not be considered as the simple sum of their actions.

The systemic organization is the ordering of training loads, as the elements of the system of training stimuli, artificially created for a specific purpose; their functioning and relationships during the training process should be based on the laws of human adaptation to intensive muscular activity.

The Principle of the Systemic Organization of Training Stimuli expresses the systemic approach. This methodological approach is in contrast with the mechanistic approach; characterized by the vision of the training planning and organization similar to the way in which a house is constructed from single bricks; where the 'bricks' are the single temporal components of the training process: training sessions, training micro-cycles.

The problem is that each training load is a part of the continuous process of the athlete's organism's morphological-functional specialization. Although the 'mechanical properties' of each single brick of a house are always the same, independently of their place in the walls of the house, the functional properties of the single elements of the training process (the training effects of training loads) are changing in relation to their place in the training process itself.

The General Principle of the Systemic Organization of Training Stimuli implies that high efficiency of training can be achieved only when the training loads are regulated in a timely fashion so that each of them effectively resolves its own particular task; all of them together ensures the achievement of the required level of special work capacity with minimum expenditure of time and energy on behalf of the athlete. Thus it entails the following three conditional factors for the correct organization of training loads:

- continuity of the training loads influence,
- concordance between the training effects of different training means scheduled in the training load, and
- positive interdependence between the training loads used in sequence (i.e. between the preceding and subsequent training load).

These conditional factors determine three inter-related principles of organizing the training process.

5.3.2. PRINCIPLE OF TRAINING STIMULI CONTINUITY

The principle of the training stimuli continuity entails that the ratio between the workloads and recovery must ensure a constant functional activity of athlete's organism during the training process.

The organism's functional activity occurs not only during the workouts, but also during the subsequent rest periods, during which the complex processes of biosynthesis, caused by the muscular work itself, are activated. Increases in the organism's current functional condition are provided by the sum of these processes.

5.3.3. PRINCIPLE OF TRAINING STIMULI CONCORDANCE

The Principle of Concordance between the training stimuli of different training means implies that their combination over time should avoid any negative effect that might be transmitted from one means to another.

This principle also implies:

- the selection of the appropriate combination of means, characterized by the required training directions and the preservation of their developmental effect through a gradual introduction of

training means with higher training potential; so as to maintain the developmental trend;
- the organization of the rational interaction between the training means having different training direction and different training potential.

The concordance between training effects plays a very important role in the preparation of high-level athletes, especially with respect to the following two cases:

1) when several problems have to be solved during the same training period, for instance, problems pertaining to special physical preparation and problems pertaining to improving technical/tactical mastery or competition mastery;

2) when the gradual intensification of the work in a specific regime and increasing the speed of execution of the competition exercise must be obtained during the training stage.

There are two ways in which training means, having different training emphasis, can be temporarily unified with each other and with other training means:

1) *Complex-Parallel Form* is characterized by the simultaneous use of training means that have different directions of their training effects; the training process is organized via the consecutive repetition in turn ('rotation') of the training means having different directions during a certain temporal period of time (usually, it is a microcycle). In this case, the acute training effects of different training means is cumulating to obtain the final complex result.

2) *Conjugate-Sequence Form* is characterized by the localization (concentration) of training means that have the same direction, in different training stages, temporally organized in the definite sequence. In this case, the training stimuli of the training means used in subsequent stages acts on the athlete's organism, which has already realized the accommodative morphological transformations (delayed training effect), provoked by the accumulated training effects of training means used in the previous stage.

5.3.4. PRINCIPLE OF POSITIVE INTERDEPENDENCE BETWEEN TRAINING STIMULI USED IN SEQUENCE

The Principle of the Positive Interdependence[50] between the different training stimuli used in sequence implies that the preceding load creates favorable conditions for achieving the training effect of the subsequent load. Besides, the subsequent loads produce the requisites to which the previous training load effects succeed; they should build upon what has gone on before, building on 'heritage'.

This principle is fundamental for the so named periodization of the training process: the subdivision of the training plan into periods; each one aimed to obtain a definite training objective.

According to this principle, a high efficiency of the training process can be achieved only when all training loads having different training emphasis are regulated in a timely fashion so that each of them effectively resolves its own particular task; all of them together ensures the achievement of the required level of special work capacity in a determined period of time (the days of competition) with minimum expenditure of time and energy on behalf of the athlete[51].

The most explicit application of all these principles can be found in the Block Training System, which represents the Conjugate-sequence form of the temporal organization of training loads having different training emphasis, during the preparatory period.

---

[50] *Positive interdependence* - the need of each other to succeed.

[51] About this issue, see the book of the Author "Programming and Organization of Training Process in Sport".

5.4. THE BLOCK TRAINING SYSTEM (BTS)

5.4.1. ORIGIN AND EVOLUTION OF BTS

The Block Training System was pioneered at the end of 1970s (before the Moscow Olympic Games) to provide an innovative model for training high level athletes in the Track & Field speed-strength disciplines. During this historical period, in the East European sports training, the improvement of sports performance was associated with the increase in the total volume of the training loads. At the end of the 1970s, the total volume of training loads performed by high level East European athletes reached the maximum limits of human capacity to withstand such loads.

At the Moscow Central State Institute of Physical Culture and Sport, where a scientific laboratory of interdisciplinary research worked on problems concerning the optimization of the training process, a team of researchers started a new research project. Their task was to identify the most suitable training models that would ensure the improvement of sports results in the strength-speed disciplines without increasing the total volume of training loads.

The initial research dedicated to this project showed that a high total volume of training loads couldn't ensure an adequate increase in sport results; most notably because the athletes used the complex-parallel form of temporal organization of training loads of different emphasis.

A high total volume of the loads, having complex composition, may not ensure a high level of training stimuli, because the training effect of one means may negatively affect the training effect of another.

The innovative idea consisted in the selective 'concentration' of training means, directing primarily towards only one training objective. This would create a 'focused' training stimulus, able to influence each of the determining factors of sport performance improvement.

In order to verify this idea in an experiment, a group of high level T&F jumpers began to use a training program which included only barbell exercises finalized at increasing the maximal strength: the barbell exercises, which were usually uniformly distributed over time, were concentrated in a limited training stage (see Figure 5.5).

The dynamic of the strength parameters, measured during the experiment, revealed for the first time, the *Long-lasting Delayed Training Effect* (LDTE). The concentrated strength loads caused a temporary deficit in the strength parameters; after the end of such stage, the strength parameters gradually returned to their initial level and, later, they reached an exceedingly high level, never achieved by the athletes in their past experience. Furthermore, the total volume of barbell exercises, carried out by each athlete in the concentrated loads stage, was less than the total volume, carried out in the whole preparatory period in the past yearly cycle, during which the SST means were uniformly distributed over time and used with other training means.

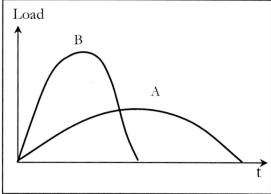

Fig. 5.5 - Scheme of concentration of strength loads: A – distributed form; B - concentrated form. The volumes of the loads are the same.

The results of the subsequent experiments showed that (Fig. 5.6):
- the formation of LDTE develops in two phases. In the first phase (t_1), in which the athlete uses the concentrated strength loads (A), the level of the strength parameters (curves f) go down. In the

second phase (t_2), where the LDTE is observed, they rapidly rise (f_1 and f_2). The lower the strength parameters fall (within an optimal range, usually a decrease in 10-12% of their initial value) during the first phase, the higher they subsequently rise in the LDTE phase (usually an increase in 20-30% of their initial value). The different dynamics between the more and the less concentrated phase A, are illustrated by the curves f_2 and f_1;

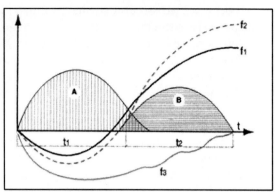

Fig. 5.6 - Basic scheme of the long-lasting delayed training effect (LDTE) of concentrated strength loads

- an excessive volume of concentrated strength loads (A) results in a significant drop in the athlete's state and, as a rule, the LDTE will not occurs with the consequence of not recovering of strength parameters (curve f_3);

- the duration of LDTE depends on the volume and on the duration of the concentrated strength loads (stage A). In general, the phase of LDTE realization (t_2) is equal to the duration of the precedent phase (t_1). The optimum duration of the concentration stage of strength loads (block A), for ensuring the fullest use of the adaptive potential of the athlete's organism and the greatest increase of strength parameters in the subsequent period, ranges from 6-12 weeks;

- during the phase of concentrated loads (A), when the strength parameters decrease (t_1), the athletes has a difficulty to execute the competition exercise with the correct technique and high level of power output;

- in the subsequent period (B), a low volume of speed-strength exercises, carried out by gradually increasing their intensity, can create a favorable condition to realize the LDTE.

From the last two observations we can depict that, in order to realize the LDTE ensuring the highest improvement in speed-strength sport performance, the stage of concentrated strength loads should be followed by two subsequent stages: in the first, the explosive strength exercises should be concentrated; in the second stage, the training exercises aimed at improving the competition exercise technique should be concentrated. In both stages, highly specific exercises should be included, they must be carried out with low volume and performed at the highest level of power output.

On the basis of these results, an innovative model of the preparation cycle of training of speed-strength sport disciplines was devised.

In the 1980s, this training

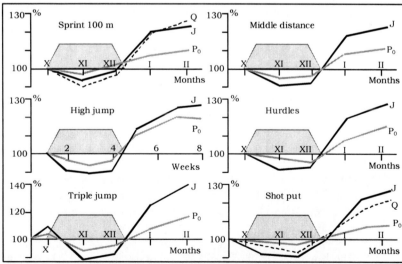

Fig. 5.7 - Examples of the long lasting delayed training effect of concentrated strength loads in the Track & Field disciplines

model was successfully used and soon became the dominant training model adopted in the training of high level Soviet athletes in the Olympic strength-speed sport disciplines[52].

This model, named 'Conjugate-Sequence System', was described for the first time in the books 'Fundamentals of the Special Strength Training in sport' and 'Programming and organization of the training process in sport', published in the 70's. Yet, the coaches and the athletes preferred to name this model as 'Block Training System', underlining in this way the importance of the concentrated strength loads 'block' in the construction of the yearly training plan (Fig 5.7).

Later, in the 80's, this system was elaborated, and successfully approved, for cyclic (endurance) sport disciplines (see Table 9). This Block Training System model has more complicated particularities, in comparison to the BTS model for speed-strength sport disciplines. However, the basic element, in both this models, is the LDTS of concentrated strength loads, used at the beginning of the preparation period.

BLOCK A BASIC STAGE	BLOCK B SPECIAL STAGE	BLOCK C COMPETITION STAGE
1. Increasing the level of Maximal Strength expressed in the main body propelling movement 2. Improving the ability to display explosive force in the specific body propelling movements 3. Improvement the ability to execute specific strength work for prolonged period of time 4. Creating the energetic base for further improvement of the specific work capacity	1. Improving the starting acceleration ability 2. Increasing the Maximal Anaerobic Power 3. Increasing the body glycolytic productivity	1. Improving the ability to maintain the optimal speed over a distance 2. Increasing the level of maximal distance speed 3. Competition and tactical preparation

Table 9 - The sequence of training objectives in the application of the Block Training System for cyclic sports

In order to apply the Block Training System successfully, it is necessary to clearly understand the meaning behind 'loads having a different training emphasis' as well as the logic founding the sequence in which these loads are arranged.

5.4.2. METHODOLOGICAL BASIS OF BTS

As it was underlined in Chapter 1, an increase in the power output of competition exercise is determined by the adaptation of the whole organism to the specific muscular work:
- increasing the functional level of physiological systems, involved in the competition exercise (increasing the athlete's motor potential);
- improving the specific motor control function (improving the athlete's capacity to realize his motor potential in the motor structure of the competition exercise).

The basic idea of BTS consists in creating the conditions for realizing these two tasks, in a determined temporal sequence:
1) achieving consecutive increases in the functional level of the organism's physiological systems, 'responsible' of increasing the athlete's specific work capacity (increase in motor potential);
2) improving the bidirectional links between these systems and the motor control system (improve-

---

[52] Verkhoshansky Y.V., Mironenko I.N., Antonova T.M. et al. The dynamic model of the athlete's condition in the yearly cycle and its role in the training process management. Theory and Practice of Physical Culture, 1983, n.5, pp 5-8

ment of the athlete's capacity to realize his motor potential in the competition exercise).

The increase in the functional level of physiological systems regards those systems which ensure the performance of the competition exercise with higher power output: in speed-strength sports, it mostly regards the neuromuscular system; in endurance, combat sports and sport games, it regards also the energy supply and cardio-vascular systems. However, the functional power of all these systems can be expressed by the same executive organ – skeletal muscles. Therefore, increasing the functional level of the neuro-muscular system is a fundamental basis for increasing the power produced by muscle contractions in the *working regime* typical of a given sports discipline. In other words, for improving the athlete's 'specific work capacity'.

The improvement of athlete's capacity to realize the motor potential in the motor structure of the competition exercise is related to setting up bidirectional links between the physiological mechanisms that ensure the mobilization of the motor potential to work in a specific regime and the CNS and the neuro-muscular mechanisms that ensure the motor control function.

These basic ideas are applied in the following training strategy (see Fig. 5.8).

In **block A**, concentrated strength loads ensure a powerful impact on the neuro-muscular system that leads to a temporal decrease in its functional power (f) and, as consequence, decreasing the athlete's specific work ability.

During the following **block B**, the long-lasting delayed training effect of concentrated strength loads leads to the progressive increase in the athlete's work ability. To fortify this increase and to direct the delayed morphological-functional transformations toward the needed way, training exercises are carried out in specific regime by gradually increasing their intensity (the level of power output).

In the **block C**, to acclimate the athlete for a complete use of his progressively growing specific work ability in the motor structure of the competition exercise, the technique work is carried out: the ex-

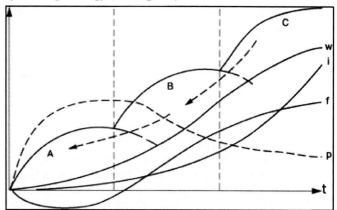

Fig. 5.8 - The conceptual model of the Block Training System: W - the power output in the specific regime of competition exercise; i - the training loads intensity; f - the functional state of the athlete's organism (of the neuro-muscular apparatus); p - the training loads volume.

The inverse outline illustrates the interdependence between previous and subsequent blocks loads (see "The Principle of Superimposition of concentrated training loads", § 5.4.2.2).

ecution of the entire competition exercise and its elements at the level of maximal power output. This work is aimed at adjusting the biodynamic structure of the competition exercise: to put it in accordance with the increased motor potential of the athlete.

It is important to underline that the Block Training System is intended only for high level athletes; the following two points may clarify why we assert that:

1) the concentration of training loads is the last way to increase the training potential of training loads; it is useful only for those athletes who have already exhausted all the other possibilities for obtaining an increase in their physical fitness level;

2) the concentration of training loads could lead to such alterations of fitness parameters to the point of creating difficulties in adjusting the biodynamic structure of competition exercise in the subse-

quent training period. Only high-level athletes, who possess a high level of technical mastery, could tolerate such alteration.

The second point also indicates the difficulties in applying the BTS in those sport disciplines, having competition exercise with a very complicated motor structure and requiring high precision of movements.

The Block Training System can be applied only as a specific training model for the given sports discipline; the model built for a sport discipline may not be used for another sport discipline:

- The power output of the competition exercise is ensured by involving different structural elements of the physiological systems, integrated into a specific functional structure. The final aim of the BTS is the enforcement of this structure through the use of concentrated training loads, which act on each of these elements in a determined sequence. In different sport disciplines, the structural elements of physiological systems involved in competition exercise may not be the same. Their difference determines not only differences between the training means used in each block, but also the general composition of the Block Training System model.

- The process of the organism's morpho-functional specialization is characterized not only by multi-lateralism (involvement of different structural elements of the physiological systems of the body), but also by heterochronism (different adaptive inertia of these systems). For this reason, the loads, which stimulate each component of the specific functional structure, must be conjugated in a determined sequence; the length of their action will not be the same.

- The length of the entire BTS program is determined by the length of the preparation period; this will vary according to the competition calendars used in different sports disciplines.

For these reasons, the Block Training System should only be presented as a practical training model for a particular sport event. The Block Training System cannot be fully described in this manual, it needs a book to illustrate its application for every sports discipline (as for example the 'Block Training System in Endurance running'). Nevertheless, in this manual the reader may find general information for setting up his own BTS.

The Block Training System is based on three principles:

1) **The Principle of Concentration** of training loads having the same emphasis in different training stages (blocks).
2) **The Principle of Subsequent Superimposition** of concentrated training loads having different training emphasis.
3) **The Principle of Temporal Priority** of concentrated strength loads in the preparation period.

5.4.2.1. PRINCIPLE OF CONCENTRATION OF LOADS HAVING THE SAME TRAINING EMPHASIS IN DIFFERENT TRAINING STAGES (BLOCKS)

This principle implies that, in the preparation period, different training means, aimed at influencing each of the determining factor of athlete's performance (power output of the competition exercise) are temporally organized via their localization (concentration) in different training stages, arranged in a definite sequence (about this sequence, see the following Principle of Superimposition).

The concentration of the training means, having the same direction of training effects, in a isolated training stage (block) ensures the formation of the *concentrated load* having a definite training emphasis. This kind of load ensures a deep training influence on the corresponding motor or physiological function of the athlete's organism; as long as its volume is not very high, due to the maximal *concordance* between the training effects of means used.

The localization of training means, having different directions, in different training stages avoids the negative influence that one training means might have on another.

The application of this principle on the SST implies:

- the concentration of loads, having the main influence on the strength component of the power output in the competition exercise, within a limited period of time (strength block);
- the temporal separation of the concentrated strength loads from the loads aimed at increasing the speed component of the power output in the competition exercise;
- the temporal separation of the strength loads from the loads aimed at achieving technical-tactical mastery.

The temporal separation of strength loads from the loads aimed at increasing the speed component of the power output in the competition exercise, as well as the loads aimed at perfecting technical-tactical mastery, is due to the phenomenon of temporary decrement in the functional characteristics of the neuromuscular apparatus during the strength block.

The figure 5.9 shows the results of the study on the relationships between the volume of SST means (resistance and jump exercises), the viscoelastic property of muscles and the control test results (the triple jump from place) of top class sprinters in the spring-summer stage of the yearly training.

To evaluate the viscoelastic property of muscles it was used the method of Seismo-mio-tonometry. This method allows to measure (with the use of seismo-sensor) the frequency of mechanical oscillation in relaxed muscle,

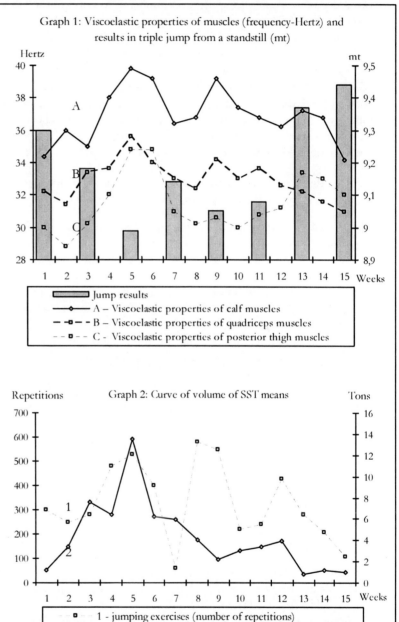

Fig. 5.9 - Relationship between the volume of strength training means (Graph 2) and the state of the sprinters motor system (Graph 1). From the PhD dissertation of A.V. Levchenko.

provoked by the blow of a falling (from the height of 35-40 cm) metallic ball (diameter 7.7 mm, weight 2 g). The frequencies of damped mechanical oscillation of the muscle tissue (in Hz) indicate the tension in the muscle.

As we can see on the graph, an increase in the volume of strength means (4th - 6th, and 8th - 9th weeks) results in an increase of muscle stiffness and a decrease in the working effect in regard to explosive efforts (results in the triple jump from place are reduced).

This means that adverse conditions for perfecting running speed are created when speed is the main task of training. Besides this, the increased training load at this time results in a decrease of the muscle contraction speed that, as a rule, creates the precondition for injuries. In this functional state, it is not wise to carry out training exercises requiring fine coordination, high power of effort and perfection of specific mechanisms of energy acquisition. Thus, the concentrated SST loads should never be combined with running at maximum speed. These tasks should be solved during subsequent training stages, in favorable conditions, created by the Long Lasting Delayed Training Effect (see § 5.4.2.3 Principle of temporal Priority of concentrated strength loads).

5.4.2.2. PRINCIPLE OF SUPERIMPOSITION OF CONCENTRATED TRAINING LOADS HAVING DIFFERENT TRAINING EMPHASIS

The Principle of Subsequent Superimposition of concentrated training loads having different training emphasis implies that:

1) the blocks of concentrated training loads having different training emphasis are arranged in a definite sequence;
2) each training block is not completely separate from the previous and the subsequent. Every subsequent block's loads must be introduced in such a way that there is a gradual replacement of the block's loads preceding it.

The concentrated training loads act on the athlete's organism not only facilitating the upsurge in the adaptive processes of corresponding physiological systems (short term training effect), but also provoking the morphological functional transformations in the systems themselves (long term training effect). Thus, in each subsequent block, the acute training effects of the training means are not only cumulative, but also superimpose on the cumulative delayed training effect of the training means used in the previous block. This way, the subsequent superimposition, of concentrated training loads having different training emphasis, generates the most significant final cumulative effect at the end of the preparatory period.

However, the previous loads, after having played their role and after having been replaced by the other loads, cannot be completely excluded from the training process: these loads begin functioning as an additional training stimulus to maintain those specific morphological transformations that they previously caused.

As shown in figure 5.10, the previous loads prepare the morpho-functional basis to increase the training effect of subsequent loads; these in turn obtain their specific objectives, supporting the further improvement of the organism's adaptive processes produced by the preceding loads; yet at a higher level of the organism's work capacity. This way, the positive interdependence between the different training loads used in sequence is ensured.

In summary, each subsequent block includes not only its own training means and the training means used in the preceding block, but also some auxiliary training means to maintain, for instance, the technique of the competition exercise execution or the body's muscular system functional state. The auxiliary SST means supporting function ensure maintenance the level of specialized work capacity, achieved during the preceding training stage. For these reasons it is more accurate to refer to the training loads of different blocks as loads which have different 'dominant emphasis'. The sequence of different training means in each block depends on the adaptive inertia of those physiological systems which are involved in the execution of the competition exercise and which should be influenced by these loads.

For example, in the BTS model for endurance running (Fig. 5.11), during the block A, the endurance work is carried out together with resistance exercises (but in different training sessions). The prolonged continuous execution of specific locomotion in the aerobic regime (at the intensity level that is slightly below the anaerobic

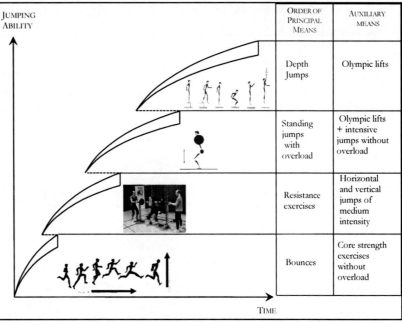

JUMPING ABILITY	ORDER OF PRINCIPAL MEANS	AUXILIARY MEANS
	Depth Jumps	Olympic lifts
	Standing jumps with overload	Olympic lifts + intensive jumps without overload
	Resistance exercises	Horizontal and vertical jumps of medium intensity
	Bounces	Core strength exercises without overload
TIME		

Fig. 5.10 - The Block Training System for improving the jumping ability (the application of Nils Holmdahl to volleyball players). The sequence of training loads having different primary emphasis, is finalized to solve the following training tasks: preliminary enforcement of the body's muscular-ligaments system → increasing maximal strength → increasing explosive strength → improvement of reactive capacity.

threshold) ensures specific morpho-functional specialization of the muscles involved in exercise: improvement of their contractile capacity and the oxidative capacity of their slow twitch fibers. In addition, these exercises are also used to activate the adaptation process in the cardiovascular system.

The prolonged continuous work, executed in the aerobic regime is an essential element of endurance training: it leads to a gradual increase in the volume of the cardiac ventricular cavity and provides the formation of particular peripheral vascular reactions linked to the optimal distribution of blood flow during the work. These reactions ensure the supply of a greater quantity of oxygen to the muscles involved in the work. It's important that the formation of these peripheral vascular reactions precedes the higher intensity training. The premature intensification of endurance training leads to the over tension of cardiovascular system and this can create the conditions which lead to cardiac dystrophy and can interfere with the normal development of the training process.

The ratio between resistance exercises and endurance exercises depends on the specific needs of a given sport. In cycling, rowing and skating, the level of the external opposition to overcome, in each body propelling movement, is higher than, for example, in endurance running. So, in the BTS model for these sports, the strength loads and aerobic loads should be superimposed in a way that the ratio between them is gradually changing during block A: at the beginning the resistance exercises dominate, then at the end the endurance ones. Thus, the load composition in blocks of BTS models for different endurance sports could vary a great deal. However, the sequence of the general training tasks to solve in blocks A, B and C, is universal (see the beginning of this paragraph), as well as the placement of the concentrated strength block in every BTS model (see the following Principle of Temporal Priority of concentrated strength loads).

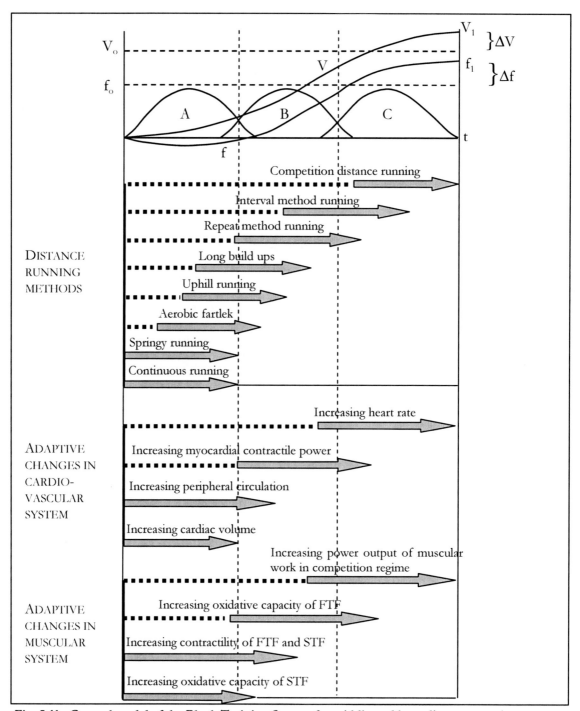

Fig. 5.11 - General model of the Block Training System for middle and long distance running.

5.4.2.3. PRINCIPLE OF TEMPORAL PRIORITY OF CONCENTRATED STRENGTH LOADS

The Principle of Temporal Priority of concentrated strength loads implies the temporal placement of concentrated strength load in Block A, in the first stage of the Block Training System program.

This principle has a crucial significance, because the Block training model is based on the LDTE of strength loads, which facilitates and emphasizes the training effect of the subsequent training loads. The LDTE of concentrated strength loads ensures the effective completion of training tasks in the subsequent stage of the yearly cycle. This way, SST loads exceed the emphasis on the Technical-Tactical and High Speed Preparation. Furthermore, the name Block Training System is historically related to the Priority Principle. In the first publications about the use of the Conjugate Sequence System in the yearly cycle, the concentrated SST load stage was presented as quadrate figure that symbolized the 'monolithic unit', named by Verkhoshansky as 'block' (see Fig. 5.7).

Concentrated strength loads are able to create a powerful impact on the neuro-muscular system provoking its profound morpho-functional reorganization, precondition for a considerable increase in the athlete's specific work capacity during subsequent training stages. Thanks to this preliminary morpho-functional preparation of the motor and other physiological systems, the following stage of intensification of the work regime doesn't lead to its overload.

In order to ensure an efficient use of the organism's energy resources in the training process, the concentrated strength loads must precede the in-depth technique and speed works: the formation of the necessary morpho-functional changes in the athlete's organism must be accomplished in advance. If the strength loads are introduced when the functional preparation level of the athlete is insufficient, they can limit the process of perfecting technique and the speed of the competition exercises. As a result, progress in sports achievement is reduced.

5.4.3. TEMPORAL ORGANIZATION OF THE SST MEANS IN BTS MODELS FOR VARIOUS SPORTS

In the BTS models for speed-strength, cyclic sports, and sport games the SST means may have the following main directions:

SPORT GROUP	SST MEANS DIRECTIONS		
	BLOCK A	BLOCK B	BLOCK C
Speed-strength sports	Increasing Maximal Strength	Increasing Explosive Strength and Starting Strength	Improving Reactive Ability
Endurance sports	Increasing Maximal Strength	Improving Local Muscular Endurance Increasing Maximal Anaerobic Power	Increasing power output of the work in specific regime
Sport games and combat sports	Increasing Maximal Strength and Static Strength Endurance	Increasing Explosive Strength Improving Local Muscular Endurance	Increasing Maximal Anaerobic Power Increasing power output of the work in specific regime

5.4.3.1. SST MEANS USED IN THE BLOCK A

Block A activates the adaptation process in the athlete's organism and provokes the subsequent morphological-functional changes in those physiological systems, which are involved in the competition exercise.

The SST means must ensure the enforcement of the working mechanism of the neuromuscular apparatus involved in the competition exercise and the increase in the strength component of power output in the key movements of the competition exercise. In the main BTS sports discipline models, the resistance exercises are focused on increasing maximal strength. They are concentrated in a way that exploits the LDTE during the subsequent block B.

In endurance sports and sports having a variable motor regime, prolonged distance exercises are also used in the aerobic regime. The intensity of these distance exercises must be gradually increased throughout the course of the block (from 'below' the anaerobic threshold to 'at' the anaerobic threshold). At the end of this block, this work can be substituted by the aerobic Fartlek.

Block A may include three stages $A_1, A_2,$ and A_3 in which different SST means are organized in conjugate-sequence form.

In speed-strength track & field sports, the Block A includes:

1) Stage A_1, also named as 'Introductory Stage', is usually used at the beginning of the yearly cycle (in the first preparation period of the yearly cycle). This stage is aimed at enforcing the main muscle synergies involved in the competition exercise. Barbell exercises, with a weight of 10 RM, are carried out according to the serial and serial-repetition methods. In addition to the barbell exercises, long bounds and multiple jumps are used according to the extensive method.

2) Stage A_2, aimed at a gradually increase in Maximal Strength of the key-movements. Specific barbell exercises, with a weight of 5 RM, are carried out using the Repeat Method. Extensive long bounds and multiple jumps are used with a lower volume than in block A_1.

3) Stage A_3, aimed at increasing the Maximal Strength in key-movements as in the Block A_2 but using the Maximal Effort Method. In this stage, only barbell exercises with a very low load volume are carried out.

In the speed-strength sports, the correct technical execution of the competition exercise must be maintained by using low volumes of specific technical exercises executed at the optimal (middle) level of power output.

In endurance sport disciplines, SST means of Block A may be used not only to increase strength capabilities, but also with the aim to improve Local Muscular Endurance.

Block A includes:

1) Stage A_1, aimed at increasing the Maximal Strength in the main muscle synergies, which ensure the force effort in the specific body propelling movement. Resistance exercises are carried out using the serial and serial-repetition methods.

2) Stage A_2, aimed at increasing the strength component of LME. Specific resistance exercises, able to ensure an increase in the contractile capacity of the muscles involved in the execution of a given sport locomotion, are carried out.

3) Stage A_3, aimed at increasing the specific 'energetic component' of LME. Specific resistance exercises (or execution of specific locomotion in more difficult conditions), able to ensure an increase in the oxidative capacity of the slow twitch fibers and able to ensure an increase in the power output of the specific work at the level of the anaerobic threshold.

In the period of the stages A_2 - A_3, resistance exercises in the aerobic regime are executed at low-middle movement rates using the interval method. The duration of the exercises is gradually increased, and the level of the external resistance is decreased.

5.4.3.2. SST MEANS USED IN THE BLOCK B

Block B is aimed at gradually increasing the power of the work in specific regime.

In speed-strength, combat sports, and sport games, the SST means are focused mostly on gradually increasing Explosive Strength (maximal explosive force effort in key-movements of the competition exercise). Intensive methods of different jump exercises are used. Preliminary competitions can be scheduled at the end of this phase.

In endurance sports, SST means are focused on increasing the speed component of LME: the contractile and oxidative capacities of the fast twitch fibers.

5.4.3.3. SST MEANS USED IN THE BLOCK C

Block C is focused on technical work at competition intensity; during this phase, the athlete should gradually achieve the maximum level of power output in the competition exercise.

The competition exercise and its elements are performed at the maximal level of power output. The execution of technical/tactical training means is aimed at the correct execution of the competition exercise. During this block, the participation in preliminary competitions is an effective element of the athlete's preparation to achieve the best result in the main competition of the season.

In certain speed-strength sports disciplines and sport games, this block may entail a low volume of shock method exercises ensure the stimulation of the neuro-muscular apparatus.

5.4.4. ORGANIZING SST MEANS IN MICRO-CYCLES WHEN CONCENTRATED STRENGTH LOADS ARE USED

As it was underlined before, within the framework of a microcycle (MC), the normal development of the adaptation process may only be ensured by an optimal proportion between the magnitude of training impact and the duration of interval between two adjacent training impacts.

This means that the strength loads of the microcycles in Block A should be temporarily organized in 'day by day' work regime that do not cause the 'collapse' of the protein re-synthesis process.

In the search for rational forms of micro-cycle construction for the BTS, post-graduate research projects (made in the interdisciplinary Laboratory of the Central Sports Research Institute at the end of 80s) explored the rational forms of training loads organization in the microcycle for skating (V. Grechman[53]) and for weight-lifting (S. Berezhnoi[54]).

The preliminary researchers (see Fig. 5.12) showed that everyday training sessions lead to intensified degradation of proteins (catabolic process, marked by the increase

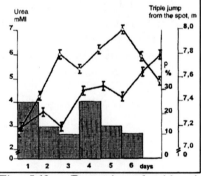

Fig. 5.12 - Dynamics of athletes' state in microcycle (skating, n=9): blood urea concentration and triple jump length. Shaded columns show training loads volume (R).

---

[53] Grechman V.V. Organizing the SST loads in the preparation period of high-level sprint skaters. PhD Dissertation, 1993

[54] Berezhnoi S.Y. The structure of Shock Micro-cycle in different training periods of the high level weightlifters. PhD dissertation, 1989

in blood urea[55]); it undermines an athlete's ability to generate explosive strength efforts (triple jump result decreased). This ability improves with the switch to protein synthesis (anabolic process, marked by the decrease in blood urea). The following phenomena were also observed:

1) A training session, carried out the day after the use of high volume strength loads, leads to an intensified expenditure of protein (catabolic effect). This occurs even if the training session includes a load with lower volume and intensity than the preceding training session and with the same training direction.

2) During the training session, carried out the third day after the high volume training load, even if moderately intensive loads are employed, protein synthesis and plastic processes (anabolic process) begin: the urea level goes down and the nuero-muscular system function begins to restore.

3) If rest is given after the first three days, the organism will fully restore to its initial state. If in following day, a large load will be repeated again, the afore-mentioned trend in the dynamics of functionality will be observed again.

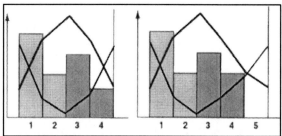

The subsequent experiments showed that a strong training impact on the organism can be ensured by the so-called 'micro-blocks' (MB - Fig. 5.13), 4 adjacent training days of loads having the same training emphasis: the first two days generate a catabolic effect (light columns), the subsequent days lead to an anabolic effect (shaded columns). The Anabolic phase, depending on the magnitude of a training impact in the initial days, can last 48-72 hours.

Fig. 5.13 - Building up of 'micro-block'. The upper line illustrates the dynamics of urea concentration in the blood, the lower line the explosive strength index.

Two days of 'developing' loads with the same training emphasis (using the highest and lowest volumes), followed by two or three days of 'support-ing' workouts (or two days of 'support' workouts and one day of rest) allows the creation of an elevated training influence on the organism; using a relatively low load volume that does not disturb the normal development of plastic reconstruction processes.

These researches allowed elaborating the following two models of the so-called 'developmental' micro-cycles: 14-day MC and 7-day MC.

The 14 day MC (Fig. 5.14) is intended for a training stage of strength loads concentration (Block A).

This MC covers three micro-blocks and, depending on the power of training impacts in the catabolic phase, provides for protein synthesis over the course of 48 or 72 hours.

The 7 day micro-cycle (Fig. 5.15) is intended for Block B. This micro-cycle makes it possible to fulfill the necessary volume of specific developing work while preserving the required level of the organism's functionality.

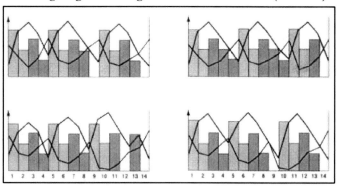

Fig. 5.14 - Variants of organization of 14-day micro-cycles

---

[55] *Urea* - the chief nitrogenous end product of protein metabolism formed in the liver from amino acids and from ammonia compounds; found in urine, blood, and lymph.

Figures 5.16 and 5.17 illustrate the dynamics of the athletes' state (8 weightlifters) in the 7 day and in the 14 day MC: Ur - urea concentration in the blood, CPC - *creatin-phospho-kinase concentration*[56] and J - the Explosive Strength level evaluated with UDS.

The volume and intensity of training

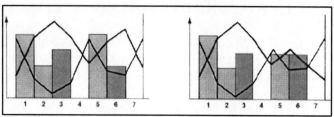

Fig. 5.15 - Variants of the organization of 7-day microcycles

loads are indicated by the following parameters: NBL - the number of barbell lifts (dark grey), CI – coefficient of intensity (light grey), which is equal to the total weight lifted during the day per the number of barbell lifts (NBL).

The MB concept has been tested by high-class bodybuilders during the muscle mass build-up stage (see Appendix 2). However, notwithstanding encouraging results, the idea of DMCs requires further experimental backing. The solution of the MC issue can be facilitated by information on the periodicity of the synthesis of protein structures in the organism; particularly via the discovery of how anabolic processes occur within 8, 14, and 17-day endogenic cycles. If a training session with a large volume of work coincides with the phase of the enhanced preparedness of the cell's regulatory apparatus for the anabolic tuning of metabolism, a favorable effect will be achieved and if it coincides with the phases of catabolic tuning, we can expect a worsening of the training effect.

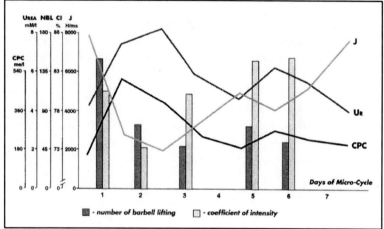

Fig. 5.16 - The connection between the athlete's state and the training loads in the 14 day training stage (for explanations see the text).

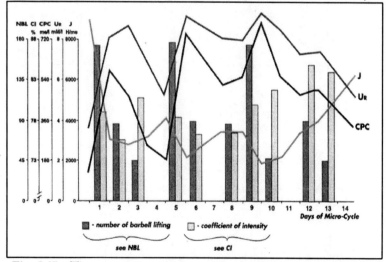

Fig. 5.17 - The connection between the athlete's state and the training loads in the 7 day microcycle (for explanations see the text)

---

[56] *Creatine phosphokinase* (CPK), also known as *Creatine kinase* (CK), or phosphocreatine kinase, is an enzyme expressed by various tissue types. It catalyses the conversion of creatine and consumes adenosine triphosphate (ATP) to create phosphocreatine and adenosine diphosphate (ADP). Elevation of CK is an indication of damage to muscle.

5.4.5. APPLYING BTS IN YEARLY CYCLE

The Block Training System does not concern the simple substitution of the traditional complex-parallel system with the conjugate sequence system. BTS is a way to solve complex training tasks: the fulfillment of athlete's preparation for a given competition. Thus, setting up the BTS model for a given sport discipline is strictly related to the specificity of the competition calendar.

On the base of the most common schema of competition calendars, the following six variants of BTS application in the yearly cycle can be proposed (see Fig. 5.18).

VARIANT I – is related to sports having two competition periods in the yearly cycle (C and C1), with the most important competition in Block C1. In this variant, SST loads are concentrated in Blocks A and A1: the volumes of the loads in Block A1 are lower compared to Block A, but their intensity is higher.

VARIANT II – is related to sports having three competition periods in the yearly cycle (at the end or during the Blocks C, C1 and C2), in which the last competition (at the end or during block C2) is the most important. This variant includes a quite long preparatory period, facilitating the realization of the whole BTS structure (Blocks A, B and C), creating the morphological- functional base for the subsequent part of the yearly cycle. Block's B1 loads are focused on increasing the ultimate power output in the specific regime. Block's A1 loads are higher in intensity compared to the loads of Block A.

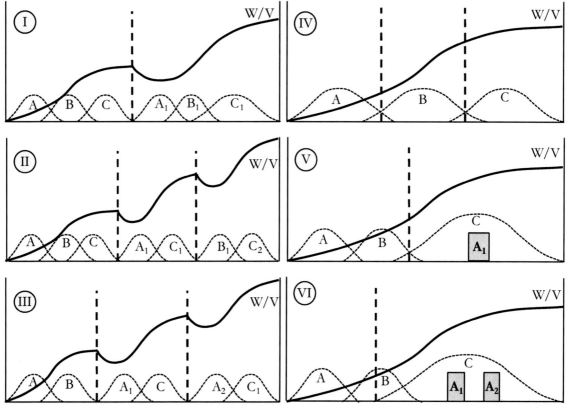

Fig. 5.18 - Placement of the strength blocks in the yearly cycle of various sports. The curve "W/V" shows the hypothetical level of the athlete's power output or speed in the competition exercise.

VARIANT III – is adapted to the yearly cycle with shorter preparatory periods compared to Variant II and with only two important competition stages (C and C1).

The preparation for the first competition (at the end or during Block C), should include the following training stages:

1) Block A - concentrated volume of strength loads;
2) Block B - specific training loads finalized at increasing the power output of muscular work in specific regime. If during Block B, the athlete is engaged in competitions, they should be considered as component of the specific training load and high level sports results should not be expected;
3) Block A1 - concentrated strength loads having an auxiliary (subsidiary) role. They are finalized at creating the optimal condition for increasing the power output of competition exercise in the following competition period (Block C1): these loads are low in volume and high in intensity.

In the preparation for the second competition (Blocks A2 - C1), the load structure (A1 - C) is repeated, but at a higher level of power output (Block A1) and at the velocity of competition exercise performance (Block C).

VARIANT IV - is related to sports having only one competition stage in the year, with the main competition at the end of block C. The training strategy, in this case, can have two variants:

1) if the competition stage (Block C) has a relatively short duration, the complete realization of the fundamental training work in Blocks A and B is achieved;
2) if the competition stage (Block C) is quite long, the function of block B can be realized through the participation in a series of preliminary competitions: in this case the competition activity will represent the main component of the specific training, focused on increasing the work power output in the specific regime.

VARIANT V - is related to sport games and combat sports, in which the yearly cycle has a quite extended preparatory period and a long continuous series of matches in the competition period. In such cases, it's possible to realize the fundamental physical preparation (blocks A and B) during the preparatory period. The subsequent competition activity (Block C) will represent the high intensity training stimuli that are able to intensify the adaptation process.

To maintain the level of the specific work capacity, obtained during blocks A and B, it's possible to include block A1 of supporting SST in the competition period.

VARIANT VI – is related to sports in which the preparation period is very short, sometimes with no clear cut distinction between the preparation and competition periods (typical, for example, for the yearly cycle of elite soccer and tennis players). In this case, the participation in competitions plays a role of high intensity training. This training begins from the second part of Block B, when the athletes usually participate in the initial matches of the season. The whole competition period represents a prolonged Block C, in which the short SST Blocks A1 and A2 are included between tournaments when appropriate.

SST IN ACYCLIC SPORTS

6.1. INTRODUCTION

This chapter illustrates the SST means and methods used in sport disciplines in which the sport results are mainly determined by the maximal expression of power in acyclic movement:

MOTOR CHARACTERISTIC OF COMPETITION ACTIVITY	EXAMPLES OF SPORT DISCIPLINES
The competition exercise as whole has acyclic motor structure.	Weight-lifting, ski jumping, Track & Field throwing (shot put, hummer and discus throw).
Main components of competition activity have acyclic motor structure.	Gymnastics, figure skating and combat sports.
The competition exercise includes acyclic component (throwing, jumping) and cyclic component (run up).	Track & Field jumping (pole-volt, high, long and triple jump) and javelin throw.
The competition activity includes acyclic components (ball passes, shoots, strokes, kicks) and cyclic components (short sprint running).	Basketball, tennis, soccer, etc.

Acyclic motor actions have an open-chain motor structure, in which the key-movement is performed only once during the competition exercise (it is not regularly repeated as in cyclic sports). Increasing the power output of the complex motor action having acyclic motor structure is linked to the improvement of athlete's skill to display a powerful concentrated force effort in the key-movement. This objective is reached by using SST means aimed at:

1) increasing the magnitude of the maximal explosive force effort, expressed in the key-movement;
2) enforcing the muscle synergies[57] involved in the competition exercise and increasing the tonus of the muscular system as whole.

Increasing the magnitude of the maximal explosive force effort, expressed in the key-movement, can be obtained using SST means aimed at increasing the Explosive Strength (see § 6.3). When an elevated level of external opposition has to be overcome in the key movement, the increase in the maximal explosive force effort can be obtained using SST means aimed at increasing Maximal Strength (see § 6.2). When the level of external opposition is low, the increase in the maximal explosive force effort is obtained using SST means aimed at increasing the High-speed Strength (see § 6.4). If the key movement includes a sharp changing direction, with a decrease and increase in movement speed, also the Reactive Ability must be improved (see § 6.3).

Enforcing the muscle synergies, involved in the competition exercise, and the increase in the tonus of muscular system as whole, are particularly important in such sport disciplines as Wrestling, Weight-lifting and Track & Field throwing. If the athletes of these sports have at their disposal a quite long preparation period, they may use the SST program 'Russian Pyramid' (see § 6.5) for accomplishing the-

---

[57] *Muscle synergy* – the concordant activity of the muscle group participating to the realization of a movement (see § 1.2.2).

se tasks. For these sport disciplines and also for other disciplines in which the increase in Maximal Strength should be accompanied by increasing the muscle mass (such as Sailing, Bobsled, Rugby, American Football), the Bodybuilding program illustrated in Appendix 2 may give ideas about the methods of using resistance exercises and their organization over the weeks (in the microcycles).

In the most part of acyclic sports, the key-movements usually include a powerful concentrated ground propulsion force effort, performed at the final phase of competition exercise or, of single technical element of the competition activity. In the Track & Field throwing and in the ball throwing movements of team sports (shoots and passes in basketball, rugby, American Football), the powerful concentrated ground propulsion force effort allows a vigorous forward drive, during a synchronized displacements of the body mass centre and the active body limb; it is the main factor for obtaining a high velocity of release. In sport games (tennis, baseball) and combat sports (boxing, karate), it is the main factor for obtaining a high potency of strokes and kicks.

Since, in the ground propulsion movements, a high level of external resistance must be overcome (the athlete's body weight), the athlete must have a sufficient level of Maximal Strength to reach a high level of power output. Therefore, Barbell Squat, which has a high training influence on the maximal strength, is the most important SST means for all acyclic sports.

In the Track & Field jumping, the main factor determining the sport result, is the ability to produce a high level of power output in the take-off movement ('jump force'). The 'jump force' can be increased by increasing the Explosive Strength and by improving the Reactive Ability, using combinations of special resistance and jump exercise, temporally organized in correct way (see the program illustrated in § 6.6). This program may be used also for improving the 'jumping ability' of the volleyball, basketball, tennis and soccer players (especially for goalkeepers).

6.2. MEANS AND METHODS FOR INCREASING MAXIMAL STRENGTH

The SST means and methods usually used for improving the Maximal Strength are the following:
1) Exercises with weights (resistance exercises executed with barbell);
2) Isometric exercises.

6.2.1. EXERCISES WITH WEIGHTS

The exercises with weights are predominantly used with:
1) Maximal effort method;
2) Repeat method;
3) Repeat-serial method.

6.2.1.1. MAXIMAL EFFORT METHOD

After an intensive warm up, the athlete performs 4-5 set with maximal weight; the duration of the rest interval between sets is free.

6.2.1.2. REPEAT METHOD

1) Execute 2-4 sets of 2-3 repetitions with the weight at 90–95% of maximum, separated by a rest pause of 4-6 minutes.
   In this exercise, two regimes of muscle work can be used: without relaxation or with relaxation of

the muscles between repetitions. When the exercise is executed with relaxation, the bar is placed on the racks for few seconds in order to instantly relax the muscles.

Both regimes are effective for increasing Maximal Strength, but the second one allows improving the ability to display the concentrated explosive strength effort and the ability to relax the muscles in the passive phases of sport movements.

2) Exercise is executed as one series of five sets (see the following table), carried out with rest intervals of 3-4 minutes. At the beginning, the athlete tries to perform the exercise according to the 1st Variant. If, after the fourth set, he feels to be not able to perform successfully the following set, the fifth set must not to be done: after the 6-8 minutes rest, the exercise is executed according to the 2nd Variant.

| SETS | 1ST VARIANT | | 2ND VARIANT | |
	WEIGHT OF OVERLOAD	NUMBER OF REPETITION IN SET	WEIGHT OF OVERLOAD	NUMBER OF REPETITION IN SET
I	90%	3	95%	2
II	95%	1	95%	1
III	97%	1	100%	1
IV	100%	1	100% plus an added weight of 1-2 kg	1
V	100% plus an added weight of 1-2 kg	1	-	-

3) Exercise is executed in yielding regime with the weight at 120-130% of maximum (the load is raised to the initial position with the help of partners). Three sets with 4-5 repetitions are done with the 3-4 minutes rests between sets.

4) Exercise is executed in combined regime, using different weights in the yielding phase and in the overcoming phase.

For example, the Barbell Squat is executed with the use of special device (hook apparatus, see Figure 6.1). The weight of barbell is 70-80 % of the maximal. The additional weights are putted on the right and left ends of the barbell, with special suspension devises - hook apparatus. The weight of barbell together with suspension devises compounds 120-140 % of the maximal.

Before the exercise begins, the bar is putted on special pillars at the height corresponding to the level of the athlete's shoulders in the standing position with the slightly flexed legs.

Fig. 6.1 - Suspension device used for additional loads in the squat

In order to initiate the exercise, the bar is secured on the shoulders taken from special pillars. Then, the yielding phase of the Squat (squat descent) is executed with a weight of 120-140% of the maximum. At the end of the yielding phase, when the suspended weights touches the floor, the suspension devices are taken off from the barbell. Then, the remaining barbell, which weight is 70-80% of RM, is lifted up from the squat position very quickly (in overcoming regime).

The bar is then once again put on the pillars and the athlete shakes the leg muscles. At this time, once again, the partners re-attach the suspension device back on to the bar.

Two to three repetitions are executed for one set with compulsory relaxation and shaking of the muscles between repetitions. In one series, there are 3 sets with 4-6 minutes rest in between them. In a single training session (or in training séance), 2-3 series are carried out with a rest of 8-10 minutes in between series. In the exercises, which involve a less number of muscle groups, duration of the rest intervals between sets can be decreased.

The exercises 2, 3 and 4 are especially effective for the development of Maximal Strength: their training influence on the athlete's organism is extremely strong. For this reason, these exercises should be used only during a limited periods of time. In speed-strength sports having explosive character of power output, these exercises must be used at the end of the preparation period for ensuring the so named 'entry in sport form'.

6.2.1.3. REPEAT-SERIAL METHOD

Repeat serial method exercises could be executed in the followings three variants.

VARIANT 1

This variant is used for increasing the Maximal Strength with a moderate increase in muscle mass. Weights equal to the 70-90% of the maximal are used. The exercise is executed in dynamic regime or in combined regime. The rest between training workouts should be 2-3 days.

Examples of using resistance exercises in dynamic regime

EXAMPLE	WEIGHT OF OVERLOAD	NUMBER OF REPETITION IN SET	NUMBER OF SETS	REST BETWEEN SETS	NUMBER OF SERIES	REST BETWEEN SERIES
I	70-80%	5-6	2-3	4-6 minutes	2-3	6-8 minutes
II	- 80% - 90% - 93-95%	10 5 2	3	4-5 minutes	2-3	6-8 minutes
III	- 70% - 80% - 85% - 90%	12 10 7 5	4	5-6 minutes	2	10 minutes

Examples of using resistance exercises in combined regime

EXAMPLE	EXERCISE	NUMBER OF REPETITION IN SET	NUMBER OF SETS	REST BETWEEN SETS	NUMBER OF SERIES	REST BETWEEN SERIES
I	The weight of overload is 75-80% of the maximal. At the beginning, slow movement in the yielding regime is executed. The lowest position is maintained for 2-3 seconds and then the overcoming movement is executed with the greatest possible speed.	2-3	2-3	4-5 minutes	2	6-8 minutes
II	The weight of overload is 60-80% of the maximal. At the beginning, there is a gradual 2-3 seconds of isometric tension build-up within the limits of 40-60% of the weight being used. After the hold, there is fast movement in overcoming regime.	4-6	2 - 4	4-6 minutes	1	

VARIANT 2

This variant of the Repeat-Serial method produces a considerable increase in muscle mass: it allows the intensification of body's metabolic processes. This variant implies an intense regime of muscle work based primarily on the glycolytic mechanism of energy production. When this mechanism is strongly involved, proteins break down is very strong: the greater the quantity of protein broken down - the stronger is their synthesis during the subsequent rest period. Their synthesis begins at rest: it develops very slowly and proceeds for about 48 to 72 hours after the heavy work. The main features of this variant of the repeat-serial method are the following:

- muscle relaxation is not required between the repetitions in one set;
- the resistance is not the greatest, but it is sufficient for the stimulation of significant muscle tension;
- the work is executed until fatigue;
- the work involves one group of muscles for 2-3 sets. In one training session 2-3 muscle groups are involved;
- the load on the muscle groups is alternated from session to session so that muscle group receives at least 72 hours of rest.

Examples of the 2nd variant

EXERCISES	WEIGHT OF OVERLOAD	NUMBER OF REPETITION IN SET	NUMBER OF SETS	REST BETWEEN SETS
I	85-90%	Until fatigue and then two additional movements are done with the help of a partner	2	Arbitrary
II	80%	8-10	3-5	2 minutes (can be increased until 5 minutes)
III	70-80%	10-12	2-3	2 minutes
IV	60-70%	15-20	3-5	5-6 minutes
V[58]	50-65%	The same number of repetitions is executed in each set but with less resistance in each subsequent set.	4-5	1-2 minutes

The optimal dosage of exercises is determined upon the number of muscle groups involved in the work. For example when doing the barbell squat, the dosage of sets number should be less and the rest between them longer than in local exercise, as for example, when doing the bench press.

In order to increase the training effect of the exercise performed according to this method, it is necessary to follow these rules:

- increasing only one variable of the training load-weight or the number of repetitions;
- increasing the number of reps and sets before increasing the weight;
- reducing the number of repetitions in accordance with increases in resistance or number of sets;
- reducing the rest pause between sets by small amounts.

This variant of the Repeat-Serial method is mainly used for promoting the development of Maximal Strength in slow movement conditions. However, it has little effectiveness in developing the Explosive Strength and the High Speed Strength. For this reason, its best use is at the beginning of a yearly cycle,

---

[58] This exercise is useful for targeting the small muscle groups which fatigue quickly when the rest pauses between sets are reduced.

with low volume. In this period, in order to maintain the level of Explosive Strength, the following jump exercise with overload can be used:

EXERCISE	JUMPS IN ONE SET	SETS	REST INTERVAL BETWEEN SETS	SERIES	REST INTERVAL BETWEEN SERIES
Consecutive Kettlebell Squat Jumps (weight of 24-36 kg) executed with sub-maximal effort.	8-10	2	2 minutes	2-3	3-5 minutes

VARIANT 3
This variant foresees the application of the Strength-Aerobic method.

FIRST EXERCISE	REST BETWEEN EXERCISES	SECOND EXERCISE	NUMBER OF COMPLEX REPS	REST BETWEEN COMPLEX REPS
Resistance exercise with a weight of 80-90% 3 sets of 3 repetitions Rest between sets 2-4 minutes	3-4 minutes	Resistance exercise for the same muscular group with a weight of 40-50% 4 sets of 15 repetitions Rest between sets 2-4 minutes	2-3	2-4 minutes

6.2.2. ISOMETRIC EXERCISES

In the execution of isometric exercises the muscle tension is increased smoothly to the maximum and maintained for 6-8 seconds. In the 2-3 sets that are done, each set involves 3-5 tensions with the rest between each not less than 1 minute. The rest pause between sets is 4-6 minutes and between each of the 2 series the rest is 6-8 minutes.

6.3. MEANS AND METHODS FOR IMPROVING EXPLOSIVE STRENGTH AND REACTIVE ABILITY

For improving Explosive Strength and Reactive Ability, it is usually used a SST means system set up by the following exercises:
1) Exercises with weights;
2) Isometric exercises;
3) Jump exercises;
4) Combination of the above exercises according to the Stimulation Method.

6.3.1. EXERCISES WITH WEIGHTS

The exercises with weight are executed in the following way: the athlete concentrates the effort at the beginning of the movement, after each repetition, the weight is put back on the support pillars with subsequent compulsory relaxation of the muscles.

Two variants of the Repeat Serial method are usually used:

Variants	Exercise	Number of Repetition in Set	Number of Sets in Series	Rest Between Sets	Series	Rest Between Series
I	The load is in the range of 60-80%. The greater the external resistances which must be overcome in competition, the greater the weight that must be used in training. The rate of executing the repetitions is not high.	5-6	2-4	4-6 minutes	2-4	6-8 minutes
II	The weight is 60-80%. At the beginning, the weight is lowered slowly (at approximately 1/3 of the working amplitude of movement). After which, the weight is quickly lowered over the remainder of the working amplitude and then moved in the opposite direction (with an instant switching from the yielding to the overcoming regime).	5-6	2-3	4-6 minutes	2-3	8-10 minutes

6.3.2. ISOMETRIC EXERCISES

Isometric exercises are executed with the joint angles corresponding to that of key movement, when the maximal force effort is reached.

The isometric exercises are executed with fast development of muscle tension up to 60-80% of the maximal. In one set there are 5-6 explosive efforts with an arbitrary rest pause. 2-4 sets are carried out, the rest between sets is 4-6 minutes. Relaxation of the muscles is necessary before during the rest intervals. Between sets, muscle lengthening and relaxation exercises are executed.

6.3.3. JUMP EXERCISES

Jump exercises, aimed at improving Explosive Strength and Reactive Ability, are usually recognized as training means for increasing the so-called explosive 'jump force'; they are:
1) Jumps with overload;
2) Single take-off jumps;
3) Bounces;
4) Depth Jumps (only for high level athletes).

The **jumps with overload** are carried out in the following two variants:

Variants	Exercise	Number of Repetition in Set	Number of Sets in Series	Rest Between Sets	Series	Rest Between Series
I	Vertical jumps with barbell. The weight of the bar is selected according to the athlete's abilities within the limits of 30-60%.	4-6	2-3	4-6 minutes	2-3	8-10 minutes
II	Consecutive Kettlebell Squat Jumps (weight -16, 24, or 32 kg, selected individually).	5-8	2-3	6-8 minutes	2-3	10-12 minutes

The **single take-off jumps** are jumps onto a box, vertical jump and long jumps. These jump exercises should be executed with maximal effort. In the double leg jumps onto a box, the height of the box should be maximal; an important element of this exercise is the active leg flexion during the flight phase.

The **bounces** foresee 3-8 take offs on one or both legs:
- three-fold bounces on one leg, from leg to leg, or on both legs;
- quintuple bounces on one leg or from leg to leg;
- eight-fold bounces from leg to leg or alternating two take- offs one after the other, by one leg and then by the other.

The single take-off jump and multiple take-offs jump are carried out according to the Repeat-Serial Method.

Exercise	Number of take offs in exercise	Number of exercises in set	Rest between exercises	Number of sets	Rest between sets	Series	Rest between series
Single take-off jumps	1	8-10	arbitrary	2-3	2-3 minutes	2-4	4-6 minutes
Multiple take-offs jump	3-8	3-4	arbitrary	2-3	4-6 minutes	2-3	6-8 minutes

The **Depth Jumps** are executed according the rules illustrated in the § 3.3.4. The height of the depth jump must not overcome 0.7 to 0.8 meters. Any further increase in height of the depth jump changes the dynamic characteristics of the push-off considerably. It is also necessary to vary the take-off after the drop down (Fig. 6.2).
The optimum dosage of Depth Jumps is 4

Fig. 6.2 - Variants of the take-off after the drop jump (depth jump).

sets of 10 jumps, for high level athletes, and 2-3 sets of 6-8 jumps for less prepared athletes. The rest between sets is filled with easy running and relaxation exercises for 6-8 minutes.
The depth jumps should be executed in a limited period of time 1-2 times per week, for high level athletes, 3 times a week.

6.3.4. STIMULATION METHOD

The Stimulation Method can be used only by athletes having an advanced level of speed-strength preparedness. In the following table are illustrated seven variants of this method. Only one of these variants can be used in a training session.
These variants have different training potentials: the training potential increases from variant I to variant IV.
The variants from IV to VII have a very high training potential: they can be used only by high level athletes; they must be introduced in the training process, gradually from the IV to the VII variant.

Variants	First Exercise	Dosage of 1st Exercise	Rest Between Exercises	Second Exercise	Dosage of 2nd Exercise	Dosage of Series
I	Barbell Squat Weight = 90% In one set are 2-3 repetitions executed slowly	2 sets with about 3-4 minutes rest.	4 - 6 minutes	Barbell Squat Weight = 30% In one set are 6-8 repetitions executed with maximal explosive effort in overcoming regime and slowly in yielding regime	3 sets with 3-4 minutes rest.	2-3 series with 8-10 min. rest.
II	Isometric exercises for local muscle group. Increase gradually isometric tension to the maximum and hold for 6 seconds	2-3 repetitions with 2-3 minutes rest	3 - 4 minutes	Explosive isometric exercise for the same muscle group. Execute 5-6 maximal dynamic explosive efforts until the 80% of maximal isometric tension.	5 - 6 repetitions with 2-3 minutes rest.	2 sets with 8-10 min. rest for one muscle group. 2-3 muscle groups can be trained in one training session
III	Isometric exercise for great muscle group Increase gradually isometric tension to the maximum and hold for 6 seconds in the position in which maximum effort is displayed in competition exercises.	2-3 repetitions with 2 minutes rest	3 - 4 minutes	Dynamic resistance exercise for the same muscle group Weight = 40 - 60% of 4-6 repetitions executed with maximal explosive effort in overcoming regime and slowly in yielding regime Rest between sets 3-4 min	2 sets with 3-4 minutes rest.	2 series with 4-6 minutes rest.
IV	Kettlebell Squat Jumps Weight = 6-24 Kg 6-8 subsequent jumps in one set	2 sets with 3-4 min rest	About 5 minutes	8 take off leg to leg bounce	5-6 bounces with 3-4 min rest	2 series with 4-6 minutes rest.
V	Barbell Squat Weight = 70-80% In one set are 5-6 repetitions executed slowly	2 sets with 3-4 minutes rest.	4 - 6 minutes	Standing Triple Jump In one set are 6-8 jumps executed with maximal effort	2-3 sets with 6-8 minutes rest	1 series
VI	Barbell Squat Weight = 80-85% In one set are 2-3 repetitions executed slowly	2 sets with 3-4 minutes rest.	3 - 5 minutes	Kettlebell Squat Jumps Weight = 16-24-32 Kg In one set are 4-6 jumps	2-3 sets with 3-4 min rest	2 series with 6-8 minutes rest.
VII	Barbell Squat Weight = 90-95% In one set are 2 repetitions	2 sets with 2-4 min rest	4-6 minutes	Depth Jump H = 0.75 m. In one set are 6-8 jumps	2 sets with 4-6 min rest	2 series with 8 - 10 minutes rest.

6.4. MEANS AND METHODS FOR INCREASING HIGH-SPEED STRENGTH

For increasing the High Speed Strength, it is usually used a SST means system set up by the following exercises:
1) Exercises with weights;
2) Jump exercises;
3) Running exercises.

The main features of the SST means and methods aimed at increasing the high-speed strength are the following:
- Specific coordinated structure of movements; the starting position corresponds to the position in which the maximal force effort is applied in the competition exercise.
- Relaxation of the muscles before and immediately after sets and in between repetitions of movements wherever possible.

The temporal organization of these exercises in the SST program must ensure their execution in a non-fatigue status.

6.4.1. EXERCISES WITH WEIGHTS

The exercises with weights are carried out according to Repeat-Serial, Stimulation and Contrast methods.

6.4.1.1. REPEAT-SERIAL METHOD

VARIANTS	EXERCISE	NUMBER OF REPETITION IN SET	NUMBER OF SETS IN SERIES	REST BETWEEN SETS	SERIES	REST BETWEEN SERIES
I	The amount of resistance is selected in the range between 50-70% in relation to the size of the external resistance which must be overcome in competition conditions. The exercise is executed at maximum speed but at a low rate (the fast movement in overcoming phase and the slowly movement in yielding phase).	6-8	2-4	3-4 minutes	2-3	6-8 minutes
II	Resistance exercise in static-dynamic regime. The weight of overload is 30%. At the beginning, there is a gradual 2-4 seconds of isometric tension build-up (the push up against limiting device) within the limits of 60-80% of the maximal isometric tension. After, there is fast movement in the overcoming regime.	4-6	2-4	Arbitrary	2-4	6-8 minutes
III	A weight of 60-65% of the maximum is used. The exercise is performed with short concentrated explosive efforts to only move the weight but not accelerate it through the maximum range possible. The regime and dosage of work is the same as in the previous variant.	4-6	2-4	Arbitrary	2-4	6-8 minutes

In all the variants of this method, the relaxation of muscles between each set is required. Between the series, active rest must be performed using swinging movements with a wide range of motion.

6.4.1.2. STIMULATION METHOD

VARIANTS	1ST EXERCISE: MAXIMAL STRENGTH	DOSAGE OF 1ST EXERCISE	REST BETWEEN EXERCISES	SECOND EXERCISE: EXPLOSIVE STRENGTH	DOSAGE OF 2ND EXERCISE	DOSAGE OF SERIES
I	Weight = 90-95% In one set are 2-3 repetitions executed slowly	2 sets with about 3-4 minutes rest.	4-6 minutes	RESISTANCE EXERCISE IN EXPLOSIVE REGIME. The weight is selected in the range between 50-70% of the maximum in relation to the size of the external resistance which must be overcome in competition conditions. In one set are 6-8 repetitions executed with maximal explosive effort in overcoming regime and slowly in yielding regime. The rate of movements is middle.	2 sets with 3-4 minutes rest.	2 series with 8-10 minutes rest.
II	Weight = 90-95% In one set are 2-3 repetitions executed slowly	2 sets with about 3-4 minutes rest	4-6 minutes	RESISTANCE EXERCISE IN STATIC-DYNAMIC REGIME. The weight of overload is 30%. At the beginning, there is a gradual 2-4 seconds of isometric tension within the limits of 60-80% of the maximal isometric tension. After, there is fast movement in the overcoming regime. In one set there are 4-6 reps with arbitrary rests.	2-4 sets with the rest intervals of 3-4 minutes.	2 series with 6-8 minutes rest.

6.4.1.3. CONTRAST METHOD

In this method, the key-movement of competition exercise is executed with maximal speed using:
- the optimum weight, it allows to imitate the muscle work regime of key-movement;
- the heavy weight, it allows to activate strength components of the force effort in key-movement;
- the facilitated weight, it allows to activate speed components of the force effort in key-movement.
In each set, the key-movement is repeated with middle-low rate: it is carried out as fast as possible only in overcoming phase. Relaxation of muscles between repetitions is obligatory.
The contrast method foresees the following variants:

VARIANTS	1ST SET	2ND SET	3RD SET	4TH SET	REST BETWEEN SETS	NUMBER OF SETS IN SERIES	REST BETWEEN SERIES
I	Heavy weight, 3-4 reps	Optimum weight, 5-7 reps	Facilitated weight, 3-4 reps	Optimum weight, 5-7 reps	2-4 minutes	2-3	8-10 minutes
II	Facilitated weight, 3-4 reps	Optimum weight, 5-7 reps	-	-	2-4 minutes	3-4	8-10 minutes
III	Optimum weight, 5-7 reps	Heavy weight, 3-4 reps	Optimum weight, 5-7 reps	-	2-4 minutes	2-3	8-10 minutes
IV	Facilitated weight, 3-4 reps	Optimum weight, 5-7 reps	Heavy weight, 3-4 reps	Optimum weight, 5-7 reps	2-4 minutes	2-3	8-10 minutes

| V | Heavy weight, 3-4 reps | Optimum weight, 5-7 reps | - | - | 2-4 minutes | 3-4 | 8-10 minutes |

6.4.2. JUMP EXERCISES

The jump exercises used for increasing the High-Speed Strength are:
1) Bounces.
2) Consecutive Jumps over T&F hurdles (see § 3.2.2.1).
Unlike the jump exercises used to increase Explosive Strength, these jump exercises should be executed without a display of great power: the emphasis should be on fast take-offs. To solve this task, the exercise must be executed with maximal speed (the time of its execution is registered by the coach), but without losing the lightness of movements.

EXERCISE	NUMBER OF REPETITIONS IN SET	REST BETWEEN REPETITIONS	SETS	REST BETWEEN SETS	SERIES	REST BETWEEN SERIES
Ten-fold jump from leg to leg or two jumps on the right and two jumps on the left leg	4-6	4-6 minutes	2-3	8-10 minutes	-	-
Eight-fold bounces from leg to leg or alternating two take-offs one after the other, by one leg and then by the other	3-4	arbitrary	2-3	4-6 minutes	2-3	6-8 minutes

6.5. SST PROGRAM FOR INCREASING MAXIMAL STRENGTH: 'PEAKING PLAN' OR 'RUSSIAN PYRAMID'

The Russian Pyramid is a 6 week routine designed for Olympic weightlifters for increasing the Maximal Strength (the weight of 1RM) in one of the specific Weightlifting exercises: Snatches, Cleans, Jerks, Cleans & Jerks, Squats (or Leg Presses), Dead-lifts and Bench Presses. The Maximal Strength increasing must be obtained ('peaked') in only one specific exercise. This program can be successfully used by power lifters to improve the sport results in one of three events: Squat, Bench Press or Deadlift.

In other sports, for example, in T&F throwing, Rugby and American Football, this program could be used to enforce the main muscle synergies involved in competition exercise.

Each primary strength building movement will be trained twice each week. **Workout 1** is the medium intensity day while **Workout 2** is the heavy day. Stagger the weakly training cycle when peaking more than one lift. Perform a different movement on each day, with no more than 2 strength building movements applied for any given session. Four to six days each week should be spent in the weight room.

	WORKOUT #1	WORKOUT #2
Week 1	70%	80%
Week 2	75%	85%
Week 3	80%	90%
Week 4	85%	95%
Week 5	75%	85%
Week 6	80%	100%+ (MAX OUT)

	Workout #1	Workout #2
Week 1		
Set 1	45% x 8-10	45% x 8-10
Set 2	55% x 6-8	55% x 6-8
Set 3	65% x 6	65% x 5
Set 4	65-70% x 6	75% x 5
Set 5	65-70% x 6	80% x 5
Set 6	65-70% x 6	80% x 5
Set 7		80% x 5
Set 8		75% x 5
Set 9		65% x 6-8
Set 10		50-55% x 8-12
Week 2		
Set 1	45% x 8-10	45% x 8-10
Set 2	55% x 6-8	55% x 6-8
Set 3	65% x 6	65% x 5
Set 4	70% x 5	75% x 4
Set 5	70-75% x 5	80% x 4
Set 6	70-75% x 5	85% x 4
Set 7		85% x 4
Set 8		85% x 4
Set 9		80% x 5
Set 10		70% x 6-8
Week 3		
Set 1	45% x 8-10	45% x 8-10
Set 2	55% x 6-8	55% x 6-8
Set 3	65% x 5	65% x 5
Set 4	70% x 4	75% x 4
Set 5	75% x 3	85% x 3
Set 6	75-80% x 3	90% x 3
Set 7	75-85% x 3	90% x 3
Set 8		80% x 5
Set 9		55-60% x 6-10

	Workout #1	Workout #2
Week 4		
Set 1	45% x 8-10	45% x 8-10
Set 2	55% x 6-8	55% x 6-8
Set 3	65% x 5	65% x 5
Set 4	75% x 4	75% x 4
Set 5	80-85% x 3	85% x 2
Set 6	80-85% x 3	90% x 2
Set 7		95% x 2
Set 8		75% x 4-6
Week 5		
Set 1	45% x 8-10	45% x 8-10
Set 2	55% x 6-8	55% x 6-8
Set 3	65% x 5	65% x 5
Set 4	75% x 5	75% x 3
Set 5	75% x 5	80% x 3
Set 6		85% x 2
Peak Week 6		
Set 1	45% x 8-10	45% x 8-10
Set 2	55% x 6-8	55% x 6-8
Set 3	65% x 5	65% x 5
Set 4	75% x 3	75% x 3
Set 5	80% x 2	85% x 2
Set 6	80% x 2	90% x 1
Set 7		95% x 1
Set 8		100% x 1
Set 9		102% x 1 Personal Best
Set 10		105% x 1

Percentages are used in order to make it more accurate and applicable to every athlete. They are also very easy to calculate, using the following daily top percentages of the Russian Pyramid.

Percentages are formulated from the athlete's maximum or 100% attempts. Do not over estimate when determining weights. In fact, it is better to underestimate them for the first few cycles.

Weightlifters should schedule their 6 week Peaking Plan for the beginning of preparation period; however, 2-3 cycles before competing under this system are recommended.

For out-of-season strength development, lengthen the cycle (up to 8-10 weeks). Instead of training all primary strength building movements in one week, begin peaking one lift on Week 1, and then start other movements on the following weeks. Increasing cycle duration is acceptable, unless training specifically for a competition.

The prime strength building movements should be placed at the beginning of each workout. Secondary exercises (assistance movements) should follow. Inter-set rests, of at least, 4-6 minutes, must be taken. Shake and massage muscles during these rest periods to restore the tissues and nerves and remove lactic acid.

Workout time should last no more than 90 minutes. The body develops best with 90 minute training periods, no more. If other tasks need to be completed, additional sessions are conducted each day.

Each individual workout has a progressive **Set/Rep scheme**. This system is referred to as '**Pyramiding**'. Resistance in the first Set of every workout can be handled easily. 100% weight cannot be trained consistently. Strength needs a strong foundation. The stronger the foundation is, the higher the PEAK. By looking at the structure of the Pyramid, it can be seen that more space lies toward its base (foundation); the summit is the PEAK which is not very big at all. If an athlete ignores lower intensity training he will eventually lose his base and never reach his PEAK.

WHAT TO EXPECT

For the first 2-3 weeks, it may seem a waste of time. Admittedly, most percentages are very light in beginning workouts. It is necessary to be patient; the intensity will begin to mount up and it has been demonstrated that all those who use this program always come out ahead. It is important to understand that it is the entire 6 week cycle that is designed to increase strength, not just one particular workout. Since training is a science that needs constant monitoring, it is necessary to work at structuring percentages and lifts especially when forcing the body to produce larger gains in strength.

WHAT FOLLOWS

This program is not based on year-round morphological rebuilding. The body and mind must rest between cycles to restore from the previous programs and prepare for future plans.

Resign maximal efforts for two weeks after every six week cycle. (Longer and more structured post-Peak phases are recommended for those who are over trained at this point, for those who have satisfactorily achieved their long sought after goals, for those who have completed a major competition, or just wish to rest). Once training starts, a pre-Peaking Plan cycle can be applied which includes low-intensity movements along with light-medium low-rep primary strength building movements. After 1-2 weeks on this program, the athlete is ready to repeat the 6 week Peaking Plan all over again! Keep in mind that in order to begin and pursue any Peaking Plan it is necessary to obtain complete restoration of muscular and nervous systems and replenish the adrenals, not to mention the mental power for abundant supplies of motivation, discipline, wisdom and patience. Aspiring athletes, desirous of ultimate power, perhaps in a rut, or just bored with the trial-&-error approach to strength gains, should give Peaking Plan a try. With persistency, patience and a lot of hard work, some surprising gains may be out there.

Weeks 1 to 4 are progressive, while Week 5 drops off slightly. This effectively cycles strength, preparing the lifter for Peak Week 6.

6.6. SST PROGRAMS FOR IMPROVING 'JUMP FORCE'

SST programs for improving 'jump force' can be used by athletes in all sports where it is necessary to jump, to run quickly, to have the ability to quickly accelerate, and to run with sharp changes in direction, etc.

When using these programs it is necessary to take into account the following:

1) The athlete should be well prepared to execute these programs. He should already have executed a finite volume of jump exercises and barbell exercises and must have the correct technique of depth jump.

2) The 'jump force' training should not be considered as an additive to other work: it must be used in special (separate) training sessions, in which it can be combined only with light work involving other muscle groups (for example, imitating technical elements executed by the trunk and arms). It should not be combined with work on perfection of sports technique and speed of movements.

The programs are based on the Complex Method that foresees using the positive interaction of the training effect of various SST means. The programs have different complexities: in the first - only two exercises are used (squat and depth jump), in the second - three exercises (squat, kettlebell squat jump and depth jump), in the third - four exercises (squat, kettlebell squat jump, vertical jump with barbell and depth jump).

Fig. 6.3 - The famous photo illustrating the jumping ability of the legendary Soviet athlete Valery Brumel (silver medal in the 1960 Olympics in Rome) who broke the high jump record five times, from 1961 to 1971.

Notes to the following three programs:

1. The height of drop down for drop jumping is in parentheses.
2. Overload weight mentioned in parentheses is percent of maximal squat (RM).
3. The rest between sets is 4-6 minutes and between series, 8-10 min.

6.6.1. PROGRAM 1: SQUAT + DEPTH JUMP

WEEK	TRAINING SESSION	EXERCISE	REPETITIONS NUMBER	SETS	SERIES
1	1	Depth jump (0.75 m.)	10	3	-
	2	Depth jump (0.75 m.)	10	4	-
2	3	Barbell squat (90-93%)	3	2-3	-
	4	Depth jump (1.10 m.)	10	4	-
3	5	1. Barbell squat (90-93%)	3	2	2
		2. Depth jump (0.75 m.)	10	2	
	6	1. Barbell squat (90-93%)	3	1	2
		2. Depth jump (0.75 m.)	10	1	

WEEK	TRAINING SESSION	EXERCISE	REPETITIONS NUMBER	SETS	SERIES
4	7	1. Barbell squat (90-93%)	3	1-2	2
		2. Depth jump (0.75 m.)	10	2	
	8	1. Barbell squat (93-95%)	3	1	3-4
		2. Depth jump (1.10 m.)	10	1	
5	9	1. Barbell squat (93-95%)	3	1	4
		2. Depth jump (1.10 m.)	10	1	
	10	1. Barbell squat (93-95%)	3	1	2
		2. Depth jump (1.10 m.)	10	2	
6	11	Depth jump (1.10 m.)	10	4	-
	12	Depth jump (1.10 m.)	10	4	-

6.6.2. PROGRAM 2: SQUAT, KETTLEBELL SQUAT JUMP, DEPTH JUMP

WEEK	TRAINING SESSION	EXERCISE	REPETITIONS NUMBER	SETS	SERIES
1	1	Depth jump (0.75 m)	10	3	-
	2	1. Depth jump (0.75 m)	10	2	1
		2. Depth jump (1.10 m)	10	2	
2	3	Kettlebell Squat jumps (24 kg)	10	4	-
	4	1. Barbell squat (90-93%)	3	2-3	1
		2. Depth jump (0.75 m)	10	3	
3	5	Depth jump (1.10 m)	10	4	-
	6	1. Barbell squat (90-93%)	3	2	3
		2. Depth jump (1.10 m)	10	1	
4	7	1. Barbell squat (90-93%)	3	2	2
		2. Kettlebell Squat jumps (24 kg)	10	2	
	8	Depth jump (1.10 m)	10	4	-
5	9	1. Barbell squat (93-95%)	3	1	2-3
		2. Kettlebell Squat jumps (24 kg)	10	1	
	10	Depth jump (1.10 m)	10	4	-
6	11	1. Barbell squat (93-95%)	3	2	2
		2. Kettlebell Squat jumps (32 kg)	10	2	
	12	1. Kettlebell Squat jumps (32 kg)	10	1	1
		2. Depth jump (0.75 m)	10	1	

6.6.3. PROGRAM 3: SQUAT, KETTLEBELL SQUAT JUMP, VERTICAL JUMP WITH BAR-BELL, DEPTH JUMP

This program is based on the principle of the strength load concentration at the beginning of training stage (Block Training System) that provides a great intensive influence on the body and causes a temporally decrease in the ability to display explosive efforts. After completion of the program, the ability to display explosive effort not only returns to the initial level but considerably exceeds this level.

WEEK	TRAINING SESSION	EXERCISE	REPETITIONS NUMBER	SETS	SERIES
1	1	1. Barbell squat (90-93%)	3	2	1
		2. Vertical jumps with bar (30-40%)	8-10	2	
	2	Depth jump (0.75 m)	10	4	-
	3	Depth jump (1.10 m)	10	4	-
2	4	1. Barbell squat (93-95%)	2-3	1	2
		2. Kettlebell Squat jumps (24 kg)	10	1	
		3. Depth jump (0.75 m)	10	2	
	5	1. Kettlebell Squat jumps (32 kg)	10	2	2
		2. Depth jump (0.75 m)	10	2	
	6	Depth jump (1.10 m)	10	4	-
3	7	1. Barbell squat (93-95%)	2-3	2	2
		2. Kettlebell Squat jumps (32 kg)	10	2	
	8	1. Barbell squat (93-95%)	2-3	2	2
		2. Kettlebell Squat jumps with (24 kg)	10	2	
		3. Depth jump (0.75 m.)	10	2	
	9	Depth jump (1.10 m)	10	4	-
4	10	1. Barbell squat (93-95%)	2-3	1	3
		2. Vertical jumps with bar (30-40%)	10	2	
	11	1. Kettlebell Squat jumps (32 kg)	10	2	2
		2. Depth jump (0.75 m)	10	2	
	12	Depth jump (1.10 m)	10	4	-
5	13	1. Barbell squat (93-95%)	2-3	1	3
		2. Vertical jumps with bar (30-40%)	10	2	
	14	1. Vertical jumps with bar (30-40%)	10	2	2
		2. Kettlebell Squat jumps (24 kg)	10	2	
	15	1. Depth jump (0.75 m)	10	2	1
		2. Depth jump (1.10 m)	10	2	

SST IN CYCLIC SPORT

7.1. INTRODUCTION

The cyclic sports are characterized by the *locomotion*[59]. Human locomotion is a cyclic progressive self-powered motion by which the athlete changes his entire body location repetitively executing the specific body propelling movement.

In cyclic sports, the main task of training is increasing maximal average speed of locomotion over the competition distance. The speed of cyclic locomotion is the result of ratio between the stride length, the distance overcome in one locomotion cycle, and the rate of cycle repetitions. Increasing the sport results is determined mainly by increasing the strides length and by improving the capacity to maintain the optimal straights length over the competition distance. The stride length is determined by the working effect of the body propelling movement and depends mostly upon the athlete's strength capabilities. The capacity to maintain optimal stride length during the execution of cyclic exercise was traditionally related to the endurance.

Cyclic sports are usually referred to as sports of endurance, with the exception of track and field sprint, which is definite as speed-strength cyclic sport. About endurance, N.A.Bernstein wrote:

"…It is based on the cooperation of all the subsystems and organs of the body. It requires a high level of co-operation of metabolism between the working organs, transport systems (the circularity system, which delivers suppliers and eliminates wastes), organ providers (respiration and digestion), and all the organs of higher command and control (the central nervous system). In fact, a hardy body should satisfy three conditions of endurance: It should have ample supplies of energy to spend when necessary. It should be able, at a proper time, to generously offer these supplies without skimping on a single unite of energy. Finally, it should be able to spend the resources with a tight, sensible frugality so then they last for the maximal amount of useful work. Briefly, to possess endurance is to have much, to spend generously, and to pay miserly. Obviously, this capacity characterizes the complex organization of the body as a whole."[60]

The sport results in cyclic sports are determined by the utmost (maximal average) power output of the work in specific regime of a given duration. The possibility to execute the muscular work for a required duration (distance length) is ensured by three energy supplying mechanism: aerobic, anaerobic lactatic and anaerobic "alactatic" or CP-mechanism. In relation to the length of competition distance, each of these mechanisms may play dominant or secondary role in ensuring the highest level of power output:

- In cyclic work of 15-30 seconds, the utmost power output is mainly ensured by the CP-mechanism, with partial involvement of anaerobic glycolysis. Longer is the competition distance (the length of work), higher is the anaerobic glycolysis involvement in obtaining the utmost power

---

[59] Locomotion "…may be defined as the action by which the body as whole moves through aerial, aquatic, or terrestrial space". Medved V. Measurement of human locomotions. CRC Press LLC, 2001

[60] N. A. Bernstein "On Dexterity and Its Development" (Translated by Mark L. Latash). In the book: "Dexterity and Its Development. Edited by Mark L. Latash and Michael T. Turvey. Lawrence Erlbaum Associates Publishers, 1996 Mahwah, New Jersey

output.

- In cyclic work of 30-60 seconds, the utmost power output is mainly ensured by glycolytic mechanism.
- In cyclic work overcoming 1 minute, the utmost power output is mainly ensured by aerobic mechanism. The anaerobic energy supplying mechanism is involved only when the work intensity overcomes the level of athlete's anaerobic threshold.
- In prolonged cyclic exercise, in which energy supplying is based mostly upon the aerobic mechanism, the so named oxygen transporting systems (respiratory and cardiovascular) play an important role. The power output of such exercise is determined not only by the capacity to consume a greatest quantity of oxygen (VO2max), but also by the muscles capacity of drawing a higher percentage of oxygen out of arterial blood and of oxidizing lactate.

Each of the three energy supplying mechanisms may be characterized by the following parameters of energy production capability:

- *Capacity*, the total quantity of producing energy;
- *Power*, the quantity of energy produced in the time unit;
- *Effectiveness*, the percentage of energy that can be utilized.

The level of energy supplying systems involvement depends on the motor structure of cyclic locomotion:

1) the magnitude of force effort and the volume of muscles (number of muscle group) involved - higher is the volume of muscles involved, higher is the involvement of energy supplying system:
    - in running, cycling and skating - the leg muscles are mostly loaded;
    - in canoeing, the upper body muscles;
    - in swimming and rowing, both legs and upper body muscles.
2) the regime of muscular contractions - different regimes of muscular contractions need different level of energy supplying:
    - in rowing and swimming - the legs and upper body muscles work in dynamic regime;
    - in skating and cycling - the legs muscles work in dynamic regime and the upper body muscles in static regime ensuring the stable body position;
    - in skiing - the upper body muscles (the trunk muscles) work both in static and dynamic regime.
3) the dynamic characteristic of force effort in body propelling movement:
    - in running, it has dynamic (explosive and ballistic) character;
    - in cycling, it has dynamic but not explosive character;
    - in skating and rowing, it has combined explosive and not explosive character. In rowing, the explosive effort is applied at the beginning of body propelling movement, while, in staking, it is applied at the end.

These differences imply different ways to economize the energy supplying during the competition exercise:

- in swimming and skiing, by optimizing inertial force;
- in cycling and running, by optimizing biomechanical characteristics of movements, which allows the non-metabolic energy recovery;
- in rowing, by using both these factors.

Traditionally, endurance was interpreted as the ability of athlete to exert himself for a long period of time or to the disposition in tolerating fatigue. Fatigue is associated with the accumulation of lactate in working skeletal muscles and the development of the so called muscle "acidosis": the increase in hydrogen ions and subsequent acidity of muscles. Thus, the main principle of endurance training was to improve the athlete's capacity to work in conditions of muscles "acidosis". As consequence, the training means, aimed at improving the endurance, have to saturate the muscles in lactic acid in order to educate the body's buffering mechanism (alkaline) to deal with it more effectively.

Since the body buffering system has limits, the sport physiologists tried to find ways for increasing artificially the body's buffering mechanism by the athlete's administering the alkaline products. However, this solution did not bring to astonishing results.

So, another training principle was proposed for improving endurance: improving the capacity in avoiding the factors which provoke fatigue instead of improving the capacity in tolerating it. This training principle was named "anti-glycolytic": it consists in the "minimization" of the glycolytic mechanism involvement in the energy supplying of competition exercise.

In the short distance endurance sport disciplines, it may be obtained by increasing the athlete's level of Maximal Anaerobic Power.

In the long distance endurance sport disciplines, it may be obtained by increasing the speed of a given locomotion (power output of specific work) at the level of anaerobic threshold; which is related to the improvement of the Local Muscular Endurance. Both these task can be solved by using appropriate SST means and methods.

The main tasks of SST in cyclic sport are:
-   increasing the working effect of the specific body propelling movement;
-   ensuring muscle's adaptation to the specific regime of executing specific locomotion (increasing the Maximal Anaerobic Power and Local Muscular Endurance).

In relation to the specific character of body propelling movement, the increase in working effect can be ensured by increasing the Maximal Strength (see § 7.2) or increasing the Explosive and High-Speed strength (see § 7.3).

The increase in Maximal Anaerobic Power (see § 7.4), can be ensured using the jumps exercises (see § 7.4.1) and executing specific locomotion in more difficult conditions (see § 7.4.2).

To improve the Local Muscular Endurance (see § 7.5), two different approaches are illustrated in the following paragraphs:
-   the first is aimed at enforcing the CP-shuttle mechanism[61] (see § 7.5.1.1). Examples of this approach are illustrated in the SST Program for rowers (see § 7.8) and in the SST Program for middle distance runners (see § 7.7).
-   the second is aimed at increasing the contractile capacity of slow twitch fibers by using static-dynamic exercises (see § 7.5.1.2).

Increasing the maximal power output in the short term cyclic motor action is related to the improvement of athlete's capacity in achieving rapidly the maximal speed at the starting acceleration. The high speed in short running and the capacity to increase it rapidly are the main factors for increasing the sport results in track & field sprint and also in sport games in which the short-distance sprinting is an important element of the competition activity: as in track & field jumps (high jump, long and triple jump), javelin throws and bobsled. The starting acceleration speed is recognized as a particular motor ability, determined by the maximal explosive force effort of the take-off movements and by the Maximal Anaerobic Power. These abilities can be improved using:
-   SST means aimed at increasing the High Speed Strength and at improving the Reactive Ability, described in § 6.3;
-   SST means aimed at increasing Maximal Anaerobic Power, described in § 7.4.

---

[61] Creatine phosphate shuttle facilitates transport of high energy phosphate from mitochondria to myofibril. (see Bessman, S.P, and Geiger. P.J. Transport of energy in muscle: the phosphorylcreatine shuttle. Science, 211, 448-452, 1981).

SST means used in track and field spring running, illustrated in this Chapter, should be used in combination with specific running exercises (see § 7.3.4). The SST program aimed at improving the starting acceleration shows how these SST means can be temporally organized (see § 7.6).

7.2. MEANS AND METHODS FOR INCREASING MAXIMAL STRENGTH

7.2.1. EXERCISES WITH WEIGHTS

Maximal Strength improvement is needed in every cyclic sports but its particularly important in those in which a great external resistance must be overcome in the main body propelling movement (Rowing, Cycling and Skating). The athletes of these sport disciplines must have a level of Maximal Strength 20-40% higher than the level of force effort employed in the specific body propelling movement.

In these sports, the Maximal Strength is an important component of athlete's capacity to express the highest level of the utmost power output during the repetitions of force effort.

For this reason, the strength training should be finalized at solving two tasks:
1) increasing Maximal Strength,
2) improving ability to repeatedly display significant strength effort.

The training methods related to the first and second aims should not be used in the same training session. It is necessary to alternate these methods in different sessions or in a week. At the beginning of preparation period, the proportion between these methods should be 1:3, and then the proportion should be gradually changed until 3:1.

For increasing the level of Maximal Strength, the cyclic sport athletes may use the same resistance training methods as in the speed-strength sports (Maximal Effort Method and Repeat Serial Method - see § 6.2.1).

In certain cyclic sports the use of Barbell Squat may create some problems. For example, in skating, where it is necessary to maintain a bent trunk position for long time during the execution of the competition exercise, the use of barbell squat could provoke:

- a creation of non-specific intra and inter-muscular coordination which hampers maintaining a trunk position without great static effort.
- a great and inadequate load on the spine, already overloaded during the execution of the specific exercise, which may cause injuries.

In such cases, it is advisable to use training devices which allow executing squat without loading the back muscles: barbell plates fastened by a strong cable to a wide belt around the waist (Fig. 7.1).

In the following tables, some examples of using different resistance exercises for increasing the Maximal Strength in various cyclic sports are illustrated.

Fig. 7.1 - Strength exercise for skaters

In Cycling, the following exercises are recommended (B.Vasiliev, S.Minakov, 1982):

VARIANTS	EXERCISE	WEIGHT OF OVERLOAD	NUMBER OF REPETITION IN SET	NUMBER OF SETS IN SERIES
I	Clean (bringing the barbell up from the ground to the shoulders)	95%	1-3	3

II	Barbell squats and half squats	80-85%	5-7	3-5
III	Barbell Squats and Half Squats	90%	1-3	3
IV	Deadlift	80-90%	3-5	5-6
V	Standing barbell calf raises		10-15	3-4
VI	Lying leg press	85-90%	5-6	3-5

In the training of rowers, to duplicate the pull of the bar in a racing scull, a front lying position, face down on a horizontal surface is assumed (Fig. 7.2).

The following variants of these exercises performing are used:

Fig. 7.2 - Strength exercises for rowers

VARIANTS	OVERLOAD WEIGHT	NUMBER OF REPETITION IN SET	NUMBER OF SETS IN SERIES	REST BETWEEN SETS	SERIES	REST BETWEEN SERIES
I	90-95%	2-3	4-6	4-6 minutes	2-3	8-10 minutes
II	85-90%	5-6	4-6	5-6 minutes	2-3	8-10 minutes
III	1) 80% 2) 90% 3) 95%	1) 10 2) 5 3) 3	3	4-6 minutes	2-3	8-10 minutes
IV	75%	10-12	3-4	2 minutes	1	-

For improving ability to repeatedly display significant strength effort, in the specific body propelling movement, the following three variants of Repeat-Serial method are used:

VARIANTS	EXERCISE	NUMBER OF REPETITION IN SET	NUMBER OF SETS IN SERIES	REST BETWEEN SETS	SERIES	REST BETWEEN SERIES
I	The movements are executed at a slow rate with resistance of 70-80%	10-15	3	4-6 minutes	3-4	8-10 minutes
II	1st set: the movements are executed at a slow rate with a resistance of 70-80%	10-15	2	6-8 minutes	2-3	8-10 minutes
	2nd set: the movements are executed at a faster rate with a resistance of 50-60%	15-20				
III	1st set: the movements are executed at a slow rate with a resistance of 70-80%	10-15	3	4-5 minutes	2	8-10 minutes
	2nd set: the movements are executed at a faster rate with a resistance of 60-70%	15-20				
	3rd set: the movements are executed with a resistance of 50-60% at a low rate but with utmost effort to display the greatest amount of effort	10-15				

7.2.2. ISOMETRIC EXERCISES

For increasing the Maximal Strength, a small volume of isometric exercises may be used, executing them in appropriate position: the force should be applied at the beginning of body propelling movement. Isometric tension is developed slowly up to the maximum; it is held for no more than 6 seconds and followed by compulsory relaxation of muscles. 6-8 tensions are carried out in one set, the rest between is arbitrary. In a training session there are 2-3 sets with a rest of 6-8 minutes between sets, during which dynamic stretching and relaxing exercises are used.

7.3. MEANS AND METHODS FOR INCREASING EXPLOSIVE AND HIGH-SPEED STRENGTH

For increasing Explosive and High-Speed strength, exercises with weights, isometric and jump exercises are used. The runners use also specific running exercises.

7.3.1. EXERCISES WITH WEIGHTS

In using exercises with weights, the predominant method is the Repeat-Serial. As with the increasing Maximal Strength, two main methods are used. In the first, the exercises are executed at a moderate rate with emphasis on initial explosive effort. In the other, the exercises are executed with a gradual increase in speed and rate of movement maintaining the initial explosive effort.

The following three variants of Repeat-Serial method are effective using the local exercises, involving small volume of muscle groups (for example, Seated Calf Rise) and the global exercises, involving large volume of muscle groups (for example, Barbell Squat):

VARIANTS	EXERCISE	NUMBER OF REPETITION IN SET	NUMBER OF SETS IN SERIES	REST BETWEEN SETS	SERIES	REST BETWEEN SERIES
I	Local exercise with weight of 50-60% is executed emphasizing the speed of the force development at the beginning of movement. The rate of executing the repetitions is not high.	10-15	3	4-6 minutes	3	8-10 minutes
II	Local exercise with weight of 20-30% is executed emphasizing the speed of the force development at the beginning of movement. The rate of executing the repetitions is not high.	15-20	2	4-5 minutes	2-3	8-10 minutes
III	Global exercise executed with maximal speed. The weight is 50-60%. The time of execution of 1 set is recorded. The key in training is to reduce the time of the set execution and reduce the time difference between the first and fourth sets.	5	4	4-6 minutes	1	-

For skaters, the following variants of Half Squat are used:

EXERCISE	VARIANTS	WEIGHT OF OVERLOAD	RATE OF REPETITIONS	NUMBER OF REPETITION IN SET	NUMBER OF SETS IN SERIES	REST BETWEEN SETS	SERIES	REST BETWEEN SERIES
HALF SQUAT	Half squat with calf rises	50-60%	middle	25-30	2	3-4 minutes	3	8-10 minutes
	Half squat without calf rises	30-40%	high	40 - 50	2-4	6-8 minutes	2-3	10-12 minutes

For rowers, the following variants are used:

VARIANTS	EXERCISE	WEIGHT	RATE OF MOVEMENTS	NUMBER OF REPETITION IN SET	NUMBER OF SETS IN SERIES	REST BETWEEN SETS	SERIES	REST BETWEEN SERIES
I		50-60%	middle	20-30	2-3	4-6 minutes	3-4	8-10 minutes
II		First set: 50-60%	middle	20-25	2-3	2-3 minutes	3-4	6-8 minutes
		Second set: 30-40%	high	30-40	4			
III		50-60%	middle	10-15	2	4-6 minutes	2-3	8-10 minutes

For cyclers, the following variants are used:

VARIANTS	EXERCISE	NUMBER OF REPETITION IN SET	NUMBER OF SETS IN SERIES
I	The series of the Barbell Squats with weight of 40-60 kg: 1st set, full Squat (slowly); 2nd set, half Squat slowly); 3rd set, full squat (slowly); 4th set, half squat (fast).	1st set, 5; 2nd set, 5; 3rd set, 8; 4th set, 5.	4
II	The series of Barbell Squats executed with maximal speed: 1st set, the weight is 40-50 kg; 2nd set, the eight is 60-80 kg; 3rd set, 40-60 kg;	7-10	3
III	Specific resistance exercise, which imitate the starting movement, executed with the weights of: 1st set, 40 kg; 2nd set, 50 kg; 3rd set, 60 kg;	8-10	3

For the athletes of different cycling disciplines, the following variants of using barbell squats were proposed by B.Vasilyev, S.Minakov, in 1982:

VARIANTS	EXERCISE	NUMBER OF REPETITION IN SET	NUMBER OF SETS IN SERIES
I – FOR THE ROAD SPRINTERS	The series of the Barbell Squats with different weights: 1st set, with middle weight (slowly); 2nd set, with high weight (fast); 3rd set, with high weight (slowly).	1st set, 7-10; 2nd set, 25-30; 3rd set, 7-10;	3
II – FOR BIKERS	The series of the Barbell Squats with different weights: 1st set, with middle weight; 2nd set, with high weight; 3rd set, with middle weight(fast); 4th set, with high weight	1st set, 25-30; 2nd set, 10-12; 3rd set, 45-50; 4th set, 30-40	4
III – FOR THE ROAD BICYCLE RACERS AND PURSUIT BIKERS	The series of the Barbell Squats with different weights: 1st set, low weight (fast); 2nd set, with high weight; 3rd set, with middle weight; 4th set, with low weight (fast); 5th set, with high weight; 6th set, middle weight.	1st set, 40-50; 2nd set, 5-7; 3rd set, 30-40; 4th set, 70-100; 5th set, 5-7; 6th set, 40-50	6

7.3.2. ISOMETRIC EXERCISES

Isometric exercises are executed with fast developments of muscle tension until 50-60% of maximal. For example, for swimmers, the isometric tensions of 1-2 seconds duration are recommended, executed 6-8 times with 10-12 seconds rest intervals. The body position should correspond to the initial phase of stroke movement (R.Rasulbekov at all, 1984).

7.3.3. JUMP EXERCISES

The Reactive Ability of leg muscles may be successfully improved using jump exercises: multiple consecutive jumps and bounces.

7.3.3.1. MULTIPLE CONSECUTIVE JUMPS

Multiple consecutive jumps are:
1) Jumps over 8-10 track and field hurdles or boxes, executed at a moderate rate with push-off on both legs.

NUMBER OF REPETITIONS IN SERIES	REST BETWEEN REPETITIONS	SERIES	REST BETWEEN SERIES
3-4	arbitrary	3-4	4-6 minutes

2) Box Jumps with two-legged take-offs executed using different box height. In rowing, box jumps at a height of 25-30 cm are used for men and 20-25 cm for women. The interval-serial and the repeat-serial methods are used in such exercises. For example:

VARIANTS	EXERCISE	NUMBER OF JUMPS IN SET / SET DURATION	NUMBER OF SETS	REST BETWEEN SETS	NUMBER OF SERIES	REST BETWEEN SERIES
I INTERVAL-SERIAL METHOD	Box Jumps are executed at moderate rate. The rate of jumps should be gradually increased until 50 jumps per minute for men and 40 jumps per minute for women and then the rate should be maintained during the series.	40-50	5-6	3-4 minutes at the beginning and then is gradually reduced to 2 minutes	2-3	10-15 minutes
II REPEAT-SERIAL METHOD	Box Jumps are executed at the beginning, at a moderate rate increasing gradually the duration of sets. Then, the movement rate is gradually increased until 50 jumps per minute for men and 40 jumps per minute for women.	For men: from 4 to 6 minutes For women: from 3 to 5 minutes	5-6	arbitrary	2-3	12-15 minutes

7.3.3.2. BOUNCES

Bounces are divided into two typologies: "short" bounces consisting in 4-6 maximum force takeoffs and "long" bounces executed for a distance of 40-100 m. with sub maximal takeoffs at a moderate rate.

The "short" bounces are executed with a double leg landing in a jump pit or on gymnastic mats:

EXERCISE	NUMBER OF EXERCISE REPETITIONS IN SERIES	REST BETWEEN REPETITIONS	SERIES	REST BETWEEN SERIES
A six-fold jump from leg to leg with maximal takeoffs and active swing movements by the free leg	6-8	arbitrary	3-4	8-10 minutes
A four to six-fold jump from place with alternation of the legs (two take offs on the right leg, two on the left leg)	4-6	arbitrary	2	8-10 minutes

The "long" bounces are executed on soft, resilient ground:

EXERCISE	NUMBER OF EXERCISE REPETITIONS IN SERIES	REST BETWEEN REPETITIONS	SERIES	REST BETWEEN SERIES
Bounces from leg to leg with sub-maximal takeoff effort. Begin with 50-60 m, gradually increasing to 100-120 m.	6-8	30-60 seconds During the rest, begin with 4-5 minutes of easy running, then 50 m of easy jumping from leg to leg, repeated 2-3 times and quiet walking.	2	10-15 minutes
Bounces from leg to leg (or two take-offs on the right leg and two take-offs on the left) with middle level takeoff effort. Begin with 100 m. and then increase it to 200 m.	3-4 at the beginning of exercise, then 6-8	4-6 minutes	2	8-10 minutes

Exercise	Number of exercise repetitions in series	Rest between repetitions	Series	Rest between series
Bounces from leg to leg (or two take-offs on the right leg and two takeoffs on the left leg) with a moderate takeoff effort. The distance is 200 m.	2	8-10 minutes	-	-

To improve the sprinting capacity, a combination of "short" and "long" bounces is used in different training sessions. The 'short' bounces promote an increase in starting acceleration speed while the 'long' bounces promote an increase in speed of run over the entire distance.

7.3.4. RUNNING EXERCISES

Running exercises are usually integrated into a training means system for track & field runners. These exercises may be useful also in track & field jumping and in sport games. The correct execution of these exercises is very important for achieving the best training effect.

7.3.4.1. LONG BUILD-UPS

Long Build-Ups (named Long Accelerations in Russia) are 100-120 m runs performed with a smooth increase in speed:
1) in the first part of exercise, maximal or sub-maximal speed is reached gradually by increasing the strides length; the distance length of the maximum speed achieving, that is initially about 3-6 strides, must be gradually increased until 6-9 strides;
2) in the second part of exercise, the speed reached is kept thanks to the inertia, the athlete should try to be relaxed while keeping the stride length with a correct technique.

The main task is the gradual increase of speed and its maintenance for a determined period without undue movement stiffness. Rest intervals must ensure a complete recovery before the next repetition.

7.3.4.2. SPRINGY RUNS

Springy or bouncy run (or bounding extensive tempo) is running exercise executed with shorter strides and with the forward impulse coming mainly from foot; it requires a more accentuated vertical push and a bounding overall action. The oscillatory movement of the recovery leg is minimized and the whole action is very relaxed. In fact, the athlete's relaxation is paramount for the correct execution of exercise; in particular the relaxation of the upper body combined with the intense work of feet muscles. Upon initiating this type of training, springy runs must be carried out on tracks with a soft surface. In the training of sprinters, it may be used over short distances (60-100 m).

7.3.4.3. BOUNDING RUNS

Bounding run is very similar to the bounce from leg to leg, but it is executed with higher strides frequency and with more "springy"; it is executed on 50 m distance as quickly as possible (with the execution time recorded). The athlete starts by pushing off from both legs as in the standing long jump, and then lands on one and then alternates the legs consecutively, trying to increase the strides frequency, but not transforming the movements in running. The dosage of exercise depend on the time of it's execution. Usually, this exercise is carried out in 2-4 series of 3-5 repetitions with arbitrary rest intervals between repetitions and 8-10 minutes interval between series.

7.3.4.4. UPHILL BOUNDING RUNS

Uphill Bounding Runs are executed similarly as the bounding runs, but with lower strides frequency. The main task of this exercise is to obtain the highest possible speed of the vertical body displacement through the accentuated take-offs of the feet, with a vigorous upward and forward movement of the thigh of swing leg.

This exercise is executed on 40-60 m distance. The uphill track slope should be selected in relation to the athlete's preparedness: the steep must not provoke the loose of the general speed character of exercise. Usually, this exercise is carried out in one series of 5-6 repetitions with 4-6 minutes of rest intervals between repetitions.

7.4. MEANS AND METHODS FOR INCREASING MAXIMAL ANAEROBIC POWER

The best exercise for increasing the Maximal Anaerobic Power is that allowing the maximal exertion of the corresponding motor function. Such exercise is usually used also as motor test. The best motor test to evaluate the Maximal Anaerobic Power was proposed by R.Margaria; it consists in running up staircase having 60° of slop, with the maximal speed, covering 2 steps every takeoff. The problem of using this test is the difficulty in finding such staircase: only Mayan Pyramids in Mexico and some escalators of metro station in the centre of Moscow have staircases with the necessary length and slope.

So, a modification of the Margaria's test was proposed using bicycle ergometer: the Wingate test. However, this kind of exercise may be considered specific only for cycling.

Several researches found high correlation of the results of Margaria's test and Wingate test with the maximal power output in take off and in leg press movement.

For increasing Maximal Anaerobic Power the following exercises are used:
1) jump exercises;
2) specific locomotion executed in more difficult conditions.

7.4.1. JUMP EXERCISES

Stadium Jumping: leg to leg bounces on stadium steps with a powerful take-off covering 2-4 steps every takeoff. The duration of work is about 8-10 seconds. This is followed by an easy run (jogging) around the stadium. The athlete comes down on another staircase while "shaking up" the leg muscles. He returns to the initial starting position with quiet walking. The repeat-serial method is used. In one series there are 4-6 repetitions of 4-6 minutes each. In the training sessions there are 3-4 series separated by 8-12 minute rest periods.

Kettlebell Squat jumps. The weight of kettlebell is 16, 24, or 32 kg and is selected individually for each athlete. One set consists in 5-6 repetitions followed by long build up at half effort and light running. In one series of 4-6 sets the rest is 3-5 minutes between sets. There are a total of 2-4 series separated by 10-12 minute rest periods.

Vertical jumps with a bar on the shoulders. A set of three-five jumps using a weight of 75-85%. After the set, there are 1-2 accelerations for 40-50 m and then quiet walking. In one series, there are 4-5 sets, 4-6 minutes each. In training session, there are 2-4 series separated by 10-12 minute rest periods.

<u>Consecutive barbell half-squat jumps</u>. The weight selected should make possible to freely execute 4-5 jumps. In one series of 4-5 sets, the rest interval is 3-5 minutes between sets. The athlete then executes one acceleration and easy vertical jumps in place, alternating the push off by one and then by the other leg and then "shaking" of leg muscles. In training session, there are 2-4 series separated by 10-12 minute rest periods.

<u>Bounces</u>. A six-fold intensive leg to leg bound executed starting in place. Maximum force with an active forward take-off is used. Returning in the initial position, athlete executes light running and "shaking" of leg muscles. In one series there are 4-6 repetitions, 3-4 minutes each. In training session, there are 2-4 series separated by 10-12 minute rest periods.

7.4.2. SPECIFIC LOCOMOTION EXECUTED IN MORE DIFFICULT CONDITIONS

<u>For cyclists</u>, overcoming a steep 60-80 m hill with maximum intensity on a large gear with a flying start is recommended. This exercise is repeated 4-6 times with a rest of 4-6 minutes in between repetitions. In training session, there are 2-4 series separated by 10-12 minute rest periods.

<u>For rowers</u>, starting acceleration at the usual rate with a hydro-brake (or towing of a motor boat) for 10-15 seconds is recommended. The movement then continues on inertia (without resistance) followed by light rowing for 2-4 minutes at the normal rate. In all, there are 4-6 bouts repeated after which there is rest for 8-10 minutes. The series is repeated 2-3 times.

<u>For skaters</u>, leg to leg bounds on a hill are recommended. In one set, 4 different exercises are executed at full strength for 8-12 seconds each. The rest period is 4 minutes in between each exercise. In all, there are 6-8 sets with a rest of 5-6 minutes in between each or 2 series of 5 sets each with a rest of 4-6 minutes in between each set. The rest between series is 8-10 minutes.

<u>The runner</u> can use the following exercises:
- Running up a steep hill with a short run-up and active forward take-offs for 15-20 m is used. On the return there is light running. Four-six sets are done in a series and each one lasts 3-4 minutes. In training session, there are 2-4 series separated by 8-10 minute rest periods.
- Running from a crouch start position with a powerful long take-off using active movement of the swing leg. A partner resists forward movement by placing his hands on the shoulders of the athletes to create active resistance against forward advancement (Fig. 7.3). This exercise is executed for 8-10 seconds and then the partner steps to the side and the running athlete continues an easy running on inertia for 25-30 m. After stopping he comes back with easy running. In one series there are 3-5 repetitions executed in 3-4 minutes each. In training session, there are 3-5 series separated by a rest period of 8-10 minutes.

Fig. 7.3 - Exercise for improving speed of starting acceleration

- Running from a standing start towing a heavy automobile wheel for 10-15 m. The take-off is active and involves a long step. When the rope attached to the wheel is unhooked from the athlete's belt there is easy running on inertia for 20-40 meters executed with free-striding and jogging on the return. In one series, there are 6-8 repeats with the rest 3-4 minutes in between each bout. In training session, there are 2-3 series separated by 10-12 minute rest periods.

7.5. MEANS AND METHODS FOR IMPROVING LOCAL MUSCULAR ENDURANCE

For improving Local Muscular Endurance the following exercises are used:
1) exercises with weights and jump exercises;
2) bounces;
3) specific locomotion executed in more difficult conditions.

7.5.1. EXERCISES WITH WEIGHT AND JUMPS EXERCISES

The exercises with weight and the jump exercises are carried out according to the following methods:
1) Interval-Serial Method using:
   - Dynamic exercises executed with muscle relaxation;
   - Static-dynamic exercises executed without muscle relaxation.
2) Complex Method.

7.5.1.1. INTERVAL-SERIAL METHOD WITH USING BARBELL JUMPS AND HIP FLEXING EXERCISE

The exercises are organized in a way which allows the loading of the PC-mechanism during each set and the stimulation of the aerobic mechanism for its recovery (between the sets and series).
During the execution of these exercises, the athlete should be motivated to maintain the given characteristics of the movements during each set: the given power of the force efforts and the rate of the movement repetitions. At the same time, he should check the moment when the execution of the exercise becomes difficult (due to the sensations of fatigue): at what set number and what repetition number it occurs. The training goal of these exercises is to gradually "delay" these sensations: to decrease the level of blood lactate accumulation during the exercise execution.
<u>Consecutive Barbell Jumps</u> (Squat Jumps or Scissor-lunge Jumps) is carried out with a weight of 40% circa. The following two variants are used:

VARIANTS	EXERCISE	DURATION OF SET	NUMBER OF SETS IN SERIES	REST BETWEEN SETS	SERIES	REST BETWEEN SERIES
I	Consecutive jumps executed with maximal effort (as higher as possible) and at the rate of one jump per second	10-12 seconds	At the beginning: 5-6 After: 6-12	At the beginning: 60 seconds After: 10 seconds	2-3	8-10 minutes
II	Consecutive jumps executed with sub-maximal effort at the rate of approximately one jump per second	20-30 seconds	At the beginning: 4-6 After: from 6 to 10	At the beginning: 60 seconds After: 30 seconds	2-3	10-16 minutes

The first variant predominantly favors the increase in power of CP-mechanism. The second variant predominantly favors the improvement in capacity of CP-mechanism. Both variants ensure the improvement of the CP-shuttle mechanism and, for this reason, effectively favor an increase in the athlete's aerobic ability.
During the training it is necessary to gradually increase the intensity of work in two different ways:
- by increasing the weight while maintaining the rate of movement;
- by raising the rate of movement using the same resistance.
The amount of weight depends on: the level of the athletes' preparedness, individual percentage of slow and fast twitch fibers in the muscles, the athlete's functional condition, the characteristics and volume of previous loads, the environmental temperature, as well as other factors. So, the weight

should be selected empirically in each particular case so that the athlete will be able to maintain the given rate of jumps (one per 1-1.5 seconds) without demonstrating an appreciable decrease in movement speed (power). So, 10-12 jumps can be executed when Variant 1 is used and 15-20 jumps in Variant 2.

The hip flexing exercise is executed with a pulley device. The forward movement of the thigh is carried out from a starting position in which the angle of the coxo-femoral joint is equal to 210°. Force production is accentuated in the early region of the movement trajectory. The overload weight is individually chosen. The rate of movements is equal to 8-10 movements in 10 sec. After each repetition of movement, the overload should touch the support during which time instantaneous muscular relaxation must occur. Each set alternates the use of one leg and then the other (the belt on the ankle is quickly changed with the help of a partner). The rate of movement should be gradually increased.

EXERCISE	NUMBER OF MOVEMENTS REPETITIONS IN ONE SET	MOVE-MENTS RATE	DURATION OF SET	NUMBER OF SETS IN SERIES	REST BE-TWEEN SETS	SERIES	REST BETWEEN SERIES
The hip flexing exercise executed with a pulley device.	10	At the beginning 8-10 movements in 10 sec	10-12 seconds	10-12 (5-6 for each leg)	Equal to the set duration	2-3	8-10 minutes

This exercise may be also executed according to all variants of the interval-serial method as described above for consecutive barbell jumps.

7.5.1.2. INTERVAL-SERIAL METHOD USING STATIC-DYNAMIC EXERCISES

This method has been proposed by V.Seluyanov and E.Myakinchenko in 2005. Static-dynamic exercises are executed slowly without full straightening in the joints. The range of movement in the joints is reduced. The exercise is executed like "swinging" up and down, spending 1-1.5 seconds in yielding phase (shortening while generating force) and 2-3 seconds in overcoming phase. It's important to avoid the accentuation of force effort at the beginning of overcoming phase. The loads are moderate, so that fatigue is reached in about 40 seconds. The exercise is carried out until the athlete perceives the muscle "burning". These exercises should be executed in one series, which can be repeated only once in 3-5 days.

The Barbell Squat, which involves grate volume of muscles, is used in the following series:

EXERCISE	WEIGHT	DURATION OF ONE SET	SETS	REST BETWEEN SETS	NUMBER OF SETS IN SERIES
Barbell Squat with reduced amplitude	10-40%	30-60 seconds (until the pain)	7-12	5-10 minutes of active rest	1-3

The resistance exercises involving low volume of muscles should be executed in the following super-series:

EXERCISES	SETS	DURATION OF ONE SET	REST BETWEEN SETS
1st Exercise	3-5	The first set - 30 seconds. After - not more than 60 seconds (until the pain).	30 seconds
2nd Exercise	3-5	The first set - 30 seconds. After - not more than 60 seconds (until the pain).	30 seconds
3rd Exercise	3-5	The first set - 30 seconds. After - not more than 60 seconds (until the pain).	30 seconds

Local static dynamic exercises can be carried out also without additional external resistance, loading only one leg by the body's weight. These exercises are executed as in the Circuit Training: one after another, without rest interval, alternating the right leg and the left leg. The super-series may include two exercises, one leg back thigh exercise and one leg squat, or four exercises, one leg Standing Calf Rises, one leg Squats, one-leg back thigh exercise and one-leg hip flexion.

VARIANT OF SUPER-SERIES USING TWO EXERCISES

SUPER-SERIES				DURATION OF SETS IN SUPERSERIES	SUPER-SERIES NUMBER
1ST SET	2ND SET	3RD SET	4TH SET		
One leg Squat with reduced amplitude (on the left leg)	One leg back thigh exercise (pushing by the right leg)	One leg Squat with reduced amplitude (on the right leg)	One leg back thigh exercise (pushing by the left leg)	30 seconds	3-6

VARIANT OF SUPER-SERIES USING FOUR EXERCISES

EXERCISE		NUMBER OF REPETITIONS IN ONE SET	DURATION OF SET	SETS NUMBER IN SERIES	REST BETWEEN SERIES	SERIES	NUMBER OF SUPER-SERIES REPETITIONS IN ONE WEEK
1st Exercise	One leg Standing Calf Rises	20-25 repetitions	30-60 seconds (until the pain)	8 (one for each leg)	3-5 minutes of active rest	2-8	2-3
2nd Exercise	One leg Squats						
3rd Exercise	One leg back thigh exercise						
4th Exercise	One leg hip flexion						

7.5.1.3. INTERVAL-SERIAL METHOD USING BODY PROPELLING MOVEMENT WITH OVERLOAD

The SST means for 'aquatic' endurance sport disciplines include specific resistance exercises executed with the use of training equipments which help to reproduce the main body propelling movement with additional external resistance.

For athletes of cyclic water sports (swimmers, rowers, canoe and kayak), the following exercises are used:

	EXERCISE	DURATION OF SETS	NUMBER OF SETS IN SERIES	REST BETWEEN SETS
I	The resistance used is 70% of maximum and the rate of work in the first minute is moderate (45-50 movements per minute). During every subsequent 30 seconds the rate is increased and in the last 30 seconds the rate is increased up to the maximum	2 minutes	8	30 seconds
II	1st set: the resistance is about 40-45% of maximum. The rate of movement at the beginning is moderate and then in the last 30 seconds the movement rate is built up to maximum.	2 minutes	3	30-60 seconds
	2nd set: the resistance is increased by 1.5 to 2 kg. The movement rate is average (in the range of 40-60 movements per minute).	1 minute		
	3rd set: an additional 1.5 to 2 kg. are added for more resistance. In this work it is necessary to preserve or even increase the rate of movement in comparison to the first set.	1 minute		

When using these exercises it is necessary to adhere to the following rules:
- in relation to the type of exercise used (number of muscles involved in the work), the level of external resistance and the intervals of rest between sets could be slightly changed (within the limits of the ranges indicated for them): the more muscle groups that are working, the greater the increase in overload and duration of work;
- during the practice of these exercises, further increases in the level of external resistance should be added only if the athlete, in executing the set, is able to maintain the optimal rate (about 45 movements per minute);
- between sets it is necessary to execute exercises for relaxation and dynamic stretching of the muscles.

In sports where a considerable level of external opposition must be overcome in body propelling movements, Interval-Serial Method is used combined to the Refusal Method. For example, the rowers may perform the pull of the bar in a racing scull, or in a front lying position, face down on a horizontal surface (see Fig. 7.2), using the following variants:

VARIANTS	EXERCISE	NUMBER OF SETS IN SERIES	REST BETWEEN SETS	SERIES	REST BETWEEN SERIES
I	Work "to refusal" with a weight of 40%	4	The rest increases as following: 10, 15, 20 minutes	1	-
II	Work "to refusal" with the weight at 40%	5-6	1 minute	2	5-6 minutes
III	Working with a weight that can be raised only 10 times (i.e. "to refusal"). After every two sets the resistance decreases by approximately 3%. The last two sets are executed with assistance from a partner who helps slightly in overcoming the weight.	5-6	Between two sets using the same weight, the rest pause is 1.5 minutes. When there is a change in weight, the rest pause is 2 minutes.	1	-

The Interval-Serial Method may give a wide range of training effect directions using the same movements but varying: the weight of overload, number of repetitions in set, number of sets, rest between sets and between series. The possibility to obtain different training effect directions by using the same training movement allows setting up a BTS model of preparation period using a specific body propelling movement as basic exercise.

For example, the swimmers may use the following sequence of specific resistance exercises.

BLOCK A:

EXERCISE	WEIGHT OF OVERLOAD	NUMBER OF REPETITION IN SET	NUMBER OF SETS	REST BETWEEN SETS	SERIES	REST BETWEEN SERIES
I	3 RM	1st set, 2-3 reps; 2nd set, 3 reps; 3rd set, 1-2 reps.	3	Between the 1st and 2nd: 30-45 seconds. Between the 2nd and 3rd: 40-60 seconds.	1	6-8 minutes
II	75-80% of maximal	10-12 reps (slow movements)	Several	During the series, the rest intervals are gradually reducing from 4 to 1-2 minutes	5	-

EXERCISE	WEIGHT OF OVERLOAD	NUMBER OF REPETITION IN SET	NUMBER OF SETS	REST BETWEEN SETS	SERIES	REST BETWEEN SERIES
III	1st set, 75-80% of maximal 2nd set, 50-60% of maximal	1st set, 10-15 reps (slow movements); 2nd set, 15-20 reps (fast movements).	2	During the series, the rest intervals are gradually reducing from 5 to 2 minutes. During the training stage, the rest intervals are gradually reducing from 4-6 to 1 minute.	5-6	8-10 minutes
IV	1) 80% of maximal 2) 70% of maximal 3) 60% of maximal	1) 10-15 reps (slow movements); 2) 15-20 reps (fast movements); 3) 10-15 reps (explosive movements with low rate).	3	During the training stage, the rest intervals are gradually reducing from 4 minutes to 2 minutes	Several	8-10 minutes

BLOCK B:

EXERCISE	WEIGHT OF OVERLOAD	NUMBER OF REPETITION IN SET	NUMBER OF SETS	REST BETWEEN SETS	SERIES	REST BETWEEN SERIES
I	Is selected individually for executing exercise during 10-12 seconds	8-10	At the beginning of the stage 5-6, after, the number of sets in series is increasing	At the beginning of training stage, 60 seconds, after, the rest intervals are gradually reducing from 60 seconds to 30 and to 10 seconds	2-3	8-10 minutes
II	Is selected individually for executing exercise during 20-32 seconds	Sufficient to execute the movements with the optimal repetition rate	At the beginning of this stage, 4-6 sets in each series are carried out. After, the number of sets in each series is increasing until 10	At the beginning of this stage, 60 seconds. After, the rest intervals between sets are decreasing until 30 sec.	2-3	10-12 minutes

During this training stage, the 'fartlek' swimming exercises are used, carried out at the AT level with 10 sec intervals of accelerations.

BLOCK C:

EXERCISE	WEIGHT OF OVERLOAD	REPETITION IN SET	MOVEMENTS RATE	SETS	REST BETWEEN SETS	SERIES	REST BETWEEN SERIES
I	50-60% of maximal	25-30	medium	2-3	At the beginning of training stage 4 minutes. After, the rest intervals are gradually reducing until 1 minute	2-3	8-10 minutes
II	30-40 % of maximal	40-50	high	2-4	At the beginning of this stage 6 minutes. After, the rest intervals between sets are decreasing until 2-3 minutes.	2-3	10-12 minutes

For rowers, the following sequence of specific resistance exercises can be used:

BLOCKS		WEIGHT OF OVERLOAD	DOSAGE	MOVEMENTS RATE	TRAINING FINALITY
A	A_1	5 - 6 RM	4-5 sets with 4-6 min rest	Slow	Increasing Fmax and Maximal Anaerobic Power. Stimulating the synthesis of contractile proteins and proteins of the ferment systems
	A_2	10 – 12 RM	6 sets with 4-6 min rest	Slow - middle	Increasing the mitochondrial oxidative power
	A_3	15 – 20 RM	3-4 sets with 6-8 min rest	Middle	Increasing the mitochondrial density
B		Customized	8-10 sets with gradually reducing rest intervals (60, 30 and 10 sec)	8-10 movements in 10-12 sec	Improving LME: increasing density and size of mitochondria in the fast switch muscle fibers
C		Customized	Repetition and Interval method with regulating the magnitude of single force effort and the movement rate	The same as in the competition regime	Improving the energy supply systems which ensures increasing the intensity level of the competition exercise

7.5.1.4. COMPLEX METHOD

The Complex Method foresees two series of different exercises in sequence executed in the same training session.

Both variants of Complex Method, illustrated in the following tables, have the same first series of resistance exercises executed, in one of the three variants proposed, with a weight of 65-75% and a rate of 33-45 repetitions per minute. The second series foresees:

1) In the first variant of the Complex Method, exercises carried out with slow movement with a weight of 80-85%.
2) In the second variant of the Complex Method, exercises carried out with fast movement with a weight of 75-85%.

COMPLEX METHOD - VARIANT 1

One super-series is performed; it includes the following two series:

FIRST SERIES				REST BETWEEN SERIES	SECOND SERIES		
EXERCISE WITH WEIGHT OF 65-75% (THE RATE IS 33-45 REPETITION PER MINUTE)					EXERCISE WITH WEIGHT OF 80-85% (EXECUTED SLOWLY)		
VARIANTS OF EXERCISE EXECUTION	DURATION OF SET	NUMBER OF SETS	REST BETWEEN SETS		NUMBER OF REPETITIONS	SETS	REST BETWEEN SETS
I	5 minutes	3	30-60 seconds	6-8 minutes	3-6	5-8	2-3 minutes
II	3 minutes	5	30-60 seconds				
III	2 minutes	10	30-60 seconds				

COMPLEX METHOD - VARIANT 2

Two - three super-series are performed; they include the following two series:

FIRST SERIES				SECOND SERIES				NUMBER OF SUPERSERIES REPETITIONS	REST BETWEEN THE SUPERSERIES REPETITIONS
EXERCISE WITH WEIGHT OF 65-75% (THE RATE IS 33-45 REPETITION PER MINUTE)				EXERCISE WITH WEIGHT OF 75-85% (10 FAST MOVEMENTS DURING THE SET)					
VARIANTS OF EXERCISE EXECUTION	DURATION OF SET	NUMBER OF SETS	REST BETWEEN SETS	DURATION OF 1ST SET	DURATION OF 2ND SET	REST BETWEEN SETS			
I	5 minutes	3	30-60 seconds						
II	3 minutes	5	30-60 seconds	30 seconds	20 seconds	1.5-2 minutes		2-3	6-8 minutes
III	2 minutes	10	30-60 seconds						

7.5.2. JUMP EXERCISES

Two variants of jump exercises are used. The 1st variant is aimed predominantly at increasing the power of CP- mechanism. The 2nd variant is aimed predominantly at increasing the capacity of CP- mechanism

VARIANT 1

EXERCISE	NUMBER OF REPETITIONS IN ONE SET	REST BETWEEN SETS	SERIES	REST BETWEEN SERIES
One of the following "short bounces" is executed with sub-maximal power output: - ten-fold jump from place with alternation of legs (2 on the right leg, 2 on the left one) or - eight-fold jump from place from leg to leg or - six-fold jumps (hops) on one leg (right and left).	4-8	15-20 seconds	2-3	8-10 minutes

VARIANT 2

EXERCISE	DURATION OF SET	SETS	REST BETWEEN SETS	SERIES	REST BETWEEN SERIES
Any form of consecutive jumps executed at a moderate intensity	25-30 seconds	4-6	60 seconds	2-3	10-12 minutes

7.5.3. SPECIFIC LOCOMOTION EXECUTED IN MORE DIFFICULT CONDITIONS

Specific locomotion executed in more difficult conditions are used according to the Interval, Repeat and Contrast Method.

7.5.3.1. INTERVAL METHOD

Swimming exercises are executed with an elastic device, which allows to swim with additional external resistance, until 25 m distance (Zenov, 1985). The following four variants of Interval method are used:

VARIANT	EXERCISE		NUMBER OF REPETITIONS	REST BETWEEN REPETITIONS
I	On the last 1.5-2.5 m of 25 m swimming, the athlete must develop the maximal traction force		10-16	1.5 minutes
II	On the last 1.5-2.5 m of 25 m swimming, the athlete must develop the maximal traction force and after, in the same blocked position, must maintain it for additional 5-15 strokes		10-15	1.5-3 minutes
III	1) Swimming only with the legs		15	75 seconds
	2) Swimming only with arms		10	80 seconds
	3) Swimming in total body coordination		20	60 seconds
IV	1) Swimming only with the legs		15	60-90 seconds
	2) Swimming only with arms		15	
	3) Swimming in total body coordination		20	

7.5.3.2. REPEAT AND REPEAT-SERIAL METHOD USING UPHILL RUNNING AND JUMPING EXERCISES

The uphill running and jumping exercises are used for improving the Local Muscular Endurance.

The uphill running is not such a simple exercise as it may appear. In sports practice, uphill running is often executed in a not correct way.

In moving the mass of the body vertically, much energy is expended, which in turn quickly results in local fatigue of leg muscles. This is why, if the athlete does not have the necessary motivation, he involuntarily goes to short steps (like jogging), creating a subjective sensation of work being accomplished. However, as a matter of fact, the athlete only increases the expenditure of energy for locomotion and, instead of using the aerobic source, he predominantly uses the glycolytic mechanism of energy supplying. As a consequence, primary emphasis of the training effect of the uphill run changes: the exercise is transformed in exhausting work of very low efficiency, wasting energy and time.

So, in all variants of uphill running it is necessary to be guided by the following methodological rule:

the main task is not the speed of locomotion but the accentuated take-off by the foot together with a vigorous upward and forward movement by the thigh of swing leg.

Choosing the right uphill track slope is of paramount importance, not just for the extent of training effect, but also for the degree of specificity of this exercise. Executing it on a steeper slope implies technical changes, such as stride frequency increase and stride length decrease that makes it less specific.

The results of a research (Fig. 7.4) showed that the increase in slope incline causes changes in execution technique of treadmill running and the increase in energetic cost. In the graphic we can observe:

- a decrease in foot contact and flight phases time;
- a decrease in length and an increase in the frequency of strides;
- a decrease in vertical and horizontal body acceleration, during the pushing phase;
- an increase in the energetic cost of running, measured by oxygen consumption.

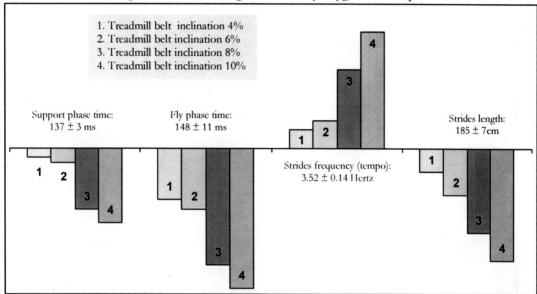

Fig. 7.4 - Changing of steps parameters in treadmill running with a speed of 6.5 m/sec (V.L.Mohnov, 1983).

As stride length is one of most important running parameters, uphill running must be executed with a low frequency and with an optimal stride length.

In uphill running it is necessary to use a direct path with different grades of the hill. The higher the speed and the shorter the distance of the run, the more abrupt (steeper) should be the inclination of the hill. Alternatively, the lower the speed and the longer the distance of the run, the less should be the steepness of the hill. The right choice of uphill track length is a crucial factor for obtaining the best training effect.

Depending on the distance length, the uphill running exercises ensure different training effects:

- Short distance (40-60 m) uphill running exercises ensure the improvement of maximum anaerobic power and Explosive Strength. The exercises must be executed at maximum speed. To avoid unintentional changes in technical form, it is advisable to perform Bounding Uphill Runs instead.
- Middle distance (150-300 m) uphill running exercises ensure an increase in the capacity of CP energy production mechanism and in the power of glycolytic anaerobic energy production mechanism, with a scarce influence on increasing aerobic capacity.
- Long distance (> 400 m) uphill running exercises ensure the maintenance of a high level of aerobic capacity and an efficient (with less energy waste) functioning of cardiovascular and cardiorespiratory systems.

Middle and long distance uphill running should be carried out at a speed of about 55-60% of the competition speed. In a training session it should be carried out as follows:
- for middle distance runners, 10 × 150 m;
- for long distance runners, 10 × 400 m.

In a training session, the middle and long distance uphill running exercises should be carried out in series of 5 repetitions. The athlete's activity, during recovery intervals after each exercise repetition, consists in:
- executing light running (like jogging) when returning to the initial starting place;
- executing 2-3 repetitions of light acceleration (50% of maximal effort) over a distance from 100 to 400 m on a flat track.

In order to improve the muscles capacity to recover mechanical energy during competition exercise, uphill bounding runs, uphill springy (bouncy) runs and light uphill bounces from leg to leg may be used. These exercises should be executed on a low degree slope.

Bounding uphill runs are carried out on a distance of 100 – 300 m, with gradual increase in the power output of push offs, using one of the three following variants:

VARIANTS	DISTANCE	NUMBER OF REPETITIONS IN SET
I	From 100-150 to 300 m	2-3
II	200 m	4-5
III	100-150 m	2-3

Uphill springy (bouncy) runs are carried out on a distance of 150 - 300 m using one of the two following variants:

VARIANTS	DISTANCE	LEVEL OF POWER OUTPUT	METHOD	NUMBER OF REPETITIONS IN SET	NUMBER OF SETS IN SERIES	SERIES
I	200-300 m	middle	Repeat	2-3	-	-
II	150-200 m	high	Repeat-serial	2-3	2-3	10-12 min

We have to remind that the execution technique of springy (bouncy) runs requires a more accentuated vertical push and a bouncy overall action, the oscillatory movement of recovery leg is minimized and the whole action is very relaxed. Athletes who have never used this type of exercise, or who are using it at the beginning of preparatory cycle, must start with executing, in the first training session, two repetitions on the 200 m distance and two repetitions on the 400 m distance. In the following training session, three repetitions of 200 m and two repetitions of 400 m should be performed. During the rest intervals, the athlete performs 2 -3 Long Build Ups, on a distance of 60-80 m, and relaxation exercises.

Light uphill bounces from leg to leg, executed on 200-800 m, are used mostly for improving the elastic quality of muscles. In training session, one series of 5 repetitions is carried out. In the rest intervals, light running (like jogging) is executed during returning to the initial starting place. After that, the athlete carries out 2-3 times light acceleration on a distance of 100-400 m.

7.5.3.3. CONTRAST METHOD

The runners use series of the following exercises:

- Uphill runs, steepness not greater than 6%;
- Running in normal conditions;
- Running in facilitated conditions (using a small down slope) with a speed 5-10% greater than maximum speed.

Distance is 60-80 m or 100-150 m. The rest intervals between repetitions are of 3-5 minutes. The series is repeated 2-3 times separated by 4-6 minute rest periods.

The swimmers use series of swimming exercises with two different "brakes" (large and small floats). The following variants of Contrast Method are used.

VARIANT 1 includes one series of 7 sets:

	EXERCISE	DISTANCE	NUMBER OF REPETITIONS IN SET
I	Swimming without brake at maximal speed (for 1-2 minutes)	25 m	2
II	Swimming with a large brake at maximal speed paying attention to the power of the pull and not trying to achieve maximum rate of strokes	25 m	4
III	Swimming with a large brake at maximum rate of strokes	12-15 m	4
IV	Swimming without brake at maximum speed (for 1-2 minutes)	25 m	2
V	Swimming with a small brake at a maximum rate of strokes	25 m	4
VI	Swimming with small brake at a maximum rate of strokes	12-15 m	4
VII	Swimming without brake at maximal speed	25 m	1

VARIANT 2 includes 4 series of 7 sets. The rest interval between sets is 1-2 minutes; between series is 2-3 minutes.

	EXERCISE	DISTANCE	NUMBER OF REPETITIONS IN SET
I	Swimming without brake at maximal speed	25 m	1
II	Swimming with a large brake at maximal speed paying attention to the power of the pull and not trying to achieve maximum rate of strokes	25 m	1
III	Swimming with a large brake at maximum rate of strokes	12-15 m	1
IV	Swimming without brake at maximum speed	25 m	1
V	Swimming with a small brake paying attention to the power of the pull and not trying to achieve maximum rate of strokes	25 m	1
VI	Swimming with small brake at a maximum rate of strokes	12-15 m	1
VII	Swimming without brake at maximal speed	25 m	1

The rowers use series of the following exercises (with rest interval of 4 minutes):
- Rowing with the tow of a cutter (motor boat), the duration of work is about 5-6 minutes;
- Normal rowing at a moderate rate of execution, the duration of work is about 5-6 minutes;
- Rowing with the pull of a motor boat. The speed is 120-128% of maximum for a distance of 250 m.

The length of the tow line should be limited to 35-60 m and the tow line should include an elastic element for damping of any sharp changes, such as slack in the line.

7.6. SST PROGRAM FOR PERFECTING THE STARTING ACCELERATION OF TRACK & FIELD SPRINTERS

The principles of this program were developed back in 1963 for Boris Zubov. He was the USSR and European record holder and Olympic Games finalist in Tokyo (1964) in the relay. Boris had great speed over the distance and finishing speed; he had no equals in the home stretch in the 200 m sprint, but his starting acceleration was very bad. He trained hard but was unsuccessful in improving the starting acceleration.

His coach (Y.Verkhoshansky) had not yet realized that sprinting over the distance and starting acceleration were determined by different abilities; nevertheless, he was able to suppose that for a good starting acceleration it was necessary to have very strong legs.

The results of using a specialized strength program, which was developed for obtaining increase in Explosive Strength, confirmed these suppositions: Boris increased the length of his first ten steps from the start by 60 centimeters. It shortened his time in the 30 m run by 0.3 sec. This was enough to establish his place on the United Track and Field Team of the USSR that took part in the USSR-USA meet in California and then went on to the Olympic Games in Japan.

Later on, the strength program became more advanced and was successfully used by hurdlers and jumpers as well as in soccer, handball, rugby, baseball, and other sports.

This program has a strong training influence on the skeletal-muscular system provoking a temporary increase in the hardness (entrapment) of muscles and a decrease in high speed running results. Therefore, it should be preceded by a less intensive, but with sufficient volume, preparatory strength work.

The program is performed two times a week for six weeks for a total of 12 training sessions, using the following exercises:
- Barbell squats with a weight of 80-90%;
- Vertical jumps with bar on the shoulders using a weight of 30-50%;
- Kettlebell Squat jumps;
- Depth jumps;
- Six-ten folds leg-to-leg jumps from place;
- Uphill bounding runs (15-25 m);
- Stadium Jumping, executed with an active take-offs (6-10) in upward and forward direction.

There are two important conditions for using this program correctly:
1) First, it is necessary to pay attention to the recommended duration of rest pauses both between sets and between series. Under no circumstances must these recommendations be neglected; economizing on time leads to a loss in training efficiency;
2) Second, during rest pauses, the same muscle groups must be active.

WEEK	TRAINING SESSION	EXERCISES (OVERLOAD WEIGHT)	SET X REPETITIONS[62]	REST BETWEEN SETS	SERIES	REST BETWEEN SERIES
1	1	Barbell Squats (85-90%)	2-3 x 5-6	4-5 minutes	2-3	8-10 minutes
	2	Barbell Squats: - (80%) - (90%) - (93-95%)	- 1 x 10 - 1 x 5 - 1 x 12	4-5 minutes	2-3	6-8 minutes
2	3	1. Vertical jumps with bar (50-60%)	2 x 6-8	4-6 min	2-3	8-10 minutes
		2. Six-fold jump from place	1 x 4-5	4-6 min. (between repeats)		
	4	Barbell Squats: - (70%) - (80%) - (85%) - (90%)	- 1 x 12 - 1 x 10 - 1 x 6-7 - 1 x 4-5	5-6 minutes	2	8-10 minutes
3	5	1. Depth Jumps (0.75 m.)	2 x 10	4-6 minutes	2-3	8-10 minutes
		2. Ten-fold jump from place	1 x 3	4-6 min. (between repeats)		
	6	1. Kettlebell Squat Jumps	3 x 8	4-6 minutes	2-3	8-10 minutes
		2. Ten-fold jump from place	1 x 3-4	4-6 (between repeats)		
4	7	1. Vertical jumps with bar (50-60%)	2 x 8	4-6 minutes	2	10-12 15 min. (after two series)
		2. Six-fold jump from place	1 x 3-4	4-6 min. (between repeats)		
		3. Uphill runs (15-25 m.)	1 x 5-6	4-6 min. (between repeats)	1	-
	8	1. Depth Jumps (0.75 m.)	4 x 10	4-6 minutes	1	15 min. (after the series)
		2. Stadium Jumps	4 x 10	arbitrary (between repeats)	2	10-12 minutes

[62] For jumping exercise, the number of repetitions indicates the number of a given jump exercise repetitions, number of sets indicates the number of series.

WEEK	TRAINING SES-SION	EXERCISES (OVER-LOAD WEIGHT)	SET X REPETI-TIONS[62]	REST BETWEEN SETS	SERIES	REST BETWEEN SERIES
5	9	1. **Barbell Squats** (93-95%)	2 x 2-3	4-6 minutes	2-3	10-12 15 (after the series)
		2. **Depth Jumps** (1.10 m.)	2 x 10	4-6 minutes		
		3. **Uphill Runs** (15-25 m.)	1 x 5-6	4-6 min. (be-tween repeats)	1	-
	10	1. **Depth Jumps** (1.10 m.)	4 x 10	4-6 10-15 min. (af-ter the series)	2-3	10-12 minutes
		2. **Stadium Jumps**:	4 x 10 (2-3)	arbitrary (be-tween repeats)		
6	11	1. **Barbell Squats** (93-95%)	2 x 2-3	4-6 minutes	2	8-10 15 min. (af-ter the se-ries)
		2. **Depth Jumps** (1.10 m.)	2 x 10	4-6 minutes		
		3. **Uphill Runs** (15-25 m.)	1 x 5-6	4-6 min. (be-tween repeats)	1	-
	12	1. **Depth Jumps** (1.10 m.)	4 x 10	10-15 minutes	1	-
		2. **Stadium Jumps**:	4 x 10	arbitrary (be-tween repeats)	2-3	10-12 minutes

7.7. SST PROGRAM FOR MIDDLE DISTANCE RUNNERS

This program is used for improving the Local Muscular Endurance, as well as for perfecting the Reactive Ability and elastic qualities of the leg muscles. As a result, there is an improvement in the ability to recover mechanical energy.

The SST program uses basically two exercises:
- consecutive Barbell Half Squat Jumps;
- consecutive Barbell Scissor-lunge jumps.

The weight of the bar used is within the limits of 35-45% allowing the athlete to execute one set of 10 jumps with sub- maximal efforts and repeat 6-10 sets without considerable fatigue.

Besides these exercises with the barbell, runners could use the hip flexing exercise executed with a pulley device (see § 7.5.1.1). The weight is selected individually allowing the athlete to execute 6-8 repetitions in 10 seconds. Ten movements are done by one leg and then the other. The optimal amount in one series is 5-6 sets on each leg (taking turns). In total, there are 2-3 series separated by a rest period of 8-10 minutes. These exercises are carried out two times a week according to the interval-serial method.

Considering that European middle distance runners have, as a rule, two competitive stages in the year, in winter and in summer, the program consists of two "strength blocks".

The first, "strength block" lasting eight weeks, takes place in December-January, and the second, of six weeks, takes place in March-April. Since the second block is executed on the basis of the morphofunctional changes that took place as a result of doing the first block program, the muscle function regime in the second block is more intense

PROGRAM FOR THE FIRST "STRENGTH BLOCK" (DECEMBER - JANUARY)

TRAINING SESSION	EXERCISE	REST BETWEEN SETS	REST BETWEEN SERIES	SETS X REPETITIONS (SERIES)
1	Half Squat jumps	60 sec	8-10 min	6 x 8 (2)
2	Scissor-lunge jumps	60 sec	8-10 min	6 x 8 (3)
3	Half Squat jumps	60 sec	8-10 min	8 x 10 (2)
4	Scissor-lunge jumps	60 sec	8-10 min	8 x 10 (3)
5	Half Squat jumps	60 sec	8-10 min	10 x 10 (2
6	Scissor-lunge jumps	30 sec	8-10 min	6 x 8 (2)
7	Half Squat jumps	30 sec	8-10 min	6 x 8 (3)
8	Scissor-lunge jumps	60 sec	10-12 min	10 x 10 (3)
9	Half Squat jumps	30 sec	8-10 min	8 x 10 (2)
10	Scissor-lunge jumps	30 sec	8-10 min	6 x 8 (2)
11	Half Squat jumps	10 sec	10-12 min	8 x 8 (3)
12	Scissor-lunge jumps	30 sec	10-12 min	10 x 10 (3)
13	Half Squat jumps	10 sec	10-12 min	8 x 10 (3)
14	Scissor-lunge jumps	10 sec	10-12 min	10 x 10 (3)
15	Half Squat jumps	10 sec	12-14 min	10 x 10 (4)
16	Scissor-lunge jumps	10 sec	12-14 min	10 x 10 (4)

PROGRAM FOR THE SECOND "STRENGTH BLOCK" (MARCH-APRIL)

TRAINING SESSION	EXERCISE	REST BETWEEN SETS	REST BETWEEN SERIES	SETS X REPETITIONS (SERIES)
1	Half Squat jumps	60 sec	8-10 min	8 x 10 (2)
2	Scissor-lunge jumps	60 sec	8-10 min	10 x 10 (3)
3	Half Squat jumps	30 sec	8-10 min	10 x 10 (2
4	Scissor-lunge jumps	60 sec	8-10 min	10 x 10 (3)
5	Half Squat jumps	30 sec	8-10 min	10 x 10 (3)
6	Scissor-lunge jumps	10 sec	10-12 min	8 x 10 (2)
7	Half Squat jumps	30 sec	8-10 min	10 x 10 (4)
8	Scissor-lunge jumps	10 sec	10-12 min	10 x 10 (3)

9	Half Squat jumps	30 sec	8-10 min	10 x 10 (4)
10	Scissor-lunge jumps	10 sec	10-12 min	10 x 10 (4
11	Half Squat jumps	10 sec	10-12 min	10 x 10 (4)
12	Scissor-lunge jumps	10 sec	10-12 min	10 x 10 (4)

This program has been experimentally tested comparing the results of two groups of runners: the experimental group, which used this program, and the control group, which was trained in the conventional way and did not use the barbell jumps in interval regime.

The training results were verified measuring: the increase in the level of strength capabilities and Local Muscular Endurance of athletes (see Fig. 7.5), and the improvement of biomechanical characteristics

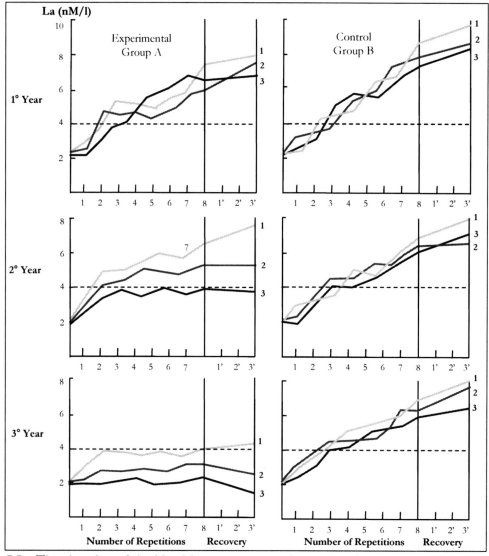

Fig. 7.5 - The changing of the blood lactate concentration during the execution of the control LME test in October (1), January (2) and July (3) of each of three years of experiment in the experimental (A) and control (B) groups.

of their running. The strength capabilities were measured using the UDS and the jump tests.

The level of Local Muscular Endurance was evaluated by the LME-test. This test consisted in executing 8 sets of consecutive half squat jumps with the bar on shoulders of 10 sec. duration, with the rest intervals of 30 seconds. Blood lactate was taken during each rest interval and 3 minutes after the conclusion of the last set. The evaluation of the Local Muscular Endurance was made on assumptions that lower is the level of blood lactate, better are the oxidative properties of muscles and the Local Muscular Endurance.

The biomechanical characteristics of running were evaluated in specific running tests, measuring stride length and strides rate at maximal speed and at speed of the anaerobic threshold.

The results showed that the athletes of experimental group achieved:

1) a higher increase in the strength capabilities than the athletes of control group: in the F_{MAX} and in the ten-fold jump from place from leg to leg.

2) a greater improvement of Local Muscular Endurance than the athletes of control group. Thus, it is possible to assert that the improvement of muscles oxidative properties in the experimental group was due to the using of barbell jumps in interval regime.

3) a greater improvement of the biomechanical characteristics of running than the athletes of control group: in the stride length at maximal speed, and at speed of the anaerobic threshold. The increase in stride frequency was insignificant.

4) better results even if their distance training load volume (1976 km), was 2.3 times less than the volume of the control group (4610 km).

7.8. SST PROGRAM FOR ROWERS

The aim of the program is increasing the strength potential of the leg extensor muscles by:

1) increasing the Maximal and Explosive Strength;
2) improving the ability to display a high level of Explosive Strength in conditions of accumulating fatigue;
3) improving the elastic properties of muscles (ability to recover mechanical energy).

The following exercises are used:
- Barbell Squat Jumps with weight of circa 40% ;
- Kettlebell Squat Jumps, the weight of kettlebell (16, 24 or 32 kg) should be individually selected;
- Box Jumps (0.30 - 0.40 m);
- Depth Jump using a height of 0.5 and 0.7 m.

The training means temporal organization is based on the principle of gradual increase in specificity and intensity of the training stimuli.

16 training sessions are executed 2 times a week for 8 weeks.

TRAINING SESSION	EXERCISES	REST BETWEEN SETS	REST BETWEEN SERIES	SETS X REPETITIONS (SERIES)
1	Barbell Squat Jumps	60 sec	8-12 min	4 x 8 (2)
2	1. Barbell Squat Jumps	60 sec	8-12 min	5 x 8 (2)
	2. Depth Jumps (0.5m)	1-2 min	5-6 min	2 x 10 (2)

TRAINING SESSION	EXERCISES	REST BETWEEN SETS	REST BETWEEN SERIES	SETS X REPETITIONS (SERIES)
3	1. Barbell Squat Jumps	60 sec	8-12 min	5 x 10 (2)
	2. Depth Jumps (0.7m)	1-2 min	5-6 min	4 x 10 (1)
4	1. Barbell Squat Jumps	60 sec	8-12 min	6 x 10 (2)
	2. Kettlebell Squat Jumps	4 min	-	4 x 10 (1)
5	1. Barbell Squat Jumps	60 sec	8-10 min	6 x 10 (3
	2. Kettlebell Squat Jumps	30 sec	-	4 x 8 (1)
6	1. Barbell Squats Jumps	30 sec	8-10 min	6 x 10 (3)
	2. Kettlebell Squat Jumps	30 sec	4-6 min	5 x 8 (2)
7	1. Barbell Squat Jumps	30 sec	8-10 min	8 x 10 (2)
	2. Kettlebell Squat Jumps	10 sec	4-6 min	6 x 10 (2)
8	1. Barbell Squat jumps	30 sec	8-10 min	10 x 10 (2)
	2. Kettlebell Squat Jumps	4-6 min	10 min	8 x 10 (2)
9	1. Barbell Squat Jumps	30 sec	8-10 min	10 x 10 (4)
	2. Kettlebell Squat Jumps	10 sec	4-6 min	8 x 10 (2)
10	1. Barbell Squat Jumps	30 sec	8-10 min	10 x 10 (3)
	2. Kettlebell Squat Jumps	10 sec	4-6 min	10 x 10 (3)
11	Barbell Squat Jumps	10 sec	8-10 min	10 x 10 (4)
12	Barbell Squat Jumps	10 sec	8-10 min	10 x 10 (4)
13	1. Barbell Squat jumps	10 sec	8-10 min	10 x 10 (3)
	2. Box Jumps at moderate rate	4 min	-	4 x 10 (1)
14	Box Jumps at higher rate	3 min	10-12 min	4 x 50 (2-3)
15	Box Jumps at highest rate	2 min	10-15 min	5 x 50 (2-3)
16	Box Jumps at highest rate	2 min	10-15 min	5 x 50 (3-4)

Some notes to the program:
1. The program should be used only by rowers with a high enough level of physical preparedness.
2. The program is finalized mainly at increasing the strength potential of leg extensor muscles, however, the need to develop specific Strength Endurance of the trunk muscles (mainly of the back), hand, arms and shoulder girdle, should not be forgotten. These works should be done two times a week in different days of the legs work:
    -   Monday, work on the leg muscles;
    -   Tuesday, work on the muscles of the trunk and arms;
    -   Thursday, work on leg muscles;
    -   Friday, work on the muscles of the trunk and arms.

The program can be varied by using the following exercises:

	EXERCISE	NUMBER OF REPETITIONS IN SET	SETS IN SERIES	REST BETWEEN SETS	SERIES	REST BETWEEN SERIES
I	Double leg jump onto a box (0.1-1.0 m) executed after run up of 3-4 steps.	10	2-4	5-6 minutes	-	-
II	Consecutive jumps over 10 hurdles (0.4-0.6 m height).	10	3	1 minute	-	-
III	Consecutive double leg jumps in place with rope skipping, executed as quickly as possible.	Set duration: 1minute	3	1 minute	-	-
IV	Pulling the bar (80% of maximum) from a face down lying position on a bench (barbell row). The bar is initially raised approximately 1/3 of the full range of motion and then lowered with a fast switching in direction and pulled up to the chest.	6-8	3	4-6 minutes	2	8-10 minutes
V	Seated row, pull back with the arms on a low pulley apparatus in the same regime of work as in the previous exercise: at first the weight is raised approximately 1/3 of the total range of motion and then is lowered with a quick switch to overcome the lifting phase of the movement, imitating the working part of the stroke. The weight is 80% of maximum.	8-10	3-4	4-6 minutes	2-3	10-12 minutes

SST IN SPORTS GAMES AND COMBAT SPORTS

8.1. INTRODUCTION

This Chapter is focused on the SST in the sports having a variable regime of muscle work, characterized by extended motor activity with sudden and frequent transitions from moderate to intense short-term exercise. Such regimes require maintaining the stability of technical/tactical skill in ever-changing and unexpected situations and in conditions of growing fatigue.

The game players engage in rapid locomotion and execution of the ball (or puck) passes, throws or strokes. In combat sport, two combatants fight against each other using striking movements (sword strikes, punches and kicks) or grappling movements.

Each of these technical elements of competition activity represents acyclic motor action, executed at the high level of power output. So, in sports having variable motor regimes, it is possible to successfully use the means and methods of SST recommended for acyclic sports (see Chapter 6). These methods are intended for the development of Maximal, Explosive, High Speed Strength and Reactive Ability. It is necessary to select the most suitable means and methods, taking into account the character of the motor activity specific to the particular sport.

High Speed Strength increase is more important in combat sports with "short contact" between adversaries (boxing, fencing, karate, taekwondo), to ensure the rapidity of striking movements.

Explosive Strength increase is important in all sport games and combat sports to increase the force effort of the body propelling movement during the execution of the specific technical elements.

Maximal Strength increase is more important in 'long contact' combat sports (judo, free and classic wrestling), where the rapid grappling movements are execute with a great external resistance. It is important also in team sports, having combat elements (contacts between players during the match), especially in rugby, American football and ice hockey.

Simultaneous increasing Explosive Strength and Reactive Ability is important in all sport games:
1) to improve the efficiency of the technical-tactical combinations (see § 8.6 - SST program to increase Explosive Strength and to improve Reactive Ability for American Football players);
2) to increase the speed of competitive running (see § 8.7 - SST program aimed at increasing the speed of competitive running for tennis players and § 8.8 - SST program aimed at increasing the speed of competitive running for basketball players);
3) to increase the jumping ability (see § 8.5 - SST programs aimed at increasing the vertical jump height in team sports);
4) to increase the power output in the ball throwing movements (see § 8.4 - SST program for improving the ball throwing power).

Distinguishing features of an athlete's preparation in variable motor regime sports is the attention directed towards the improvement in technical-tactical mastery. It is advisable to use the Conjugate method to simultaneously solve tasks of technical-tactical and special strength preparation (see § 8.2).

The task of SST in sports having variable motor regimes is to increase the athlete's strength capabilities, as well as improve the athlete's ability to effectively use his strength potential and to maintain the necessary level of work capacity in competitive conditions.

Competition activity in sport games has intermittent character: short phases of highly intense activity, which involve mainly the CP energy supplying mechanism, are followed by short phases of low intensity activity (or rest intervals as, for example, in tennis), during which the aerobic processes ensures the restitution of the anaerobic sources.

Most part of sport games has alactat-aerobic character of the energy supplying during the matches. In team sports where the competition rules provide for the substitution of players during the game (especially in hockey), the glycolytic energy supply mechanism has fundamental importance.

Metabolic models of combat sports depend on the character of 'contact' between adversaries during competition. In the combat sports with "short" contact between adversaries (boxing, fencing, karate, taekwondo), the CP - mechanism plays a dominant role; in combat sports with longer contact between adversaries (judo, free and classic wrestling) - glycolytic mechanism. Notwithstanding these differences, the improvement of specific work capacity in all these sports is ensured by increasing:

1) the Maximal Anaerobic Power, that allows performing the active phase of competition activity without or with limited accumulation of 'oxygen debt';

2) the aerobic capacity to eliminate 'oxygen debt' during the less intensive phases of competition activity, using lactate as the substratum of oxygenation and improvement of the Local Muscular Endurance.

Maximal Anaerobic Power and Local Muscular Endurance may be improved through the use of SST means described in Chapter 7 (SST in cyclic sports). However, in sport games and combat sports, the main part of these SST means should be specific exercises (technical-tactical elements) executed with additional resistance (see § 8.2). Wrestlers may use specific exercises with a partner of a heavier weight category or with a specific device, heavy sacks, and the adversary's 'effigy'. Boxers may use the Shadow Boxing with dumbbells. Sport game players may use specific short term exercises (technical/tactical elements) performed at maximal speed with additional external resistance.

For preliminary preparation of the muscular system to the work in specific regime (§ 8.3), the jumping exercises executed in interval regime (§ 8.3.1) the Strength-aerobic method (§ 8.3.2) and Circuit method (§ 8.3.3) are used.

8.2. SST MEANS AND METHODS AIMED AT INTENSIFYING MUSCULAR SYSTEM WORK IN SPECIFIC REGIME

For intensifying muscular system work in specific regime, the Conjugate Method is used; it foresees specific exercises with additional external resistance.

For wrestlers, throws of a mannequin (puppet) in various variants of the interval method are used. Wrestlers use specific exercises with overloads (heavy sacks, the adversary's 'effigy') or with a partner of a heavier weight category can be introduced.

The following variants are used for increasing the Maximal Anaerobic Power.

EXERCISE		NUMBER OF REPETITIONS IN SERIES	REST BETWEEN REPETITIONS	SERIES	REST BETWEEN SERIES
The throws executed at maximal rate for 15 seconds	Light weight class	6	2 minutes	2-3	6-8 minutes
	Middle weight class	6	2 minutes	2-3	8-9 minutes
	Heavy weight class	3	2-2.5 minutes	2-3	9-10 minutes

The following variants are used for improving the glycolytic mechanism.

TRAINING TASK	EXERCISE DURATION	NUMBER OF EXERCISE REPETITIONS IN SERIES	REST BETWEEN REPETITIONS	SERIES	REST BETWEEN SERIES
Increasing the glycolytic *power*	30-50 seconds	3	1.5-2 minutes	3-4	For lightweight class wrestlers, 13-15 minutes. For middle weight class wresters, 16-18 minutes. For heavyweight class wrestlers, up to 20 minutes.
Increasing the glycolytic *capacity*	1.5-2 minutes	3	2 minutes after two first repetitions and 1 minute after the third repetition	3	

For boxers, Shadow Boxing with dumbbells is used. The weight of dumbbells ranges from 250g to 2kg. It is very important to select the optimal weight for every athlete in relation to his level of physical preparedness and body weight. Dumbbells that are too heavy will interfere with patterns for normal boxing. It is, therefore, advisable that only very strong boxers classified in the heavy-weight category use dumbbells weighing 1-2kg.

In sports games the Conjugate method is used by performing technical-tactical actions while using the loaded waist coats weighing 5-8 kg.

For ice hockey players, the following variants of technical-tactical actions are used.

EXERCISE	EXERCISE DURATION	NUMBER OF EXERCISE REPETITIONS IN SERIES	REST BETWEEN REPETITIONS	SERIES
Zone attack. The formation of the players as follows: 11, 22, 33, 32, and 4 x 3. The speed is 90-95% of maximum and there are 3-4 breaks with changes in direction at maximum speed and 3-4 with a defensive pressing action.	20-40 seconds	4-7	2.5-3.5 minutes	1
An attack with a numerical advantage (5 on 4 players, 5 on 3 players). Speed is 60-80% of maximum which includes a defensive press and a fast break.	60-80 seconds	5-7	2 minutes after two first repetitions and 1 minute after the third repetition	1

For soccer players, the following technical actions are used:

VARIANTS	EXERCISE	EXERCISE DURATION	REST BETWEEN REPETITIONS	NUMBER OF EXERCISE REPETITIONS IN SERIES	SERIES	REST BETWEEN SERIES
I	Dribbling the ball for 15 m. circling 2 posts, 4-5 m. apart. Dribbling 5-6 m. and passing the ball to break free for a shot on goal (10 m.).	6-7 seconds	80-90 seconds	8-10	4-5	6 minutes
II	Break away (10 m.), dribbling the ball for 15 m. with a shot on goal. Break away to score a goal (10 m) and taking a shot on goal.					

Variants	Exercise	Exercise Duration	Rest between repetitions	Number of exercise repetitions in series	Series	Rest between series
III	Fast break-away (10 m.), dribbling the ball for 15 m. and circling 2 posts 4-5m apart. Then dribbling for 5 m and taking a shot on goal.					

For basketball players, the following technical actions are used:

Exercise	Exercise Duration	Number of exercise repetitions in series	Rest between repetitions	Series	Rest between series
Different variants of ball dribbling and circling of players finishing with a shot	8-10 seconds	6-8	2-3 minutes	2-4	5-6 minutes

In all ball games, the performance of the specific tactical combinations with maximal intensity (i.e. the work duration should not overcome 10 second) and the rest intervals between them of appropriate duration: the Repeat-Serial and the Interval method are used.

The methods of carrying out these exercises can be various in relations to the training tasks: For gradual improving the Local Muscular Endurance, the following sequence of using these exercises can be applied:

Methods	First stage	Second stage	Third stage
Rest intervals between exercises	10-15 seconds	10-20 seconds	Until 30 seconds
Duration of one series	6-8 minutes	7-8 minutes	6-8 minutes
Cardiac frequency during the series execution	Until 180 beats/min	Not less than 130 bets/min	160 beats/min
Number of series	7-9	7-8	7-9
Rest interval between series	40-60 seconds	60-90 seconds	3-4 minutes
Cardiac frequency before the following series execution	Not less than 125 beats/min	Not less than 130 beats/min	105-110 beats/min

8.3. SST MEANS AND METHODS AIMED AT PREPARING MUSCULAR SYSTEM TO WORK IN SPECIFIC REGIME

8.3.1. JUMP EXERCISES

For improving the Local Muscular Endurance, good results could be obtained by carrying out a complex of five jumping exercises in place. Two such complexes are shown in Fig. 3.4 - § 3.2.1.2.

Each exercise is repeated 10 times, the rest between sets is about 1.5 minutes. Rest includes light running. The whole complex takes 10 minutes. They promote the improvement of coordination and strengthening of the trunk muscles. In training, the composition of exercises in the complexes should vary.

Another variant of the jump complex is with high loads; six exercises with maximum effort at takeoff and limited intervals of rest (Fig. 8.1):

1) Barbell Squat Jumps for 8 repetitions.
2) A ten-fold jump from leg to leg for 2 repetitions.
3) Kettlebell Squat jumps for 8-10 reps.
4) Double leg half squat jumps while remaining in place for 10-12 repetitions.
5) Jumps on to a box 40-50 cm high with a double leg take-off for 4-6 repetitions.
6) Six or ten-fold jumps (2 on the left leg and 2 on the right) for 1 repetition.

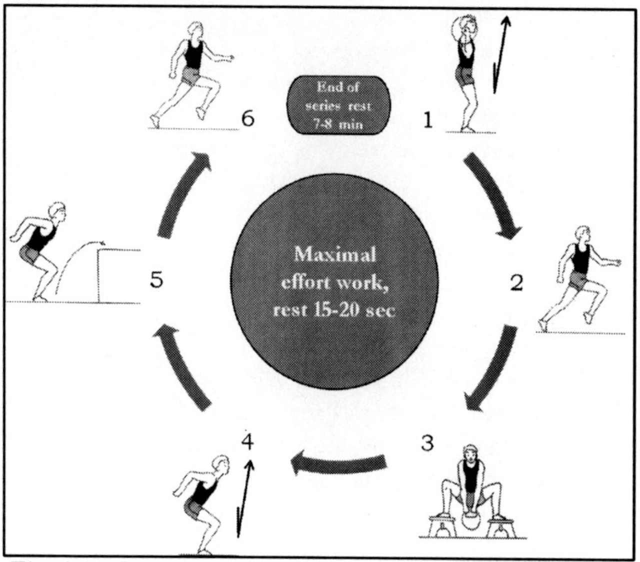

The rest between exercises is 15-20 seconds. In all, there are 2-4 series separated by a rest of 6-8 minutes.

Fig. 8.1 - Complex of jumping strength exercises

8.3.2. STRENGTH-AEROBIC METHOD

The main characteristic of the Strength-Aerobic method is in the enforcement of strength of the fast as well as the slow muscle fibers; while primarily using the aerobic source of energy acquisition for the work.

FIRST VARIANT

Executing two subsequent series of exercises for the same muscle groups in the following order:

	EXERCISE		NUMBER OF REPETITION IN SET	NUMBER OF SETS IN SERIES	REST BETWEEN SETS	SERIES	REST BETWEEN SERIES
I	Exercise executed at maximum effort with the weight at 80-90% of RM		3	3	2-4 minutes	1	-
II	Exercise executed slowly with the weight at 40-50% of RM Work intensity is checked according to pulse, which should have a frequency between 120-140 beats per minutes	First variant	15	4	2-3 minutes	2-4	5-6 minutes
		Second variant	Duration of set: 15-20 sec.	5-6	20-30 seconds		

SECOND VARIANT

Eight to ten exercises involving various muscle groups are executed. The weight used for each exercise should allow work to be done at a low rate for 30-60 seconds without obvious fatigue. The rest between exercises is 1 minute, which includes relaxation of the muscles. The pulse should not exceed 120-140 beats per minute. When the complex of exercises is selected it is necessary to be guided by the following rules:

- First, the muscle groups that carry the main load in the competition activity should be loaded (stressed).

- Second, three consecutive exercises should not be executed by the same muscle groups.

For wrestlers, the following complex of 10 exercises can be effective (Fig. 8.2):

1) Barbell squat.
2) Bench press.
3) Trunk raises (sit-ups) from a supine lying position, with the legs fixed in place.
4) Bent arm flies (Raising dumbbells sideways in a back lying position.)
5) Straight leg dead lift. (Pulling with the trunk keeping the legs straight.
6) Side bends with the bar on the shoulders.
7) Bent arm pullover in a lying position.
8) Barbell curl using a supinated grip.
9) Bent over barbell row pulling the bar to the chest. Legs remain straight.
10) Overhead press (military press from the chest).

Fig. 8.2 - Complex of strength exercises for wrestlers

The entire complex is executed in 20 minutes. It effectively promotes development of Maximal Strength as well as Strength Endurance.

8.3.3. CIRCUIT METHOD

VARIANT 1

Eight stations of exercises are performed in which the work interval is 60 seconds and the rest interval is 60 seconds. The following exercises are used (Fig. 8.3):

1) Squats with a 20 kg barbell disc held on the shoulders.
2) Jumps in place from a deep crouch position.
3) Arm flexion and extension in a front support position (push-ups).
4) Jump-out of a half squat with the feet shoulder width apart and at the same time, push the bar off the chest to an overhead position [jump with an overhead press]. The exercise can also be done from a lunge position (the scissor lunge), similar to a push-press.
5) In a seated position with legs up and in

Fig. 8.3 - First variant of circuit method of strength training

front, execute cross movements of the legs from side to side with simultaneous movement to the other side with the arms holding a 25 kg disc.
6) Double leg jumps jumping as high as possible in place.
7) Lifting the bar from the ground to the chest (clean). Do not touch the floor;
8) Run with a combination of acceleration and acrobatic exercises such as jumping, rolling and somersaulting.

VARIANT 2

Six stations are used. There is no rest between exercises and the rate of execution is maximal (Fig. 8.4).
1) Arm flexion and extension in a front support position - 20 reps (push-ups);
2) Double leg jumps over 10-12 medicine balls - 3 reps;
3) Overhead medicine ball throwing to a partner - 10-15 throws;
4) Leg circles while lying flat on the back. The legs do not touch the floor - 10 reps to each side;
5) Single leg jumps over 10-12 medicine balls - 2 reps on each leg; and
6) Acrobatic exercises - 3 body rolls and a forward somersault.

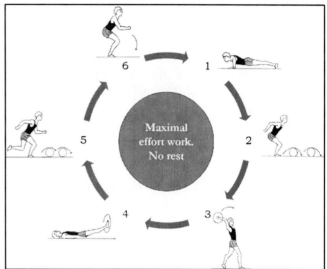

Fig. 8.4 - Second variant of circuit method of strength training

VARIANT 3

Circuit training with six stations. The time of working on each exercise is 15-20 seconds at a maximum rate. Transition to the following stations takes 8-10 seconds.
1) Vertical jumps in place bringing the knees up toward the chest;
2) Lifting the bar weighing 40-50 kg from the ground to the chest (clean);
3) Standing triceps extension with a barbell disc weighing 20-25 kg;
4) Jerk of the bar weighing 40-50 kg from the chest (military press);
5) Jump onto a box 60-70 cm high;
6) Snatch with a bar weighing 30-40 kg.
The circuit is repeated 2-4 times with a rest of 6-8 minutes in between.

8.4. SST PROGRAM FOR IMPROVING BALL THROWING POWER

This program includes the combination of light and heavy weight throwing using a special training apparatus that allows executing specific throwing movement in Shock Regime (see Fig. 8.5). To select the weight it is necessary to measure the maximum effort that can be displayed by the player in the starting position for the ball throw. The light

weight is equal 40% and the heavy one, 80% of this value. For example, if the maximum effort is 20 kg, the training weights will be equal to 8 kg and 18 kg respectively.

The work should be executed using the Repeat-Serial method. One series includes the heavy exercise and the light weight exercise with the first exercise executed with the heavy weight. For example, a series of 1x4 with heavy weight and then 2x7 with light weight means that in the beginning, one set of 4 reps with heavy weight and then 2 sets of 7 reps with light weight are executed. The rest interval between sets is 1-2 min. The series can be repeated several times with a rest interval of 4-6 min in between. When the maximum effort in the starting position for the ball throwing is improved, the training weights should be increased accordingly.

Fig. 8.5 - Throwing exercises in Shock regime

1ST WEEK:

TRAINING DAYS	1ST EXERCISES WITH HEAVY WEIGHT	2ND EXERCISES WITH LIGHT WEIGHT	SERIES
1	1 set of 4 repetitions	2 sets of 7 repetitions	2
2	1 set of 4 repetitions	3 sets of 7 repetitions	2
3	1 set of 4 repetitions	3 sets of 7 repetitions	2
4	1 set of 4 repetitions	4 sets of 8 repetitions	2
5	1 set of 4 repetitions	2 sets of 3 repetitions	2

2ND WEEK:

TRAINING DAYS	1ST EXERCISES WITH HEAVY WEIGHT	2ND EXERCISES WITH LIGHT WEIGHT	SERIES
1	1 set of 4 repetitions	3 sets of 7 repetitions	2
2	1 set of 4 repetitions	3 sets of 7 repetitions	2
3	1 set of 5 repetitions	3 sets of 8 repetitions	2
4	1 set of 5 repetitions	5 sets of 8 repetitions	2
5	1 set of 5 repetitions	3 sets of 8 repetitions	2

3RD WEEK:

TRAINING DAYS	1ST EXERCISES WITH HEAVY WEIGHT	2ND EXERCISES WITH LIGHT WEIGHT	SERIES
1	1 set of 4 repetitions	2 sets of 7 repetitions	2
	1 set of 4 repetitions	3 sets of 7 repetitions	1
2	1 set of 5 repetitions	2 sets of 7 repetitions	2
	1 set of 5 repetitions	3 sets of 7 repetitions	1
3	1 set of 6 repetitions	3 sets of 8 repetitions	2
	1 set of 6 repetitions	2 sets of 8 repetitions	1

4	1 set of 6 repetitions	3 sets of 8 repetitions	2
	1 set of 6 repetitions	2 sets of 8 repetitions	1
5	1 set of 6 repetitions	3 sets of 8 repetitions	2
	1 set of 6 repetitions	2 sets of 8 repetitions	1

4TH WEEK:

TRAINING DAYS	1ST EXERCISES WITH HEAVY WEIGHT	2ND EXERCISES WITH LIGHT WEIGHT	SERIES
1	1 set of 4 repetitions	3 sets of 7 repetitions	3
2	1 set of 4 repetitions	3 sets of 7 repetitions	3
3	1 set of 4 repetitions	2 sets of 8 repetitions	3
	1 set of 4 repetitions	3 sets of 8 repetitions	1
4	1 set of 4 repetitions	2 sets of 8 repetitions	2
	1 set of 4 repetitions	3 sets of 8 repetitions	1
5	1 set of 5 repetitions	2 sets of 8 repetitions	3
	1 set of 5 repetitions	3 sets of 8 repetitions	1

5TH WEEK:

TRAINING DAYS	1ST EXERCISES WITH HEAVY WEIGHT	2ND EXERCISES WITH LIGHT WEIGHT	SERIES
1	1 set of 5 repetitions	2 sets of 8 repetitions	4
2	1 set of 5 repetitions	2 sets of 8 repetitions	4
3	1 set of 6 repetitions	1 set of 8 repetitions	2
	1 set of 6 repetitions	2 sets of 8 repetitions	3
4	1 set of 6 repetitions	1 set of 8 repetitions	2
	1 set of 6 repetitions	2 sets of 8 repetitions	3
5	1 set of 6 repetitions	1 sets of 8 repetitions	2
	1 set of 6 repetitions	2 sets of 8 repetitions	3

6TH WEEK:

TRAINING DAYS	1ST EXERCISES WITH HEAVY WEIGHT	2ND EXERCISES WITH LIGHT WEIGHT	SERIES
1	1 set of 5 repetitions	2 sets of 7 repetitions	2
	1 set of 5 repetitions	3 sets of 7 repetitions	1
2	1 set of 5 repetitions	2 sets of 7 repetitions	2
	1 set of 5 repetitions	3 sets of 7 repetitions	1
3	1 set of 5 repetitions	2 sets of 8 repetitions	2
	1 set of 5 repetitions	3 sets of 8 repetitions	1
4	1 set of 5 repetitions	2 sets of 8 repetitions	2
	1 set of 5 repetitions	3 sets of 8 repetitions	1

Important additional information about the program:

- It is possible that players will lose "the feeling of the ball" the feel of the throw) when the strength program is used (especially beginning the 3rd week). This is a natural result of the strength training. The coach must explain the cause of this phenomenon to players. He must also tell them that it is a temporary phenomenon and that the "feeling of throwing" will come back when the program is completed.
- The low ability to throw the ball as a result of the strength training should be kept in mind when technical-tactical mastery is an aim of training.
- The weeks following the strength program play an important role in the training process. First of all, the load on the muscles of the throwing arm must be excluded during the first week. Then the power of throwing should be increased gradually. As a rule, 2-3 weeks is enough for the restoration of the feeling of throwing.

8.5. SST PROGRAMS FOR INCREASING VERTICAL JUMP

These three training programs were elaborated for volleyball players, but could also be used by the basketball and soccer players that need to increase the height of jumps during competition.

- Program 1, for average level players.
- Program 2, for high level players in the preparatory stage of training;
- Program 3, for high level players during the pre-competitive stage of the yearly cycle.

8.5.1. PROGRAM FOR AVERAGE LEVEL ATHLETES

The duration of this program is 4 weeks, done 3 times a week. In total, there are 12 training sessions. The program consists only of depth jumps. Each jump series consists of 10 jumps.

WEEK	DAY	DEPTH JUMP HEIGHT	DOSAGE
1	1	0.60	3 x 10
	2	0.60	3 x 10
	3	0.70	3 x 10
2	4	0.70	4 x 10
	5	0.75	4 x 10
	6	0.75	4 x 10
3	7	0.75	4 x 10
	8	0.75	4 x 10

Week	Day	Depth Jump Height	Dosage
	9	0.75	4 x 10
	10	0.80	4 x 10
4	11	1.10	4 x 10
	12	1.10	4 x 10

The recommended dose of strength work is related to the athlete and how well he executes the technique of the drop jump (drop down in the depth jump). This determines the optimal load limit, which should be reached gradually, and which should not be exceeded.

The depth jumps in each session should be preceded by a special warm up, which includes double leg vertical jumping and some sub-maximal force take-offs following a jump down from a small height (0.3 to 0.4 meters).

The rest between jump series is arbitrary. The jumps are executed repeatedly as is convenient for the athlete, who should not increase the interval of rest between jumps.

The amount of rest between the jump series should be regulated by the working state of the athlete. The break between series should not be targeted for reduction or for an increase. The following series should begin after the athlete has a sensation of readiness to continue jumping. Three to five times is enough for this. The rest between series should not be a passive one. Exercises for relaxation, shaking up of the muscles and slow light running, promote restoration of muscle work capacity.

8.5.2. PROGRAM FOR PREPARATORY STAGE OF HIGH LEVEL ATHLETES

The duration of this program is 6 weeks, executed 2 times a week. In all there are 12 training sessions. The program includes the following exercises:

- Barbell squats using various weights;
- Vertical jumps with the bar on the shoulders using different weights;
- Double leg vertical jumps for height after a 2-3 step approach. The athlete should endeavor to touch by hand the highest point possible on a basketball backboard (or some other place).
- Depth jump from various heights.

Week	Day	Exercise	Dosage
1	1	Barbell squats (85-90%)	2-3 x 5-6 Series are repeated 2-3 times. Rest between sets is 4-6 min, between series, 6-8 min.
	2	Barbell squats (80%)	3 x 8-10 Series are repeated 2 times. Rest between sets is 4-6 min., between series, 8-10 min.
2	3	1. Barbell squats (90-93%) 2. Vertical jumps with bar (40-50%)	2 x 2-3 2-3 x 6-8 Series is repeated 2 times. Rest between sets is 3-4 min, between series, 8-10 min.

WEEK	DAY	EXERCISE	DOSAGE
3	4	1. Barbell squats (90-95%) 2. Vertical jumps with bar (40-50%)	2 x 2-3 2 x 6 Series is repeated 3 times. Rest between sets is 3-4 min, between series, 8-10 min.
	5	1. Vertical jumps with bar (60-70%) 2. Double leg squat jumps	2 x 8 2 x 8 Series are repeated 2 times. Rest between sets is 3-4 min, between series, 8-10 min
	6	1. Barbell squats (90-95%) 2. Double leg squat jumps	2 x 2-3 2 x 8 Series are repeated 2-3 times. Rest between sets is 4-5 min., between series, 8-10 min.
4	7	1. Depth jumps (0.5m) 2. Double leg squat jumps	2 x 8 2 x 8 Series are repeated 2 times. Rest between sets and rests between series, 4-6 min
	8	1. Depth jumps (0.7 m.) 2. Double leg squat jumps	2 x 8 2 x 10 Series are repeated 2 times. Rest between sets 4-6 min.
5	9	1. Barbell squats (90-95%) 2. Depth jumps (0.75 m.)	2 x 2-3 2 x 10 Series are repeated 2 times. Rest between sets, 4-6 min, between series, 10-12 min.
	10	1. Depth jumps (0.75 m.) 2. Depth jumps (1.10 m.)	2 x 10 2 x 10 Rest between sets is 4-6 min
6	11	1. Barbell squats (90-95%) 2. Depth jumps (0.75 m.)	2 x 2-3 2 x 10 Series are repeated 2 times. Rest between sets is 4-6 min, between series, 8-10 min.
	12	1. Depth jumps (0.75 m.) 2. Depth jumps (1.10 m.)	1 x 10 3 x 10 Rest between sets is 4-6 min.

8.5.3. PROGRAMS FOR PRE-COMPETITION STAGE OF HIGH LEVEL ATHLETES

This program is 4 weeks long and is executed 3 times a week. In all, there are 12 training sessions. The program includes the same exercises as in the previous programs.

WEEK	DAY	EXERCISE	DOSAGE
1	1	Barbell squats (85-90%)	2-3 x 5-6 Series are repeated 2 times. Rest between sets is 4-6 min, between series, 6-8 min.

WEEK	DAY	EXERCISE	DOSAGE
	2	1. Barbell squats (90-93%) 2. Vertical jumps with bar (40-50%) on the shoulders	1-2 x 2-3 2 x 6-8 Series are repeated 2 times. Rest between sets is 4-6 min, between series, 8-10 min.
	3	Barbell squats with bar (80%)	3 x 8-10 Series are repeated 2 times. Rest between sets is 4-6 min, between series 8-10 min
2	4	1. Barbell squats (90-95%) 2. Vertical jumps with bar (40-50%)	2 x 2-3 2 x 6 Series are repeated 2-3 times. Rest between sets, 4-6 min, between series, 10-12 min.
	5	1. Barbell squats (90-95%) 2. Double leg squat jumps	2 x 2-3 2 x 8 Series are repeated 2-3 times. Rest between sets, 4-6 min, between series, 8-10 min.
	6	1. Depth jumps (0.75 m.) 2. Depth jumps (1.10 m.)	2 x 10 2 x 10 Rest between sets is 4-6 min
3	7	1. Vertical jumps with bar (60-70%) 2. Double leg squat jumps	2 x 8 2 x 8 Series are repeated 2-3 times. Rest between sets is, 4-6 min, between series, 8-10 min.
	8	1. Barbell squats (90-95%) 2. Depth jumps (0.75 m.)	2 x 2-3 2 x 10 Series are repeated 2 times. Rest between sets is 4-6 min, between series, 8-10 min.
	9	1. Depth jumps (0.75 m.) 2. Depth jumps (1.10 m.)	1 x 10 3 x 10 Rest between sets is 4-6 min.
4	10	1. Barbell squats (90-95%) 2. Depth jumps (0.75 m.)	1 x 2-3 1 x 10 Series are repeated 4 times. Rest between sets is 4-6 min., between series, 10-12 min.
	11	1. Vertical jumps with bar (60-70%) 2. Double leg squat jumps	1 x 6-8 1 x 8-10 Series are repeated 4 times. Rest between sets is 4-6 min, between series, 8-10 min.
	12	1. Depth jumps (0.75 m.) 2. Depth jumps (1.10 m.)	2 x 10 2 x 10 Rest between sets is 4-6 min.

It is important to underline some characteristics of the training effect of this program to understand better what kind of results can be achieved.

The training effect of program 3 is shown in the graphs of Fig. 8.6. The changes in Maximal Strength (Po) and Explosive Strength (J) in the Leg Press and Seated Calf Raise were measured by UDS. After the end of this program, the UDS tests continued up to the day of competition.

The concentrated load resulted in a sharp reduction in the speed-strength indicators. After this, the functional indicators returned to the initial level and then considerably exceeded it.

This phenomenon has been illustrated in Chapter 5. At the time of the main competitions (the 10th week) the functional indicators reached their maximum significance.

It follows to add that the team using the program 3 (Group A) had good results in the competition. The other team that used the traditional method of training (Group B) reached modest results.

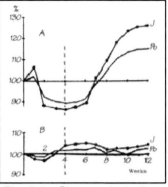

Fig. 8.6 - Changes in indicators of Maximal (Po) and Explosive (J) Strength of the volleyball players in the experimental group (A) and control group (B).

8.6. SST PROGRAM FOR INCREASING EXPLOSIVE STRENGTH AND IMPROVING REACTIVE ABILITY OF AMERICAN FOOTBALL PLAYERS

This program was elaborated for high level American Football players of the "New York Giants" club. This program is rather demanding, but it is specially designed for the talented athlete with strong resolve who has chosen American football.

This program, with some additions and changes, can be successfully used by athletes in handball, baseball, rugby and other sports

where it is necessary not only to be fast, but also to overcome high external opposition during the contacts with opponents.

The objective of this program is to increase the capacity to perform the speed-strength play actions, realized in specific conditions of fatigue that are developed during the game.

The program is designed for 12 weeks in which the training sessions are carried out twice weekly for the first eight weeks. From the 9th week on, workouts are executed three times a week, from day 17-28.

Four primary exercises are used in this program:
1) Barbell Squat;
2) Consecutive Barbell Jumps (Barbell Half-Squat Jumps and Barbell Scissor-lunge Jumps);
3) Depth jumps;
4) Box Jumps.

The loads used in the program are as follows:
- the weight of the bar is indicated in % of maximum, as for example "barbell squats (80%)". This means a weight equal to 80% of the maximum weight (1RM) the athlete can handle for 1 squat;
- the dosage of 8 x 10 (2) means that 2 series are executed. In each series there are 8 sets of 10 repetitions.

WEEK	TRAINING SESSION	EXERCISES (LOAD WEIGHT) AND REST INTERVALS	SET NUMBER X REPETITION NUMBER (SERIES NUMBER)
1	1	1. **Barbell Squats** (90%). Rest is 4-5 min between sets 2. Rest 6-8 min before the following exercise execution 3. **Barbell Squats** (80%). Rest is 2 min between sets.	2-4 x 5 2-3 x 10-12
	2	1. **Barbell Squats** (93-95%). Rest is 4-5 min between sets 2. Rest 6-8 min before the following exercise execution 3. **Barbell Squats** (80%). Rest is 2-3 min between sets	2-4 x 3 3-5 x 8-10
2	3	1. **Barbell Squats** (93-95%). Rest is 4-6 min. between sets. 2. Rest 6-8 min before the following exercise execution. 3. **Barbell Squats** (85%)[63]. Rest between sets is arbitrary	3-5 x 2-3 2 x 8 (+2-3)
	4	**Barbell Squats**: - (80%) - (90%) - (90-95)% Rest between sets is 4-5 min This series is repeated 2-3 times. Rest is 6-8 min between series	(2-3) 1 x 10 1 x 5 1 x 2
3	5	1. **Barbell Squats** (93-95%). Rest is 4-6 min. between sets 2. Rest 6-8 min before the following exercise execution. 3. **Barbell Squats** (80%) Rest is 2-3 min between sets	3-5 x 2-3 3-5 x 8-10
	6	**Barbell Squats**: - (70%) - (80%) - (85%) Rest between sets is 5-6 min. This series is repeated 2-3 times. Rest is 8-10 min between series	(2-3) 1 x 12 1 x 10 1 x 7
4	7	**Consecutive Barbell Jumps** (40%) Rest interval between sets is 60 sec. Rest interval between series is 8-12 min	5 x 8 (2)
	8	**Barbell Squats** (85-90%) using the interval method[64]	4-5 x 1-3
5	9	**Consecutive Barbell Jumps** (40%) Rest interval between sets is 60 sec. Rest interval between series is 8-12 min	8 x 8 (2)
	10	**Barbell Squats** (95%) using the interval method (See 8th day program)	4-5 x 1-3

[63] After completion of the last repetition in the squat with the weight at 85%, it is necessary to do 2-3 additional repetitions.

[64] In the interval method it is possible to execute one series of several sets consisting of 1-2 repetitions using a heavy weight (85-90%) and with limited rest pauses. At the end of the series, the number of repetitions decreases and the duration of rest pauses increases. For example, in the first set of 3 repetitions the rest pause is 30-40 seconds; in the second set of 2-3 repetitions the rest pause is 40-60 seconds; in the third set consisting of 1-2 repetitions, the rest pauses is 60-90 seconds and in the in the 4th set there is one repetition.

Week	Training Session	Exercises (load weight) and rest intervals	Set number x repetition number (series number)

6	11	1. **Depth Jumps** (0.75 m.)
		2. **Depth Jumps** (1.10 m.)
		3. Rest 10-12 min before the following exercise execution.
		4. **Consecutive Barbell Jumps** (40%)
		    Rest between sets is 60 sec.
		    Rest between series is 10-12 min
			2 x 10
			1 x 10
			
			8 x 10 (6)

	12	1. **Depth Jumps** (0.75 m.)
		2. **Depth Jumps** (1.10 m.)
		3. Rest 8-10 min before the following exercise execution..
		4. **Consecutive Barbell Jumps** (40%)
		    Rest between sets is 30 sec.
		    Rest between series is 8-12 min.
			2 x 10
			2 x 10
			
			6 x 8 (2)

7	13	1. **Depth Jumps** (0.75 m.)
		2. **Depth Jumps** (1.10 m.)
		3. Rest 8-10 min before the following exercise execution
		4. **Consecutive Barbell Jumps** (40%)
		    Rest between sets is 60 sec.
		    Rest between series is 8-12 min.
			3 x 10
			1 x 10
			
			10 x 10 (2-3)

	14	1. **Depth Jumps** (0.75 m.)
		2. Rest 8-10 min before the following exercise execution
		3. **Consecutive Barbell Jumps** (40%)
		    Rest interval between sets is 30 sec.
		    Rest interval between series is 8-12 min.
			4 x 10
			
			8 x 8 (2)

8	15	1. **Depth Jumps** (0.75 m.)
		2. **Depth Jumps** (1.10 m.)
		3. Rest 8-10 min before the following exercise execution
		4. **Consecutive Barbell Jumps** (40%)
		    Rest interval between sets is 10 sec.
		    Rest between series is 8-12 min.
			2 x 10
			2 x 10
			
			6 x 10 (2)

	16	1. **Depth Jumps** (0.75 m.)
		2. **Depth Jumps** (1.10m.)
		3. Rest 6-8 min before the following exercise execution
		4. **Consecutive Barbell Jumps** (40%)
		    Rest interval between sets is 30 sec.
		    Rest between series is 8-12 min.
			2 x 10
			2 x 10
			
			8 x 10 (2-3)

9	17	1. **Depth Jumps** (1.10 m.)
		2. Rest 8-10 min before the following exercise execution
		3. **Consecutive Barbell Jumps** (40%)
		    Rest interval between sets is 30 sec.
		    Rest between series is 8- 12 min.
			4 x 10
			
			8 x 10 (2-3)

	18	1. **Depth Jumps** (0.75 m.)
		2. Rest 8-10 min before the following exercise execution
		3. **Consecutive Barbell Jumps** (40%)
		    Rest interval between sets is 30 sec.
		    Rest interval between series is 8-12 min.
			4 x 10
			
			10 x 10 (2-3)

WEEK	TRAINING SESSION	EXERCISES (LOAD WEIGHT) AND REST INTERVALS	SET NUMBER X REPETITION NUMBER (SERIES NUMBER)
	19	**Box Jumps** (0.4 - 0.5 m.) Rest between sets is 3-4 min. Rest between series is 10-12 min.	4 x 40 (2)
10	20	1. **Depth Jumps** (1.10 m.) 2. Rest 8-10 min before the following exercise execution 3. **Consecutive Barbell Jumps** (40%) 　Rest interval between sets is 10 sec. 　Rest between series is 8-12 min.	4 x 10 10 x 10 (2)
	21	1. **Depth jumps** (0.75 m.) 2. Rest 8-10 min before the following exercise execution 3. **Consecutive Barbell Jumps** (40%) 　Rest between sets is 10 sec. 　Rest between series is 10-12 min.	4 x 10 10 x 10 (2-3)
	22	**Box Jumps** (0.5-0.6 m.) Rest between sets is 3-4 min. Rest between series is 10-15 min.	6 x 40 (2)
11	23	1. **Depth Jumps** (1.10 m.) 2. Rest 8-10 min before the following exercise execution 3. **Consecutive Barbell Jumps** (40%) 　Rest interval between sets is 10 sec. 　Rest interval between series is 8-12 min	4 x 10 10 x 10 (2-3)
	24	1. **Depth Jumps** (0.75 m.) 2. Rest 8-10 min before the following exercise execution 3. **Consecutive Barbell Jumps** (40%) 　Rest interval between sets is 10 sec. 　Rest interval between series is 10-15 min	4 x 10 10 x 10 (3-4)
	25	**Box Jumps** (0.7-0.8 m.) Rest interval between sets is 2-3 min. Rest interval between series is 10-15 min.	5 x 50 (3)
12	26	**Consecutive Barbell Jumps** (40%) Rest interval between sets is 10 sec. Rest interval between series is 10-15 min.	10 x 10 (3-4)
	27	**Consecutive Barbell Jumps** (40%) Rest interval between sets is 10 sec. Rest interval between series is 10-15 min.	10 x 10 (3-4)
	27	**Consecutive Barbell Jumps** (40%) Rest interval between sets is 10 sec. Rest interval between series is 10-15 min.	10 x 10 (3-4)
	28	**Box Jumps** (0.7-0.8m.) Rest interval between sets is 2 min. Rest between series is 10-15 min.	6 x 50 (3)

Notes to the program:
1.　The program is intended for athletes with good preliminary preparedness and having great muscle strength.

2. The program is for improving the leg movements. For the arm, shoulder-girdle and trunk movements, additional strength programs should be used.

It is important to pay attention to the following:

- the program is constructed on the principle of gradually increasing the specificity and intensity of the load;
- rearranging the means or their placement in the program is not recommended. In this program, each training workout prepares the body for the effective execution of the following workout;
- in the Interval-Serial method each work out in one set is executed with maximum intensity;
- jumping out of a squat with the bar can be executed in two variants: feet shoulder width apart or in the "scissor-lunge position" with alternation of the legs;
- when maximal leg strength is increased, the weight used in the Barbell Squat Jumps must also be increased and should be about 40% of maximum when doing a Barbell Squat;
- when using the Interval method, the rest pause between series is very important for preservation of the specific work capacity of the athlete during the training session. Small volume work with the intensity at 60-70% of maximum oxygen consumption, executed by the same groups of muscles is expedient (see recommendations in the program for rowers).

8.7. SST PROGRAM AIMED AT INCREASING SPEED OF TENNIS DISPLACEMENTS

This program was elaborate in the 80th for the soviet tennis players. At that time, the soviet tennis players didn't use the Barbell Squat with high weights, because this means were usually associated with the increase in muscle mass and a negative influence on speed. Notwithstanding this, the soviet track and field sprinters successfully used Barbell Squat already from the 60th. To avoid the negative influence of this exercise on the speed ability, at the end of 70th, the BTS model of training loads organization was adopted. In this model, the barbell exercises were separated from the speed running exercises and were used in a special training stage, which preceded the speed and technical work.

The SST program for tennis players illustrated in this paragraph is based on that BTS model for track and field sprinters, but it foresees lower volume of loads, shorter length of blocks and the execution of specific tennis exercises (drills) during the last block.

The following 4 groups of exercises are used:
1) Resistance exercises (exercises with barbell);
2) Jump exercises;
3) Sprint running exercises;
4) Tennis running exercises (game displacements) - Tennis drills.

Resistance exercises include:

- Barbell Squat;
- Barbell Calf Rises (Standing Calf Rises and Seated Calf Rises in equal proportion);
- Consecutive Barbell Jumps (Barbell Half-Squat Jumps and Barbell Scissor-lunge Jumps in equal proportion).

Jump exercises include:

- Consecutive multiple jumps: double leg jumps over low hurdles and 'slalom' jumps - double and single-leg jumps advancing along the length of the bench (see Fig. 3.8, § 3.2.2.1); gymnastics bench usually has a height of 1 m, width of 50 cm and length of 2.5 m circa.

- Long Bounces - leg to leg bounces carried out with moderate intensity on a distance of 40-60 m;
- Short Bounces - leg to leg jumps from place (single, triple, five-fold, and ten-fold) carried out with maximal power output;
- Single take-off jumps.

Sprint running exercises include:

- Long Build Ups for 80-100 m;
- Short start accelerations (for 15-20 m.) executed with maximal effort from a standing and crouch start;
- Bounding runs at maximal speed on the 50 m. distance.

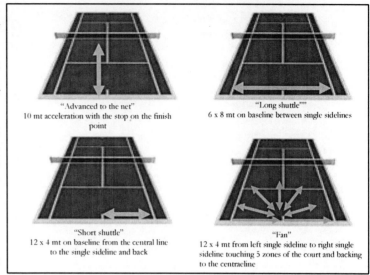

Fig. 8.7 - Schema of the tennis drills. The changes of direction in the left-right replacements must be executed without rotation of body – the athlete must always see the net.

Specific running exercises (game displacements) include the following tennis drills (see Fig. 8.7):

- "Advance to the net" - starting acceleration on the distance of 10 m with stop on a finish point (touching the net);
- "Long Shuttle" - running on a baseline (6 x 8 m) with 5 side-to-side (left-right) changes of direction;
- "Short shuttle" - running on a baseline (12 x 4 m) with 11 side-to-side (left-right) changes of direction;
- "Fan"- running from left single baseline to right single baseline touching 5 zones of the court and backing to the centerline (12 x 4 m.) with 11 changes of direction.

Tennis drills are executed with the racket in hand. The changes of directions are executed with touching the flow by the racket; the athlete must not turn over, he must always face toward the net.

The SST work is carried out as a special workout separated from the technical training on a court.

The program lasts 9 weeks, subdivided into the following 4 stages:

	INTRODUCTORY STAGE (3 weeks)	MAXIMAL STRENGTH STAGE (2 weeks)	SPEED-STRENGTH STAGE (2 weeks)	SPECIFIC SPEED STAGE (2 weeks)
RESISTANCE EXERCISES	10-5 RM Barbell Squats and Calf rises, Consecutive Barbell Squat Jumps with weight of 20 RM	5-1 RM Barbell Squats and Calf Raises	-	-
JUMPS AND BOUNCES	Jumps and bounds executed with sub-maximal effort and the control of execution technique	-	Jump exercises and bounds executed with maximal effort	-

	INTRODUCTORY STAGE (3 weeks)	MAXIMAL STRENGTH STAGE (2 weeks)	SPEED-STRENGTH STAGE (2 weeks)	SPECIFIC SPEED STAGE (2 weeks)
RUNNING EXERCISES	Running exercises executed during warm up with sub-maximal effort and the control of execution technique	Running exercises executed during warm up with sub-maximal effort and the control of execution technique	Sprint exercises executed with maximal effort: Long Build Ups, 50 m Bounding runs, 10-20 m start accelerations	Sprint exercises executed with maximal effort: Long Build Ups, 50 m Bounding runs, 10-20 m start accelerations.
SPECIFIC TENNIS DRILLS	-	-	Some specific tennis drills executed with sub-maximal effort	Specific high speed tennis drills executed with maximal effort

8.7.1. SCHEMATIC WORK OUT OF INTRODUCTORY STAGE (3 WEEKS, 9 WORKOUTS)

The goal of this stage is preparing the muscular system for the intense SST work of the subsequent stages as well as improving the technique of exercises execution.

1. WARM UP	1. Continuous running with gradual increase of speed	10 minutes
	2. Articular gymnastic (see note 1)	10 minutes
	3. Running exercise (see note 2)	10 minutes
2. JUMP EXERCISES AND BOUNCES	1. 'Slalom' double leg jumps of 8-12 take-offs, over gymnastic bench (see note 4).	4-6 repetitions
	2. 'Long' (40-60 m.) leg to leg bounces carried out with moderate intensity (see note 3)	3-4 repetitions
3. EXERCISES WITH BARBELL	1. Barbell squat with the weight at 10RM (see note 5)	3-4 sets of 10 reps
	2. Calf Raises with the weight at 10RM	2-4 sets of 10 reps or 2-3 sets of 10-15 reps
	3. Consecutive Barbell Jumps with the weight of 20RM	2-3 x 15
4. COOL DOWN	Light slow running, exercises for relaxation and stretching exercises for core muscles	10 min

Notes to the program:
1. Articular gymnastic is described in the Appendix 3.
2. Running exercises, used in warm up, include the following series:
   - run with high lifting of the thigh (high knees);
   - run with a heel kickback (butt kicks);
   - springy run;
   - long build up.

   The series is carried out 3-5 times with a middle level of power output paying attention to correct technical performance and nimbleness of movements. For tennis players, it is especially important to execute these exercises without increasing the muscular tension in upper body: arms and shoulders must be very relaxed. The first three exercises are executed on the distance of 20-30m, long build ups are executed on a distance of 60-100 m with a middle level effort.
3. 'Long' bounces are introduced in the program from the second week; they include the series of following exercises:
   - Leg to leg bounce;
   - Bounce with alternating 2 take offs on the left leg and 2 take-offs on the right leg;

- Bounce with alternating 3 take offs on the left leg and 3 take-offs on the right leg;
- Bounce on the right leg;
- Bounce on the left leg;
- Two legs take off bounces ("Frog").

'Long' bounces are executed on a soft, resilient flow with not maximal effort on a distance, which allows the athlete to perform exercise without losing the nimbleness of movements. During two weeks, these distances should be gradually increased; the number of series is increased from 1 to 3-4.

4. 'Slalom' double leg jumps (of 8-12 take-offs) over gymnastics bench advancing to jumping over the length of the bench are executed with middle effort, trying to maintain the arms and shoulders relaxed;
5. In the barbell exercises, a gradual transition is done from the weight of 10 RM to the weight of 5 RM;
6. Between repetitions of strength and jump exercises, the athlete executes easy running, light build ups and abdominal exercises;
7. During this stage, the athlete can have the leg muscles soreness (DOMS), which is a result of using jumps and bounces. This pain will pass during the following stage, in which only Barbell exercises will be used.

8.7.2. SCHEMATIC WORK OUT OF MAXIMAL STRENGTH STAGE (2 WEEKS, 6 WORKOUTS)

The main goal of this stage is increasing the Maximal Strength of leg flexion muscles.
In the barbell exercises, a gradual transition is done: from the weight of 5 RM used at the end of precedent stage, to the weight of 3RM. In the last workouts of this stage, the athletes may use the Maximal Effort method.

FIRST WEEK (3 WORKOUTS)

1. WARM UP	1. Continuous running with gradual increase of speed 2. Articular gymnastic 3. Trunk rotations with a barbell disc in the hands 4. Running exercises	10 minutes 10 minutes 5 minutes 5 minutes
2. EXERCISES WITH BARBELL	1. Barbell squat with weight of 5-3RM 2. Calf Raise with weight of 5-3RM	3 series of 5-3 reps 3 series of 5-3 reps
3. COOL DOWN	Light slow running, exercises for relaxation and stretching exercises for core muscle	10-15 min

SECOND WEEK (3 WORKOUTS)

1. WARM UP	1. Continuous running with gradual increase of speed 2. Articular gymnastic 3. Trunk rotations with a barbell disc in the hands 4. Running exercises	10 minutes 10 minutes 5 minutes 5 minutes
2. BARBELL EXERCISES	1. Barbell squat with weight of 3-1RM 2. Barbell Calf Raises with weight of 3-1RM	3 sets of 3-1 reps 3 sets of 3-2 reps
3. COOL DOWN	Light slow running, exercises for relaxation and stretching exercises for core muscle	10-15 min

In this stage, the training sessions are very short. However, the athlete must not execute other exercises, only some upper body exercises with weights and abdominal exercises may be used. The training on a court foresees only low intensity exercises on a half-court. In the days between the strength workouts, the athlete may execute prolonged aerobic cross running and after, stretching exercises for core muscles (Yoga exercises in lying position).

8.7.3. SCHEMATIC WORK OUT OF SPEED-STRENGTH STAGE (2 WEEKS, 6 WORKOUTS)

The goal of this stage is perfecting the ability to display Explosive Strength.

1. WARM UP	1. Continuous running with gradual increase of speed 2. Articular gymnastic 3. Running exercises	20 min 10 min 10 min
2. SPRINT EXERCISES	1. Long Build Ups for 80-100 m 2. Short start accelerations for 10-15 m. 3. Short start accelerations from a standing and crouch start for 15-20 m. 3. Bounding runs for 50 m 4. Some specific tennis drills executed with sub-maximal effort (at the end of this stage)	See note 1
3. JUMP EXERCISES	1. Single take-off jumps on the stairs. 2. Leg to leg jumps: single, triple, five-fold, ten-fold 3. Double leg jump exercises over 10 low hurdles (1 m)	See note 2
4. COOL DOWN	Light slow running, exercises for relaxation and stretching exercises for core muscles	10 min

Notes:
1. Sprint exercises are executed with the repeat-serial method: 3-4 series with a duration of rest intervals which ensures a complete recovery. During this stage, the level of effort should be gradually increased from the middle to the maximal.
2. Jump exercises are executed with maximal effort and the results must be recorded. In the 10 consecutive jumps over the hurdles, the result is the minimal time of execution. In the leg-to leg-jumps, the result is the maximal length. In each single take-off jump on a stairs, the athlete must jump on the highest stair. Each exercise is repeated until the athlete is able to increase the result (usually, not more than 5 repetitions). The rest intervals between repetitions must ensure a complete recovery.

8.7.4. SCHEMATIC WORK OUT OF SPECIFIC SPEED STAGE (2 WEEKS, 3 WORKOUTS)

The objective or this stage is perfecting specific speed ability.
FIRST WEEK (3 WORKOUTS).

1. WARM UP	1. Continuous running with gradual increase of speed 2. Articular gymnastic 3. Running exercises	15 min 10 min 5 min
2. SPRINT EXERCISES	1. Long Build Ups for 80-100 m 2. Short start accelerations crouch start for 8-10 m. 3. Short start accelerations from a standing and crouch start for 10-15 m. 3. Bounding runs for 50 m	See note 1

	"Advance to the net" "Long Shuttle" "Fan" "Short Shuttle"	
3. TENNIS DRILLS	"Advance to the net" "Long Shuttle" "Fan" "Short Shuttle"	See note 2
4. COOL DOWN	Light slow running, exercises for relaxation and stretching exercises for core muscle	10 minute

SECOND WEEK (3 WORKOUTS).

1. WARM UP	1. Continuous running with gradual increase of speed 2. Articular gymnastic 3. Running exercises	15 min 10 min 5 min
2. SPRINT EXERCISES	1. Short start accelerations for 10-15 m. 2. Standing and crouch starts for 10-15 m. from different initial positions (facing forward, backwards, sideways in relation to the direction of movement) 3. Bounding runs for 50 m for time	See note 1
3. TENNIS DRILLS	1. "Advance to the net" 2. "Long Shuttle" 3. "Fan" 4. "Short Shuttle"	See note 2
4. COOL DOWN	Light slow running, exercises for relaxation and stretching exercises for core muscle	10 minute

Notes to the program:

1. Long build ups are executed with sub-maximal and maximal effort, according to the repetition method. Short start accelerations and Bounding runs are executed with maximal effort. Short start accelerations are executed from the frontal, lateral starting positions. Each exercise is repeated until the athlete is able to increase the result (usually, from 3 to 5 repetitions).

2. Specific Tennis Drills are executed with maximal speed. The rest pauses between repetitions are sufficient for total restoration. Each exercise is repeated until the athlete is able to increase the result. After, the long interval of recovery is done and the series is repeated. If, in the second series, the athlete improves the results of exercises execution, the series is repeated for the third time. The competitive method may be used: two athletes are executed the same exercise on the same tennis court.

To control the effectiveness of this program, a study was carried out in the natural

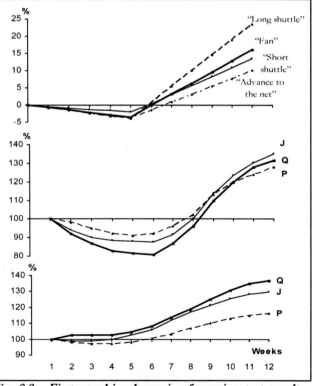

Fig. 8.8 - First graphic: dynamic of running test results. Second: dynamic of strength capabilities - leg press. Third: dynamic of strength capabilities - seated calf rise. (N. Verkhoshansky, 1984)

conditions of training of middle-level tennis players. In the illustration (Fig. 8.8):
- the 1st graph shows the dynamics of special motor tests ("Long shuttle", "Short shuttle, "Fan" and "Advance to the net");
- the 2nd graph shows the dynamic of the Maximal (Po), Explosive (J) and Starting (Q) Strength in the isometric Leg Extension;
- the 3rd graph shows the dynamic of the Maximal (Po), Explosive (J) and Starting (Q) Strength in the isometric Seated Calf Rises.

During the concentrated stages of SST loads (during the introductory and the maximal strength training stages), the results of speed tests and strength parameters of Leg Extension both decreased. During the speed-strength training stage, they return to the initial level and, during the speed training stage, they considerably exceed it: the maximal increase was obtained in the Explosive Strength, for 35%, and in the results of test "Long Shuttle", for 25%. The strength parameters of Seated Calf Rise didn't decrease during the concentrated strength stage, but their final increase exceeded the initial level for more than 30% (in Explosive and Starting Strength).

This program was adapted for the high level players and successfully used by the soviet national tennis team at the end of 80th. In the year cycle, the whole program may be used 1-2 times, in the periods when the athlete is not involved in important competitions. The reduced 6 weeks-variant of this program may be used; it doesn't include the introductory stage.

8.7.5. INTEGRATING THE PROGRAM IN THE TRAINING PLAN OF PREPARATION PERIOD

The program can be incorporated in the following variant of Block Training System program:

BLOCK A
Introductory stage (Strength – Aerobic work of high volume and of low - medium intensity):
1) Legs strength exercises (Barbell Squats, Calf Raises and other) that must be executed with a gradual increase in overload weight during this training stage: from 10 RM to 5 RM (Monday and Thursday). The upper body strength exercises may be performed as the traditional general exercises (Bench Press and Pullover), as well as certain resistance exercises used by T&F throwers (as illustrated in figure 8.9).

Fig. 8.9 - Examples of the Track & Field throwers upper body exercises, which can be useful for tennis players

2) Extensive long bounds and jumps (Tuesday and Friday).
3) Prolonged aerobic running (Wednesday and Saturday).
The first training session, which is long and hard, must be carried out separately from the tennis training sessions. The second and third training session (séances) could be carried out after the tennis training session. During this and the subsequent block, the tennis training volume and intensity must be very low.
Maximal Strength stage (high intensity - low volume strength work and Aerobic Fartlek):
1) Leg extension strength exercises (Barbell Squats, Calf Raises) and upper body exercises for large

muscle groups with 5-2 RM overload weight and isometric exercises executed in the position of the contact between racquet and ball during the volè strokes and service (Monday, Wednesday, Friday or only Monday and Thursday training sessions, separated from tennis training).

2) Prolonged aerobic running of the preceding block should be gradually substituted by Aerobic Fartlek (Tuesday, Thursday, Saturday or only Tuesday and Friday).

BLOCK B (Explosive Strength and Maximal Anaerobic Power):

1) Legs explosive strength exercises and upper body explosive strength exercises with medicine balls (Monday, Wednesday, Friday or only Monday and Thursday training sessions separated from tennis training sessions). The upper body exercises of block B must be explosive strength resistance exercises similar to the specific technical elements: throwing of overloaded tennis racquets by strokes movements and by the final service movement executed with maximal power effort (the shock method may be used for the final service movement, see figure 8.10).

Fig. 8.10 - Shock Method specific exercises for the final movement of service

2) Track and field sprint exercises (Tuesday, Thursday, Saturday or only Tuesday and Friday).

BLOCK C (high intensity specific speed and power work):

1) Specific speed and explosive strength exercises executed with the repetition method (long rest intervals) and serial - repetition method.

2) Specific running exercises and tactical combinations executed with maximal speed (serial-repetition training method and interval training method).

3) The execution of the service with maximal power output and control of the ball placement.

4) All physical preparation training of block C must be carried out on tennis court before the planed technical – tactical training.

8.8. SST PROGRAM FOR BASKETBALL PLAYERS AIMED AT INCREASING THE SPEED OF SPECIFIC RUNNING

This program is a variant of the precedent program for tennis players, adapted for basketball.

The program may be useful for the middle level basketball players and especially for very high athletes, who usually have problems with agility. The program is aimed only at increasing the speed of short-term game displacements with changing direction; it doesn't include the SST means aimed at increasing the vertical jump height (Depth Jump and Vertical jump with barbell).

The program foresees the use of following four groups of exercises:

1) Resistance exercises (exercises with barbell);
2) Jump exercises;
3) Sprint running exercises;
4) Specific running exercises (game displacements) - Basketball drills.

The first three groups include the same exercises as the program for tennis players.

Specific running exercises (game displacements) include the Basketball drills: short speed running exercises (not more than 15 sec) with specific trajectories and changes of direction.

The SST work is carried out as a workout separated from basketball training session.

The program is based on the BTS; it consists of 9 weeks, subdivided into the following 4 stages:

TRAINING MEANS	INTRODUCTORY STAGE (3 WEEKS)	MAXIMAL STRENGTH STAGE (2 WEEKS)	SPEED-STRENGTH STAGE (2 WEEKS)	SPECIFIC SPEED STAGE (2 WEEKS)
RESISTANCE EXERCISES	10-5 RM Barbell Squats and Calf rises, Consecutive Barbell Jumps (20RM)	5-1 RM Barbell Squats and Calf raises	-	-
JUMPS AND BOUNCES	Jumps and bounds executed with sub- maximal effort and the control of execution technique	-	Jump exercises and bounds executed with maximal effort	-
RUNNING EXERCISES	Running exercises executed during warm up with sub- maximal effort and the control of execution technique	Running exercises executed during warm up with sub- maximal effort and the control of execution technique	Sprint Running exercises executed with maximal effort: Long Build Ups, 50 m Bounding runs 10-20 m start accelerations	Running (sprint) exercises executed with maximal effort: Long Build Ups, 50 m Bounding runs 10-20 m start accelerations
SPECIFIC BASKETBALL DRILLS	-	-	Some specific basketball drills executed with sub-maximal effort	Specific basketball drills

8.8.1. SCHEMATIC WORK OUT OF INTRODUCTORY STAGE (3 WEEKS, 9 WORKOUTS)

1. WARM UP	1. Continuous running with gradual increase of speed 2. Articular gymnastics 3. Running exercises	10 minutes 10 minutes 10 minutes
2. JUMP EXERCISES AND BOUNCES	1. Double leg jumps (of 8-12 take-offs) over gymnastic bench advancing to jumping over the length of the bench. 2. "Long" (40-60 m.) leg to leg bounces carried out with moderate intensity (from the second week – see note 3).	4-6 repetitions From 1 to 3-4 series
3. EXERCISES WITH THE BARBELL	1. Barbell squat with the weight at 10RM 2. Calf Raises with the weight at 10RM 3. Barbell Squat Jumps with a weight of 20RM	3-4 sets of 10 reps 2-4 sets of 10 reps or 2-3 sets of 10-15 reps 2-3 sets of 15 reps
4. COOL DOWN	Light slow running, exercises for relaxation and stretching exercises for core muscle	10 minutes

8.8.2. SCHEMATIC WORK OUT OF MAXIMAL STRENGTH STAGE (2 WEEKS, 6 WORKOUTS)

1. WARM UP	1. Continuous running with gradual increase of speed 2. Articular gymnastic 3. Running exercises	20 minutes 10 minutes 5 minutes
2. EXERCISES WITH THE BARBELL	1. Barbell squat (the weight is increasing from 5-3RM) 2. Calf Raises (the weight is increasing from 5-3RM) 3. Barbell Squat Jumps with a weight of 20RM	3 sets of 3-4 reps 3 sets of 3-4 reps 3 sets of 15 reps
3. COOL DOWN	Light slow running, exercises for relaxation and stretching exercises for core muscle	10 min

8.8.3. SCHEMATIC WORK OUT OF SPEED-STRENGTH STAGE (2 WEEK, 6 WORKOUTS)

1. WARM UP	1. Continuous running with gradual increase of speed 2. General developmental gymnastic exercises, executed with light dynamic stretching and relaxation of the muscles 3. Running exercises.	20 min 10 min 10 min
2. SPRINT EXERCISES	1. Long Build Ups for 80-100 m 2. Short start accelerations for 10-15 m. 3. Short start accelerations from a standing and crouch start for 15-20 m. 3. Bounding runs for 50 m for time 4. Some specific drills executed with sub-maximal effort (at the end of this stage)	See note 1
3. JUMP EXERCISES	1. Single take-off jumps on the stairs 2. Leg to leg jumps: single, triple, five-fold, ten-fold 3. Double leg jump exercises over 10 low hurdles (1 m)	See note 2
4. COOL DOWN	Light slow running, exercises for relaxation and stretching exercises for core muscle	10 min

Notes:
1. Sprint Exercises are executed with the repeat-serial method: 3-4 series with rest intervals ensuring a complete recovery. During this stage, the level of effort in each exercise should be gradually increased, from low-middle to maximal.
2. Jump exercises are executed with maximal effort (the result should be measured). Each exercise is repeated until the athlete is able to increase it. The rest intervals between repetitions must ensure a complete recovery.
3. Between the jumping and running practice, the athlete could execute exercises with the ball (dribbling, passing, shots from different positions and free throws).

8.8.4. SCHEMATIC WORK OUT OF SPECIFIC SPEED STAGE (2 WEEKS, 6 WORKOUTS)

1. WARM UP	1. Continuous running with gradual increase of speed 2. Articular gymnastic 3. Running exercises	20 min 10 min 10 min
2. SPRINT EXERCISES	1. Long Build Ups for 80-100 m 2. Short start accelerations for 10-15 m.	See note 1

	3. Short start accelerations from a standing and crouch start for 15-20 m. 3. Bounding runs for 50 m for time	
3. SPECIFIC BASKETBALL DRILLS	The short speed running exercises (not more than 15 sec) with the specific trajectories and changes of direction	See note 2
4. COOL DOWN	Light slow running, exercises for relaxation and stretching exercises for core muscle	10 min

Notes:

1. Long build ups are executed with sub-maximal and maximal effort, according to the repetition method. Short start accelerations and Bounding runs are executed with maximal effort. Each exercise is repeated until the athlete is able to increase the result (usually, from 3 to 5 repetitions).

2. Specific Basketball Drills are executed with maximal speed. The competitive method is used for stimulating the athlete's interest to be first to the finish line. Between runs there are rest pauses, sufficient for total restoration. Each exercise is repeated until the athlete is able to increase the result.

8.8.5. INTEGRATING THE PROGRAM IN THE TRAINING PLAN OF PREPARATION PERIOD

The program could be incorporated in the following variant of the Block Training System program for basketball players.

BLOCK A

Introductory stage (strength – aerobic work of high volume and of low - medium intensity):
1) Legs strength exercises (Barbell Squats, Calf Rises and other) and upper body strength exercises that must be executed with a gradual increase in overload weight during this training stage: from10 RM to 5 RM (Monday and Thursday).
2) Extensive long bounds and jumps (Tuesday and Friday).
3) Prolonged aerobic running (Wednesday and Saturday).
The first training session, which is long and hard, must be carried out separately from the basketball training sessions. The second and third training session (séances) could be carried out after the basketball training session. During this and the subsequent block, the basketball training volume and intensity must not be high.
Maximal Strength stage (high intensity - low volume strength work and Aerobic Fartlek):
1) Leg extension strength exercises (Barbell Squats, Calf Rises) and some upper body exercises for large muscle groups (as Bench Press and Pullover) with 5 – 2 RM overload weight (Monday, Wednesday, Friday or only Monday and Thursday training sessions separate from basketball training).
2) Prolonged aerobic running of the preceding block should be gradually substituted by Aerobic Fartlek (Tuesday, Thursday, Saturday or only Tuesday and Friday).

BLOCK B

Increasing Explosive Strength and Maximal Anaerobic Power:
1) Legs explosive strength exercises: Barbell Squat Jumps; Russian Kettlebell jumps; intensive bounds and jumps. At the end of this block, intensive bounds and jumps can be replaced by 2 - 4 series of 10 Depth Jumps.
2) Explosive strength upper body exercises with medicine balls (Monday, Wednesday, Friday or only

Monday and Thursday training sessions separated from the basketball training sessions). The upper body exercises of block B must be explosive strength resistance exercises similar to the specific technical elements of basketball: chest passes and overhead passes with medicine balls executed with maximal power effort. These exercises may also be executed in a seated position, without loading the legs. The upper body shock method exercise could also be used: as, for example, the maximal reactive explosive efforts in the inclined Bench Press: throwing the barbell after it's landing in the athlete's hands (in Smith Machine).

3) 20-30 m distance uphill running executed with complete recovery after each repetition. During the recovery phases, athletes must execute light running accelerations (Tuesday, Thursday, Saturday or only Tuesday and Friday).

BLOCK C

High intensity specific speed and power work:

1) Specific speed and explosive strength exercises (10 – 20 m starts, basketball jumps and shots) executed with the repetition method (long rest intervals) and serial - repetition method. The "classic" Depth jumps of the preceding block must be replaced by Depth jumps with subsequent jump shot.

2) Specific tactical combinations executed with maximal speed (serial-repetition training method and interval training method), chest passes and overhead passes executed with maximal power effort.

All physical preparation training of block C must be carried out on the basketball court before the planed technical-tactical training.

APPENDIX 1: TRADITIONAL SST EXERCISES USED BY SOVIET TRACK & FIELD ATHLETES

The figures illustrating the exercises are taken from the book "Equipments and specific exercises in Track&Field" (edited by B.G. Alabin and M.P. Krivonosov), Moscow, "Fiskultura and Sport", 1976. In this book two sport training experts and T&F coaches, V.G.Alabin, PhD and M.P Krivonosov, PhD, summarized the multiyear training experiences of 20 leading soviet coaches in Track& Field disciplines.

I.1. POLE VAULT

Sergey Bubka - Soviet/Ukrainian pole-vaulter. Repeatedly voted the world's best athlete, Bubka won 6 consecutive IAAF World Championships, Olympics gold and broke the world record for men's pole vaulting 35 times (17 outdoor and 18 indoor records). He was the first to clear 6.0 meters and the first and only (as of March 2010) to clear 6.10 meters (20 ft).

I.2.   TRIPLE JUMP

Viktor Saneyev - Soviet triple jumper, who dominated the triple jump during the late 1960s and '70s. He won four Olympic medals; three gold (1968, 1972 and 1976) and one silver medals (1980).

I.3.   HUMMER THROW

Yuriy Sedykh - Soviet/Ukrainian athlete who represented the USSR, specializing in the hammer throw. He won Olympic gold medals at the 1976 and 1980 Summer Olympics as well as taking first at the 1986 Goodwill Games and the 1991 World Championships in Athletics.

I.4.   SHOT PUT

Natalya Lisovskaya - Soviet athlete who competed mainly in the shot put. She competed for the USSR in the 1988 Summer Olympics held in Seoul, South Korea where she won the gold medal. Lisovskaya holds the world record in the women's shot put with a throw of 22.63 meters, which she achieved on June 7, 1987 in Moscow, Russia. She also has the four farthest throws of all time by a female shot putter.

I.5.   JAVELIN THROW

Jānis Lūsis - Latvian / Soviet athlete who competed in javelin throw in four Summer Olympics for the USSR team, winning bronze in 1964 Olympics, gold in 1968 Olympics and silver in 1972 Olympics.

I.6. DISCUS THROW

Faina Melnik - Ukrainian-born Soviet discus thrower, a 1972 Summer Olympics champion in the discus event. She is considered to be one of the most dominant track and field athletes of the 1970s. Melnik set the world record twice and held the first ranking in women's discus from 1971–77, the third longest world's first ranking streak in women's track and field history.

I.7.   SPECIAL STRENGTH PREPAREDNESS OF SOVIET THROWERS

ATHLETE	SPORT RESULT (M)	BENCH PRESS (KG)	SQUAT (KG)	STANDING LONG JUMP (M)	STANDING ALTERNATE TRIPLE JUMP (M)	REVERSAL THROWING (M)
Sergey Gavryushin	Shot put 22.09	1RM - 250	3RM - 260	3.62	10.00	-
Sergey Smirnov	Shot put 22.24	1RM - 240	1RM - 310	3.50	10.20	23
Romas Ubartas	Discus throw 70.06	1RM - 250	1RM - 280	3.65	10.60	23.10
Natalya Lisovskaya	Shot put 22.63 (WR)	5RM - 140	5RM - 180	2.93	-	23.5

APPENDIX 2: 'ULTRA MASS' BODYBUILDING PROGRAM TO OVERCOME MUSCLE GROWTH STAGNATION

This program was designed for advanced bodybuilders who have reached a stagnation phase, mass barrier, or plateau in training. This training program could also be used by high level athletes of those sports disciplines that require increasing muscle mass as a condition for Maximal Strength increasing.

II.1. WHY PLATEAUS ARE REACHED DURING THE PROCESS OF INCREASING MUSCLE MASS

There are two main reasons:

1. OVERTRAINING DUE TO LENGTHY AND INTENSIVE TRAINING

If the plateau was caused by overtraining, the time for preparation should be longer (3-5 weeks), and should utilize more pronounced recovery measures. Restoration methods are useful, such as hiking in the mountains or walks along the seashore, biking, swimming and other forms of physical relaxation. You should also change the place of your workouts, decrease the number of strength exercises, and make this training fun. At the end of this period you should feel the desire to begin intense training again.

2. MONOTONOUS TRAINING

A lack of variety in exercises, the sequence of exercises, the gym, and the overall training plan. Limited exercises, the improper choice of weight, and a non-optimal balance between weight and the number of reps within the set also contribute to stagnation.

If the plateau was caused by a monotonous training regime, before starting this program you should precede it for 2-3 weeks with a low (30-50% of normal) training program. During this period, this program should include a moderate volume of strength exercises with light weight, swimming or other means of relaxation which you enjoy and are fun. These will prepare you for the intensive training program to come.

II.2. HOW TO OVERCOME THE STAGNATION OF THE INCREASE IN MUSCLE MASS

To overcome the stagnation of the increase in muscle mass, you may use the nontraditional form of the training load organization in microcycles that involve very strong muscle action. This organizational format is based on the principle of the training loads 'super-position': the application of two workouts using the same exercises in each workout.

The training load of the second day can entail less volume than the first day, but because it includes two days in a row of training the same muscle group, it still provides strong stimulation. This is optimal for maximizing the effect of training and recovery on building muscle mass.

The traditional bodybuilding system as proposed by Weider, Kennedy and others, is designed to work one muscle group and then rest it for 48-72 hours. Only then will the muscle be worked again.

The principle of the training loads 'super-position', tested in many weightlifting, power lifting, and bodybuilding regimes can serve to greatly fortify the previous concepts.

On the first day the athlete will carry out basic exercises for a specific muscle group. On the second day, he will perform many isolation exercises for the same muscle group. These muscles are then given 72 hours for optimal restoration.

This method is not a contradiction to the classical ways of bodybuilding training, but is rather a further advancement of this basic philosophy and should be used in addition to the processes already proposed for overcoming a plateau in building muscle mass.

VARIANT 1 – 4 DAYS MICROCYCLE

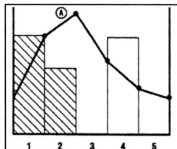

In this variant of practical application, the principle of 'super-position' of the training load is realized in such a way as shown in Fig. II.1. On the first day, basic exercises, performed at a high load (volume and intensity), are applied to specific muscle groups. This leads to an increase in protein breakdown (catabolic process) in the muscles stressed.

On the second day, the training load is again targeted towards the same muscle group as day one (Fig. II.1). In spite of the training load being less than the first day, the second day's training increases the breakdown of the proteins in muscle again, even more than on the first day. Following training, the catabolic action can be observed through measurements of metabolic by-product levels such as histidine, CPK, lactate, ammonia and others.

Fig. II.1 - Super-Position Training on Days 1-2. A – marks the rise and fall of metabolic by-products.

After the third day (a day of rest for the particular muscle group), all biochemical processes begin to normalize. A more plastic process within muscles (the synthesis of proteins) is observed. On day four, when a different muscle group is worked, the muscles trained on days 1 and 2 continue the normalization process and activation of muscle synthesis.

VARIANT 2 - 9 DAYS MICROCYCLE

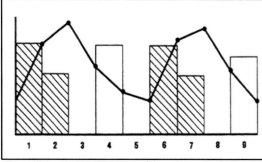

The organization (setting up) of the training load in the microcycles with a developing character is oriented towards the development of muscle mass. Such a micro-cycle includes two micro-blocks (Fig. II.2). These cycles last 9 days and are characterized by intensive training loads directed towards a specific muscle group on days 1-2 and 6-7. Such training results in an increased breakdown of the muscle proteins plus a build-up of excess metabolites. This stress is most important to achieve optimal growth.

On days 3 and 8 the body switches off the catabolic process to switch over to one of anabolic action, in-

Fig. II.2 - Super-Position Training on Days 1-2 and 6-7. Days 3 and 8 are transitional. Days 4-5 and 8-9 are anabolic.

creasing the synthesis of the proteins. This is a super-compensation of the energetic resources of the body which are necessary for the synthesis of proteins on days 4-5 and 9.

It is important to point out that the 'super-position' principle within a nine day micro-cycle should be used by advanced athletes during special periods of training, for example, when a Mass Barrier must be avoided or broken.

This method should not be used for a long time, and certainly not by beginners. The entire program consisting of 10 micro-cyc1es incorporates a variety of principles within the organization of the training, with a tendency towards a gradual stepwise improvement in loads from one micro-cyc1e to the next. The idea of the Variety principle in this case is a switch off from a micro-cycle which is strong to one of moderate influence or action on the body. The strong action on the body within a developing micro-cycle means conditioning that provides mostly for the breakdown of the muscle.

A moderate action macro-cycle is a restoration or recovery micro-cycle which is designed mostly for the activation or synthesis of muscle proteins. (Developing & Recovery Micro-cycle).

II.3. GENERAL DESCRIPTION OF THE TRAINING PROGRAM

The following program is a solution to breaking through a mass barrier due to cases 1 and 2 listed above. In Bodybuilding, this program can be included in a preparation period lasting five months, divided into muscle building and cutting up blocks, with the first Block aimed at building muscle strength and size.

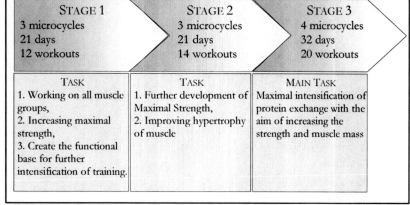

STAGE 1	STAGE 2	STAGE 3
3 microcycles 21 days 12 workouts	3 microcycles 21 days 14 workouts	4 microcycles 32 days 20 workouts
TASK	TASK	MAIN TASK
1. Working on all muscle groups, 2. Increasing maximal strength, 3. Create the functional base for further intensification of training.	1. Further development of Maximal Strength, 2. Improving hypertrophy of muscle	Maximal intensification of protein exchange with the aim of increasing the strength and muscle mass

Fig. II.3 - Scheme of the training program

- Slow movements are executed in overcoming and yielding regimes;
- The overload weight should be near 80% of maximum;
- The weight lifted for 8 – 12 reps;
- A tempo is 40-70 seconds for each set;
- The rest period between each set should be not longer than 2 minutes and can be 30 seconds or less.

The second Block must be aimed at the maximum definition and vascularity of the muscles for the ultimate ripped appearance.

The mass building program, regarding the first Block, is designed for 11 weeks and includes 10 micro-cycles for a total of 46 training sessions combined in three stages. (Fig. II.3).

II.4. STAGE 1 (STRENGTH ORIENTED)

The goal of this stage of training is to prepare for the intensive training in future cyc1es. The task is to work on all musc1e groups, increase the Maximal Strength and create a functional base for further intensification of training. This stage includes three micro-cycles of 7 days each (Fig. II.4).

Training builds on the traditional body-

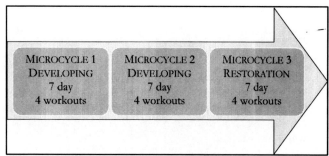

MICROCYCLE 1 DEVELOPING 7 day 4 workouts	MICROCYCLE 2 DEVELOPING 7 day 4 workouts	MICROCYCLE 3 RESTORATION 7 day 4 workouts

Fig. II.4 - Scheme of the Stage 1 (21 days)

building format of the split system. Each muscle group will be worked two times each with a recovery interval of 48-72 hours.

Micro-cycles 1 and 2 are of a developing character. Training with a great load and using basic exercises with great resistance (weight) is applied here.

Micro-cycle 3 is a recovery micro-cycle. The training load in this week decreases, due to decreasing the weight by 20-30%. The goal of this week is the activation of the restoration process.

MICRO-CYCLE 1 & 2 (DEVELOPING)

MONDAY		
1. Squats (using "rest-pause")	1-3 sets	3-6 reps[65]
2. Bench Presses	1	10
	3-4	3-6
3. Combination: Lying Bent Arm Pullover and Lying French Press	3-4	5-7
4. Combination: Bent Arm Flies and Lying Triceps Press	4-6	(2-4)+(2-3)
5. Abdominal Exercises	Hard	

TUESDAY		
1. Dead Lift	1	10
	2	4-8
2. Bent Rows with wide grip	1	10
	3	4-8
3. Press Behind Neck (wide grip)	1-2	10
	2	5-8
4. Preacher Curls	2	6-10
5. Abdominal Exercises	Light	

FRIDAY		
1. Squats	1	10
	3-4	4-8
2. Bench Press (using 'rest pause')	2-3	4-6
3. Triceps Parallel Bar Dip (w/load)	3-4	5-7
4 Abdominal Exercises	Hard	

SATURDAY		
1. Good Mornings with figured grip (see fig. II.6)	2-3	4-8[66]
2. Bent Rows with wide grip	4	6

---

[65] Rest-Pause Principle. Example: Bench Press for 1-3 reps at a weight of 90-95% with limited pauses. Rest 30-45 seconds. Again perform 2- 3 reps. Rest for 40-60 seconds. Then perform 2- 3 reps. Rest 60-90 seconds. Finish with one final rep.

[66] Figured grip as seen in Fig. II.5.

3. Combination: Seated Triceps Press (from chest and behind neck)	4-6	4-6
4. Barbell Curls (using cheating)	3-4	4-6+(2-1)[67]
5. Abdominals	Light	

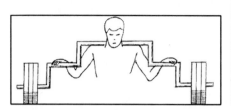

Fig. II.5 - Figured Barbell

Fig. II.6 - Bend forward (Good Morning) touch rubber surface and rebound

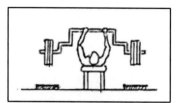

Fig. II.7 - Bench Press with Figured Barbell with shock

MICRO-CYCLE 3 (RESTORATIVE)

MONDAY AND THURSDAY		
1. Squats	3-4 sets	6-8 reps
2. Bench Presses	3-4	4-8
3. Combination: Lying Bent Arm Pullover and Lying French Press	2-3	6-8
4. Triceps Parallel Bar Dip	2-3	6-8
5. Abdominals	Hard	

TUESDAY AND FRIDAY		
1. Dead Lifts	4 sets	6-8 reps
2. Bent Rows (with wide grip)	4	6-8
3. Press Behind Neck	4	6-8
4. Barbell Curls	4	6-8
5. Abdominals	Light	

II.5. STAGE 2 (TRADITIONAL MASS SPLIT-SYSTEM)

Further improvement of Maximal Strength and hypertrophy of muscles.

This stage includes three weeks of micro-cycles (Fig. II.8).

In the first two micro-cycles (4 and 5), the training is based on a 5 workout split system. The principle for this micro-cycle is that each muscle group will be worked twice each week.

The fifth workout is for more deep work on one muscle group which is lagging and demands priority training.

In micro-cycle 4, more detailed focus on the leg and chest muscles are undertaken. In micro-cycle 5,

---

[67] In this combination, the first 3-4 reps are barbell curls with a weight of 3-4 SRM in each set.. If this combination is followed immediately with 1 or 2 lifts using cheating principle, the cheating principle uses the muscles of the back and legs.

the muscles of the back and upper body (arms and shoulders) are targeted, micro-cycle 6 is for recovery, and is the same as micro-cycle 3 of the first stage. Based on the four day split-system, a decreased weight and volume of the load is utilized. Additional recovery means are also applied.

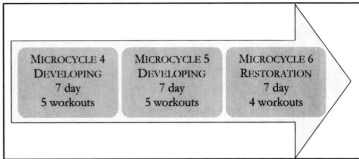

| MICROCYCLE 4 DEVELOPING 7 day 5 workouts | MICROCYCLE 5 DEVELOPING 7 day 5 workouts | MICROCYCLE 6 RESTORATION 7 day 4 workouts |

Fig. II.8 - Scheme of the Stage 2 "Split System" (21 days)

MICROCYCLE 4 (DEVELOPING)

MONDAY		
1. Squats	1-3 sets	8-10 reps
2. Bench Press (rest-pause) or Lying Triceps Extension	3-4	6-8
3. Combination: Bent Arm Pullovers and French Presses	3-4	4-6
4. Seated Toe Raises	4-5	6-10
5. Abdominals	Hard	

TUESDAY AND SATURDAY		
1. Dead Lifts	2-3 sets	6-8 reps
2. Bent Rows (wide grip)	2-3	6-8
3. Press Behind Neck	3-4	8-10
4. Preacher Curls	2-3	6-8
5. Abdominals	Light	

WEDNESDAY		
1. Inclined Bench Press (wide grip)	4 sets	6-9 reps
2. Dumbell Flies	4	6-8
3. Parallel Bar Dip	4	6-8
4. Abdominals	Light	

FRIDAY		
1. Squats (rest-pause)	3-5 sets	6-8 reps
2. Bench Presses (see fig. II.7)	2-3	8-12
3. Combination: Bent Arm Pullovers and French Presses	3-4	4-6
4. Calf Machine Raises	4-6	8-10
5. Abdominals	Light	

MICROCYCLE 5 (DEVELOPING)

MONDAY		
1. Dead Lifts	1 3-4	10 4-6
2. Bent Rows (wide grip)	1 2-3	10 6-8
3. Dumbell Rows	3-5	6-8
4. Preacher Curls	2-3	6-10
5. Barbell Curls (cheating)	1-3	6-8+(1-2)
6. Abdominals	Hard	

TUESDAY AND THURSDAY		
1. Squats	1 3-4	10 8-10
2. Bench Presses (see fig. II.7)	2-3	8-10
3. Combination: Bent Arm Pullovers and French Presses	3-4	4-6
4. Parallel Bar Dips	4	4-6
5. Abdominals	Light	

WEDNESDAY		
1. Good Mornings with Figured Grip (see fig. II.6)	2-3	4-6
2. Press Behind Neck	2-3	6-8
3. Barbell Upright Rows	3-4	6-8
4. Dumbell Lateral Raises	3-4	6-8
5. Bent Over Lateral Raise	3-4	4-6

FRIDAY		
1. Dead Lifts	1	6-8
2. Bent Rows (wide grip, cheating)	2-3	4-6+(1-3)
3. Dumbell Rows	3-5	6-8
4. Preacher Curls	2-3	6-8
5. Barbell Curls (cheating)	1-2	6-8+(1-2)
6. Abdominals	Hard	

MICROCYCLE 6 (RESTORATIVE)

MONDAY AND THURSDAY		
1. Squats	3-4	6-8
2. Bench Presses	3-4	4-6
3. Combination: Lying Bent Arm Pullovers and French Presses	2-3	6-8

4. Triceps Parallel Bar Dips	2-3	6-8
5. Abdominals	Hard	

TUESDAY AND FRIDAY		
1. Dead Lifts	4 sets	6-8 reps
2. Bent Rows (wide grip)	4	6-8
3. Press Behind Neck	4	6
4. Barbell Curls	4	6
5. Abdominals	Light	

II.6. STAGE 3 ('SUPER-POSITION')

The main task is to maximize the intensification of the organism's protein exchange to further improve strength and muscle mass. The stage lasts for 32 days and it includes 20 training sessions. Four microcycles (Fig. II.9) are included in this stage. Microcycles 7 and 9 last nine days. These have a developing (building up) character. They consist of a

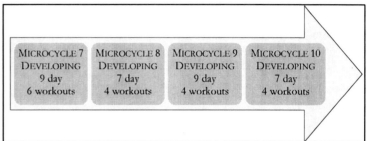

Fig. II.9 - Scheme of the Stage 3 "Super-position" (32 days)

training session which is based on the training load principle of 'super-position'.

Microcycles 8 and 10 last 7 days. These are recovery oriented. Training the same muscle group two days in a row (1-2 and 6-7).

Microcycle 7 is mostly for leg and chest muscles.

Microcycle 9 targets the back and shoulder muscles. On the first day of the two-day training sequence you will use basic exercises. On the second day you will utilize more isolation exercises.

Microcycles 8 and 10 activate protein synthesis and muscle hypertrophy. They build on the principle of the 4-day split system and decrease the training load in comparison to microcycles 7 and 9.

In all microcycles of this program, the range of sets and reps depends on the athlete's level of preparation and how he feels in that day.

The weight of resistance is chosen according to the individual level of preparedness in that day. The weight chosen should be one where the athlete is able to lift 6-8 times, (6RM, 7RM, and 8RM).

Rest between sets in the first stage should be from 1.5 to 3 minutes, with a tendency to decrease the rest time by the end of the stage.

MICROCYCLE 7 (DEVELOPING LEGS & CHEST)

DAYS 1 AND 6		
1. Squats (rest pause)	4-5 sets	6-10 reps
2. Bench Presses (see fig. II.7)	3-4	8-12
3. Decline Press	2-3	6-10
4. Parallel Bar Dips	3-4	6-8

5. Combination: Bent Arm Pullover and French Presses	3-4	6-8
6. Abdominals	Light	

DAYS 2 AND 7		
1. Leg Presses	3-5 sets	8-10 reps
2. Leg Extensions	2-3	8-12
3. Leg Curls	2-3	6-10
4. Dumbell Bench Press	3-5	6-8
5. Incline Dumbell Flies	3-4	6-8
6. Triceps Pushdown	3-5	6-8

DAYS 3 AND 8: REST

DAYS 4 AND 9		
1. Dead Lift	1	10
	4-5	3-5
2. Bent Rows (wide grip)	1	10
	2-3	3-5
3. Behind Neck Press (wide grip)	1-2	8-10
4. Preacher Curls	3-4	6-10
5. Abdominals	Hard	

DAY 5: REST

MICROCYCLE 8 (RESTORATIVE)

DAYS 2 AND 5		
1. Squats	3-4	6-10
2. Bench Presses (see fig. II.7)	3-4	4-6
3. Combination: Bent Arm Pullovers and Lying French Presses	2-3	6-8
4. Parallel Bar Dip	2-3	6-8
5. Abdominals	Hard	

DAYS 3 AND 6		
1. Dead Lifts	4	6-8
2. Bent Rows (wide grip)	4	6-8
3. Presses Behind Neck	4	8-10
4. Barbell Curls	4	6-8
5. Abdominals	Light	

DAYS 4 AND 7: REST

MICROCYCLE 9 (DEVELOPING BACK & SHOULDERS)

DAYS 1 AND 6		
1. Dead Lifts	1 4	10 3-6
2. Bent Rows (wide grip)	1 3-4	10 4-6
3. Pull Downs	3-4	8-10
4. Presses Behind Neck (wide grip)	4-5	6-10
5. Barbell Curls (cheating)	1-3	4-6+(1-2)
6. Abdominals	Hard	

DAYS 2 AND 7		
1. Good Mornings with Figured Grip	4	6-8
2. Behind Neck Pulldowns	3-4	6-10
3. Seated Cable Pulls	4-5	6-10
4. Barbell Upright Rows	4-5	6-8
5. Bent Over Lateral Raises	3-5	6-8
6. Preacher Curls	4-5	6-10

II.7. PREVENTIVE MEASURES AGAINST FUTURE STAGNATION OF MUSCLE MASS INCREASE

To prevent the stagnation of the increase in muscle mass it is possible to use the following non-traditional 3 day microcycle model.

II.7.1. MODEL OF INTENSIVE 3-DAY MICROCYCLE FINALIZED TO INCREASE MUSCLE MASS

The following three day on/one day off workout cycle is done at maximum intensity until failure of the muscle in each set. The fourth day is a recovery day of rest. The next day you can continue the training cycle listed above. It is essential that each set be performed until failure point is reached, for it is only at this point where strength endurance lactic acid characteristics are most pronounced, leading to maximum muscle mass increase.

One or two warm-up sets in addition to your general warm-up should be done before the first exercise for each muscle group to reduce the chance of strain or injury.

MONDAY		
Flat Bench Press	3 sets	8-12 reps
Incline Dumbell Press	2	8-10
Decline Dumbell Flies	2	8-10
Cross Bench Dumbell Pullovers	2-3	10-12

Standing Barbell Curl	3 sets	8-12 reps
Incline Dumbell Curls	2-3	8-10
Cable Concentration Curls	2-3	10-15
Abdominals	Hard	

TUESDAY		
Behind Neck Pull Downs	3 sets	8-12 reps
Seated Cable Rows	2-3	8-10
T-Bar Rows	3	8-10
Seated Press Behind Neck (wide)	4 sets	6-10 reps
Dumbell Side Laterals	3	8-12
Dumbell Bent Over Laterals	3	8-12
Calves	Hard	

WEDNESDAY		
Squats or Leg Press	4-5 sets	8-12 reps
Leg Extensions	3-4	8-10
Leg Curls	3	8-12
Lying Barbell Triceps Extensions	2 sets	8-12 reps
Close Grip Bench Press	2	8-10
Dumbell Kickbacks	2	8-10
Cable Pushdowns	3	8-10
Barbell Reverse Curls	3 sets	6-10 reps
Barbell Wrist Curls	3	10-15
Barbell Reverse Wrist Curls	2	10-15
Barbell Reverse Curls	3 sets	6-10 reps

APPENDIX 3: QUESTIONS AND ANSWERS ABOUT WARM-UP[68]

III.1. WHAT DOES WARM-UP MEAN AND WHY IS IT NECESSARY?

Warm-up is a compulsory workout which traditionally must precede any kind of intense motor activity. In sports physiology literature, the Warm-up is defined as a complex of physical exercises which prepares the athlete for competition or a training session; it ensures the acceleration of the introductory processes to activity and facilitates performance improvement. The rule to execute Warm-up before training or competition was introduced into sports practice a long time before physiologists had justified it (1). Yet, in defining the basic rules of the Warm out execution, scientific arguments played an essential role (16).

From a physiological point of view, the necessity to execute Warm-up is related with the inertia of the organism's physiological functions: transition from an everyday activity to an intense muscular activity requires a certain period of time. This time is necessary for the functional activation of specific mobilizing mechanisms in the vegetative (autonomic) systems and the central nervous system. Accordingly, an efficacious execution of training or competition activity should be preceded by a designed training load aimed at the preliminary activation of the above-mentioned processes - 'putting them behind the starting line' (16).

The general action of the Warm-up consist of the activation of the sympathetic-adrenaline system, which, through specific hormones, mobilizes glycogen reserves and stimulates the efficient activity of the heart, lungs, blood vessels and the blood itself. In this way, the increase in activity of all components of the oxygen transport system is obtaining (the amplification of the capillary system in lungs, heart and skeletal muscles as well as increasing blood temperature) which ensures an improvement in the organism's energy supplying function (17). This increase in the activity of the organism's vegetative (autonomic) system, leaving traces of increased nerve center sensitivity, ensures the higher excitability of the respiratory and thermo-regulation centers and regulation centers of the cardiovascular and motor systems activity. Afterwards, in relation to the changes in the general condition of the organism (regarding the activity of the energy supply, hormonal and the neuro-muscular systems), it is necessary to recall the 'motor engram' of the movements, which form the basis of the subsequent training session.

For this reason, the Warm-up should include two parts – general and specific. The first part (general) is mainly aimed at the organism's general activation, the preparation of the locomotory system as a whole, and of single muscular groups. The second part of the Warm-up is mainly aimed at the activation of the specific motor control function, related to the subsequent physical activity.

As it is traditionally acknowledged, Warm Up consists in the three subsequent phases, which include the following activities:

1) prolonged cyclic exercise executed in aerobic regime, aimed at increase of body temperature (the warming out load (WL);

2) general articulation gymnastic exercises, executed with dynamic muscle stretching or, as it became

---

[68] Based on the article: 'The Scientific and Methodological Fundamentals of the Warm-Up in Elite Level Sports', Natalia Verkhoshansky, ('Basi scientifico-metodologiche e problemi attuali del riscaldamento nello sport di alta prestazione'), 'Atletica Studi', n 3/4, 2003 - Italy.

a popular in the last years, exercises of static stretching;

3) specific exercises, which corresponds to the exercises, included in the following activity, in regards their motor structure, but executed at the lower level of power output.

Even though the Warm-up includes three consecutive phases aimed at solving different problems, it represents a unitary process with a single purpose: the preparation of the athlete's organism for the subsequent load. For this reason, all the different groups of exercises used in the Warm-up should be efficacious. Yet, each of these groups contributes to the global result not directly, but in the organic dependence on each other. This is why the efficacy of each of them can be assessed separately in an objective way, only by considering the influence of others, according to the global result of warm-up, through the increase in specific work output level at the moment of the execution of the subsequent work.

III.2. WHAT ARE THE REAL PROBLEMS INVOLVED IN CARRYING OUT THE WARM-UP CORRECTLY?

Even though it is stated in physiology manuals that the general part of the Warm-up should be similar for every kind of sport, research results show that each sport discipline has its specific needs in the general part of the Warm-up as well (11, 15).

In modern sports practice the Warm-up is often executed with exercises that the athlete is usually accustomed to during the first years of sports practice; and continues to repeat them without ever questioning their effectiveness. Warm-up temporal parameters used by athletes in different sports disciplines can differ from each other greatly. For example, a thrower's Warm-up (very often completely neglected) is quite different from a track and field sprinters' Warm-up, which could last up to 60 minutes (4). Athletes of the same discipline can also go about a Warm-up differently, for example, in Weightlifting, a Warm-up can last from 2 minutes to half an hour (20).

Also, there is one tendency which has been emerging over the last years. In the 1980s the appearance of a social-economic and cultural phenomenon likes 'Fitness' exerted its influence on many aspects of Olympic sports athlete preparation. The difference between training in amateur sport and Fitness, and high-level athlete training gave rise to methodological questions which needed some explanation. Two questions in particular regarding the rules of Warm-up exercise emerged.

The first question to be clarified concerns the length and the intensity of the warming up load (WL), aimed at increasing body temperature. In some of the literature, it has been confirmed that an elite athlete's WL should be longer and more intense than a beginner's WL (5). However, the authors advise everybody to run for five minutes at a moderate speed; this they say is usually enough for both beginners and experts. The activation of perspiration is considered the criterion for deciding whether the exercise has been completed. (5,6) Other publications regarding high level sport, on the contrary, have stated that a longer WL is necessary - anything from 15 up to 30 minutes; the intensity can be gradually increased to reach 60-80% of the maximal agonistic level (4, 12, 15, 16).

What has actually been observed in practice, in certain sports, is that there is a tendency to underestimate the importance of the increasing the whole body temperature (4) and to replace it with an increasing the local temperature of the muscular groups involved in the carrying out subsequent activity (20).

The second question under recent discussion concerns the choice of exercises to be used during the second phase of Warm up, i.e. immediately after execution of WL. "Dynamic rhythmic articular gymnastic exercises with light muscle stretching have always been a part of sports Warm-up, but since people began speaking about 'stretching', static maximal stretching has completely replaces them, also in those sports disciplines in which a great flexibility is not necessary" (7). Nowadays, however, the legitimacy of such a replacement raises serious doubts among the experts (8, 7, 5).

It has been observed that Russian athletes as well as many Eastern Europe athletes – unlike athletes in the West – do not stop in stretching static positions, immediately after Warm-up running, but rather, prefer to perform dynamic gymnastic exercises. It is also odd that in Russian, instead of the term which is equivalent to Warm-up, usually used in the Anglo-Saxon world, there is another word, - разминка, - derived from the verb разминать, comparable to the meaning of the English verb to knead (bread).

In recent years, people have often talked about the mysterious "Russian Warm-up" trying to understand what it is, essentially, and the advantages it has over 'Western style Warm-up'. (23) However, for those who have observed athletes training for many years, there is nothing particularly 'national' in the 'Russian Warm-up'. In fact, until 20 years ago, it represented the 'traditional Warm-up' used all over the world.

Information which clarifies these two problems and assists the reader to formulate his/her own opinions regarding how to perform the Warm up, is presented in the following questions and answers.

III.3. WHY DO WE NEED TO INCREASE BODY TEMPERATURE BEFORE INTENSE PHYSICAL ACTIVITY?

The reason why the body needs to Warm-up before beginning muscular work is based on the fact that an increase in body temperature (hyperthermia) is considered as the main condition that ensures increasing physical work output (16). The most studied aspect of the preparatory action of hyperthermia is its influence on the contractile capacity of the muscles. (Astrand, Rodhal 1969; Bennet 1975, Nadel 1985, cit. from 6).

In Asmussen's classic research (cit. from 17), a direct connection between the body's hypothermic level and physical work output is illustrated – the higher the temperature reached during Warm-up, the higher the output indicator in the execution of subsequent short work of maximal power.

Later research demonstrated that an increase in deep body temperature ensures the proportional increase in results of the subsequent short speed strength exercise: a 2° increase corresponds to 7%; a 1° increase to 3-5%. The lowest increase in temperature leads to the lowest increase in results (10, 4).

III.4. WHAT IS THE NECESSARY OPTIMAL LEVEL IN MUSCLE TEMPERATURE AND WHAT IS THE BEST WAY TO REACH IT?

Optimal body temperature at which the best power index and movement coordination are registered, ranges from 39° to 39.5 °C – at this temperature all the physiological processes in the organism take place at maximal intensity (Israel 1959, Kirsch; Kayser 1983, Cit from 4).

Yet, there is also a belief (4) that warming-up the body to 39 °C is only necessary in cases when maximum expressions of speed and speed strength are required to be reached following a workout. That is, the increase in body temperature up to 39° C does not seem to be an obligatory condition if the speed-strength exercises executed at the level of maximal power output is not required in subsequent training session. However, the data regarding the optimal level of Warm-up in such cases is not available. In some publications, (6) authors discuss the need to increase the body temperature level by 1°C to 38 °C without there being any evidence of this need.

How body temperature is increased is very important. Research shows that the 'passive' local Warm-up of muscles (through massage, hot compresses, infrared rays, ultrasound and diathermy) does not result in the same increase in work output, reached through a workout load Warm-up (16, 17). The fact that the replacement of the warming up load (WL) or the shortening of its length in favor of the application of means to Warm-up local muscles is pointless: it is made evident by the characteristics of the thermoregulation system of the human organism (16). This system does not possess its own executive organs; the preservation of thermal homeostasis is realized by the joint functioning of three systems – circulatory, respiratory and secretory (17). Muscles serve as a source of warmth through muscular work, yet it is only the warming up of the body's core that leads to a steady warming up of its periphery i.e., the muscles themselves. Quick local muscular warming-up (for example, through local massage) causes subsequent rapid cooling-down, because it is through the blood that warmth is transmitted to the body core: venous blood, by taking the warmth away from its producer, the muscles, cools them quickly, transferring this warmth to heart, the core. Only if the body's core warms up, will the warmth pass from the blood to its periphery, the skin, for cooling down.

Regarding the influence of temperature on the activity of the central nervous system, it is well-known (12, 16) that, even though an increase in the temperature of single neurons leads to an increase in speed reaching proprioceptive stimulation and information volume, brain work output increases only if the generated hyperthermia has an endogenous origin; increasing the external radiation of warmth has the opposite effect.

All this confirms the importance of *activating the whole blood circulatory system as an essential physiological mechanism which ensures an increase in the body temperature and the positive effect of warming-up in general.*

III.5. HOW LONG SHOULD THE WARMING-UP LOAD LAST AND HOW INTENSE SHOULD IT BE?

As Asmussen demonstrated (cit. from 17), the higher the intensity and the longer the duration of the warming-up load (WL), the higher the level of work output in a subsequent work. In his research, the higher the power of the WL (in the interval from 400 to 1600 kg m per minute), the higher the body temperature (from 37° to 40° C); but muscle temperature only reached the steady maximum level of 39° C after ten minutes, while the internal (rectal) temperature was reached after thirteen minutes.

The subsequent research on the dynamics of increases in the deep body temperature of an athlete in an aerobic workout with different power exertion (10, 16), confirmed that the higher the power of the WL, the higher the working hyperthermia. Nevertheless, the time to stabilize core temperature, as well as muscle temperature, does not depend on the level of the executed work power; it forms on average about 20 minutes later. Performing WL at the same power for more than 20 minutes does not increase core temperature (Fig. III.1).

The comparison between the modification of deep body temperature and perspiration during the prolonged WL of moderate power (15, 16) showed that the appearance of the first drops of perspiration cannot be considered as a criterion for putting an end to Warm-up loads - under normal conditions of external temperature, the first drop of perspiration appears after about 2-5 minutes of work while the body core warm-up is completed only after 20-25 minutes (Fig. III.2).

This means that if <u>an athlete does not have to face a subsequent training session or competition with maximal power output (that is, if body temperature does not need to be increased to 39° C), then he/she can execute the WL at a lower intensity, but its duration should not be shortened.</u>

Regarding the necessary value of the WL power (intensity), the German researchers W. Joch and S. Ukert (4) showed that the necessary Warm-up level (39° C) can be reached by using a 20 minute load on the bicycle ergometer, which includes two phases: ten minutes of pedaling with a constant intensity (power) level of 200 Watt in a first phase; the second phase with an increasing number of thrusts on the pedal, from 80 to 100 turns per minute and up to the maximal value (about 188 turns per minute).

A modification of the power and the length of the WL at the opposite extremes respectively did not produce positive effects. A prolonged workout of up to 45 minutes at a low intensity (130 Watt) allowed for an increase in temperature of only 0.6° C. A short WL, which included a 23-24 second workout period at the highest power, allowed for a more significant 1.3° C (0.9° C in women) increase in temperature, which still, did not reach the desired optimal level of 39° C.

Therefore, it can be seen that the reported data in its entirety confirms that the choice of WL power has a particular meaning for the performance level of the subsequent motor activity – the lack of sufficient WL power does not have to be compensated for by increasing its length. Besides, if the maximal power of WL is kept for an insufficient length of time, this does not allow the organism sufficient preparation, necessary for any subsequent work.

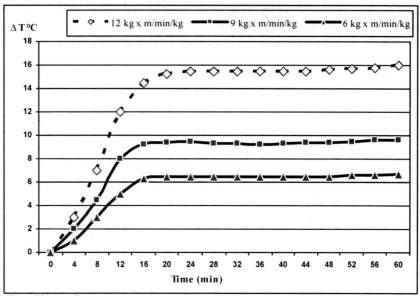

Fig. III.1 - Dynamics of increase in body deep temperature of the same athlete during the work on cyclo-ergometer with different power (Bobkov G.A. 1978).

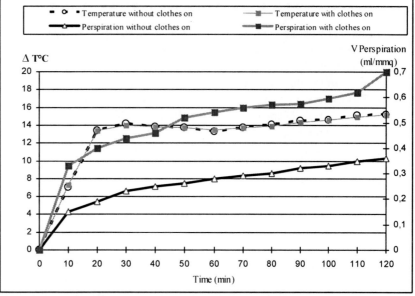

Fig. III.2 - Dynamics of the increase in body deep temperature (left abscissa) and in perspiration (right abscissa) during the work executed by the same athlete without his clothes on and with his heavy clothes on (Ioffe L.A., Bobkov G.A. 1988)

W. Joch and S. Ukert (4) believe that an insufficient intensity in exercise performance is an essential shortcoming in current Warm-up methodology in track & field throwing. The influence of such a

Warm-up on body temperature and on the performance of subsequent speed strength exercises (shot put and maximal explosive effort on Arm-Press machines) showed that it was not possible to increase temperatures up to 39° C, nor was there any significant improvement in control exercises.

III.6. CAN WARM-UP LENGTH BE REDUCED UNDER INCREASED ENVIRON-MENTAL TEMPERATURES OR BY USING HEAVY CLOTHING?

The degree of warming-up the body's core depends on work power and under medium thermal conditions (from less than 10° to 20° C); it does not depend on the degree of heat insulation. This means that it is not possible to reduce WL time despite the use of heavy clothing (16). Besides, heat insulation increases perspiration and organism dehydration which has a negative influence on work output. In a comparative research on the dynamics of the modification of deep body temperature and the perspiration of an athlete with/without clothes on (see Fig. III.2), it was observed that in both cases deep temperatures coincided, as well as the time it took to reach maximum temperatures – the only differences registered were the times of the onset of perspiration (15).

By increasing work power (higher than 100% level of VO2 max), and considerably increasing the temperature, particularly the humidity of the surrounding environment, the organism's 'cooling system' is exponentially not able to overcome excess heat and deep temperature increases. (16). Yet, the increase in surrounding environmental temperature cannot be sufficient reason for eliminating warming-up completely – we need only to reduce WL intensity in the first part of the Warm up (5).

III.7. CAN WE USE TEAM SPORTS AS WARMING-UP LOADS?

Traditional Russian rules of Warm up execution do not suggest using non-continuous exercises without uniform intensity such as the warming up load. Opinion regarding this aspect of the Warm up is shared in the West. According to T. Kurz (4), it is wrong to begin the Warm-up with high intensity exercises - an intense beginning reduces the athlete's work output, contributing towards a faster increase in blood lactate concentration. Different/intermittent modifications of work power have a neurologically dangerous disorganizing effect. The author confirms the traditional warm up rules that start the Warm-up with low intensity exercises, gradually building up to the basic level of intensity of exercises which form the load and are subsequently executed.

At this point in the discussion, the results of a research conducted on the modification of psychophysiological indexes deserve attention. The condition of 33 young (14-16 year old) Russian wrestlers was studied after the execution of a Warm-up at different intensities (9). Fig. III.3 represents the percentage modification dynamics of the indexes of the athletes' psycho-physiological condition after the execution of several Warm-ups at different intensities.

The increase in the average intensity of Warm-ups used by athletes with heartbeats ranging from 120 to 164 beats per minute, improved in accordance with the indexes of the young athletes' condition in all the parameters studied, particularly with respect to the sector of 132-138 heartbeats per minute. The Warm up executed at these intensity levels ensured: the best SNC condition (the maximal hand strength dynamometry and the highest perceptible light frequency), the highest level of muscle elasticity (myothonometry indexes), and the athletes' best general emotional condition (Galvanic Skin Response Index).

Deterioration in these psycho-physiological characteristics after the Warm-up at a medium intensity was noticed, corresponding to a heart rate level of below 180 beats per minute. The use of team sports as a Warm-up increased the heart rate to 150 beats per minute, causing the sudden fall of all the parameters studied.

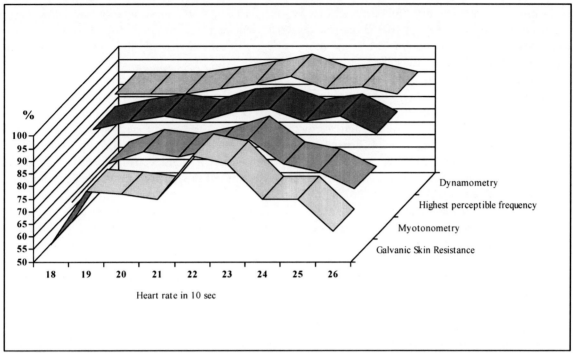

Fig. III.3 - Dynamics of parameters of athletes' psycho-physiological condition after the warm-up, depending on the different level of heart rate. (Bashkirov V. F., Novikov A.A., Zunuspekov S. K. 1991 – modified).

While carry out the above-mentioned experiment, there were nine injuries: three of them - two at the beginning of the training and one at the end - after the execution of a low intensity warm-up, and six of them - during the first part of training, preceded by a Warm-up set at an intensity which was too high. These injuries could be related (especially, those which occurred at a low intensity low level) to two psycho-physiological indexes: myothonometry and maximal perceptible light frequency. The low myothonometry indexes indicated that the athlete's muscles were rigid both in the case of the low intensity Warm up as well as in the Warm up that was too intensive. The low index of maximal perceptible light frequency indicated that the athletes were not able to effectively control their movements. Furthermore, the low index of Galvanic Skin Response observed in these two cases, indicated the suboptimal emotional arousal level of the athletes.

III.8. HOW SHOULD WL PARAMETERS BE ADAPTED TO THE ACTIVITY TO BE UNDERTAKEN AND THE ATHLETE'S INDIVIDUAL NEEDS?

It is well-known that the duration and the intensity of the Warm-up as well as the interval between the Warm-up and the main activity are determined by the following factors (7):
-   the type of follow-up exercise,
-   external conditions (temperature and air humidity),
-   athlete's characteristics and emotional conditions.

With regard to women, during the period of ovulation and in the 3-4 days before the beginning of menstruation, Warm-up intensity can be reduced by 15-20% without negative effects in virtue of hyperthermia, a characteristic typical during periods of ovulation and menstruation (10, 16).

It is well-known that the positive influence of the Warm-up before long-distance races is not as great compared to middle and short distances races (16, 17). In fact, the question about how the Warm-up in the various sports disciplines should be designed remains open: which temporal parameters should be set? which loads should be used? and to what degree of intensity should they be fixed? At this point in time these questions are still waiting for answers.

In the literature, it has been highlighted that a large part of the theories concerning the use of the Warm-up are only based on logical reasoning. Everybody thinks that they know them and in virtue of the power of persuasion, they do not raise any doubts regarding the concepts used to justify them. The experiments carried out demonstrated conflicting results. Research in different sports disciplines were often compared, but the individual needs of each discipline regarding the Warm-up (not only in the specific part but in the general part as well), are often different. This is mainly because of the differences in the kind of work required and in the characteristics of the athletes' functional condition in the various disciplines (11).

The influence of temperature increase on the whole organism should not be confined to the simple sum of the effects on single tissues and organs. Different kinds of work are limited by different factors; the thermoregulation processes, the capacity to execute workouts with different intensities and duration. These factors mainly depend on each other within the vegetative systems. During the workout, whose limiting factor is the capacity to save on the vegetative resources of muscular activity, body core Warm-up is undesirable because it damages muscular efficiency (16).

From this, we know that the Warm-up is a phenomenon that concerns different aspects of each sports discipline which in turn has specific needs that must be addressed in the general part of the Warm-up. In the presence of general rules concerning its execution, both the general, as well as the specific part, should be designed and carried out in different ways according to the subsequent kind of muscular work.

III.9. STATIC STRETCHING VS. DYNAMIC STRETCHING: WHICH IS THE BEST METHOD FOR WARM UP?

An essential topic dealt with by supporters of static stretching in the Warm-up is that this method causes fewer injuries – *"the ballistic dynamic stretching is not recommended if the subject who is training, executes sudden forward-backward movements; the potential danger of muscular accidents connected to a too quick passage from shortening to stretching"* (6).

Yet, in sports practice, the opposite opinion has become common for many years. For example, in the 1960s Igor Ter-Ovanesyan[69], the ex-holder of the world long-jump record and more than one time holder of the Soviet long-jump record, who also competed successfully in the sprint dis-

Igor Ter-Ovanesyan, Olympic medalist and world record holder in long jump. Coach of the Soviet national jumpers' team and since 2001 at the head of Methodological Council of all Russian National Olympic Teams coaches.

---

[69] Igor Ter-Ovanesyan has been Olympic medalist in long jump, participated in Olympic Games five times (1956, 1960, 1964, 1968, 1972) and twice won a bronze medal (in 1960 and 1964). He beat the world record in 1962 (8.31 meters) and 1967 in Mexico City (8.35 meters). After retiring from his active career, he became coach of the Soviet national jumpers' team. Since 2001 he has been at the head of Methodological Council of all Russian National Olympic Teams coaches.

cipline, wrote: "... *it is essential not to stretch and not to loosen up the muscles too much. Through my experience I know that in the Warm-up it is better to execute stretching exercises as little as possible; using mainly swings, whose nature corresponds to natural sports movements the most*"(18).

In the beginning, these conflicting opinions were expressed in the following rhetorical question: *Which is the best method for developing the flexibility that should be applied in the Warm-up to reduce the possibility of injuries and to increase the performance of the subsequent sports activity?*

A detailed comparative analysis of a great deal of data in the last 30 years, regarding methods to develop flexibility, was conducted by G. Wydra. (8) He came to the conclusion that it is not possible to answer the question, *'which is the most efficacious method to develop flexibility?'*. Unequivocally and yet, in his opinion, dynamic exercises are more suitable than static ones for Warm-up.

In fact, different authors report the same experimental data regarding the immediate negative effect of the static stretching on the performance of subsequent sports activity: 15 minutes of stretching the hip flexors and extensors caused the sprint time results to worsen by 40 meters. A similar group of exercises had a negative influence on vertical jump results in which there was a 4% decrease (Henning et al., 1994. cit from 7). This data confirms the material T.Kurz, reported on (5) concerning the negative influence of the static stretching on strength maximal indexes (Kokkonen et al 1998) and the activity of articular reflexes (Rosenhaum, Henning 1995).

K Wienmann. and A. Klee (7), however, set out the object of the discussion by presenting the problem in a different way – is *the development of flexibility the aim of using the stretching exercises during Warm-up?*

In the authors' opinion, the mistake lies in the same logic illustrated in our preliminary remarks, that is, if stretching exercises lead to an improvement in flexibility, then we need to use them in the Warm-up to reduce the risk of accidents in subsequent workout loads. The question is that we need to distinguish between the immediate effect of stretching exercises and their training effect on flexibility in general.

Improvement in flexibility requires the execution of a forced passive stretching of muscles. Its maximum value should be reached, the threshold of which is represented by a sensation of pain. According to the detailed analysis of the maximum static stretching affects on the structural composition of myofibrils, the authors deduced that this effect is similar to the effect of the isometric strength exercise.

Gilles Cometti with co-authors J. Ungaro & L. G. Alberti came to the same conclusion on the basis of numerous research data: static stretching is a hard load for the muscles'; its 'passive' structure creates the conditions leading to the formation of micro-injuries inside the muscle fibers (22).

G. Cometti et alt (21), as well as K. Wienmann & A. Klee. (7), came to the conclusion that "..*the systematic training, aimed at developing flexibility, really leads to the improvement in joint mobility (joints movement extension) with a decrease in passive stiffness and muscle tone. Yet, the intensive static stretching in the Warm-up phase, causes an effect, which is just the opposite to the one that we usually hope to obtain: instead of an increase in performance and a decrease in dangers of injuries, what actually takes place is a worsening of the performance and an increase in the danger of injuries*".

Gilles Cometti famous researcher of the Dijon University, great innovator in the field of sport methodology.

S.Tubanski (24) sums up other European authors' different facts and opinions regarding static stretching and its use in the Warm-up:

- Stretching exercises, executed before speed-strength sport activity, can lead to a deterioration of the performance, which has a limiting effect on sports results and does not have an effect on accident prevention.

- In the Warm-up programs for speed-strength sports athletes, the dynamic stretching exercises are preferred to passive stretching exercises.

According to K. Wiemann and A. Klee (7), in the Warm-up, five static or dynamic light exercises, used very cautiously and with sub-maximal stretching are enough to reach a positive effect- a general increase in mobility and elimination of passive muscle tension. This, in the authors' opinion, should also concern the athletes of those disciplines, in which an increased extension of the basic sports gesture in the execution of the exercise (gymnastics, hurdles, javelin throwing) is required; these athletes have to train the development of a specific flexibility only during the provided training sessions and not in the Warm-up.

Regarding the last statement, Gilles Cometti et alt (21) believe, on the contrary, that the Warm-up program should consider the specific needs of these sports disciplines: it is better not to exclude specific stretching exercises from the Warm-up of athletes engaged in sports disciplines who need to perform considerable speed-strength efforts in the positions of maximal movement extension; as for example, in hurdles, sprint and javelin throwing. But, these stretching exercises should not be executed as classi-

Fig. III.4 - Specific warm-up exercises with muscles stretching for runners-hurdlers.

cal static stretching, but as specific dynamic, 'springing' exercises (Figs III.4 and III.5)[70].

Research results showed, therefore, that, from the point of view of the influence on the passive structure of muscles, in the Warm-up, the use of static

Fig. III.5 - Specific warm-up exercises with muscles stretching for javelin throwers

stretching with muscle maximal stretching has no advantages in comparison with the traditional dynamic exercises. Yet, it still poses the question:

do the traditional dynamic exercises present any advantages in comparison with the static stretching and are these advantages determined only by their influence on the passive structure of the muscles?

To answer this question it is necessary to closely analyze 'traditional dynamic exercises.'

III.10. WHAT ARE THE 'TRADITIONAL DYNAMIC WARM-UP EXERCISES'?

Gilles Cometti tried to reconstruct some aspects of the so-called Warm Up 'à la russe', analyzing a contribution to the Russian journal 'Legkaya Atletica' ('Track & Field'), published in the 1960s, in which some innovations to the traditional Warm up method were proposed (23).

Unfortunately, the entire description of the 'Russian style Warm up' exercises were not to be found in this journal, since they were obviously the ABC of the Rus-

Warm up gymnastic at school

[70] The figures are taken from 'Equipment and specific exercises in Track & Field' (edited by B.G. Alabin and M.P. Krivonosov), Moscow, "Fiskultura and Sport", 1976.

sian and Eastern European coaches. Regarding the methods of carrying out Warm ups, Russian coaches (always former-elite athletes of the same sports discipline) usually started to learn from their first coaches during childhood, who in turn, also learned this method from their coaches.

Three groups of exercises are included in the 'traditional Warm-up gymnastics':

1) Concatenated cyclic 'pendulum' repetitions of voluntary anatomic movements in the most important articulations of the body (flexion-extension, abduction-adduction and rotation).

2) Additional dynamic stretching of the muscle groups, which are involved in the basic competition movements with increase in extensions, in the shape of *springy flexing* (in knee-bends, leaning, half-hanging, etc)

3) Relaxation exercises in the shape of movements of ballistic swings with the extremities (limbs) free from support or with the trunk alternating muscular relaxation with tension and passive stretching (inertial).

The first group of exercises (General Developing Exercises[71] of the traditional European gymnastics) have been known for more than a century as the Articular Gymnastics, for example, Muller's gymnastics system (Lieut. J.P. Muller, of Denmark, 'My System', 1904). It is odd that many of these exercises are very similar in form to the Indian Hadha Yoga series of dynamic exercises (3), which are also the base form of curative gymnastics (Kinesiotherapy) and several modern Fitness products (such as Pilates or Kallanetics).

There are some peculiarities in the execution technique of articular gymnastic exercises used by athletes during the Warm-up, which differentiate it from its early traditional form; its movements can be defined as 'rigid'. The articular gymnastic exercises, used in the athletes' warm up, should be executed gradually increasing the extension of movements, keeping the muscles relaxed during the passive phases of the movements. This peculiarity gives the movements a more marked swinging, ballistic characteristic, when the change of direction takes place together with a little inertial stretching of muscles that were previously relaxed.

We can clearly see from some traditional rules about the use of articular gymnastics that is considered above all a means for improving the blood circulation in the furthest parts of the body and in the adjacent articulation tissues. For example, an essential principle, which determines the sequence in the execution of exercises, is 'from the periphery to the core' principle (from the distant parts of the body to more central ones) and from one part of the body to another (from the lower body to the upper body or vice versa). Exercises that ensure movements for the muscular groups used first of all in the main part of the training session should end the Warm-up. (5)

Considering that for every part of the body there is a certain number of articular gymnastic exercises, in beginners' training, it is advisable to frequently change the order in which they are performed so as to avoid monotony (5). On the contrary, high-level athletes often choose exercises, that they prefer and form their personal selection, the repetition of which can become a sort of standardized ritual before the competition (e.g. see the drawings of the wrestlers warm up 'ritual'), which helps to prepare them

Fig. III.6 - "Ritual" warm up of wrestlers

---

[71] General Developing Exercises - in Russian, ОРУ, общеразвивающие упражнения.

both psychologically and physically for the performance in competition (4, 21), see Fig. III.6.

An important role is played by exercises for trunk muscles and above all for back muscles, which are often neglected because it is thought, erroneously, that, there will not be any need for arm movements, if the main work in the training involves legs. What is usually forgotten is the importance of improving the condition of vertebral disks and ligaments - extremely vulnerable parts of the body. The traditional wide arm swings, scapular-humeral and coxo-femoral joint rotations, flexions and trunk rotations are often used in corrective gymnastics; special exercises for the treatment and the prophylaxis of scoliosis and osteochondros of the vertebral column. (13). Not less important is the condition of the trunk muscular system to preserve the stable position of the back; it determines the main biomechanical parameters of sports technique - the projection of the body's center of mass in relation to the support, (14).

The general influence of the Warm-up on the athlete's condition depends on the choice of rhythm and the duration of the exercise execution: it can be relaxing (slow and long lasting) or tonic (dynamic, short and quick) (18, 5).

In the second group there are some exercises which are usually defined as 'static-dynamic stretching'. The technique to execute these kinds of exercises differs from the static stretching exercises; it includes a cyclic change of the degree of muscle stretching, a 'springing' in certain 'stretched' position (Fig. III.7). With this kind of exercise, the athlete reaches the level of the longest stretch for only a short period of time; the passive absolute maximum value should not be reached too soon. The group of exercises which have just

Fig. III.7- Springing exercises.

been referred to is considered dangerous if used in the Warm-up. And yet it is the amateur who runs these risks in pursuit of fitness and not the athlete who has good training experience (e.g., high-level athletes, who train almost every day for years).

As G. Cometti underlines (21), 'springing' movements represent an essential element of dynamic muscle stretching, through which a better effect on the capacity of reactive performance can be obtained without any reduction of speed strength. And yet, we should be more careful to monitor the execution technique of these exercises; they place higher coordinative demands on the athlete. The trainer has to inform the athlete that the springing movements should be executed cautiously, in a measured way and never if any sensation of pain is experienced. The point is that, in executing single muscle stretching exercises, it is very important to avoid reflex tension by stretching the antagonist. This is why there are particular rules in Yoga, which include the combination of a stretching phase, characterized by slow and long exhalations, with a relaxation phase – characterized by inhalation (3). An awareness of motor sensation control should be reached during the execution of stretching exercises in the warm-up - this requires a certain experience. Thanks to the development of this practice, the level of the athlete's general motor knowledge becomes greater, showing the capacity to effectively control voluntary movements, as well as the specific ability to relax, important in both speed strength and endurance sports disciplines.

The third group, ballistic exercises (swings), helps to eliminate the possible negative action of the previous static-dynamic stretching on the passive structure of the muscles, such as any 'remaining tension' (Fig. III.8). This is reached through the combination of a phase of light stretching with a phase of deeper relaxation during the movement of inertia and also through leg and arm shaking.

In the literature, it is thought that these dynamic stretching exercises also increase accident risk. (6). Yet, Ter Ovanesjan classifies them as relaxation exercises (18). In fact, the effect of any exercise depends on the mental statement directive with which it is executed.

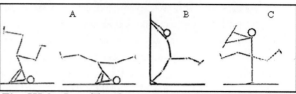

Fig. III.8 - Igor Ter-Ovanesjan's draws of his favorite dynamic warm-up exercises (18).

<u>The ballistic swings during Warm-ups should be executed, not to increase the extension of the movement, but to relax muscles, to 'loosen' any 'remaining tension.'</u>

The essential requirements of Warm-up exercises can be traced back to three basic rules regarding their execution:

1) Uniform rhythm and 'nimbleness' in the execution of movements, which exclude forced high speed, excessive tension.
2) Gradual increase in movement extension (amplitude/range of motion).
3) Scrupulous control of relaxation; on no account should control of movement be lost during the execution of spring and swing exercises.

It is recommended to group the ballistic movements in series of 10-12 repetitions for each leg and 5-6 repetitions for each arm: the athlete should execute the number of series necessary to reach the maximum of voluntary movements in every direction (5).

In spite of the apparent easiness of these exercises, it is essential to observe and reinforce the correct execution technique. The effectiveness of these exercises essentially depends not only on the time and the rhythm of their execution but also on the capacity to relax the muscles during the inertial phases of movements.

Muscle relaxation between each phase of the cycle, and the capacity to control movement extension and motor sensations are very important for the general effect of warm-up gymnastics (19, 2). For example, Igor Ter Ovanesjan wrote (18) that he was able to reach the optimal physical condition, taking part successfully in 100 and 200 m sprint races the same day, because, in his opinion, he did warm-up exercises *"...composedly: not only to Warm up muscles, but ... 'listening' to myself all the time, trying hard to understand how they affect me"*.

In his drawings there are three "favorite" exercises, which he used in Warm-ups before a 100 m race (Fig. III.9): dynamic stretching (A), springing (B) and ballistic (C) movements.

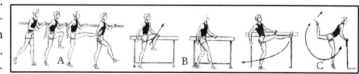

Fig. III.9 - Ballistic exercises ("swings").

III.11. WHAT ADVANTAGES DO TRADITIONAL DYNAMIC GYMNASTICS HAVE OVER STATIC STRETCHING?

The term dynamic stretching is very often used to refer to articular gymnastics as well. As we shall see, this term is too limited and therefore cannot be considered correct. The physiological action of traditional dynamic articular gymnastics should have the following characteristics:

1) Activation of SNC motor area by increasing the flow of afferent impulses by the joint proprioceptors which means a general improvement in the coordination of movements;
2) Improvement in blood circulation through the activation of local blood circulation in the articulations and the release of their additional reserves, deposited in the blood, with rich hemoglobin;
3) Improvement in the condition of trunk muscles (respiratory muscles and back muscles), vertebral

disks and the whole control system of motor cerebro-spinal reflexes, correction of posture, prevention of accidents and alteration of vertebral column function;

4) Decrease in passive muscle tension through the rhythmic change from relaxation to tension.

As we can see, the assumed effect of these exercises should not be limited to muscle stretching with all its positive consequences. Besides, the functions of all the different parts of the warm-up cannot be clearly identified since they interact with each other, strengthening this and preserving that in the passage from one phase to another. The passage to the dynamic exercises immediately after the warming-up load helps to attenuate the decrease in the frequency of cardiac contractions, ready to start relaxation during the long stretching phase.

Concerning the additional activation of the blood circulation and the improvement of trophic processes in articulation and ligaments, the advantages of dynamic movements compared to static movements are absolutely evident. (5). The warming-up effect, reached in the first part of the Warm-up, which improves the activity of all the systems in the organism, is accentuated and realized through the dynamic exercises, which stimulate this process towards a greater specificity, selecting the final part of the main competition gesture.

Without any doubt, all the advantages of the traditional Warm-up exercises explained here, are based on theoretical considerations. Up until now, nobody has demonstrated the real effect of their use with specific testing showing how they wholly correspond to what has been supposed in theory; in addition, up until now, nobody has proven it to be wrong. Yet, it is possible that the absence of experimental confirmation of these theories does not show that they are not correct, but only that there is a lack of data derived from direct experimentation control.

The traditional dynamic Warm-up exercises were a systemic part of the only process of athletic preparation of training and competition over many years of trial and error and over several generations of trainers and athletes;. The gradual acquisition of the correct execution of exercise often took place at the same time as the acquisition of other important elements of training including the increase in the level of the athlete's own expertise and mastery of his/her sports discipline.

The replacement of the Warm-up, of the traditional dynamic exercises with the static stretching highlights the reductive tendency to simplify the utility of athletic preparation to meet the level of amateur athletes. And yet, the substantial differences between elite sport and amateur sport should not be forgotten. Fitness and high level athletic preparation are two are extremely different specific sectors of man's motor activity. In their essence they face different problems and choose different methods for solving them. For those who practice 'fitness' and mass forms of physical activity, it is possible to organize a warm-up with the easiest positions of stretching rather than pay attention to the detail of dynamic exercises and their execution techniques. And yet, for high-level athletes paying attention to detail is essential.

III.12. CONCLUSIONS: WHAT DO WE REALLY KNOW ABOUT THE CORRECT WAY TO WARM UP?

1) The Warm-up for athletes appears to be a series of physical exercises. They are made up of well-defined consecutive phases, determined by the need to activate and synchronize basic physiological mechanisms. These mechanisms facilitate the execution of the muscular workout that is to follow. The so-called general part of the Warm-up, as well as the subsequent specific part, should be organized and executed in relation to the kind of subsequent training workout as well as the athlete's level of preparation.

2) The general part of the Warm-up for high-level athletes is different from the Warm-up designed

for those who wish to maintain a healthy lifestyle. Fitness offers a great variety of forms of physical activity On the other hand high level athletes require a more precise definition of the basic Warm-up parameters in relation to the type of training or competition load they require, especially if they aim to reach the maximal results in speed strength exercises.

3) The first phase of the general part of the Warm-up is focused on the organism's general warming-up, which ensures an increase in the athlete's performance – improvement in the contractile capacity of the muscles and the function of the organism's oxygen supply. An essential physiological mechanism of the athlete's performance improvement during Warm-up, is an increase in body temperature which can only be obtained by activating the whole blood circulation through the execution of continuous muscular work.

Research results show that in the speed-strength sports (or before SST training sessions):

- the warming load (WL) should be continuous and long enough (20 minutes) so that the increase in body temperature is stable. The higher the value of subsequent work power, the higher its average intensity should be. However, it should not go beyond the athlete's individual anaerobic threshold level;
- the choice of WL power is particularly important for the performance of the subsequent motor activity –insufficient WL power should not be compensated for by prolonging its duration. Besides, if the maximum power of the WL is not of a sufficient duration, it does not ensure the organism's necessary preparation for the subsequent workout;
- if the athlete does not have to prepare for a training session or competition, in which he has to reach his maximal results, he/she can carry out a WL at a lower intensity, without reducing the overall length and duration of the workout.
- the increase in WL intensity should be gradual, so that only at the end of the workout the level of training and competition work power is reached.

4) The second phase of the general part of the Warm-up should first of all ensure a decrease in passive muscle tension as well as the improvement of the local blood circulation; but not the development of flexibility. The theoretical analysis of the means used to reach this aim, and the methods and data of specialized research, show that the most suitable exercises aimed at solving these problems, are the traditional dynamic exercises of articular gymnastics.

To increase the active extension of specific movements, a few stretching exercises can be used, followed by the relaxation exercises (swings).

The positive effect of the exercises of the second phase of the general Warm-up essentially depends on the quality of their execution.

5) An analysis of the literature shows that the execution methodology of the Warm-up in high-level sport is an on-going question, which needs further research. What is less clear are the questions connected to the exact choice of the warming up load, its duration and intensity in relation to the actual form of the subsequent training session or competition.

To conclude, it needs to be highlighted that the Warm-up in elite sports can lead the athlete's organism to reach a high physical level, training it and preparing it for competition as well as, requiring the athlete's contribution of specialized motor knowledge and specific experiences. The trainer's professional problem is not only to correctly sequence the exercises and teach the athlete to perform them in a systematic way, but also to lead him/her to learn how to 'listen to' his/her body, to recognize its condition and to have the ability to manage it with efficiency.

III.13. BIBLIOGRAPHY

1. Billat V. L'apport de la science dans l'environment sportif:l'exemple de la course de fond. STAPS, 2001, 54, 23-43 (in French).

2. Fox E.L., Mathews D.K. The Physiological Basis of Physical Education and Athletics. Philadelphia. Saunders Co., 1981, p.282.

3. Iyengar B.K.S. Light on Yoga, Schocken Books; Revised edition (January 3, 1995), trade paperback ,p.544.

4. Joch W., Uckert S. Kriterien fur ein Wirkungsvolles Aufwarmen. Leistungssport, 3, 2001(in German).

5. Kurz Th. Science of Sports Training. Stadion Publishing Company. Tnc.USA, 2001,p.426.

6. Michelli L.J., Jenkins M. The Sports Medicine Bible. Harper Perrenial, A Division of Harper Collins Publishers, 1995,p.391.

7. Wiemann K., Klee A. Die Bedeutung von Dehnen und Stretching in der Aufwarophase vor Hochstleistungen. Leistungssport, 4, 2000,p.5,(in German).

8. Wydra G. Stretching. Ein Uberblick uber den aktuellen Stand def Forschung. Sportwissenschaft, 4, 1997, pp.409-427, (in German).

9. Bashkirov B., Novikov A., Zunuspekov B. Warm Up as the optimising factor of the yang wrestlers psychophysiological indexes and injuries prevention. Theory and Practice of Physical Culture, 11,1991, pp.51-54,(in Russian).

10. Bobkov G. et al.. The report on the Pan-Soviet Symposium "The physiological and clinical problems of the human and animal organisms' adaptation to the hypoxia, hyperthermia, hypo-dynamia to specific means of recovery" 1978, p.100. (in Russian).

11. Bobkov G. et all. The report on the Pan-Soviet Technical-Scientific Conference "The system of complex valuation of the elite athletes preparedness" Moscow. 1979, p.-15. (in Russian)

12. Bobkov G., loffe L. e al. In the book: "The factors limiting the improvement of the high level athletes work capacity". Moscow, 1987, pp.5-7.(in Russian)

13. Dubrovsky V. Cinesiotherapy: manual for students. – Moscow, 1998,p.-608. (in Russian)

14. Zatziorsky V., Aruin A., Selujanov V. Biomechanics of the human motor apparatus. Moscow. 1981.p.-141. (in Russian)

15. Joffe L. e al. The report on the XXIII pan-Soviet conference of Sport Medicine "Ways of improving the effectiveness of the medicine control of the elite athletes" Moscow., 1987, p. 54. (in Russian)

16. Joffe L., Bobkov G. Thermo-regulative aspects of Warm Up (revue). Theory and Practice of Physical Culture, 4, 1988, pp.24-28. (in Russian)

17. Kotz J. Pre-competition condition and Warm Up in "Physiology of Sport" Moscow. 1986, pp.27-32. (in Russian).

18. Ter-Ovanesyan I. About Warm Up, "tuning" and new sensations. Track and Field, n.5 1966, pp.10-11.(in Russian)

19. Farfel V. "Physiology of Sport" Moscow, 1960.p. 384. (in Russian)

20. Chajrulin R. "The culture of the pre-competition Warm Up in Weightlifting". Theory and Practice of Physical Culture, n. 7. 1990, pp.33-34. (in Russian)

21. Cometti G., Ungaro L., Alberti G. Stretching and Sports Performance (part 1). SDS - Rivista di Cultura Sportiva. n. 62 - 63 (2004), pp. 47 –59. (in Italian).

22. Cometti G., Ungaro L., Alberti G. Stretching and the sport performance (the second part). SDS - Rivista di Cultura Sportiva. n. 60 - 61 (2004), pp. 33 – 39. (in Italian).

23. Cometti G., Ungaro L., Alberti G. Warm Up and sports performance. SDS - Rivista di Cultura Sportiva. n. 64 - 65. (2005) (in Italian).

24. Tubanski S. Aufwòrmeffekte von Stretching in Sportarten und Disziplinen mit Schnelkraftanforderungen. Leistungssport,n. 2, 2005, pp.20-23 (in German).

APPENDIX 4: THE CONTRIBUTION OF YURI VERKHOSHANSKY TO THE DEVELOPMENT OF SPORT SCIENCE

IV.1. MAIN PARADIGMS OF THE TRADITIONAL THEORY AND METHODOLOGY OF SPORTS TRAINING

Traditional Eastern European sports theory and methodology viewed the training process as a *preparation for competition*. The three main components of the training process consisted of technical and tactical preparation, psychological preparation and finally, physical preparation.

Physical preparation methodology in particular was based on the objective of honing the athlete's physical attributes. The manner in which this could be achieved in the training process was derived from the concept of '*human motor abilities*'. This concept was formulated on the basis of the following theoretical observations:

1) Human motor function versatility is based on a hypothetical mechanism. This mechanism allows activation and synthesis of the basic *motor abilities*. The different motor abilities being: strength, speed, endurance, agility and joint mobility. Abilities can take precedence over each other in varying degrees in sport according to the type of movement required.

2) Each of motor abilities is individually regulated by a specific physiological mechanism, which governs its expression and development.

3) Improvement in motor ability necessitates using appropriate means and methods. This process is called *education* and is specific to each of motor abilities.

4) It is possible to obtain the desired specific combination of motor abilities through developing each one of them separately and then combining them into new 'hybrid' abilities.

In the 1950s and 1960s, these aforementioned concepts were applied to the field of sports training methodology. According to this approach, any type of sports activity is characterized by a combination of different motor abilities called physical qualities. When physical qualities are combined, certain characteristics take precedence. The first is that the emphasis will be placed on the most outstanding physical quality necessary in a given sport. The second characteristic being there will be a specific combination of secondary qualities that are necessary to compliment the expression of the primary physical quality.

These theoretical observations determined the way traditional training methodology was developed. During the 1970s most research was based on the belief that each physical quality could be evaluated by a motor test. Consequently a systemic approach was implemented in sport training methodology. Because of this, in each sports discipline the structure models of athletes' special physical preparedness were elaborated based on a statistical analysis of motor test results. In addition, physical preparation training means and methods were classified and structured. The basis for this classification focused on the capacity to improve a given physical quality.

Taking these things into account, the athlete's physical preparation comprised of two components: the General Physical Preparation (GPP) and the Special Physical Preparation (SPP). The first is focused on the development of each particular physical quality through the appropriate means and methods. The goal of SPP is to integrate the physical qualities that are developed individually in a specific structure. This is accomplished by using distinct exercises analogous to the competition technique.

At the time, resistance exercises were seen as a training means to develop strength motor ability specifically. Special Strength Training (SST) was an important part of physical preparation for those sports events in which strength is the outstanding motor ability. Olympic weight-lifters and throwing event athletes in track and field utilized SST specifically in their training. In other sports disciplines these exercises were considered only to be used for general physical preparation.

The dominant methodological doctrine at the time with regard to the organization of sports training was Matveyev's[72] concept of *Periodization*. This concept was formulated in the book "The problem of Periodization in the Training Process", published in 1964. Soon after its publication, it became the foundational concept of sport training methodology. Matveyev's second book entitled, "Fundamentals of Sport Training", published in 1977 further elaborated on these concepts.

The ideas presented were revolutionary. For the first time, sport training was analyzed as a unified process: *"The preparation of the athlete represents a multilateral process using the whole totality of the factors (means, methods and the particular conditions of training), which allow to influence purposefully the athlete's development and to ensure the necessary level of his readiness for sport achievements."[73].*

Lev Pavlovich Matveyev (1925 – 2006)

According to Matveyev's Periodization concept:

"The integrity of the training process is ensured by a definite basis- structure, which determines the relatively stable order through the gathering all its components (its portions, its parts and its links), the regularity of their interrelation and their sequence…The modern opinions about the fundamentals of the training process organization are related to the acknowledgement of the following three levels in its structure:

- *The level of Micro-structure – it is the structure of the single training lesson (training session) and the structure of several training sessions (micro-cycles);*
- *The level of Mesostructure- it is the structure of the middle- length training cycles (mesocycles), which includes the relatively definite chain of microcycles;*
- *The level of macrostructure – it is the structure of the big training cycles (macrocycles), such as half-year cycle, yearly cycle and multiyear cycles"[74].*

"…The training cycles represents a relatively complete repetitive sequence of training process chains and stages (training sessions, training stages and training periods), taking turns in rotation. Each subsequent cycle represents a partial repetition of the precedent, but, at the same time, …it includes partially renewed contents(training mean and methods) and a higher level of training load.."[75].

---

[72] Lev Pavlovich Matveyev (1925 – 2006), professor, Dr. Hab., founder of the pedagogic school in the field of Physical Education, Physical Culture and Sport Training, author of the basic manuals for the students of all Soviet institutes of physical culture and sport: "Theory and Methodology of Physical Education" (1967), "Fundamentals of Sport Training" (1977), "Theory and Methodology of Physical Culture" (1991), "Theory and Methodology of Sport" (1992). His carrier is strictly related to the Moscow's Central Institute of Physical Culture and Sport, where he worked all his life (55 years). In 1950 he graduated, in 1954 he completed a post-graduate study and began to work in the Theory and methodology of Physical Education Department. In 1955 he defended his PhD thesis; in 1965 he was graduated as Doctor Habilitatus. He worked as docent, professor, chair of Theory and Methodology of Physical Education and as vice-director of the Moscow's Central Institute of Physical Culture and Sport.

[73] L.Matveev, "Fundamentals of Sport Training", Moscow, Fiscultura e Sport, 1977, page 20.

[74] L.Matveev, "Fundamentals of Sport Training", Moscow, Fiscultura e Sport, 1977, page 224 - 225.

[75] L.Matveev, "Fundamentals of the sport training", Moscow, Fiscultura e Sport, 1977, page 84.

The fundamental principle of sport training was the unity of the general and specific preparation. The overall aim of sports training was formulated as follows: "*…Achieving the highest sport results represents the way to harmoniously develop the physical capacities of an athlete and his inner world; to use the sport activity as a factor for the <u>harmonious development of a person, his education according to the needs of society</u>.*" With specific regard to physical preparation, this principle was applied as the principle of Complex (all-embracing) Development of the athlete's physical qualities. This principle prescribes that the 'education' of all physical qualities should be done in the same training session (complex manner) or in the same microcycle (complex-parallel manner).

It is important to understand the cultural viewpoint of the times. Traditional sports training theory was based on the pedagogical approach. First and foremost the sports training process was regarded as teaching and educating a harmonious person. Improvement of the athlete's physical preparedness was to be obtained through the 'education, 'hybridization' and 'transfer' of their physical qualities.

IV.2. PARADIGM CHANGE IN THE THEORY AND METHODOLOGY OF SPORTS TRAINING

The study and application of training theory became more pragmatic when winning Olympic gold medals became the most important goal of a country's political and social achievements. Once this became the case, the primary focus of sports training became the improvement of Olympic competitors' results. Olympic athletes began to be increasingly more professional, distinguishing them more and more from the previous generations of athletes. They were no longer considered as being 'harmoniously developed individuals'. They now were considered highly adapted individuals trained for competition at the highest level of Olympic sports. Physiologists began to refer to them jokingly as the

'new human species' or *Homo Olympicus*. On specific occasion before the Moscow Olympic Games, Western journalists referred to Olympic athletes as 'modern gladiators'. However, Professor Vladimir Kouznetsov [76] offered a more venerable connotation calling them the 'gifts of the 21st century'.

Kouznetsov wrote that elite sport was a continuous experiment. This experiment was represented by athletes, coaches and scientists who were carefully chosen specialists in their field. He postulated that humanity is seeking the ultimate limits of what the human organism is capable of achieving, and the optimal way of reaching this goal. At the laboratory of Human Potential and Reserves, Kouznetsov

Vladimir Kouznetsov (1931-1986), Russian athlete and sports scientist. The photo on the right was taken for the "Olympic Revue" in 1985, shortly before his unexpected death

[76] Vladimir Kouznetsov (1931-1986), Russian athlete and sports scientist. On four occasions he was crowned the Soviet national javelin champion. He challenged the national record eight times, improving it by 10m. His won his last title in 1964. He would soon after obtain his PhD in defense. When he was still successfully competing as an athlete, he became the head coach of the Soviet national javelin team. After retiring, he began working at the Central Institute of Scientific Research for Physical Culture and Sport and eventually became its deputy Director of Research. At the end of the 1970s, he created Anthropomaximology, the science which studies the extreme capacities of the human organism.

chose elite athletes, "*naturally gifted in the activity under consideration and who have undergone years of intensive and specialized training, perfecting their natural talents*". These athletes were the focus of his study. The results of these studies demonstrated, that "*in order to establish universal laws governing an optimal regulation of the human system, … scientific data obtained from world champions and record-holders of the past, …did not provide results of universal validity as had been hoped*". Furthermore, Kouznetsov postulated that modern champions are in the process of "*reaching a point of development where their performances lie within the sphere of universal laws.*"[77].

In the 1970s, the standard of sports achievements had increased to such a degree that sports results accessible to only a few phenomenally talented athletes between the 1930s and 1950s, were now merely the basic requirements of the average athlete. It would be necessary for the modern day coach to find more efficacious training methods for this new generation of athletes. Thus, a revolution of traditional Soviet sports training methodology was afoot. In order to achieve the ambitious new standards of athletic performance, analysis based on the training of athletes in the 1950s and 60s was no longer valid. The entire system needed to be revised.

By the end of 1970s, one fundamental truth had become undeniable: "*to compete better, you must train more*". When the training load volume of elite athletes had been increased to extremes, sports scientists began to search for new ways of achieving improved sports results. Investigation in this domain diverged into two groups of scientists. One group began researching how to artificially improve athletes' specific work capacity. This facilitated the possibility of increasing the training load volume, while also augmenting the ability of the athlete to recover from the training. Their focus was on the study of the physiological factors that determine an increase in sports results. This research shifted the focus of the sports training process, and looked at it from a physiological standpoint or 'from within". Unfortunately, these studies also helped to open the Pandora's box of doping in modern sport.

Another group of scientists started to search for ways of optimizing the training process. Their goal was to find out how sports results could be improved without increasing the volume of training loads. An approach based methodology which focused on maximizing specifications, and individualizing an athlete's preparation was proposed. For elite athletes who already possessed a high standard of technical skill and motor ability, it was necessary to elaborate specific sets of parameters with regard to each sports discipline. These parameters would represent the determining factors specific for improving the results of each discipline. It was necessary to select the training means that influenced each of these factors, and implement them into optimal training loads and properly organized training schedules[78].

How the training parameters were determined evolved throughout the research as scientists learned more about the influence of human physiology on performance. Rather than focusing on the physical qualities that needed to be improved through 'education' or 'hybridization', their focal point turned to the purely physiological factors of performance. Specifically, the factors that had the most influence on improving sports results. From this research the scientists could analyze specific training methods in depth and extrapolate the relevant data to be applied to training.

As the atom lost its place as the base element of matter in nuclear physics, so did the parameters of physical qualities lose its status as being the base 'element' in the structure of an athlete's physical pre-

---

[77] Vladimir Kouznetsov "The Olympic Games and the Future of Mankind" Olympic Revue, n. 208, 1985

[78] This approach is similar to the basic approach currently used in the modern Optimal Control Theory, the science of maximizing the returns from minimizing the costs of the operation of physical, social, and economic processes. Process optimization is the discipline of adjusting a process so as to optimize a specified set of parameters without violating any constraints.

paredness. Scientists even began to shy away from using the word 'education' when referring to the influence of training loads on the athlete's body. However, the concepts of 'education', 'hybridization' and 'transfer' of physical qualities still remained the corner-stone of the traditional Soviet sports training methodology.

What was the reason for this? As T. Kuhn wrote, *"Scientists have neither needed to be nor wanted to be philosophers. It is, in periods of acknowledged crisis that scientists have turned to philosophical analysis as a device for unlocking the riddles of their field"*[79]. It can be said that the "period of acknowledged crisis" at the time with regard to discussions concerning traditional sports training theory, had to do with the Block Training System. Because this system was understood as the 'periodization of physical qualities', it was restricted to the concepts of traditional training methodology. The traditional understanding of 'physical qualities' and 'periodization' made it virtually impossible for a coach to implement the BTS effectively. This was specifically evident when attempting to select the training loads for each of the 'blocks'. Limited by the structures of traditional understanding, the result was a simply ineffective training plan. In order to develop an efficient BTS model for a given sports discipline, it was necessary to look at the training process from another perspective.

Y. Verkhoshansky himself even had difficulty recognizing the crisis. In fact, in 1970, he still used the traditional theoretical-methodological approach[80]. He did this despite the fact that the fundamentals of the new approach had already been presented in his articles published in the 1960s. He revisited this issue only in the 80', during his work on the BTS model for endurance sports[81]. This issue was analyzed for the first time in 'The Fundamentals of Special Physical Preparation in Sport', published in 1988.

Verkhoshansky was convinced that the Physiology of Human Adaptation was the way to the development of the sport science rather than the pedagogical approach of the Instructional Theory. *"...The unique and correct path to the formulation of effective and practical principles of sports training is through the clarification of the laws of the human body's adaptation to loaded muscular activity as well as to the laws of the process of achieving sports mastery in line with the analytical conclusions after many years of practical experience"*[82].

This conceptual divergence became a turning point in sports training theory and methodology. The new training model of Y.Verkhoshansky, which had been considered 'apocryphal' from the traditional perspective[83], could be validated only once this approach was introduced.

---

[79] Kuhn T.S. The Structure of Scientific Revolutions, University of Chicago Press, Chicago, 1962.

[80] Chapter 1.3.4 'General ideas about the structure of the athlete's physical preparedness' in 'Fundamentals of Special Strength Training in Sport' (1977), presented in the book 'Supertraining' (1999), Chapter 23 'Characteristics of Physical Fitness'.

[81] Articles published in "Sport science bulletin" ("Nauchno-sportivny vestnik"): The problems of the development of endurance, 1984 (together with Charieva A,A.); Endurance as determining factor of the movements speed in cyclic sports, 1988; The system of annual training in the middle distance running, 1989 (together with Zaleev E.N.); Improving the special endurance of the high level ice-hockey players and Programming the special physical preparation of the high level hockey players in the annual cycle,1988, 1989 (together with Tihonov V.V, Charieva A.A and Lasarev V.V). Article published in the book "The problems of skating sport", Moscow, 1989: The role and placement of the special strength preparation in cyclic sports.

[82] see Addendum of 'Supertraining' (Sixth edition expanded version)

[83] see the article of Peter Chine, 'The priority of the biological aspect in the theory of training,' (published by "The Canadian Athletic Coaching Centre" with permission from "Modern Athlete and Coach"). Unfortunately, in this paper, the early publications of Y.Verkhoshansky about the theoretical base of sport training have not been considered.

It may seem that the difference between the newly introduced concepts and the traditional attitudes towards the sports training process were superficial and insignificant. It is important to understand that the correct understanding of the practical innovations introduced by Verkhoshansky was impeded by the 'paradigm shift' in the theoretical discussions. This was imperceptible to many sports training theorists. Verkhoshansky's opponents in fact, did not attempt to discuss how to apply the physiology of adaptation in sports training methodology. They simply continued to disagree with his Block Training model.

The words of Thomas Kuhn help to illustrate the psychological struggle of the scientist who can not come to terms with change: "...*Led by a new paradigm, scientists adopt new instruments and look in new places.... see new and different things when looking with familiar instruments in places where they have looked before. It is as if the professional community has suddenly been transported to another planet where familiar objects are seen in a different light and are joined by unfamiliar ones as well. ...Novelty emerges only with difficulty, manifested by resistance, against a background of expectations. The process of paradigm change is closely tied to the nature of perceptual (conceptual) change in an individual. The emergence of a new paradigm breaks with one tradition of scientific practice that is perceived to have gone completely astray and introduces a new practice conducted according to different rules and within a different universe of discourse*"[84].

Great effort will be made to explain in more detail for those readers who need to find a 'corner-stone' of reference for how the perceptual and conceptual changes in the understanding the fundamental theory of sports training can influence the practical approach of an athletes' preparation.

IV.3.   CHANGES IN THE BASIC THEORETICAL ISSUES

In his approach, Y. Verkhoshansky used two basic theoretical benchmarks: N. Bernstein's Theory of the Self-regulated Motor System and P. Anokhin's Theory of the Functional System.

"...*These two scientists were considered as the founders of the theory of self-regulation of activity in the former Soviet Union. They developed the model for the self-regulation using actual physiological data... The activity is regarded as goal oriented human behavior which is organized by a conscious goal and regulated as a system... Psycho-physiological functional state is developed to provide activity, as a complicated multi-component system which includes behavioral, psychological, physiological, and bioenergetics components. These components interact with one another and are organized by the goal into a self-regulative system. Thus all components of the system interact in such a way to provide the goal of the activity.*"[85]

Basically Y. Verkhoshansky's approach can be summed up as follows:

1) The sports result is the working effect of competition exercise. Performing at the highest level of athleticism requires a mastery of coordinated and precise movements. These movements represent complex motor actions, a system of movements aimed at solving a defined motor task. Two factors determine the ability to attain the desired goals of sport through complex motor action. The first factor is motor control. Motor Control aims to optimize the harmony of the movement system during the performance of exercise. The second factor is physiological. Physiological factors endeavor to create a stable form of mutual connections between the physiological systems. When this is achieved, performing the competition exercise with the needed biodynamic characteristics becomes possible.

2) Increasing the sports result through the training process is a direct result of attaining the desired outcome of an athlete's adaptation. The training process consists of the systematic use of training

---

[84] Kuhn, T.S. The Structure of Scientific Revolutions, University of Chicago Press, Chicago 1962.

[85] Karpoukhina A.M., One-Jang Jeng. "System approach to psycho-physiological evaluation and regulation of the human state during performance". www.scienceshopswales.org.uk

exercises. The utilization of training exercises has two goals. Primarily they must increase the athlete's motor potential. This is done by generating adaptation stimuli which ensures at the functional level, a gradual increase of the physiological systems involved in the competition exercise. It is also important to note that they must also ensure a gradual adaptation of the motor control system to the modified conditions of the athlete's morphology.

3) Increasing the elite athletes' motor potential can only be ensured by highly intensive and highly specialized adaptation stimuli. This can only be reproduced in the training process by a system of training means which are properly organized throughout the training year, and specific to the athlete's competitive event.

These issues will now be examined in detail.

IV.3.1. THE BASIC MECHANISM ENSURING VERSATILITY OF HUMAN MOTOR FUNCTION

The essence of sports activity lies in the movement of the human body. According to N. Bernstein[86], *"Movements are not chains of details, but structures which are differentiates into details: they are structurally whole, simultaneously exhibiting a high degree of differentiations of elements and differing in the particular forms of the relationships between these elements...."*[87]. They are products of a programmed brain model ('the desired future model'), which determines their final result, the goal of motor action.

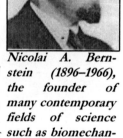

The sports result reached by athletes during competition, represents the working effect of complex motor action (competition exercise). It represents the movement system focused on achieving a defined goal. To achieve this goal, each single movement is aggregated into a system.

"... The organization of single movements into a system is accomplished through the selective gathering of single actions of the working mechanisms of the human body[88] . *In this system, single actions are interrelated and are managed by the motor control mechanism, based on the hierarchical principle"*[89].

Nicolai A. Bernstein (1896–1966), the founder of many contemporary fields of science such as biomechanics and motor control.

To achieve the goal of complex motor action (sports competition exercise), the athlete adheres to the movement system according to pre-determined biodynamic characteristics, which Yuri Verkhoshansky called the *biodynamic structure of sports exercise*: it is the part of general strength field (i.e. the sum of all the external and internal forces involving the body while it undertakes a given motor task).

"Biodynamic structure constitutes the basic framework of the movement system, determining its spatial-

---

[86] "...It has often been stated that the ideas of Bernstein, relevant to many disciplines that constitute the science of human movement, placed him 20-50 years ahead of his time. Many psychologists, anatomists, biomechanists, and even philosophers, have been inspired by his work..." G.J. Van Ingen Schenau and A.J. Van Soest, 'On the biomechanical Basis of Dexterity", in 'Dexterity and its development', Lawrence Erlbaum Associates, Inc., 1996.

[87] Bernstein N.A. Studies of the Biodynamics of Walking, Running and Jumping, 1940. In: Human Motor Actions: Bernstein reassessed Advances in psychology, n.17, Chapter III, Biodynamics of locomotion.

[88] Working mechanisms of the human body (mainly muscle-agonists and muscular synergies, able to produce traction force and anatomically predetermined to achieve movements via limb leverages) are the innate functional components of the human motor apparatus, used to accomplish human motor actions, as independent control units (see Chapter 1).

[89] Verkhoshansky Y. "Fundamentals of Special Physical Preparation in Sport", Moscow, 1988

temporal characteristics and the working effect of sport exercise"[90].

Since every movement represents the interaction between the human body and the environment; complex motor action includes *'the complex of all interactions between internal and external forces, formed during the solving of motor tasks'* (N. Bernstein, 1945). The biodynamic structure of sports exercise is a part of the general strength field, i.e., the sum of all the external and internal forces engaging the body while it undertakes a given motor task. The question is, in what way the human body is able to overcome these external and internal forces and perform sports exercises with the desired dynamic structure.

The answer might be found by implementing Anokhin's theory of the Functional Systems. This theory explains the basis of the physiological mechanism that ensures the organism's interaction with the environment, including human motor action.

Pyotr K. Anokhin (1898-1974) the leading Russian biologist and physiologist of Russian Science Academy.

"...Functional Systems were put forward by P.K. Anokhin[91] *as an alternative to the predominant concept of reflexes. Contrary to reflexes, <u>the endpoints of functional systems are not actions themselves but adaptive results of these actions</u>. This conceptual shift requires an understanding of the biological mechanism for matching results of actions to adaptive requirements of an organism, which are stored as anticipatory models in the nervous system"*[92].

This concept means that any interaction between the organism and the external environment, triggers off the formation of the organism's functional system, 'focused on' and 'determined by' its goal. To achieve this goal, the 'selectively identified' structural elements in the organism's physiological systems are activated and aggregated (integrated) into the functional system.

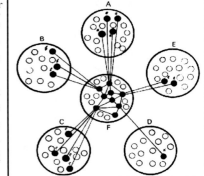

'... Organisms as a whole are composed of many well interrelated functional systems, connected by neurological, hormonal and informational mechanisms. These functional systems often belong to different organism structures; but their synergetic function ensures both the organism's homeostasis and adaptations to the environment.[93]'

The human body's physiological systems (cardio-vascular, hormonal and neuro-muscular) represent the so-called 'morphological substrate' of functional systems.

"...Figuratively speaking, the morphological substrate represents only

Fig. IV.1 - Anokhin's famous scheme illustrates the process of organ "fragmentation" during the formation of functional system. A, B, C, and D are the organs in which the 'individualization' of the structural elements a, b, c, and d occurs. These elements undergo an accelerated growth and consolidation in the the integrated functional system (Anokhin P.K., 1973.)

[90] Y.Verkhoshansky "Fundamentals of Special Strength Training in Sport", Moscow, 1970, 1977

[91] Pyotr K. Anokhin (1898-1974) a leading Russian biologist and physiologist at the USSR Science Academy was the creator of the new Russian scientific school of Physiology. He developed the theory of functional systems which linked the subtle neuro-physiological mechanisms to the integral activity of an individual. According to this concept, a functional system is '...a combination of processes and mechanisms, dynamically formed into a system in a particular situation. This system can lead to an adaptive result which is optimal for the organism at that moment in time'. P.K. Anokhin, 'The functional system theory as a prerequisite to the construction of physiological cybernetics', in: Academy of Science in the USSR, Moscow, 1962, pp. 74-79

[92] Redko V. G., Prokhorov D. V., Burtsev M. S.. "Theory of Functional Systems, Adaptive Critics and Neural Networks".

[93] K.V. Sudacov ,"The systemic construction of human functions", 1999.

the keyboard of a piano: different functional systems play a variety of tunes on these keys to satisfy different human needs... To maintain the useful adaptive result at the optimal level (or to return this result to the optimal level, in the case of deviation), each functional system selectively gathers: different organs and tissues,: combinations of neural elements and hormonal influences and if necessary, specific behavioral forms as well. It is important to note, that the same organs, according to their diverse "free levels" may be included in different functional systems." (see Fig. IV.1).

Returning to human motor action (sports exercise), it represents the movement system (with its inherent biodynamic structure), produced by the force-efforts of working mechanisms of the human body. These force-efforts are produced by muscular contractions. In relation to the working regime, these muscular contractions can be ensured by different energy-supply mechanisms or any of their combinations. These mechanisms are located in the sarcoplasmic reticulum and mitochondria of muscle fibres, but they involve all the physiological systems of the human body (cardio-vascular, hormonal and neuro-muscular) in different proportions. In this way, the outcome of each human motor action is a product of the functional system, which selectively aggregates different organs and tissues (or the same organs and tissues, according to their different functional 'free level'), the combinations of neural elements, and hormonal influences.

Therefore, the versatility of the human motor function is based not on the "synthesis" of different basic motor abilities, but on the ability to create any type of functional system, 'to play any kind of melody' on the 'keyboard' of the human body.

Y. Verkhoshansky wrote *"...Human movement, in its spatial-temporal, quantitative and qualitative expressions, can be seen as the transformation of an idea into a reality, ensured by the entire complex of the physiological systems of the human body... The qualitative parameter of movement (fast, strong, prolonged) is determined by the current functional state and the functional capabilities of the athlete's body, and by the athlete's motivation to execute the particular movement with a given qualitative effect (the semantic structure and the final goal of the motor action). Thus, it is unproductive to search for the specific physiological mechanism of each motor ability. The basis of forming and improving human motor skills is the 'purposeful' adaptation effect, the integrated adaptive reaction, which leads to the morphological-functional specialization of the human organism as a whole..... The general physical qualities, which are known as strength, speed, and endurance, can only represent theoretical categories concerning the general qualitative characteristics of the human motor function..."*[94].

These general categories could be used to characterize the motor function of an individual: different people have, genetically, different motor abilities. Yet, whether they are fast, strong or resistant depends on the kind of motor activity they are undertaking, and the functional levels of the organism's physiological systems involved in this activity. Therefore, quantitatively, these capacities may be evaluated only relatively to a given motor activity.

These categories can characterize all kind of sports activity. In different sports disciplines, there may be a need for specific capacities to perform competition exercises to the maximum, to overcome external opposition, or to resist fatigue. Yet, it must be understood that in different disciplines, these capacities are ensured by different physiological factors; in each sports discipline the working effect of competition exercise is ensured by its own functional structure.

IV.3.2. SPORT TRAINING - THE PROCESS OF ADAPTATION

"... The endpoints of functional systems are not actions themselves but adaptive results of these actions. This conceptual shift requires an understanding of the biological mechanism for matching results of actions to adap-

---

[94] Verkhoshansky Y. "Fundamentals of Special Physical Preparation in Sport", Moscow, 1988

tive requirements of an organism, which are stored as anticipatory models in the nervous system."[95]

Initially, the theory of Functional Systems concerned the formation process of the elementary behavioral forms of the organism during its *ontogenesis*[96] or, in another words, the process of the organism's adaptation to specific life conditions, determined by the necessity to survive. Later, through the research conducted at Anokhin's Russian Academy Institute of Science for Normal Physiology (headed by academic K.V.Sudakov), this theory was applied to a much wider field:

"… The results of adaptation which form different functional systems can be displayed in the molecular, cellular, homeostatic, behavioral, and psychological levels of a single being, as well as when these beings are gathered in populations and societies" and can be displayed also *"…in the process of an individual's learning: automatism and the temporal loss of different skills."*[97].

The sports training process is also a process of human adaptation. Yet, this is not the 'natural' adaptation process determined by the organism's need to survive in a new environment, but rather, an artificially organized adaptation process: *"the process of human adaptation to strenuous muscular activity, determined by the need to improve sports result"*[98].

If the performance of a complex motor action is ensured by the involvement of the elements of the organism's different physiological systems, enhanced in a specific functional system, it is logical to suppose that 'during the athlete's systematic training, which leads to improving the result of his/her sport, the elements of the physiological systems undergo an accelerated adaptive transformation. This transformation ensures the stabilization of the functional characteristics of the elements of the physiological systems at a higher level. This way, on the basis of the functional system, the stable form of mutual interaction between the organism's physiological systems is established in the athlete's organism.'

Verkhoshansky called this stable form Specialized Morphological-Functional Structure (SMFS), which *"…ensures an optimal level of the athlete's specific work capacity under the practical conditions of training and competition activities"*. In other words, it represents the basic structure of an athlete's physical preparedness, his motor potential. It means that an increase in the force characteristics of a given movement is obtained by the *"mutable changes in the central nervous, sympathetic and somatic spheres of the athlete's organism. The strength field, created while the competition exercise is in progress (interrelations between the external and internal forces) objectively reflect the entity, the direction and the stability of the adaptation processes in the athlete's organism as a whole."* [99]..

Therefore, the biodynamic structure of the competition exercise, which ensures the needed working effect of competition exercise, *"… represents the result of the human organism's adaptation to the new specific conditions (a new interaction with the external environment)'. Consequently '…sports achievements are produced by purposeful human adaptive behavior, which is determined by the defined conditions accompanying the process of solving a defined motor task…"*[100].

---

[95] V. G Red'ko, D. V. Prokhorov, M. S.. Burtsev, Theory of Functional Systems, Adaptive Critics and Neural Networks, in Anticipatory Behaviour in Adaptive Learning Systems, Springer Berlin / Heidelberg, 2007. About this issue see also L. Pickehain "The importance of I. P. Pavlov for the development of neuroscience". in "Integrative Psychological and Behavioural Science", Volume 34, Number 2, 1999.

[96] *Ontogenesis* (ontos - present participle of 'to be', genesis - 'creation') describes the origin and the development of an organism from the fertilized egg to its mature form.

[97] K.V Sudacov, The Systemic Construction of the Human Functions, 1999.

[98] Y.Verkhoshansky, Fundamentals of Special Physical Preparation, Moscow, 1988

[99] Y.Verkhoshansky. The regularities of the process of achieving sports mastery, in Theory and Practice of Physical Culture, 1966, n 11, page 19.

[100] Y.Verkhoshansky. The regularities of the process of achieving sports mastery, in Theory and Practice of Phys-

Already by the 1960s, Verkhoshansky had written:

"...the process of improving sports mastery could be seen from the point view of the relationship between the human organism and the environment... It is important to take into account that this relationship is realized not as a 'discrete arc', rather as a "closed curve", based on the 'feed-back' mechanism (N.Bernstein, P. Anochin). The athlete's organism, united by these external and internal relationships, represents a dynamic system. This whole system consists of numerous elementary systems, characterized by their mobile multiform functions and relationships. The state of this dynamic system can be modified by the influence of external 'coercion.' This way, sport training (intensified motor activity) changes the organism's external and internal relationships or, more precisely, complicates them. The consequent adaptive structural-functional reconstructions in the human organism create a new and higher level of work capacity. From a cybernetic standpoint, therefore, the process of improving sports mastery means the transfer of the dynamic system to a new condition of a superior qualitative level. The improvement in sports results represents the visual expression of the improvement in a specific work capacity."

Some years later, Verkhoshansky, on the basis of this idea, introduced Programming, a new approach to managing the process of the dynamic system's 'transfer' to a higher level, and a new innovative method of planning the training process, yet before investigating Programming, it is necessary to clarify other important issues regarding the training process itself.

IV.4. CHANGES IN THE METHODOLOGICAL APPROACH

IV.4.1. MAIN COMPONENTS OF THE TRAINING PROCESS

"According to the theory of functional systems, whenever there is any deviation of activity away from the system's normal life activity (e.g., loss of equilibrium between the levels of the elements within the system), these functional elements automatically mobilize and revert to their respective levels. The sums of the mechanisms responsible for the organism's return to its normal level of activity; prevails in a number of deviating mechanisms. This is the universal rule of the organism's normal functional activity." (Sudakov K.V.,1999).

This rule means that the repetitive achievement of the complex motor action's goal, leading to an increase of its working effect, provoke the morphological-functional growth in those physiological system's elements that are integrated in the Functional System. Thus, the systematic repetition of the whole competition exercise, trying to achieve its goal, ensures the gradual increase in sport results through the coherent functional increase of the elements of the morphological substrate of the functional system, involved in the competition exercise accomplishment.

However, it's also logical to suppose that not only the systematic repetition of the whole competition exercise, but also the systematic use of the training means, which are able to enforce each element of the morphological substrate of the functional system, could ensure the increase in the working effect of the competition exercise.

In fact, the main training method used by coaches when the development of sports training methodology was at its beginning, was the repetition of competition exercise, or its main elements, with the control and correction of its technical execution. However, very soon coaches began to use different training means and methods of preparation to improve the performance of the competition exercise. At the beginning, it was the performance of the competition exercises of other sport disciplines. The next step included only selected elements of sport's competition, similar to one's own. After that, coaches started to include, in the preparation of their athletes, additional training means and methods used in other sport disciplines (from Weightlifting or Track & Field jumping and running/sprinting).

ical Culture, 1966, n 11, page 19.

According to Verkhoshansky, an athlete's preparation for competition should include two interrelated components aimed at:

1) increasing the athlete's 'motor potential' (physical preparation);
2) improving the capacity to use motor potential during the performance of specific competition exercises (Technical/Tactical Preparation).

As early as the 1960s, analyzing the biodynamic structure of the competition exercise, in regards to a large group of track and field jumpers having different levels of sport results (from beginners to Olympic record holders), Y.Verkhoshansky came to the conclusion that *"the process of achieving sports mastery consisted of improving an athlete's ability to realize his constantly increasing motor potential in the motor structure of a given competition exercise."*[101].

An increase in the athlete's 'motor potential' is based on the mechanisms of adaptation which allow the morphological-functional specialization of the human body to a specific muscle activity. The performance of each training exercise causes a specific adaptive reaction in the involved elements of the organism's physiological systems - a process of enzymatic and structural protein synthesis in the tissues of the organs is set in motion. *"... the energetic super-compensation that takes place after a pre-determined follow-up period at the end of the muscular work is of prime importance"* (Jakovlev, 1976).

The organic substrates that are consumed during exercise performance do not return to the same level during the subsequent rest period: the process of their re-synthesis always goes through a phase of super-compensation. Multiple repetitions of this process, spaced at set intervals, reach a stable morphological change in the organism's structures that are involved in the exercise performance; this change represents the basis of the morphological-functional specialization of the athlete's organism and an increase in his/her motor potential.

Improving the capacity to use the motor potential during the performance of a specific competition exercise is also based on the mechanism of adaptation related to the formation of the self–regulated motor system and the process of motor learning. In the case of elite athletes possessing a stable level of technical mastery, improving the capacity to use the motor potential is based on perfecting the technical performance of competition exercise in relation to the enforcement of the organism's physiological systems.

The role of these two components in the training process depends on the sport: the peculiar characteristics of the competition exercises. The contribution of each component differs according to the coordination difficulties of the competition exercise and the degree of impact between the human body and the external environment during the execution of the exercise itself.

Finding ways of combining these two different processes, in every sport, without causing any negative effects between them - due to different mechanisms in the combined training process - is the greatest challenge in sports training methodology.

According to Y.Verkhoshansky, in the process of the athlete's preparation for competition, the increase in motor potential must anticipate the improvement of the capacity to use it during the performance of the competition exercise. This idea confirms his important empirical discovery: the necessity to increase the athlete's level of special physical preparedness before he starts to improve the technical execution of the of the competition exercise.

This is the basic idea behind the Block Training System: increasing the athlete's motor potential (Block A) and gradually improving his capacity to use this potential in a specific regime (Block B and C).

---

[101] Y. Verkhoshansky. 'The regularities of the process of achieving sports mastery', in Theory and Practice of Physical Culture, 1966, n 11, p.19.

IV.4.2. SPECIAL PHYSICAL PREPARATION: TASKS AND CONTENTS

Increasing the athlete's motor potential is ensured through the use of the means and methods of Special Physical Preparation.

According to the traditional methodological approach, all of the different physical preparation means that are used in the training process must be classified on the basis of their capacity to emphasize the improvement of different physical qualities (motor abilities).

The new approach establishes that in order to obtain an increase in motor potential (the athlete's increase in special physical preparedness), all the different physical preparation training means (loads) must be structured in relation to their capacity to emphasize the enforcement of the organism's Specialized Morpho-Functional Structure through the intensification of the adaptation process in each one of its structural elements. In other words, the main mechanism of the increase in motor potential is the accentuation of the adaptive processes in each element of the main competition exercises Functional System through the use of different training means (or loads).

"...Thus, two points of view could be evidenced in regard to the increasing of the Special Physical Preparedness of an athlete: physiological and psycho-pedagogical. The first consider the special work capacity (motor potential) and its increasing as a result of the forming of the specific morphological-functional structure of the athlete's organism; the second – as a result of development of motor abilities. Each of these considerations regards the same phenomenon, but from different points of view. So, we don't want to set them against each other. However, it should be clear, that the special physical preparedness of the athlete represent not the complex of his motor abilities, but the stable functional state of his organism, which could be only described (relatively) in terms of motor abilities "[102].

According to Verkhoshansky, the motor abilities (physical qualities) may not be used as universal elements of the structure of an athlete's physical preparedness (physical fitness) that lead the direction of training loads. In fact, when coaches of different sports are talking about the improvement of "strength", "speed", or "endurance", they could purport different things (training aims and training methods); because, in different sport discipline the capacities to be strong (or fast or resistant to fatigue) could ensured by different physiological mechanisms.

Each training means represents an appropriate exercise, or another complex motor action based on the formation of the Functional System, which is in turn determined by the purpose of the exercise. The specific training exercises must be designed so that their performance provokes the selected (targeted) adaptive reaction in those organism's physiological structures that are involved also in the accomplishment of the competition exercises.

"The most important factor for improving elite athletes' sports results is the motor potential. Only very intensive training stimuli can influence the body's physiological systems involved in the specific sports activity. The elite athletes' organisms only respond through adequate adaptive reactions to selected external influences (training loads).Such intensive and highly specialized adaptation stimuli can only be reproduced 'artificially' in a training process using training means and schedules expressly designed and elaborated for a given sport" (see note 98).

HOW THE TRAINING MEANS SYSTEM CAN BE CREATED?

According to the principle of the dynamic correspondence of training means to the motor structure of competition exercise, the specific training means should, first of all, possess a spatial-temporal structure, similar to the competition exercise; secondly, they should be performed implementing the appropriate muscle work regime. In selecting the means, three steps should be followed:

1. Step 1 - Analyzing the competition exercise (or the competition activity) and identifying the specif-

---

[102] Y. Verkhoshansky 'Fundamentals of Special Physical Preparation' Moscow, 1988.

ic technical parameters which ensure the high level performance of the competition exercise; for instance, take-off power, starting acceleration speed, stride-length and frequency. Biomechanical research regarding the sports discipline is appropriate.

2. Step 2 - Analyzing each of these specific technical parameters and identifying the physiological factors that ensure their improvement. For this step, reference to physiological research could be helpful.

3. Step 3 - Selecting training means and methods to enhance physiological parameters. The analysis of relevant publications regarding sports discipline and training methodologies of similar sports might be useful but the criteria of the principle of dynamic correspondence should be remembered when choosing the means and methods to apply to one's own sport.

The system of training means should hierarchically combine the training means of differing motor potential and differing levels of specificity. The increase of each element of the specific performance structure must be obtained through the use of the corresponding training mean or the complex of training means, united in the sub-system. For example, in order to increase the Explosive Strength expressed in the take-off movement, which represents an important element of the performance structure of Track & Field jumpers, it's necessary to use two different training means: barbell squats and jumping exercises. So, these two training means represent the training means sub-system finalized towards the increase in Explosive Strength.

From this standpoint, there is not a rigid division between SPP and GPP means: all physical preparation training methods should be applied with a specific aim or purpose in mind. When the training means are used as elements of a system, the training specificity depends not only upon the specificity of a single exercise but on the role of the exercise in the entire system of training means: every exercise, which may not seem to be very specific to a sport discipline, can instead be efficacious as an element of the entire specific system of training means. Thus, prolonged aerobic running, which has little in common with the competition activity of sport games, or barbell exercises, which have little in common with the competition activity of track and field long distance runners, can instead be useful for increasing the sport result as elements of the specific system of training means.

So, the training means, which are usually associated with General Physical Preparation, are not finalized towards the improvement of general physical qualities, but represents the part of the entire system of Special Physical Preparation, aimed towards the preliminary enforcement of the athlete's organism's structures involved in the execution of the specific training exercises; for instance, increasing the traction force (strength) of the most important muscle groups (prime movers), the elastic property of the muscles, and the tonus of entire muscular system. This ensures the fundamental preparation of the athlete's body for the intensive specific loads and the avoidance of injuries.

Weight exercises (the so-called strength exercises) represent an essential element of the training means system in every sport. The main aim of these exercises is not so much to increase strength abilities but rather, to intensify work on the muscular system in a specific regime. The implementation of specific resistance exercises in the training process facilitates an increase in the intensity of the training stimuli on the organism, creating the conditions which exacerbate the interaction between the body and the external environment. Increasing the level of external opposition above the level experienced during the execution of every sports movement, represents the universal way of increasing the functional elements of the specialized structure.

IV.4.3. SCHEDULING DIFFERENT MEANS IN THE TRAINING PROCESS (TEMPORAL OR-GANISATION)

What is the mechanism that facilitates the increase in an athlete's level of physical preparedness when different training means and methods are united in a system and used in combination?

Sport training methodology answers this question through the concept of the cumulative training effect. Each training means causes a reaction in the organism after its implementation; this is known as the training effect. Different training means and methods (different loads) cause different kinds of reactions, or training effects, in the organism, or, as it is referred to in Western literature, have different training load emphasis. If, in the training process, several training means (loads) are implemented, their training effects accumulate; this results in the so-called *cumulative training effect*.

For instance, Y.Verkhoshansky's research showed the increase in take-off Explosive Strength was obtained by the cumulative training effect of the barbell and jump exercises. This accumulation is obtained, both, when different training means are used within the same session or in subsequent training sessions.

Scheduling the different training means in the training process is the most complicated problem of sports training methodology. Up until now, this problem has been solved on the basis of empirical research analysis. According to the results, the accumulation of the training effects of different loads is obtained using three forms of temporal organization:

- *complex* (in the same training session), mainly suitable for children;
- *complex-parallel* (with 'rotation' of different training means during the microcycle), mainly suitable for medium-level athletes;
- *conjugate-sequence* (the consecutive superimposition of the training effects of loads of different emphasis, concentrated over limited periods), mainly suitable for elite athletes.

For the new methodological approach, the main matter is the transfer of the Specialized Morphological-Functional Structure (SMFS) at a higher level. This approach requires two preliminary actions:

1) the identification of specially selected training means able to enforce each SMFS structural element;

2) the definition of the temporal organization of these training means (as the training loads having different emphasis) in a unified training process.

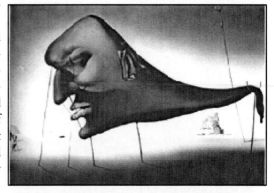

The process of solving this problem, employing images, may be illustrated by the following analogy:

…imagine a multiform three-dimensional construction (biodynamic structure of competition exercise), touching the ground (human body) in several points (morphologic substrate of the functional system) with supports – vertical props of different heights (Specialized Morpho-Functional Structure). In the limited period of time (preparatory period) this entire construction must be lifted above the ground to the highest possible level without collapsing. How can this be done?... Start by gradually lengthening one leg after another:

- If it is an unreliable construction, it is necessary to lengthen each support millimeter by millimeter very carefully- moving around from one support to another (complex form)
- if it is a more reliable construction, each support could be lengthened a little more after each move or 'effort', but it will take more time. There will be fewer 'rotations' per unit time (complex-parallel form).

- if this construction is very large and strong, much more time will be needed to lengthen each support, and before starting, the ground under each one will also need to be re-enforced (conjugate-sequence form).

This analogy does not wholly reflect the real situation. In the training process, there is another problem to be solved: in which order or sequence have the supports to be lengthened? In fact, the Functional Structures of different competition exercises involve diverse elements of multiple physiological systems of the human organism in varying proportions. Every physiological system of the human organism has its own inherent 'adaptive inertia' - the time necessary to give the adaptive response to training load stimuli and to obtain the necessary morphological-functional reconstruction. Furthermore, each training means represents a complex motor action, the accomplishment of which is based on the formation of a functional system: *"each functional system has its own specific rhythm of activity, strictly related to the rhythms of activity of other connected functional systems"* Sudakov K.V., 1999.

Therefore, the training means with different emphasis should be used in the correct sequence:

- for the implementation of the complex organization of training means having different emphasis, it is necessary to arrange them in the appropriate sequence in each individual training session;
- for the implementation of the complex-parallel temporal organization, it is necessary to arrange the rotation of these means in the appropriate sequence in each individual microcycle, in relation to their immediate or acute training effect.
- for the implementation of the conjugate-sequence form (BTS), it is necessary to localize these means into the concentrated loading periods having different training emphasis (Blocks A, B and C) arranged in appropriate sequence, in relation to their long term training effects (the time required to obtain the morphological-functional change in an athlete's organism).

Each form of the conjugate-sequence temporal organization of the loads of different emphasis may be displayed in the form of training models. These training models are not universal, but must be elaborated specifically for each sport's competition calendar. Yet, the creative coach, who already understands the system of training means for his sport, may successfully adapt the training models of similar sports to his own.

So, in regards to the Block Training System, the substance of this innovation is not merely the simple substitution of the complex-parallel form with the conjugate-sequence form of temporal organization of the training loads finalized to the improvement of different *motor abilities*, as seems to be the understanding of many coaches. In the Block Training System, the training loads of different emphasis should be finalized to increase *different parameters* of the Specialized Morpho-Functional Structure, which ensures an increased power output in the competition exercise specific to the sport. If one is unaware of the physiological parameters included in this structure, one is unable to elaborate upon the model of the Block Training System for a specific sport.

Of course, to refer to these parameters, the coaches of the same sport may use the terms "speed", "strength" and "endurance", implying more detailed physiological indexes. However, the coaches of different sports, using these terms to indicate the training loads emphasis, could imply absolutely different training means and methods, especially in regards the terms "speed" and "endurance". For this reason the definition of the BTS as 'periodization of physical qualities' is a simplification. It is not wrong but neither is quite right. It is like Plato's definition of a human being as 'a featherless biped with broad nails'[103].

---

[103] When the philosophers of Plato's Academy claimed that the best definition of a human was a "featherless biped", Diogenes, the Cynic is said to have exhibited a plucked chicken and declared "Here is Plato's Man." The Platonists promptly changed their definition to "a featherless biped with broad nails".

IV.5. CHANGES IN TRAINING PROCESS PLANNING APPROACH

IV.5.1. HISTORICAL BACKGROUND

Before talking about this issue, it's necessary to make a long historical excursus, returning in the 60's, when Y.Verkhoshansky had a passing acquaintance with the ideas of N.Bernstein and encountered him personally. We can say that the personality of Bernstein has played a decisive role in Verkhoshansky's professional growth as a scientist, just like the personality of Dyachkov has played a decisive role in his growth as a sport coach.

What mostly stunned Verkhoshansky was Bernstein's capacity to find the roots of studied matters.

In 1991, Y.Verkhoshansky wrote about his last visit to the deadly ill Bernstein, the 16th of December 1965: *"As always, Nicolai Alexandrovich is attentive, well-disposed, laconic and exclusively concrete in the issue of discussion. "What would happen if this graph would go not this way, but differently, for example, like this"- he asks me and his red pencil draws the sure-hand line on my draft. I am confused and embarrassed, because "like this" cannot be. I am searching the words to answer, but notice his crafty and testing glance and understand that it is a joke, but not a simple joke: it is an examination on my vision of the basic idea of this graph.... In the evening of the 31ˢᵗ of December, I call Nicolai Alexandrovich to wish him a Happy New Year, but nobody answer. Some days later, I was told about his death. Probably, I was one of the last of his guest, if not the last."*[104].

The personality of N. Bernstein, *"an intellectual titan, sending a challenge to almighty nonentities"*, had an enormous influence on the Y.Verkhoshansky's mind. The most important thing that he acquired from Bernstein was the idea that to solve even an utilitarian problem such as the problem of sport training planning, was necessary to use the most innovative scientific approach, an innovative way of thinking.

M. L. Latash the pupil of N.Bernstein wrote: *"It has to be noted that even though Bernstein himself died, his ideas and way of thinking – did not. So, one may discuss with Nikolai the Great and tell him: at this point you are right, but here you are obviously wrong! Then Nikolai Alexandrovich would smile wisely from the old photo* (photo on the right*), as if he wanted to say: Read it once more, please! And usually he is right! Well, sometimes his particular statements might be regarded as slightly outdated, indeed, but his way of thinking remains instructive and fertile still today!"*[105].

What does Bernstein's way of thinking regard? First of all, it regards a systemic thinking: applying a systemic approach to the analysis of the human motor function.

N.Bernstein had revealed the greatest mystery of nature: the basic principle of human motor coordination, the mechanism of human dexterity. In his book "Coordination and Regulation of Movement", published in 1947 in the USSR, he formulated the theory of a self-organizing system in which body movements are coordinated, or assembled, in response to specific tasks. The method that he used to study human movements became the fundament of biomechanics: the study of the movements through the application of mechanical principles. The basic mechanism of coordination and control of the human voluntary movements, which he discovered, became the fundament of a new science of effective organization: cybernetics.

---

[104] Y.Verkhoshansky. Some strokes to the portrait of scientist. Theory and practice of Physical Culture, №3 1991
[105] Mark Latash. Progress in Motor Control. Volume 1: Bernstein's Traditions in Movement Studies. Human Kinetic, 1998.

"...The term 'cybernetics' itself was, of course, introduced by Norbert Wiener, who defined it descriptively as the theory of relationships and control in the living organism and the machine...Cybernetics is based, above all, on the concept of system: a certain material object which consists of other objects which are called subsystems of such system.... The cybernetics studies the organization of the systems in space and time, that is, it studies how subsystems are connected into a system and how the change of state of some subsystems influences the state of other subsystems....Cybernetics is pre-eminent when the system under scrutiny is involved in a closed signal loop, where an action by the system in an environment causes some change in the environment and such change manifest itself to the system via information, or feedback, causing the system to adapt to new conditions: the system changes its behavior. This 'circular causal' relationship is necessary and sufficient for a cybernetic perspective"[106].

In the works of N.Bernstein, *"Relevant data, concerning the priority of introducing the notion of feedback in the process of active voluntary human movements, were available twelve years before the known Wiener's publication. Bernstein demonstrated how the problems of general physiology can be explored in terms of the structural analysis of movements. He dealt with the most important aspects of the vital activity of higher organisms and how this has been accorded the place in physiology and, when it developed, promised to be of the greatest value in cybernetics and in the exact mathematical formulation of a physiological theory of motor behavior."*[107].

Unfortunately, in the absurd theatre of life of the soviet totalitarian regime, a scientist could be favored or felled by government just for ideological reasons, i.e. the opinions based on the biased and one-sided ideological interpretation of his ideas, without understanding their real scientific meanings by the ignorant ideologists.

"At that time in Soviet Russia the most outstanding scientist was the Nobel Prize winner – I. P. Pavlov. Furthermore, the science in soviet Russia (and not only in Russia, and not only at that time) was strongly influenced by politics, so it was not safe to propagate other views other than Pavlov's. Nevertheless, Bernstein has chosen his own way in science. In 1935 he wrote a book in which he aurgued with Pavlov's views. It was finally ready to be printed, but at that time Pavlov died and Bernstein decided not to publish it, because Pavlov would have no possibility to discuss. It seems that this book went lost.

Until 1947 Bernstein worked at the National Central Institute of Physical Culture in Moscow, where he was the head of the scientific department. In 1947 he won a very prestigious national prize (the so called Stalin prize) for his famous book "O postroyenii dvizheniy" (On construction of movements), in which he presented a five-level system of movements' construction. Regrettably, somewhat later he was accused of being a cosmopolitan and deprived of his job. Fortunately enough, it was impossible to prevent him to think. Here his fate reminds the history of I. Newton, who made his most important discoveries in 1665 and 1666, when there was a plague in Cambridge and the university was closed. Also Bernstein, deprived of the possibility of experimental work and direct contact with the Institute, created a new branch of science: physiology of activity. Apart from this, he turned to cybernetics, because just then he saw great capabilities – at that time yet "sleeping" – of this branch of science.

After the Second World War, in the West motor science was falling down, and in Soviet Russia the views not consistent with Pavlov's theory were suppressed. For this reason, the Bernstein's historic ideas were not allowed to grow and flourish, as they deserved. After his death in 1966 it seemed that Bernstein's heritage could be lost. At the end of his life he still managed to authorize the book "The Co-ordination and Regula-

---

[106] V. Turchin. The phenomenon of science. A cybernetic approach to human evolution. New York, Columbia University Press, 1977.

[107] M. Vukobratovic, M.Jovanovic. Nikolai Alexandrovich Bernstein – pioneer in control and cybernetics. International Journal of Humanoid Robotics. Vol.7, Issue 1 (2010), pp.213-222.

tion of Movements" – until 1996 the only book by Bernstein published in English. His not numerous disciples dispersed all over the world, and in Russia the main "motor science makers" were followers of Pavlov's stream of thinking."[108].

This explains why, for a long time, the ideas of N.Bernstein were quite unknown both in the Soviet Union and in the West and why the cybernetics development was not related with the name of Bernstein. Also the cybernetics was felled by soviet ideologists, who definite it as a 'reactionary pseudo-science', 'an ideological weapon of imperialist reaction'[109].

"The early 1950s - the time when cybernetics and information theory became known to the Soviet reader - were the wrong moment to propagate in the Soviet Union ideas originated in the West. That applied not only to political doctrines, but to scientific theories and engineering approaches as well. In the Cold War wave of anti-American propaganda of the early 1950s, nearly a dozen sharply critical articles appeared in Soviet academic journals and popular periodicals, attacking cybernetics and information theory as products of the American imperialist ideology and totally ignoring Russian traditions in these fields. ... Cybernetics was labeled a "pseudo-science produced by science reactionaries and philosophizing ignoramuses, prisoners of idealism and metaphysics.

In March 1953, with the death of Stalin, the Soviet Union entered a new era. The political "thaw" brought significant changes to all spheres of Soviet life, including science and technology. The period of forced isolation of Soviet science and technology from its Western counterpart came to an end. The division into "socialist" and "capitalist" science no longer held; claims were made for the universality of science across political borders. The Soviet leadership embarked on a course of rapid assimilation of modern Western scientific and technological advances"[110] .

"Wienner's book was published in the USSR in 1958 and became very popular. At the end of the 1950s and the beginning of the 1960s, there was a cybernetics boom in the USSR. Many scientific-research institutions were organized. Cybernetics departments in universities, laboratories, cathedras, scientific journals, etc. were created. Many people were involved in this activity."[111].

"Cybernetics conquers the imagination through the frightening audacity and originality of its ideas and, at the same time, by its amazing simplicity and persuasivity. Cybernetics set the beginning of the Renaissance epoch in the soviet biological sciences and the process of returning to be free in a creative thinking"[112] – wrote Y.Verkhoshansky about these years.

Just in this historical period, the soviet scientists discovered that the basic principles of cybernetics, which were explored by N.Bernstein still in the 40th.

Exactly in those times, Yuri Verkhoshansky made the first attempts to apply the cybernetics principles on planning and organizing the training process in sport; he elaborated the main directions of development of the future researches in this field. So, today, those who try to analyze the sports training process by applying the theory of Dynamic Systems must know what Y.Verkhoshansky had already written about this issue more than 40 years ago.

---

[108] M. Latash. Progress in Motor Control. Volume 1: Bernstein's Traditions in Movement Studies. Human Kinetic, 1998.

[109] Definition of Cybernetics in the "Short Philosophic Vocabulary"(Mark Rozental' and Pavel Iudin, eds., Kratkii filosofskii slovar' , Moscow: Gospolitizdat, 1954)

[110] D. Mindell, J. Segal, S. Gerovitch. Cybernetics and Information Theory in the United States, France and the Soviet Union. In the book: Mark Walker, Science and Ideology: A Comparative History. Routledge, London, 2003, pages 66-95

[111] T. Medvedeva. Cyberneticd and the Russian intellectual tradition. http://www.stu.ru

[112] Y. Verkhoshansky. Some strokes to the portrait of scientist. Theory and practice of Physical Culture, №3 1991

IV.5.2. WHY ARE THE RESULTS OF TRAINING NOT SIMPLE TO PREDICT?

Verkhoshansky wrote that the training process should be viewed not as a relationship between 'coach' and 'athlete', as is believed by the pedagogical thought. On the contrary, it should be viewed as a relationship between the training influences proposed by the coach and the reaction of the athlete's organism these influences. The following is part of the article published in 1966:

"...The principle scheme of this empirically implemented process, (dating back to the time of ancient gymnasiums of Greece), is illustrated in Fig. IV.2. Notwithstanding the fact that modern coaches know infinitely more about the mechanisms of the development of this process, with respect to the ancient Greeks, empiricism and a degree of vagueness is inherent in their work. In fact, it is still impossible to clearly determine the contents of the block 'Program' and the block 'Complex of training influences': some of the most experienced coaches achieve great mastery in this art; but the results of their practical experiences only indicate the target of scientific research; this is not the optimal basis for programming a training process in the truest sense of the word.

Is there an explanation for this? Fundamental to the Process Management is to receive information regarding events happening in a controlled system. In the case of controlling the training process, the subject of control should be the relationship between all the blocks presented in the following figure. However, present knowledge is limited to the regulation of feedback between the block 'Immediate Effect' and the block 'Reaction of the Body'. Concerning feedback between the 'Final Purposeful Effect' and the 'Program', and the feedback between the 'Functional Adaptation' and the 'Reaction of the Body', it is intuition or abstract ideas that guide us.

The problem is that the Control Process is based on the comparison (the evaluation of differences) between the real and the benchmark parameters of the system state. It presupposes the possibility of a quantitative verification of the existing values of the regulated parameters and the level of their distinction with the benchmarked values (references) during the process development. If the above approach is to be applied in trying to manage the training process, the greatest difficulties to be overcome are the parameters of the output system (their entity and benchmarked values); they need to be defined and deserve further clarification.

There is nothing incoherent about the fact that an evaluation of the real state of the parameters and the benchmark values has not been tested up until now. In terms of cybernetics, the human organism is defined as

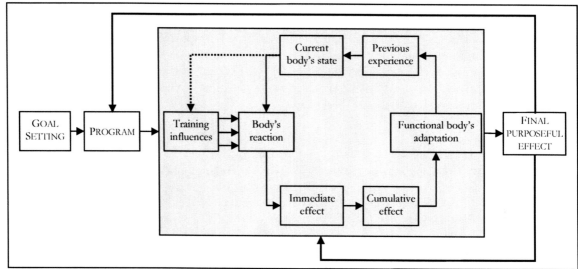

Fig. IV.2 - Outline of the training process

a statistically determined system (W. R. Ashby[113]). This means that the management of such a system (the regulation of its behavioral mechanism under externally given influential factors) has a stochastic character, that is, the result of input action (the output system) is not straight forward and predictable. It is precisely for these reasons that empirical attempts at programming a training process have so far been unsuccessful. To reverse this stasis, improved technical resources are needed. They would facilitate the identification of qualitative measures related to specific biological processes. These biological processes in turn would require new statistical methods of analysis. Only then will there be any hope of obtaining credibility.

Therefore, in spite of these obstacles, we should try to produce a qualitative description of this process of attaining sports mastery. A first phase in this research we could begin with a quantitative description based on objective experimental data. To successfully move in this direction, we need to examine the implementation of a mathematical method to quantitatively describe this process and to create benchmark models (at least approximately).

During the second phase of this research, we should formalize this process of attaining sports mastery and elaborate the quantitative schemes of actions (complexes of single influences) that guarantee an optimal regime of training management. Since this endeavor is in its first phases, the objectives should be as follows:

1. to study the biomechanical and physiological mechanisms of a given sports exercises which determine their variability and their evolution during the improvement of sports results;

2. to define a specific direction and the dynamics of adaptive reconstructions of an athlete's body during the entire process of attaining sports mastery.

Research aimed at obtaining the above objectives must explicitly reveal the qualitative aspects of the studied processes with precision in relation to externally influential factors and should regard the following three systemic levels:

1) the physiological systems of the athlete's organism;

2) the entire athlete's organism as a dynamic system;

3) the system - organism/environment."

IV.5.3. THE CONCEPT OF PROGRAMMING THE TRAINING PROCESS

In the 1960s, Y. Verkhoshansky introduced the concept of Programming the Training Process. Basically, the systemic-structural methodological approach was proposed for use in the field of sports training. At the time, this approach had only just begun to penetrate all fields of scientific research and productive activity. Today this 'methodological pattern' to realize objectives connected to any 'development project' is known in business and even in spatial programs as System Analysis & Design and Structured Process Modeling.

The term 'programming' is often associated with the creation of computer software. However, this term was used in the Motor Control Theory long before the advent of the computer era. In science, the term programming has a more general meaning, for example: *"…in applied mathematics, the theoretical branch existed for a long time; it was referred to as 'the theory of programming' (linear programming, non-linear programming … and so on). This branch has no relationship with the programming of computer software: it is aimed at the development of theoretical methods in order to optimize different processes…* [114]".

Basically, programming envisages:

1) the individualization and the evaluation of objectives;

2) the identification of means which ensure the attainment of these objectives;

---

[113] W. Ross Ashby, An introduction to Cybernetic, Chapman & Hall, London, 1956. See also: W.R. Ashby. Requisite variety and its implications for the control of complex systems, Cybernetic 1 (1958), 1-17.

[114] Smirnov M. "Programming" or "Construction?" Theory and Practice of Physical Culture. 1999, 12

3) the elaboration of the general and detailed model of the developmental process through the use of these means;

4) the process of 'product release' and its management on the basis of the verifications of the half-way results compared with a programmed model.

In the context of Sports Training Methodology, the term programming has a more precise meaning compared to the setting up of any training program: it means the specific way of compiling a program. In practice, to develop training plans on the basis of programming methodology it is necessary to:

1) identify objectives in practical terms, specifying the difference between the result of the preceding competition and the possible target result of ensuing competitions, and the period of time available, that is from the date of the commencement of the training period to the date of the competition;

2) evaluate the actual physical state of the athlete before the initiation of the process; identify the levels lacking in the state parameters based on the quantitative meaning of the performance model, which ensures the attainment of these objectives;

3) identify the training means and methods available to ensure the rise of these parameters (an analysis of specialized literature could form the basis);

4) identify the total volume of training loads necessary (regarding the different training means directions) on the basis of analyzing training load parameters obtained by the athlete in the previous yearly cycle, recorded in his/her training diary;

5) select the strategy to distribute the total volume of these loads over the period of time available; divide them into training stages, microcycles, and training sessions.

Obviously, it is necessary to clarify at least two highly important issues before being able to put this methodology into practice:

- the quantitative structure of performance in a given sports discipline and its structural qualitative model;

- the benchmarked development model of the structural parameters changing under the influence of training loads.

In fact, these two issues were the most important objectives of Verkhoshansky's research during the final ten years of his work in Russia.

IV.5.4. DIFFERENCES BETWEEN THE CONCEPTS OF PROGRAMMING AND PERIODIZATION

In Western Europe and the United States of America, where, until recently, the history of the development of Soviet sports science was unknown, the difference between the concepts of Periodization and Programming was still unclear.

Usually, periodization and programming are associated with terms that are normally used for practical activities that generally make up the planning of the training process: 'periodization'– the subdivision of the training process into periods and 'programming' – the compilation of training programs within these periods. Nevertheless, the understanding of these terms does not correspond to the content

of the two different methodological concepts: Periodization according to L.Matveyev[115] and Programming according to Y.Verkhoshansky[116] (in the photo, Verkhoshansky and Matveyev at beginning of the 70s.)

The problem is that *a concept* is something conceived in the mind, an abstract or a generic idea generalized from particular instances. In this case, it is first a basic idea around which the training process must be planned and implemented. Secondly, it is the reasoning behind an idea i.e., a strategy, or a proposal which places a particular emphasis on the benefits it proposes to bring about. Therefore, the concept of planning the training process has two aspects: *how and why*. The 'how', can be expressed in two ways: *the general rules* on which the training process should be *planned*, and *the model* (a representative form, style, or pattern), a standard setting out showing *how it has to be done*.

Unfortunately, the present interpretation of Periodization and Programming does not take into consideration the above-mentioned aspects; they are often misconstrued - or confused.

In the West, periodization has been the focus of numerous articles, in which the authors also give general definitions of it. Perhaps the most appropriate definition of periodization that has been offered up to this moment in time is the following: *'a cyclical approach to training in which periodic changes in training parameters (volume, intensity, loading, exercise selection, etc) are planned so that the athlete achieves optimal performance at the appropriate time'*[117].

However, the concept of Periodization, introduced by L.Matveyev, is understood only as 'how' without 'why', i.e., only as the necessity to 'periodize' the training process: *'...His work validated the concept of Periodization that is, that the annual training plan should be divided into training phases, each phase having a specific training objective mostly physiological [!?]. And that the phases of the annual plan should be subdivided into even smaller training phases, called macro-cycles (of 2-6 weeks' duration) and microcycles (a week's training)'*[118].

In another definition, periodization is attributed some characteristics that do not correspond to Matveyev's concept of Periodization at all: *"...in terms of the game theory, periodization is the use of planned unpredictability to manipulate or outmaneuver another player - which in this case is the body's adaptive mechanism."*[119]. In fact, this definition corresponds more closely to Verkhoshansky's concept of Programming.

At the same time, it is difficult to find a definition concerning Programming as a specific concept. Usually, it is understood as only "how" without "why", i.e., only as a Block model for the preparatory cycle construction proposed by Verkhoshansky. Nevertheless, the essential points of Programming, as a methodological approach to the optimal management of the training process in sport, was presented for the first time in November, 1965 at the Moscow Conference "Cybernetics and Sport" in the presence of N.A.Bernstein, the main source of inspiration behind this concept. The innovative model of the annual preparatory cycle construction based on the BTS was developed over the years between the 1970s and 1980s in a search for a solution to the problem of optimizing an elite athlete training process.

For the majority of Western readers, the existence of the contradiction between Periodization and

[115] Matveev L.P. The problem of Periodization in Sports Training, Moscow, "Physical Culture and Sport", 1964.

[116] Verkhoshansky Y.V. "Programming and organization of training processes", Moscow, "Physical Culture and Sport", first edition, 1977, second edition, 1985 .

[117] G. Gregory Haff 'Roundtable Discussion: Periodization of Training: Part 1' in National Strength and Conditioning Association, Volume 26, Number 1, pp 50–69, 2004.

[118] The father of periodization – Tudor Bompa', Interview by John Shepherd, in Athletics Weekly.

[119] S. Plisk, 'Periodization: Fancy Name for a Basic Concept', in Olympic Coach 16(2): pp.14-17, 2004.

Programming only came to public attention when an article written by Verkhoshansky (it was published in the Russian journal 'Theory and Practice of Physical Culture and Sport' in 1996) was translated into English and illustrated on the internet entitled 'The End of Periodization...'. It has been observed in different articles and internet forums that the meaning of the word 'periodization', as used by Verkhoshansky, was not understood correctly. Perhaps the reason for this depends on the fact that for readers in the West, this article was only the tip of the iceberg, the last point of a discussion which had been going on among Russian academics for some time. Western readers could not be blamed for not knowing the background to this problem and, for this reason could not understand the criticism of Verkhoshansky arguments.

Criticism of Periodization is understood not as a criticism of Matveyev's concept, but as a criticism of Matveyev's preparatory cycle model. For instance: *"I read such an article and was very disappointed to realize the author confused loading patterns with the periodization of training! There have been a number of articles recently, touting 'the end of periodization'. These, to me, just supplant linear periodization with undulating periodization"*[120].

One pertinent observation could explain the cause of such confusion: *"... If there is one self-limiting tendency between strength and conditioning among professionals, it is that we often focus on numerical models rather than on an underlying strategy when designing programs."*[121]

However, if Matveyev's concept of Periodization is understood as a general strategy, only needing to 'periodize' the training process, (and Verkhoshansky criticizes Periodization as this strategy), the readers may join T.Bompa and exclaim: *"...if periodized training is ineffective, what is there left to us? We either have periodization or chaos!"*[122].

At this point it is necessary to clarify the background to the contention in order to answer these questions. L. Matveyev set out the concept of Periodization in "The problem of Periodization in the Training Process", published in 1964. T.Bompa was absolutely right when he wrote: *"Matveyev was the first author to really statistically analyze what the Soviet athletes used in training for the 1952 Olympic Games"*. On the basis of this analysis, L.Matveev identified some general characteristics regarding the implementation of their training processes.

It is logical to assume that, since these athletes had achieved such excellent results, the characteristics of the training process could be used for other athletes. In fact, L. Matveyev developed the general rules and the model of organizing training loads over a yearly cycle. However, this model and these rules still do not represent the concept of Periodization. Periodization as a concept was formulated when Matveyev explained 'why', more precisely; the rules were interpreted as 'laws of the training process', based on two theoretical benchmarks: the 'laws of sports form development' and the 'laws of the education of physical qualities'. In another words, L. Matveyev introduced not only the general rules, which imposed 'cyclisation' on the training process and explained how to implement this 'cyclisation'; he also made the first attempt to explain why the training process should be 'cyclised' and 'periodized' in a certain manner.

The problem is that, the results of these attempts were *postulated as axiomatic*[123], and as such the con-

---

[120] T. Bompa 'Periodization from a sports science point of view', Sports Coaching: an interview with periodization coach Tudor Bompa.

[121] S. S. Plisk, M. H. Stone. 'Periodization Strategies', in Strength and Conditioning Journal. 2003, Vol. 25, Number 6, pp. 19–37.

[122] T. Bompa 'Periodization from a sports science point of view'.

[123] *Postulate as an axiom* is a proposition that has not been proved or demonstrated but is considered to be either self-evident or subject to necessary decision.

cept of Periodization was considered the theoretical foundation of the Methodology of Sports Training tout court. As a consequence, L.Matveyev's book was regarded as the basic manual for teaching this methodology to sports coaches in the Soviet Union. Matveyev's model of the yearly cycle was imposed as the only correct method. However...

In the 1970s, the level of sports achievements and the volumes of training loads used by elite level athletes had radically increased compared with the 1950s; coaches and scientists had begun to search for new ways of improving their sports results. As a result, Y. Verkhoshansky elaborated a new model of organizing training loads into a yearly cycle.

Independently from Verkhoshansky, Anatoly Bondarchuk had proposed a similar training model for Track&Field throwers. Unfortunately, his proposal only dealt with the 'how': the 'why' was not expressed clearly, with the using the same terms and, in consequence, the same paradigm as Matveyev's concept of Periodization.

Instead, Verkhoshansky had gone further with the concept of Programming, developing not only the new 'how' but putting forward a new 'why' - the new methodological approach to training planning.

This conceptual innovation was presented in the theoretical observations of 'Programming and organization of the training process', and in articles published in the 1980s. By the end of 1970, Y.Verkhoshansky had evidence of at least two differences between his concepts and those of L.Matveyev.

1) the training process is inherent to the 'cause/effect'' character, therefore, its implementation cannot have 'laws', but can have 'principles' or 'rules', which can be re–elaborated whenever there are changes in training process conditions. For this reason, the training model proposed by Matveyev could not be the only model: alternative and more effective ones were possible. L.Matveyev partly accepted this criticism; he did not perceive the difference between 'laws' and 'principles' in the theoretical discussion, but he did accept that his model could be variable and, therefore, could be improved on, yet, only within certain limits. It was Verkhoshansky's model that would overcome these limits.

2) Y.Verkhoshansky demonstrated different ways of interpreting the nature of the training process in sport and stated that the rules of implementing the training process should be based, primarily, on the 'laws' of human adaptation to strenuous physical activity. This was in contrast to L.Matveyev's belief; he accepted the specific role of adaptation mechanisms in the sports training process, but

Moscow, 1989. National Institute of Physical Culture and Sports Sciences, the first sport medicine course in the former Soviet Union organized by the USSR Sports Committee and AICEP. On the left, Y. Verkhoshansky illustrates the Block Training System. On the right, after the lecture, with Dr James Stoxen DC (left) and Dr Steven Press DC PhD (right).

did not accept sports training as an adaptation process: "*In explaining the sports improvement process, and the phenomena related to this improvement, priority should be given not to the Theory of Adaptation, but to the Theory of Development*"[124], "*Adaptation could be one aspect of development, but not necessarily a component*"[125].

Prof. Y.Verkhoshansky (left) with Prof. Atko-Meeme Viru, (right), the author of the book "Adaptation in Sport", and Prof. Carmelo Bosco (between them), the leading Italian scientist in sports physiology.

Regarding the adaptation process, L.Matveyev, only wrote about Canadian endocrinologist H. Selye's Theory of the Stress Syndrome in his theoretical discourses about adaptation. According to some commentators, H.Selye was considered the first to demonstrate the existence of biological stress. He did much important factual research on the hypothetical non-specific response of the organism to stressors. While Selye was aware of specific response: he did not recognize the role and the many aspects of *glucocorticoids*[126] in this response.

Returning to the Verkhoshansky's article 'The End of Periodization...', it's possible to say, that this article was Verkhoshansky's last desperate attempt to invite his colleagues into a discussion. Notwithstanding the fact that first applications of the Block Training System were successfully used in sports practice, this model was strongly criticized by L. Matveyev. He didn't accept the father researches of this model. Furthermore, he did not understand the novelty of Programming. Up until then, his apologists were considering the Programming concept as "*...an apparent novelty, introducing new terms, abstract graphic constructions, and considerations of a critical character*"[127].

Such a contradictory intellectual climate did not encourage Russian experts in sports training to make the necessary theoretical analyses. The absence of any theoretical analysis could have led to stagnation in the development of theoretical aspects and, as a consequence, a progressive slowing down in the practical aspects of sports training.

In order to better understand the difference between the concept of Periodization and the concept of Programming, Y. Verkhoshansky recently suggested[128] that it would be useful to remember a sketch used by T. Kuhn in Gestalt psychology to illustrate the 'paradigm shift' phenomena - the vision of two alter-

[124] L.Matveyev, about the 'sports form' in Theory& Practice of Physical Culture and Sport 1991, n.2, p. 19-23.)

[125] L. Matveyev., The categories of 'development', 'adaptation' and 'education' in the Theory of Physical Culture and Sport. Theory and Practice of Physical Culture, 1999. n. 1, p. 33.

[126] *Glucocorticoid* - a hormone that predominantly affects the metabolism of carbohydrates and, to a lesser extent, fats and proteins (and has other effects). Glucocorticoids are made in the outside portion (the cortex) of the adrenal gland and chemically classed as steroids. Cortisol is the major natural glucocorticoid.

[127] Platonov V. N., Super-compensation, training loads, adaptation and other issues in Sports Science. SdS - Scuola dello Sport, 2005 (Rome - Italy).

[128] Y.Verkhoshansky, N.Verkhoshansky, The paradigm shift in the methodology of sports training. SDS-Rivista di Cultura Sportiva, 2003 (Rome - Italy).

native images represented by a duck and a rabbit (see the figure of Thomas Kuhn's illustration of the mechanism of the 'paradigm shift'. He used the phenomenon of duck-rabbit optical illusion to demonstrate the way in which a paradigm shift could cause one to see the same information in an entirely different way).

It is possible to say that the most important difference between the concept of Periodization and the concept of Programming, is based on the different way of 'seeing' the same object-microcycle.

According to the concept of Periodization, the microcycle is the basic structural element of the training process. In fact, the most important objectives of the research were based on this conception, the elaboration of the microcycle models for each type of training period in a given sport. The training plan could then be 'constructed' from these microcycles, like different calibrated 'bricks', located within an undulating tier along a time axle towards the competition date. Regarding the day of competition, the level of the athlete's performance was impossible to predict, but it was necessary to guarantee its progressive improvement and the achievement of maximal 'angle' increasing.

According to the concept of Programming, the microcycle, as well as the training process as a whole, is seen from different points of view. This concept was elaborated for elite athletes whose sports achievements and training loads had attained the maxim level of human physical capabilities. The progressive improvement in the level of an athlete's performance, in an effort to obtain the maxim 'angle' of increasing during the preparatory cycle cannot always be guaranteed; the human organism responds to increasing external influences with adequate accommodation restructuring only within the limits of its Current Adaptation Reserve (CAR).

"CAR volume has a definite limit according to specialized studies, based on two factors: the adaptation (functional reserve of the sympathetic-adrenal and hypophysial-adrenocorticoid systems), and the absolute level of adaptation (morpho-functional) restructuring, which has already been achieved in the body. CAR volume decreases with an increase in sports mastery, that is, according to the degree of genetically conditioned limits of adaptation capabilities, long term adaptation to sports activity can be presented as an uninterrupted cyclical and mutable event, combined with CAR exhaustion and restoration in the body"[129].

Therefore, according to the concept of Programming, the most important temporal measure of the training process in elite level sport is not a microcycle, but rather a Great Adaptive Cycle, aimed at realizing CAR. For this reason, we should start planning the training 'from the end', from the definition of the total volume of training loads necessary to achieve CAR (this volume could be indicated by the volume of the loads 'assimilated' by the athlete in the previous preparatory period). A microcycle represents the working forms of training loads distribution over time, determined by the general strategy of their temporal organization. This strategy can be chosen by a coach as the complex-parallel organization of the different emphasis loads or as their conjugate-sequence organization (BTS).

The Verkhoshnsky's concept of exhaustion and restoration of the athlete's Current Adaptive Reserve may be confused with Matveyev's concept of formation, stabilization and loss of 'sports form': another 'rabbit/duck' situation in discussions surrounding Periodization and Programming.

According to Y.Verkhoshansky: "...adaptation reserves present in the body can be seen in cases of injury (Yakovlev, Prokop, Beckman, Letunov, Garkavi). Frequently, even at the end of the 1950s, the adaptation ability concept, the loss of energy during stress, and its possible recovery, was used to explain the dynamics of sports achievements during training. Three phases were defined (Prokop):

1) adaptation phase - increase in the athlete's skills;
2) highest sport working phase;
3) re-adaptation phase.

---

[129] See the Addendum of 'Super training', Sixth edition expanded version, Italy - 2009.

L.Matveyev eventually adopted this idea, interpreting these phases as the phases of formation, stabilization and loss of sports form without any kind of physiological explanation".

More precisely, L.Matveyev did not accept changes in sports form phases as an adaptation process; his sports form standards were taken from sports results obtained from athletes during competition.

Therefore, the difference, between the concept of Periodization and the concept of Programming, regards not the model of the training load scheduling (temporal organization), but the general theoretical approach to analyzing the training process and the general methodological approach to training planning.

According to the concept of Periodization, the training process is seen as 'a microcycle chain', that is, a cumulative structure, 'the whole' which is 'the sum of its parts'. On the other hand, according to the Programming concept, the training process is seen not as a *'microcycle chain', but as a structure which is divided into microcycles*[130]: a hierarchical system of training influences on the organism, organized over time, which can only be diversified within the microcycle.

The concept of Programming is based on systemic thinking: a discipline for seeing wholes, recognizing patterns and interrelationships, and learning how to structure those interrelationships in more effective and efficient ways. *"The substance of the process of improving sports mastery is to transfer the dynamic system's condition to a new qualitative level"*; the training process aimed at 'transferring' the dynamic system, the athlete's preparedness, to a higher level within the CAR limits of the athlete's organism is seen as a 'whole' system of training influence. Since, the 'whole' is not the sum of its parts, but rather the product of their interaction, every change in one of its parts can modify the 'whole' provoking the phenomenon of 'emergence'[131].

Therefore, the programming of training must be seen as a *systemic process*, which *"involves the definition of a problem, the searching of alternative solutions in general through a model, and the selection of the best alternative that will eventually determine the course of action"*.

The elaboration of a training plan, then, is seen not as the 'construction' of microcycles, or a goods train with a string of wagons, but as the solution of a more complex problem - how to accommodate so many passengers into a limited number of railway carriages, providing maximum comfort for each and every one of them.

For those *"... who do not see the difference between the concept of programming the training process, introduced by Verkhoshansky and the concept of constructing the training process..."*, professor M. Smirnov (National University of Pedagogy, Novosibirsk, Russia) wrote[132]: *"...the difference not only exists, but it actually distinguishes the direction towards which, unfortunately, the theory of sports training is moving today, away from the correct direction that we must maintain if we want this theory to progress.*

The 'construction' of the training process concerns the formulation of some training loads and later the verification of the results of the employment of these loads, using motor tests. Regarding 'programming', the scientifically justified parameters of the loads are used and the results of their influence may be anticipated from the beginning.

Furthermore, with respect to the use of 'construction', the most experienced trainers, who heed the training

---

[130] Paraphrase of the Bernstein's words: 'Movements are not chains of details, but structures which are differentiated into details', N.A. Bernstein, Studies of Bio-dynamics of Walking, Running and Jumping, 1940.

[131] *Emergence* - new properties arising in systems as a result of the interaction at a basic level (properties which are not inherent to its separate elements, but arise as a result of the gathering of these elements in the whole system). In the philosophy of systems theory and science, emergence is the way complex systems and patterns arise out of a multiplicity of relatively simple interactions. Emergence is central to the theories of integrative levels and complex systems.

[132] M. Smirnov, 'Programming' or 'Construction'? Theory and Practice of Physical Culture. 1999,p.12.

process structure, commit a significant error: the relationship of the planned load is connected to sporting re-sult dynamics, but not to the dynamics of change within the reserves of organism.

This question remain unanswered: At what price has the standard result been attained? It is in the absence of such information that leads to overtraining; the multiple repetitive occurrences of overtraining lead, as is well-known, to permanent pathological mutations in the athlete's organism.".

CPSIA information can be obtained at www.ICGtesting.com
Printed in the USA
BVOW05s2235261015

424158BV00005B/20/P